THE
RUIN
OF THE
ROMAN
EMPIRE

ALSO BY JAMES J. O'DONNELL

Augustine: A New Biography

THE
RUIN
OF THE
ROMAN
EMPIRE

JAMES J. O'DONNELL

ecco

An Imprint of HarperCollinsPublishers

THE RUIN OF THE ROMAN EMPIRE. Copyright © 2008 by James J. O'Donnell.
All rights reserved. Printed in the United States of America. No part of this
book may be used or reproduced in any manner whatsoever without written
permission except in the case of brief quotations embodied in critical articles
and reviews. For information, address HarperCollins Publishers, 10 East 53rd
Street, New York, NY 10022.

HarperCollins books may be purchased for educational, business, or sales
promotional use. For information, please write: Special Markets Department,
HarperCollins Publishers, 10 East 53rd Street, New York, NY 10022.

FIRST EDITION

Designed by Cassandra J. Pappas

Library of Congress Cataloging-in-Publication Data is available
upon request.

ISBN: 978-0-06-078737-0

08 09 10 11 12   OV/RRD   10 9 8 7 6 5 4 3 2 1

This is Ann's book

CONTENTS

PREFACE

An American soldier posted in Anbar province during the twilight war over the remains of Saddam's Mesopotamian kingdom might have been surprised to learn he was defending the westernmost frontiers of the ancient Persian empire against raiders, smugglers, and worse coming from the eastern reaches of the ancient Roman empire. This painful recycling of history should make him—and us—want to know what unhealable wound, what recurrent pathology, what cause too deep for journalists and politicians to discern draws men and women to their deaths again and again in such a place. The history of Rome, as has often been true in the past, has much to teach us.

The reign of Caesar Augustus consolidated and secured Roman domination in the lands around the Mediterranean. For 200 years after he died in 14 CE, the prosperity and the pomposity of the empire were wondrous to behold. Then, through a long series of lost opportunities, blunders, and wars, Augustus's heirs first showed that they could sustain their inheritance in time of crisis, then worked to release their world from ancient confrontations, and then in a tragic reversal bludgeoned into dust the opportunities Rome had created. This book tells the story of the central, tragic episode, when the mighty Roman empire, unable to understand itself or its world, chose to be true to its past ambitions and accomplishments and so brought itself to ruin. The figure of the emperor Justinian looms over the ruins, a figure mighty for his accomplishments, yet tragic for the calamities that his reign both saw and spawned.

The stories I weave together here will be unfamiliar to most readers. Specialists will disagree with at least some of what I venture and debate it

heatedly, as they (and I) should. Nonspecialists should expect some surprises. Because I mean to tell a fresh story with old materials, I have also
tried to recount the whole of it for the benefit of the reader who knows
none of it.

There are borders and boundaries being overrun and reinforced on
every page of this book, so it may be relevant to admit that I was born
about five miles outside the outermost boundary of the Roman empire
in Germany; grew up within a few miles of the U.S.-Mexico border in El
Paso (attending high school in a structure built by Jesuits hiding out from
an anticlerical revolution in Mexico); once owned, in the farthest west
of Ireland, a farm that my ancestors acquired when they were on the run
from the British after the battle of Kinsale; and have other family reasons
for knowing a lot about the history of Ukraine, the nation whose name
means "borderland." Is it personal bias or scholarly judgment that makes
me say that great capitals and bustling cities are all well and good, but that
the constructive and creative energies of humankind are often best seen
among the mixtures and minglings of peoples at the margins of nations
and empires? I leave it to my readers to decide.

I have meditated and written this book in some unusual places, on
travels to every continent save one, in the intermissions of my unscholarly
duties as provost of a great university that has long understood itself to
have a global responsibility. Because my professional role now makes me
think in very concrete terms about shaping institutions to serve a more
democratically understood humankind, it was doubly important to explore and tell this story, not just for readers, but also so that I can do my
own job better.

THE
RUIN
OF THE
ROMAN
EMPIRE

Overture

The night sky changes every night yet never seems to change, as the seasons bring the same stars in the same constellations on the same day of the year, age after age. The sky defines the calendar, for the stars never fail. For many thousands of years, until the smoke and light of human fires and human ingenuity began to plunder the night of its glory, the order and regularity of the stars surveyed and guided civilized life below.

The anomalies of the night offered hints. The planets (the word comes from the Greek for "wanderers") followed paths just unpredictable enough to challenge the mathematical abilities of generations, until Copernicus found a simpler model. It was easier to believe that the planets were the chariots of gods—for gods were notoriously whimsical and footloose—than to study the ancient mathematical models. Watchers below easily gave religious readings to other occasional anomalies of the night. Comets, shooting stars, the shimmer of the aurora borealis—all were safer to ascribe to divinity than to a blind material order. For us, the silence and darkness are beautiful, the stars a beautiful adornment; for the ancients, the night was terrifying and familiar and mysteriously well ordered.

Sitting beneath these stars and thinking in these ways, civilized humankind went about its business without grasping what evidence the skies bore against its habitual ways of thinking. Unable to measure the vast distances that separated the heavenly bodies patent before their eyes, they took the dimensions of this planet—or, rather, of Eurasia and northern Africa—as the measure of space. Incapable of grasping the evidence of the skies as a sign of the great age of the world and the long revolu-

*tions that bring us our flickering moment of consciousness, they mea-
sured time by the span of human memory and the stories of a few dozen
generations.*

*Small wonder that they understood their world so poorly. Small
wonder as well that even when we know better in principle and when
we can grasp the age and reach of the universe, we still fail to explore
and explain this world on a scale expansive enough to make it genuinely
intelligible. Science measures boldly the unimaginably large and small
of the cosmos, the breathtakingly fast and unspeakably slow movements
of bodies. History struggles to contain those universes in its imagination
while observing in minute detail as well. Historians struggle to think of
human experience in a way both congruent with the experience of mortals and expansive enough to offer real explanation.*

*The sky of the Greeks and Romans, carrying the names of their gods
and heroes in arbitrary patterns of stars, still passes over our heads at
night. The Great Bear and Little Bear circle each other at the top of the
sky, while Orion and his dog go hunting in the fall. They will do so long
after all of us now alive are gone, long after all our descendants have
destroyed themselves with nuclear fission or automotive exhausts. The
ancient communities that put those names on the sky have already disappeared or altered beyond recognition, and yet they continue to shape the
world in which we live.*

*This is a book about changes on earth below that left ancient heroes
marooned in the sky, stripped of their celestial powers. If we can understand those changes—and what has not changed—we may have a better
chance of avoiding calamities of our own.*

*We will begin with a man who thought that the world below the stars
was flat.*

COSMAS THE VOYAGER

The two visitors, skillful and knowledgeable merchants, found the obelisk
and the throne facing west, away from the sea. They stood at the gate of
the city of Adoulis, a trading town on the Red Sea coast of what is now
Eritrea. The land's distinctive products were ivory from elephants, horn
from rhinoceroses, and tortoiseshell. Both obelisk and throne pointed up
into the mountains, toward the great city of Axum, more than 100 miles

away in what was already called Ethiopia. Their inscriptions honored the Hellenistic king Ptolemy III Euergetes ("Benefactor"), by then dead for about 750 years. Ptolemy had probably never come this far south, but these lands still paid tribute—you could call it a tax, or you could call it protection money—to Egypt when they were not at war with the Egyptians.

The throne was cut from a single piece of gleaming white marble. The visitors were surprised to see this, because they knew of such stone only in the Mediterranean, from the island of Proconnesus in the Sea of Marmara near Constantinople. The throne's base was square, with four delicate columns at the corners and one more supporting the seat at the center. The obelisk was carved of basalt on a square base and stood behind the throne. Both objects were inscribed in Greek.

The manuscript illustration we have of the scene (a copy of an original from an eyewitness) makes it hard to get at their sizes, but the throne was perhaps human-size, and the obelisk not out of scale with it. In a future era, Mussolini would take another of Axum's obelisks from Ethiopia to Italy to stand as a token of his imperial aspirations in Rome. A few years ago its fragments were disassembled and returned to Ethiopia.

Mountainous Axum was a venerable Christian city by then (the 520s CE), and if any place on the planet could ever reasonably claim to be the home of the Ark of the Covenant, Axum would be it. Ellatzbaas, king of the Axumites, was as Christian as his ancestors had been for a century at least, though his brand of Christianity was falling out of favor elsewhere and would gradually lose touch with most of the Christian worlds in the years to come. Now Ellatzbaas prepared to descend from his capital 7,000 feet above sea level and go to war across the Red Sea against the Himyarites, dwellers in what is now Yemen. Fastidious in preserving and proclaiming royal glories, he sent to Adoulis to have the inscriptions on the throne copied for him and placed at the gates of Adoulis. This required craftsmanship and intelligence and led Asbas, the governor there, to ask our two traveling merchants to do the copying for him.

They were Menas, who later became a monk in Sinai and died there; and Cosmas, who came from Alexandria. From their visit, Cosmas kept his own copy of the inscriptions, and he included them in his descriptive twelve-volume book about such places. The two travelers also found sculptured images of Heracles and Hermes on the back of the throne and disagreed over their symbolic interpretation. They represented power and wealth to the merchant who would become a monk, but Cosmas thought they stood for deeds and words instead. Merchants like Menas and Cosmas traveled to Adoulis because they knew that sellers brought incense down from the mountains there and that one could buy it at a good price to transport across and around Arabia to Roman and Persian markets. This was good business, supplementing what Yemen produced across the water.

Cosmas returned to Alexandria to write his stories, and that's why we know of him. *Christian Topography,* his lavish illustrated book, is something that only a man of substance and wealth could have produced, and it survives in three medieval copies. One, made in Constantinople in the ninth century, now resides in the Vatican library; two others were made in the eleventh century. The one from Cappadocia, deep in Asia Minor, has migrated to Sinai in Egypt; the one from Mount Athos, that monastic metropolis west of Constantinople, is in Florence's Laurentian library. What they share is an abundance of illustrations, all going back to Cosmas's original, pictures that supplement the wonders he sought to describe in words. The Florentine manuscript bears the name *Cosmas* added in a later hand, so that's what we call him, but most medieval readers knew him only as he wanted to be known: as "just a Christian," anonymous and devout. His contemporaries, though, found anonymity to be precious and polemical, a sign of a man taking sides in the religious quarrels of the time.

Cosmas and his comrade were both sophisticated, experienced travelers, yet Adoulis still felt like the end of the earth to them. We can see instead that it was more accurately the center of the human universe; that when they were there, it was a cockfighting pit of geopolitical rivalry. The Himyarite realm lay not far away across the strait of Bab el Mandeb. At the narrowest point of the strait, just where it squeezed the passage down to the Indian Ocean, the Red Sea was no more than twenty miles wide, with an island midway across. Himyar was an ancient land, variously contending for control with nearby Saba (the biblical Sheba) and with the Ethiopians across the water. From of old, the land there was fertile, its richness enhanced by the fabulous Marib dam, a third of a mile long and rising fifteen feet above water level, feeding a system of canals that ensured a regular, reliable water supply to the region. Inscriptions, not necessarily legendary, say it was built in the seventh century BCE, but the dam was undoubtedly renewed, expanded, and strengthened as time passed and craft grew. There was a serious dam break in 450 CE, and Cosmas may not have known when he wrote his story in the late 540s that another also occurred in 542. The last, and most catastrophic, occurred in 570, and with it came the end of agricultural prosperity and Himyarite domination.

At the moment of Cosmas's visit to Axum, however, the Himyarite nation was still formidable. Its kingdom was Jewish in a world where Christianity was more and more the officially sponsored religion, even at the fringes of empire. (To be fair, however, the label "Jewish" may over-state its resemblance to other communities that venerated the books of Moses.) In 518, one skirmish between Ethiopians and Himyarites led to something like a civil war between Christians and Jews in Yemen, during which there was an anti-Christian pogrom by the leader Yusuf Ashaar, nicknamed Dhu Nuwas ("the man with a ponytail"). He concluded the conflict with a massacre of Christians in Najran in the early 520s. One ac-count alleged that Dhu Nuwas ordered 20,000 Christians thrown into pits of boiling oil for refusing to convert to Judaism. Under this man with the ponytail, the Himyarites savored a fleeting, doomed independence.

Then Ellatzbaas launched his invasion from Ethiopia, beginning with a solemn Mass in Axum cathedral, followed by the blessing of a fleet of seventy ships from Adoulis, and ending by establishing a puppet regime in Himyar that he controlled.

Ellatzbaas didn't act entirely on his own. Behind him lay the support and ambitions of the emperor Justin I, the monarch of Constantinople far to the north. Axum controlled Himyar for about ten years, until a Chris-tian regime acceptable to Justin replaced it, one that lasted until 575. Then Persian forces detached Yemen from Rome once for all. Now, in the 520s, Justin saw a larger map and knew that Persian trading posts had spread from the Persian Gulf around the Omani coast and then stretched toward Yemen. To him, securing the Red Sea as a Roman lake felt like necessary strategic resistance to Persian expansionism. But when we read of Roman and Persian conflict in this period, there were always good businessmen like Cosmas who paid only as much attention to geopolitics as necessary to keep their ships moving profitably.

Their interest was piqued when they learned that every two years King Ellatzbaas sent merchants farther inland, on a six-month trek to a land of gold called Sasou, near the Blue Nile. There they traded beef, salt, and iron for gold in a cumbersome ritual of barter with customers with whom they had no language in common.

Cosmas the merchant was from Alexandria; he was a man who most likely owned his ships and directed their courses while profiting from their cargoes. His city was Greek and so was his tongue, though he may also have known some of the native Egyptian language that we now call Coptic; a merchant who ranged so far in the ancient world would surely have made himself understood in many languages and dialects.

Businessmen like Cosmas did not concern themselves with the un-glamorous bulk cargoes of their world. Behind and beneath them, farmers tilled the land for grain where possible, hoping for a tenfold return on what they planted, yet often settling for fivefold or less and driven to the brink of starvation in years when the seed grain barely reproduced itself. The regular grain shipments north from Africa, whether from Carthage to Rome or from Alexandria to Constantinople, were state-managed and burdensome, risky for all. Whenever the harvest was late or shipping was disrupted by weather, fear of famine led to riots in the big cities. Instead of being subject to state-controlled prices—paltry rewards for such risk—Cosmas and others like him became cunning arbitrageurs, matching the lightest and least bulky cargoes with the greatest opportunities for increasing value over distance. Luxury goods—gems, spices, and silks—were the best business. Merchants delivered amber from the Baltic seacoast south to the Mediterranean, across many borders, for centuries. Spices were always profitable wherever they could be gotten. The wise men of the gospels may have been powerful, but their gifts of gold, frankincense, and myrrh were just the sort of thing you expected to arrive on camelback across the desert, most likely from Yemen. Elegant fabrics from the very Far East already making their way along the many paths of the silk route (and by other routes west) were another profitable line.

Neither Cosmas nor his contemporaries would have spoken of the Roman empire as a free-trade zone, or praised the blessings of a single currency usable across many lands and ports, like today's dollar or euro, but that was part of what the Roman empire had accomplished. Ancient currency in particular was always at risk of degradation, as cheaper and cheaper metals were used and people lost faith in the value of coins in cir-culation, but 200 years before Cosmas's time, the emperor Constantine had stabilized the currency to create this world, and a few years before

Cosmas sailed, the emperor Anastasius I had reimposed discipline and so created fresh prosperity again. What we now call infrastructure benefited from Roman rule as well, as roads and bridges were maintained, harbors were kept up, and security in and away from cities was generally excellent.

Merchantry was in the main for Greeks, Jews, and Syrians; thus the economic benefits were primarily felt in the eastern Mediterranean. How the business world looked from farther east is harder to say, but we know about an anonymous Persian adventurer who landed on the island of Jotaba, at the mouth of the Gulf of Aqaba. For a few years in the late fifth century, he managed to expel the Roman customs officers and take over the regulation of trade himself, with grudging support from Constantinople. An empire can make life difficult for entrepreneurs, but it cannot live without them.

Then, as now, merchant life required sober judgment, decisive bargaining, and a fair amount of luck. We know enough of Cosmas's career to see that he had all three. During more than a quarter century he sailed three challenging seas. His home waters were the Mediterranean, north and west from Alexandria, and the Red Sea, via the Nile and ancient canals, reaching down the Sinai to the opening of the Indian Ocean, beyond the straits of Bab el Mandeb. He seems also to have navigated the Persian Gulf, from the mouths of the Tigris and Euphrates down to the Strait of Hormuz. By the time Cosmas entered the trade, these reaches of salt water all had a long history of commerce, supported by robust institutions of port management, banking, customs duties, and even credit. Alexandria had been doing business from its dazzling seafront for 800 years, and the Phoenicians had made the Mediterranean their own long before. There are signs that sailors made it all the way from Mesopotamia to India, beginning as early as the reign of Sargon of Akkad, the great lord of the Sumerians in the third millennium BCE, a figure who lived even farther in Cosmas's past than Cosmas does in ours. Greek and Roman civilization remained mostly trapped inside the Mediterranean, where you could sail from anywhere to anywhere without leaving sight of land, and where you huddled ashore for the winter months.

Merchants like Cosmas also knew their way around land, since by definition the commodities that shipped best were also easy to carry ashore and sell at high prices. In addition to his voyages at sea, we have reason to think he made his way inland to the Mesopotamian cities of Nisibis, Edessa, Harran, and Dara—names that will recur in these pages—where Roman and Persian influences rubbed one another most contentiously. Nisibis, now Nusaybin in Turkish Kurdistan, between the Euphrates and Tigris in upper Mesopotamia, was the site of religious schools that Cosmas knew well. Yet it was nearby Edessa (modern Urfa in southeastern Turkey) that boasted the most famous market fairs in the region and thus provided a merchant's greatest financial rewards. The border may have been fought over repeatedly, but it was always porous to travelers and traders. The fairs may have brought Cosmas here, but the scholars of Edessa diverted and instructed him.

In all our reference books, Cosmas's name is a mouthful: Cosmas Indicopleustes, or "Cosmas who has sailed to the Indies." This name wasn't one he ever heard; someone attached it at a later date, inaccurately—his book of wonders makes it clear that he himself never crossed the Indian Ocean or saw south Asia. But like many sailors before and since, he didn't mind leaving an exaggerated impression of his exploits. The giveaway is his story of how one day in the sixth century, sailing down the Red Sea, he and his men saw a flight of unfamiliar birds, including an albatross, twice the size of any hawk they had ever seen, and they were all afraid, for they sensed that this meant the open ocean was near. Here, as at Gibraltar, the ocean beyond the sheltered sea they knew terrified Mediterranean sailors because the technologies of sailing and navigation that preserved life in enclosed bodies of water fell short of what it took to sail beyond sight of land. Another 1,000 years would pass before Mediterranean sailors could venture successfully out on the Atlantic, though others who lived in sight of the oceans had been bolder. The Irish and Scandinavians anticipated them in the north, and other traders plied flourishing routes from Arabia to the East Indies to China.

Some brave souls made it from Cosmas's world to Sri Lanka, coming back with tales about the lands that lay beyond. We know this partly because Roman goods appear in India in appreciable quantities, and scattered finds have been made in Indonesia, Malaysia, and even Vietnam. Sri Lanka was then called Taprobane, and Romans knew there was a church of Persian Christians there, whose priest had been ordained in Persia itself, and the churchgoers could participate in the whole of the Christian liturgy. Most natives there were not much taken with this imported religion and preferred their own cults. One native temple housed a giant hyacinth plant the size of a towering pine tree that shone in the sun from afar. Sri Lanka itself was a trading post for sailors from Rome, Arabia, and Persia to the west; from southeast Asia to the east; and from the Indian subcontinent to the north, gathering silk, aloe, sandalwood, and the like from the lands to the east and north and passing them on to buyers from the west.

Cosmas tells a story from that end of the world going back to his own early days, around 515 CE, when Sopatros the Roman, traveling with Ethiopians, arrived in Sri Lanka the same day as a Persian ship. The merchants from the two ships held a contest before the local king, each seeking to prove that his monarch, the *imperator Romanorum* or the shah of shahs, was the greatest. In this merchant realm, money was decisive: the Roman gold was heavier and better crafted to appeal to the eye. The king gave Sopatros the honors on the spot and his people made Sopatros the centerpiece of a great feast. They took him out and seated him on an elephant and had him paraded about the palace grounds with music and dancing on all sides. Sopatros probably did good business on that trip.

How did Cosmas know that story? He heard it from Sopatros 2,500 miles from Sri Lanka, there at Adoulis, perhaps on the same trip during which he and Menas came upon the obelisk and throne. He heard more stories from Sopatros then, about elephants in droves, and even used as cavalry mounts in battle. Cosmas's bestiary offers many word pictures of creatures from the ends of the earth, and illustrates most of them: rhinoceros, buffalo, camelopard (giraffe), yak, monokeros ("one-horn," in Latin *unicornis*—in all probability the rhinoceros, slimmed down and glamorized in the retelling), boar, hippopotamus ("river horse," which he makes look just like a horse, and admits he hasn't seen), seal, dolphin, and tortoise. Cosmas doesn't mention the tigers that others saw north of the Caspian Sea. He lived too soon to tell us the story of Xuan Zang, the Buddhist monk from the court of China who explored deep into India in the sixth or early seventh century, looking for the roots of his own enlightenment. Xuan Zang came west out of China on the silk roads, then south through the mountains of the Hindu Kush, almost far enough to meet men like our Alexandrian merchant's friends.

Cosmas the Christian lets us know that he wrote several books. The one we'd really like to have is his volume on geography, in which he provided the most detailed observations of the worlds he traveled through. He

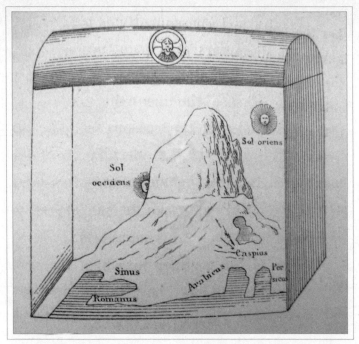

Cosmas illustrates a flat earth, resembling the tabernacle of the ancient Hebrews. Note the sun scooting behind the Alps.

also wrote on astronomy—the course of the stars in the unchanging sky—before turning to the book we *have* read, in twelve volumes. Its theme is not quite geography, not quite theology, but something in between,[1] for Cosmas has a particular point to make. He remains the only authentic, sincere, and argumentative flat-earther from his era of whom we have a record. We moderns used to be taught that flat-earthers were critics of Christopher Columbus, but that's not quite accurate. Columbus's opponents were, more accurately, "big-earthers," who argued that if he sailed from Spain to Japan westbound, he would die of thirst and exposure before he ever reached his goal. A true flat-earth theory is quite rare. Few people were so obtuse as to believe such a thing, especially in Alexandria, the capital of ancient natural science. In this context, Cosmas seems to us unusually misguided, with a flat-earth doctrine springing from religious obsession.

He, "just a Christian," as he described himself, was shocked by the existence of "false Christians" who did not understand how the world is constructed, and who preached false doctrine. He tells us he wrote in Alexandria, addressing himself to a friend who had come from Jerusalem and encouraged him to write. Cosmas complains to us of his weak eyesight and poor digestion, and laments that he has not the fine education that others have, yet he plunges into his theories. His topic is the tabernacle the Jews built in the desert at their God's command.

Cosmas learned all that is true on this subject from the "most holy Patrikios," who came from the land of the Chaldeans. Now this Patrikios, son of Abbas, was (at the time Cosmas wrote) the *katholikos*—something between pope and patriarch—of the Christian church in Persia, though Cosmas may have met him in Alexandria or closer to the frontier. In the Christian church of the time, Patrikios led the faction usually called Nestorian, named after a patriarch of Constantinople who never actually preached the doctrines attributed to him. This is oddly appropriate, for the Nestorians never preached them either, but were nonetheless separated from other branches of Christianity. Patrikios did at one point travel to Alexandria, accompanied by a disciple—a visit mentioned by Cosmas because it lets him make the point that just as Abraham came from the land of the Chaldees to bring the true faith to the Egyptians, so too did Patrikios.

The lesson Cosmas ascribes to this master is that the Jewish tabernacle, rather in the shape of an old, round-topped New England barn, was constructed as a model of the whole universe. The tabernacle floor is the flat earth, and the visible sky arches above. The sun, if you must know, rises in the east, sets in the west, and then scoots around to the north, behind the Alps, to return to the east for the next day's rise. Cosmas even has the pictures to prove just how intelligently designed this world is.

What is striking about his flat-earth doctrine is the way it uses the authority of a book to stand truth on its head. Cosmas sounds deferential and humble. He praises a book that teaches a true and unchanging fact about the world, and then applies his modest interpretative skills to reveal that fact, even though we now know the truth is the reverse. The authoritative book lets him remake his world in whatever image he chooses.

We have a good idea what Cosmas was attacking—that is, what drove him to say such ridiculous things. The leading philosopher in Alexandria was a man we call John Philoponos. Philoponos is a nickname—"lover of toil," literally—given to people marked for their zeal for Christianity. In both Beirut and Alexandria, the two great university cities of the eastern Mediterranean, the *philoponoi* were, in the words of one scholar, "rather officious and pious intellectuals, bent on sniffing out the remains of paganism"[2]. In John Philoponos's case, intellect and zeal took him to the heights of academe, where his reputation was assailed from several directions. All philosophy of this time was at least nominally Platonic, though the follower of Socrates might have had difficulty recognizing his ideas in their "modern" or what we later termed "neo-Platonic" form, and Philoponos was quite modern. He was also, as many Alexandria philosophers before him had been, going back to Clement of Alexandria over 300 years earlier, Christian.

When Cosmas expresses outrage over this combination of new religion and old philosophy, he is the crank and Philoponos the establishment figure. Philoponos, a man of substance whose work we have come to appreciate more and more with each generation of scholarship,[3] taught that the world was a sphere, an idea descending from the best traditions of Alexandrine science. This earned him criticism from Cosmas the flat-earther, and also the more thoughtful rebuke of Simplicius of Athens, a traditionalist philosopher not much taken with Christianity. Simplicius attacked Philoponos for refusing to accept that the world was eternal—for insisting that it had a created beginning and would also have an end. No matter that for the wrong reasons Philoponos was closer to correct about the world than either of his main critics: being right is rarely enough to win the day for philosophers.

We now must leave Philoponos and Cosmas at their loggerheads, for we have no other texts that allow us to overhear them wrangling, though at some remove they must have continued to do so. Philoponos moved increasingly from philosophy to pure theology after writing his books on the (non-)eternity of the world in the 530s. At just about the time Cosmas crafted his *Christian Topography* at the end of the 540s, Philoponos wrote an extensive commentary "on the creation of the world." He lived and worked another twenty years, producing a book on the trinity in about 567, before he disappears from view. Cosmas vanishes as well, but we can allow his afterimage to linger in the pages that follow, a man of broad horizons if narrow mind. We will meet others like him.

The Alexandria that Cosmas and Philoponos knew as a home of merchants, philosophers, monks, and more had been a place of civilization, contention, and shortsightedness for more than 800 years, and arguably the most civilized place in the Greco-Roman world for most of that time. Within a century, neither the intellectual descendants of Cosmas nor those of Philoponos would have much standing in the community in which they worked. We can take that as a measure of what would soon be lost, but we should also see how prosperous and untroubled the city still was in the sixth century.

THE VIEW FROM ALEXANDRIA

The great lighthouse called the Pharos stood on a narrow spit of land a mile or so from the coastline. The same engineers who built this mighty tower had also stretched a seawall back to the shore and created two harbors side by side, thus making possible the wealth of the port city that flourished after Alexander's conquests. If we walked out along that wall with Cosmas and looked to the horizons, how would we see the world that seemed to him so stable and assured? It was a world of two empires, Roman and Persian; and of long-reigning and proud rulers, Justinian and Khusro. But the doings of emperors were of little direct consequence for their peoples, who generally stayed out of their way. When one emperor died or was overthrown, every citizen of Alexandria knew that he would have precisely nothing to do with the succession and exactly no control over the workings of imperial government. Such a monster was best treated as Odysseus did the Cyclops—by trying not to provoke him, and, should the emperor notice you, relying on wit rather than force to escape his clutches. But the world was too big for emperors to control, and a traveler like Cosmas knew that world better than most emperors did. What did he see?

At farthest remove, Cosmas knew about the land he called "Tzinista" and we call China. Silks and other precious goods came from there, but he could imagine his world untouched by their prosperity and prospects. In the late sixth century and the early seventh century, the short-lived Sui dynasty and the more promising Tang that followed may be said to have inaugurated classical Chinese civilization. The first construction of the canal connecting the Yellow and Yangtze rivers was just then coming to completion, linking the agricultural prosperity of the south to the cultural and political centers in the north. In the same period, Roman religion

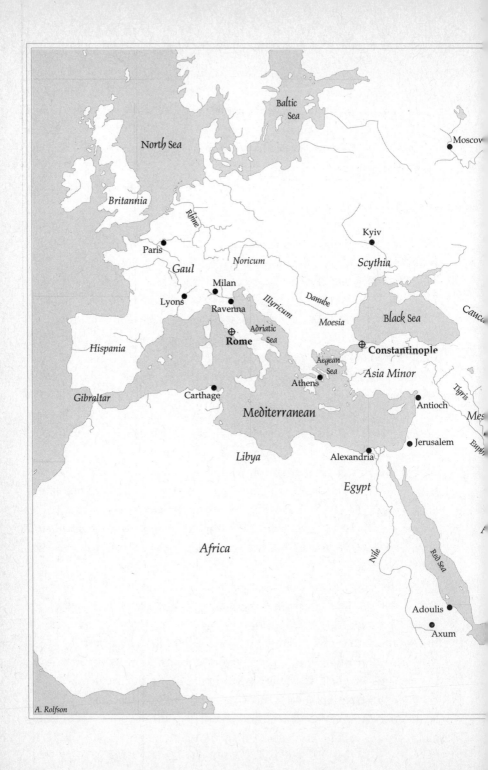

A. Rolfson

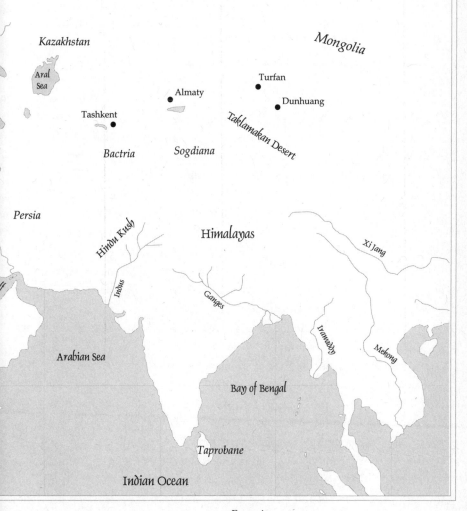

EURASIA

Kazakhstan

Mongolia

Aral
Sea

Turfan

Almaty

Dunhuang

Tashkent

Taklamakan Desert

Bactria

Sogdiana

Persia

Hindu Kush

Himalayas

Xi Jang

Indus

Ganges

Irrawaddy

Mekong

Arabian Sea

Bay of Bengal

Taprobane

Indian Ocean

Eurasia.

passed along the silk route and into China, and so the Nestorians consecrated a church in the Tang capital of Changan in 638. Many Nestorian
manuscripts have been found at Turfan and Dunhuang, on the edges of
the Taklamakan desert at the heart of the Silk Road. Meanwhile, the once
fashionable Roman new-age cult of Manicheism slid in quietly. China sent
no similar cultural products or practices to the Mediterranean.

Closer at hand, the Gupta empire in India was deteriorating, but the
states that succeeded it were, if less coherently gathered together, doubtless more prosperous and attractive in the reports carried of them to the
west by traders and adventurers. From India at this time comes the story of
Barlaam and Ioasaph, which we have in a Greek version from the early seventh century.[4] Ostensibly a story of a Christian holy man and his princely
convert, it is really a thinly veiled Christian version of the story of the
Buddha. Latins venerated the piety of the Buddhist saints on November
27, Greeks August 26, and Barlaam and Ioasaph's story circulated widely
in Christendom, eventually taking shape in the 1870s as the tale of Kundry
and the title character in Wagner's *Parsifal*. Cosmas's vague awareness—
as other westerners had been vaguely aware for centuries—of the Brach-
manes (Brahmin) of India is one sign of the cultural bridge over which that
story would travel.

Cosmas's wider world he measured thus: to go from China through
the land of the Huns to Bactria, you would travel for 150 days, following
the silk route through the desert of Taklamakan and the mountains of the
Hindu Kush. Merchantry and religion traveled together, so monks began
to decorate the great caves of Dunhuang and fill them with books, making
that desert an improbable cultural home between societies for more than
500 years. From there another eighty days (each day a thirty-mile march)
would take you across Persia to the frontier and Nisibis. From there you
continued to Seleucia on the Mediterranean, and then another 150 days
would take you around the sea. Cosmas's reckoning adds up to about
12,000 miles for those 400 days. In fact, such a route would take you only
about 7,000 miles, but a full year might well elapse, given the conditions
of road and weather over such diverse territory.

If you stretched a string from China to Rome, it would run through
Persia. Persia is the true middle kingdom; and the center of the world in
more ways than one was and still is Mesopotamia, the land between the
Euphrates and Tigris rivers. The first humans to leave Africa and colonize

the Eurasian landmass are now thought to have crossed the strait of Bab el Mandeb, back where we first met Cosmas. In the Karacadag Mountains of southeastern Turkey, some of their descendants cultivated for the first time the grass that became standard wheat, which today feeds the cultures of Europe and western Asia.

Mesopotamia is the heart of modern Iraq. The lands to its east over the Zagros Mountains—the highlands of classical Persia and modern Iran— are its natural partners. The lower Tigris valley in particular remains in social and religious contact with Persia, particularly with the minority Shiite sect of Islam, a connection so ancient that only American politicians could possibly be surprised to learn of it. The agricultural prosperity and trading links of Mesopotamia well supplement the highland farming of Persia, and since the first millennium BCE, with the domestication of the camel and the Arabian breeding of the durable one-hump species, the caravan routes that stretched across the desert from the Euphrates to Syria created and strengthened a link that offered profit and possibility on all sides. The defenses that Persian warriors could offer against steppe marauders from beyond had the effect of assuring Mesopotamia a long and comfortable history.

But Mesopotamia and the Mediterranean are too close for comfort, too far apart for ease, and the fault line between their lands and peoples is ancient and unhealed. Two such prosperous and commercially minded worlds so close together had to interact—but long stretches of desert made a permanent bond untenable. Creating a civil society or polity to link the two has perplexed visionaries for millennia. From Alexander the Great to Crassus to Julian the Apostate, nothing was so certain in the ancient world as that the boundary between the dominions of the Mediterranean and of Persia was contested, unsettled, and unsettling.

For Cosmas, planning his merchant ventures from the comfort and prosperity of Alexandria, the borderland between Rome's realms and Persia was what mattered. A chain of important frontier cities, changing hands from time to time and marked by a distinctive border culture, grew up and prospered—even when they changed hands. These cities spoke neither Greek nor Persian, but a Semitic variant of Aramaic. Today we call that language Syriac, but we must be careful not to overspecify. That language, long spoken along the Mediterranean coast from Palestine up along both sides of Mount Lebanon and out through the heartlands around

Heliopolis (modern Baalbek) in the Bekaa valley, Apamea (Homs), and Damascus, spread naturally north and east as well. Antioch (modern Antakya, Turkey) to the north was its big-city home in the Roman world, and the busy countryside of prosperous towns and villages between Antioch and Aleppo spoke it as well, as did the forts and market towns east to and beyond the Persian frontier. The people who spoke Syriac formed a society nominally subject to Rome, but by the sixth century it was increasingly independent in matters of culture and community.

In Cosmas's day, the prosperity of that world was enough to make a businessman's mouth water. Gaza on the Mediterranean coast was already a trading post, and Caesarea (destroyed by a Mamluk sultan in the thir-teenth century) and Berytus (Beirut) farther north combined commerce and culture. Beirut had flourished since at least the fourteenth century BCE, with a handsome harbor halfway between Antioch and Gaza (about a week's travel in either direction for those with the best pack animals), a city sure that Poseidon would look after it. Caesarea was the home of the finest library of early Christianity, and Berytus was the center of Roman legal education for the eastern Mediterranean.

In Palestine, Jerusalem was a religious zealot's amusement park, but other cities mixed populations and people. The "ten cities" of Palestine were famous for their prosperity and civic pride. Neapolis became modern Nablus and was the home of the Samaritans, while Scythopolis (Beat Shean) was a monastic center that thrived in its border world.

Scythopolis exemplified provincial success. At its height around 500 CE it was a local capital with perhaps 30,000 inhabitants.[5] Thirty springs made it a well-watered oasis on the way inland from the coast to the Jordan valley, and even when it later housed mainly monks, they harvested date palms and produced linen to make themselves independent and comfortable. Archaeology shows us a sixth-century monastery there with church and meeting hall on either side of a central courtyard and cells and kitchens around it. A floor mosaic depicts traditional scenes of farm and animal life. By then long settled, it had been hellenized enough to feature a marketplace (agora) and a theater at the foot of the hill on whose summit the first settlers had taken refuge. Conventional Mediterranean buildings surrounded the agora; the temple of Zeus was destroyed in the fourth century, and one of the baths went out of use in the early sixth cen-tury. Two Samaritan brothers, Silvanos and Sallustios, replaced this bath

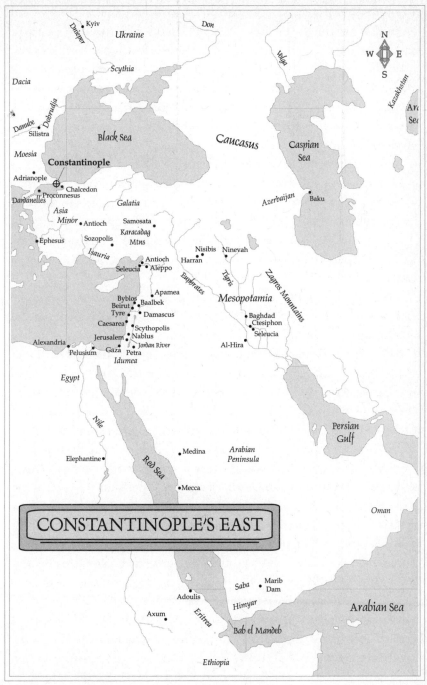

Constantinople's East.

with a large hall. One of the brothers was lynched in 529 by Christians in the murderous suppression of a Samaritan rebellion of which we will hear more.

By the end of the sixth century, there were at least four new churches in Scythopolis, and the city was losing its rectilinear Roman shape as shops and workshops filled in what had once been grander public spaces. Meanwhile, public bathing was abandoned at the same time as private housing crept into the city center. By the 720s, that great hall of the Samaritan brothers was rebuilt as a crowded souk by the caliph Hisham, and though it was destroyed a few years later, it completed in its time the transition from the old Mediterranean city style to the new Muslim model. Scholars will continue to disagree whether this remaking of the city is change or decline, but the medieval Islamic world prospered while doing its buying and selling in a souk rather than in an agora or a forum.

North and east of Palestine the businessman-traveler came to Edessa, a very old city (thought by Muslims to be the birthplace of Abraham) refounded under the successors of Alexander and one of the oldest sites of Christianity. Everyone believed Edessa's King Abgar had received a letter from Jesus himself, preserved and eagerly read into the sixth century. Even Justinian's skeptical historian Procopius gives credit to the story. Edessa was also home to the widely regarded Bardesanes, a widely influential teacher of Christian doctrine around 200 CE. East again, and one came to the borderlands proper and another old city, Nisibis. In the sixth century it was usually on the Persian side of the frontier, and the place to which Roman citizens seeking refuge from religious oppression (Christians out of favor with Constantinople or traditionalists not able to toe the Christian line) would flee. At Nisibis there flourished the largest Christian school of the Nestorians—whom their enemies sometimes called, confusingly, Jews—led by Mar Aba, who is probably the same man known in Greek as Patrikios, who taught Cosmas his doctrine of the tabernacle. These Nestorians had taken up business there when the intolerant emperor Zeno closed the predecessor school at Edessa in 489 and left them no choice but to do business in a more tolerant empire.[6] Not far from Nisibis was Daraa, a defensive city that the Roman emperor Anastasius I built around 500, much to the distress of the Persians. That anxiety cast a shadow forward through the next century.

South of the frontier zone was Arabia, if we can see it as Cosmas and his contemporaries would see it. In antiquity they inhabited the perimeter of Arabia, but the center of the peninsula, then and now, was not entirely barren; for centuries, Mediterranean and Persian culture sent out shoots into the interior, traces of which can still be found. Arabia survived in antiquity at the fringe of Roman and Persian worlds on its wits, on commerce, and on rumors of the world beyond. The Romans had created their own province, inland from Palestine: it consisted mainly of a Roman road running north and south more or less as did the Hejaz railway built by the Ottomans and plagued by Lawrence of Arabia, from Damascus to Medina. Long before Lawrence, this was the path of the camel caravan that annually ran down from Damascus to Mecca for the hajj, or pilgrimage. The Nabateans once ruled there from their curious fortress of Petra, a city hidden in a valley approached by narrow defiles, until the Romans made their power unshakable in the second century and the Nabateans' economic influence faded. As late as the sixth century a substantial Christian church (not rediscovered until 1990) dazzled the eye in that remote fastness with its mosaics and marbles, adjoined by a huge baptistery. The terrain turned the Roman road into the natural boundary between cultivated lands and desert. Rome's soldiers moved easily up and down the highway and fanned out eastward to terrify and control the desert dwellers, thus ensuring settled agriculture and consistent tax paying to the west.

Within the Arab community, there were more settled and prosperous tribes, reaching out into the more intractable desert, marginal desert dwellers—forerunners of the modern bedouin. Along the western line of Arabia from the Roman frontier south toward Mecca, the Ghassanid family had the power, monopolizing all dealing with the Romans. They so prospered that other Arabs thought of them as Romans. The Lakhmids were the first family of the frontier between the Persians and Arabia and played a similar role, reaching to the city of Hira almost within sight of the Euphrates, near where Syria and Iraq come together today. If you were a Roman used to cities and government, you thought of these Arabs as dubious folk, and when you chose to honor al-Harith, the prince of the Ghassanids, and tried to use him as your cat's-paw in controlling the lands beyond the borders, you knew you were taking a risk. Eventually you would find him and his son, al-Mundhir, too inclined to go their own way and you would call them traitors.

If you were bedouin of the desert, however, you saw the Ghassanids and the Lakhmids as people who knew how to navigate the world of empires and armies and how to maintain their strength and identity. They were good protectors, partners, and employers—a source of stability.

Cosmas's Alexandria was the mother city of Egypt. An ancient and unbroken line of civilization—of agriculture, of urban life, and of temples—continued into the sixth century. In cities and among elites, Greek all but supplanted the native language (Coptic), and Greek-branded Christianity had made broad inroads. Coptic (its name derived from the name of the land, "Aegyptos") appeared first in written texts in the fifth century CE, by then fully Christianized itself. The survival of Coptic from that day until now has gone hand in hand with the survival of Christianity under many forms of Islamic rule.

Christian temple busters had been effective enough, particularly in Alexandria (Cairo would not become powerful until the Islamic period), but from the Nile delta south a line of pyramids great and small served as reminders of a very old past, standing watch on the ridge where the cultivated land of the valley, watered by the Nile's annual floods, gave way to the desert upland. One fourth- or fifth-century Egyptian, Horapollon, wrote plays, commentaries on the ancient poets, and a work on temples. Then he (or possibly a son or grandson of the same name) wrote an extensive book explaining the meaning of the Egyptian hieroglyphic language and its religious symbolism. He occasionally got things right, but only occasionally. Horapollon's father, Asclepiades, had traveled widely, writing, apparently, a synoptic treatise on all the religious ideas of the Greek world. He had lingered particularly at Heliopolis (Baalbek), studying its faceless idols, remnants of an ancient Semitic religion. *His* brother, Heraiscus, was said to have a more practical religious talent: the ability to tell at a glance which sacred statues were actually inhabited by divine spirits. He would sniff them and then either walk away or fall, on the spot, into a religious trance in the presence of the divine.

A sober contemporary of that family, the businessman Dioscoros from the modest city of Aphrodito (Aphrodite's town, back when the landscape was given Greek names), left a trove of documents that reveal prosperous provinciality far up the Nile. From him we have leases and loans, receipts and wills, petitions and depositions—a whole range of documentation that once pervaded the Roman empire but that has all but disappeared, leaving us with only a fragmentary sense of the way this meticulous, businesslike world worked. Thanks to Dioscoros, we know that a donkey sold for a little more than half a year's earnings for a farmer, making it the ideal capital investment (and much cheaper than a boat). It would eat about two percent of its load of wheat in a day and carry that wheat twenty-five miles or more. This is the scale at which a camel was an expensive purchase, reserved only for long-haul shipments by the rich, and horses and mules were for government officials and soldiers. Most of the Mediterranean world lived among donkeys.

Dioscoros's modern biographer compares him to a Japanese minor court poet or a Chinese official. But that runs the risk of encouraging us to look down on him. To see a man like Dioscoros whole, you need to see him from below, from the village perspective in which he appeared as a great man. Dioscoros dazzled that audience by combining a good head for business and book learning (from a good education in Alexandria) and also by writing poems:

> *I always want to dance. I always want to play the lyre.*
> *I strike up my lyre to praise the solemn festival with my words.*
> *The Bacchae have cast a spell on me.*[7]

That traditionalist Dioscoros who wrote of the Bacchae surely attended Christian services regularly. When he was in Alexandria he could have attended the church of the Evangelists, later dedicated to saints Cyrus and John. This was originally the temple of Isis and Manetho, hastily converted for Christian use in 391 when sacrifice was banned. (Curiously enough, the cures that occurred thanks to the protection of the old gods continued under the new management.)

Now, Dioscoros *was* a minor figure compared with the members of the Apion family. Based in Oxyrhynchus ("sharp-nosed," from a fish found there) on the middle Nile 100 miles south of Cairo, the Apiones were local landlords and—during the sixth century—grandees of imperial stature. The wealthy daughter of the murdered philosopher Boethius went into exile at Constantinople and found it advantageous to marry one of her own daughters into the Apion dynasty. One Apion was the praetorian prefect (roughly equivalent to a prime minister) for the east under the emperor Anastasius, but it was Flavius Apion II who dominated his part of Egypt as few others had done since the time of the pharaohs. He served Justinian at court and as a general, before spending most of his career from the 550s to the 570s doing what ancient gentlemen did best: controlling his home turf. His family owned 75,000 acres of precious, river-watered land in his home district and maintained an extensive private staff that practically amounted to a government. The people who lived under this dominion were sharecroppers at best, and might have been forgiven for thinking they were virtual slaves on their own land.

The emergence of this kind of superrich family subtly undermined imperial authority. They were no longer one of several dividing up the power in a region and sharing a sense of rivalry and patriotism, but were now far more dominant as a family unit and growing unconcerned with matters beyond their personal ken. Like Dioscoros, the Apiones also left a huge trove of documents unearthed in modern times, where we can read memos from a senior estate steward to a junior colleague, resolving a quarrel over the use of a cistern or ordering a boat repair for a trip downriver to Alexandria.[8]

Much as the cities of Ireland had to wait for the Vikings to come by sea and "discover" the virtues of the ports of Dublin, Waterford, Cork, and Limerick, so Alexandria was brought to glory by conquering Alexander and his successors from far away. For them, linking Egypt with the Mediterranean world was an obvious step and building the city and port of Alexandria the obvious way to do it, after the many generations of Egyptian rulers who had been content with their riverine world and the tribute that came overland from the east.

Alexandria and Egypt were natural magnets for Jews, some of whom settled there before Romans were even heard of, at Elephantine far south on the Nile at the first cataract. They were probably planted there as a military garrison in the pay of the Persians, when the great kings dominated Egypt long before the time of Augustus, and they kept up their rituals in astonishing isolation from Jerusalem. And where there were Jews, from very early times there were usually Christians. While Athens remained doggedly faithful to its traditions and its irreligion until the threat of brute force intervened, Alexandria was more cosmopolitan and diverse at every period. There were ugly moments, as in the early 400s when a Christian mob murdered Hypatia, an intellectual prodigy who refused to accept or acknowledge the new creed. But prevailing powers usually forget the violence they had used to clear their paths, and so by the sixth century it was possible to think of Alexandria as a place that had naturally and uncomplicatedly endured in its role as the great city of the Mediterranean world. Rome and Constantinople had imperial pomp, but Alexandria had urban flair—think of staid Berlin or Washington compared with cosmopolitan Paris or New York. The ships still came and went, while caravans brought Mesopotamian and Syrian trade over land. The Nile also brought men and commerce, some of it from the Red Sea voyages of Cosmas and his kind.

Alexandria never forgot that across the Mediterranean and up through the Aegean lay the path to Constantinople—a city we will visit in later pages. On the hierarchy of Greek cities headed by Alexandria, with Ephesus, Smyrna, and Antioch proudly following, and then the only somewhat lesser but still noble communities of Byblos, Berytus, Tyre, Sidon, Caesarea, and Gaza (all recalling long histories), that ancient city of Byzantion had long dwelled in an obscurity from which it was finally rousted by the devastating generosity of emperors.

Constantine gave one hostage to fortune in founding his city. He chose the location in part to keep closer watch on military affairs along the lower Danube. Underdeveloped in classical antiquity, broken up into small regions and communities, with few cities, the world south of the Danube was easy to destabilize, but the hinterland of an immensely wealthy capital should be secure and impregnable. Suddenly the Balkans and their politics were both an opportunity and a menace for the empire. The region became and would remain a central recruiting area for soldiers and even emperors, but it was also a regular source of threat to imperial safety. The long-term development of the Slavic Balkans is unimaginable without the tempting sight of fat Constantinople to the southeast, positively begging to be blackmailed or plundered.

But Alexandria and Antioch were the real capital cities of the eastern Mediterranean, the former with Egyptian (that is to say, Coptic) hinterlands, the latter surrounded by Syriac-speakers. Had Constantine not intervened by creating his new capital, a post-Roman Mediterranean no longer in touch with Latin-speaking Italy would have seen Greek culture and language in the east diminish. Had Alexandria and Antioch been left to grow and dominate their regions unchecked, Islam might never have taken the form or achieved the strength it did. Or at least it probably would

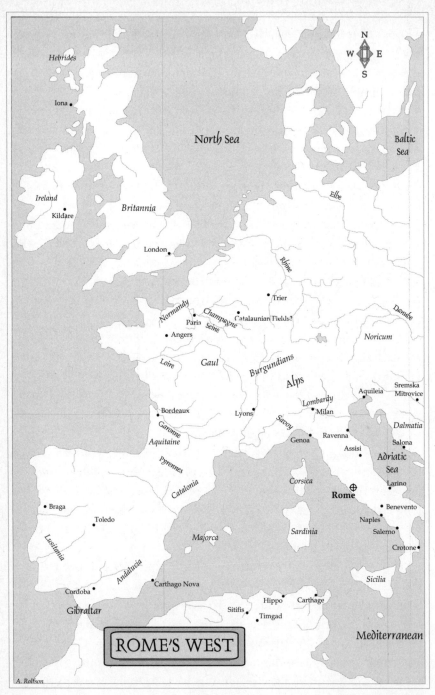

Rome's west.

have allied itself with one of the two eastern cities in a contest against the other that would have shaped a far different world.

Constantinople, while drawing wealth away from Alexandria and Antioch, ensured survival for speakers of Greek, and gave them opportunities for prosperity and comfort.[9] Even after Constantine's city fell to the Turks in 1453, the Greek language flourished in and around the Aegean basin for the 400 years modern nationalism took to rediscover it. Today's Greek language is an extraordinary mix of ethnic, cultural, and social influences: the ancient high-prestige language of Plato and Demosthenes, the continuing vernacular used in Christian scripture and liturgy, all amalgamated long after antiquity's end.

In matters of government and religion, Alexandria did what it needed to do to remain on good terms with Constantinople, if always with reservations. And so the city thrived as the sort of place where a merchant with religious ideas could fancy himself a writer and produce a large book, lavishly illustrated, to promote what he had to say. As ever with ancient sources, we need to remember how much has been lost, to think of how many other merchants were writing books of their own, and to consider what the philosophers and monks were doing to fertilize the pool of ideas ever in circulation. Athens in the fifth or early sixth century may have boasted traditionalist intellectuals of great acuity, but for the real action, it was Alexandria or nowhere.

Nothing suggests that Cosmas ever traveled west from Alexandria; nor did he have reason to. If you lived anywhere east and south of Constantinople, around the eastern Mediterranean to Alexandria, you had little cause to think of the people who lived west of your world: the people who spoke Latin. They were stuck in an earlier time, in a world of stunted development by comparison with the sophistication and prosperity of the east. The cities of the western provinces were still in the hands of a small elite, drawing their power from agricultural holdings, and populated with tradesmen, craftsmen, slaves, and those who might have been better off if they were slaves. No western city had ever achieved the kind of economic independence that was commonplace among even modest communities in the eastern Mediterranean, and thus none developed the robust bourgeoisie of professionals, local merchants, and aspirants to higher things that marks a true city. The only upwardly mobile people in western cities of late antiquity were the clergy. Outside the cities, mere county seats for their surrounding agricultural communities, the countryside operated far too much like a plantation society for its own good, and it advanced astonishingly little in economic and social terms during the five centuries from Augustus to Justinian. Out in the wild, brigands, derelicts, marauders, and holy men proliferated—dispossessed people with no natural economy in which to find a fresh home.

Cosmas, like all ancients, was certain that the Pillars of Hercules stood at the westernmost end of the known world. Nothing in his milieu would make him think westward travel might be worthwhile. For him, the west might as well have not existed. We, however, will make our own visit that way soon enough.

LIVING IN A MATERIAL WORLD

In some future age, people will say history began with the twentieth century, for it will be the earliest period from which they'll have sound and motion recordings to capture the flavor of life. To apprehend comparable flavor for the late antique world requires imagination and attention to often scant scraps of detail preserved in surviving sources.

Let's start with *flavor* itself. What did men and women eat in this late antique Mediterranean world?[10] Bread, of course, with a little olive oil. Olives themselves could be cured and saved with salt, with vinegar or honey vinegar, and with brine. Milk was more for those in northern climes, where it didn't spoil as quickly, but cheese was common everywhere. Meat and fish were luxuries, but if you were in a great city near the water, seafood was at least somewhat familiar. Strabo the geographer tells us that every year there was a run of bonito, a type of mackerel, in great shoals descending the Bosporus toward the Mediterranean, driven by currents close to the shore of what would become Constantinople. And when did people eat? Custom in late antiquity shifted away from the midday main meal of traditional Rome toward an evening main meal, at least at Constantinople.

And in a great city, there were luxuries unimaginable elsewhere. Those luxuries were for the rich, of course, and if you were a ruler, you would rate even scarcer rarities. In Italy, that meant salmon fished from the Rhine and carp from the Danube, but still Italian wine—at one point Verona's vintage was the most fashionable.[11] If you were regal, rich, or both, you could season what you ate with spices. They were also useful to balance the humors in the blood; for example, the game birds and roast meats of a luxurious table in January were to be seasoned with the hottest spices, such as pepper, cinnamon, and mustard, so that their warming properties would counterbalance the cold, moist phlegm of the body. Herbs provided the flavorings of choice, with every corner of the garden scoured for everything with a distinctive taste. Our herb and spice racks are full of parsley, mint, basil, coriander, and more because our ancestors could not find or afford stronger stuff. Rarer spices commanded high prices for their negligible weight, and they were often formed into enticing shapes to lure buyers. To this day, if you travel to the souk of Aleppo and find the stands full of spices sculptured into elegant castles for sale, you are only inches away from the premodern world. Cinnamon and its cousin cassia traveled all the way from Sri Lanka and China. With ginger they were the best-known most abundantly sold spices. Pepper came from southern India.[12] Exotic fruit would not become fashionable and available until Islamic times; the Greco-Roman Mediterranean settled for apples, pears, cherries, apricots, plums, peaches, and of course grapes. Honey was the sweetener of choice, because sugar was known only in Persia and northern India, and would not become universal and addictive until modern times.

Slightly less elegant and also less expensive was the Spanish fish sauce called *garum*, made by steeping fish eggs and entrails in brine. *Garum* increased in popularity through late antiquity, and we know that an Italian traveler, Liutprand of Cremona, saw it as late as the tenth century in Constantinople.

The meats of preference included buffalo, oxen, goat, sheep, and pig (our beef cattle were unknown), and the lower classes could sometimes afford sausages made from the butchered leavings. The taste for wild game was more catholic: deer, gazelle, wild goat, wild boar, bear, and more commonly hare. Medical writers liked to recommend chicken, but there was not an abundant supply. The list of game birds seems endless: ancient Romans knew duck, goose, quail, pigeon, partridge, peahen, and crane, and enjoyed many of their eggs.

The choice of a beverage was simple: either water or wine. The rich at Constantinople could afford to sneer at the aqueduct water that came from many miles away, and a western visitor agreed that it tasted salty and bad. Better to drink wine. Sweet wines were preferred to dry, and retsina, or resinated wine, was practical and popular from an early date. Retsina was named for the pine resin that waterproofed the earthen wine vats and also helped stabilize it and prevent spoilage. Wines like these were generally "cut" at least fifty-fifty with water—so they lasted longer and addled the drinker less.

The people of late antiquity drank, ate, and sometimes did not eat. Some people who read this book know what it is like to go to bed hungry, but few will know what it is like to spend your whole life without the assurance that you will not face grinding, incessant hunger next month or next year. Poverty and famine tormented many people in ancient times. The great moral risk for the student of ancient history is that we too easily inure ourselves to its brutalities and miseries because we admire what the rich and powerful were able to accomplish.

So the chronicle of Joshua the Stylite tells us of one famine around the frontier city of Edessa in the years 499–501.[13] Two harvests failed in 499. First a swarm of locusts savaged the wheat, and then a few weeks later the millet did not get the weather it needed. The price of bread rose immediately, and people began to sell their possessions just to buy it. Many fled the region, while others flocked into the city and became beggars. Disease was rampant and—the story goes—some people were reduced to eating the flesh of the dead. Desperate farm people tried eating lees, the sediment remaining after grapes were pressed for wine, while city folk tried roots and leaves. They all knew the dread of looking at emptied larders while knowing that months remained until the next growing season could possibly bring relief.

The other perils of the body were scarcely less threatening. Disease could take even the strong in a matter of hours or days. Yet we will meet a few nonagenarians in this book, for if you survived childhood robustly and had adequate nourishment, your chances of long life were decent, although old age was thought to begin in your forties.

Being a woman or child could win you either sympathy or abuse, but few advantages. Children whose parents could not afford their support were left outside to die or, less often, for generous passersby to rescue and raise. Exposure was condemned by pious Christian emperors in the fourth century, but the practice continued widely until well into the sixth century.

Justinian ruled—in an unenforceable law—that foundlings could not be enslaved. The kindest treatment we see was the growing habit of presenting unwanted infants to monasteries to be brought up in religion.

Chastity, under the lightly Christianized Roman ideal, was a woman's task, and failure to defend against sexual assault was a mild disgrace at best and too often a source of lasting shame. The convent provided little in the way of refuge. Although Saint Augustine remonstrated in his *City of God* that rape victims had not sinned, four decades later Pope Leo I still refused to allow religious women who had been sexually assaulted to reside with and be counted entirely among the "virgins of God." Instead, they were assigned a separate, middle place somewhere between the "real" virgins and the women who turned to religion in widowhood. Childbearing was still a deadly risk for mother and infant, a sad fact that demographers today can calculate from too many tombstones bearing names of young matrons and babies. Marriage in such a world was terrifying to many women, and the alternative of religious chastity, when offered, must have seemed literally a godsend to some.

You probably lived where you were born, and you rarely traveled. You spoke the dialect of your village or town and expected outsiders to be difficult to understand, but visitors were so interesting that you and they would find a way to communicate. Not all travel was desirable, for some led to warfare and some to slavery. If you lived inside the boundaries of the Roman empire or its successor states, you were reasonably safe, though slave raiders were seen on the fringes of Roman Africa from time to time. Rome also regularly went shopping for slaves across the lower Danube, while never quite comprehending that this buccaneering attitude might arouse deep resentment. Romans captured other slaves in the war on the Persian front, but some of their own were lost that way as well.

Clothing varied by climate. The Roman toga was long gone except as a form of fancy dress for a very few. Tunic and cloak were the usual combination, with the brooch as a standard form of ostentatious jewelry for both sexes. Women were covered down to the ground, while men wore shorter tunics, for the Gaulish fashion for trousers had been thought effeminate and never caught on. Women covered their hair for ceremony but not for every day. People who wore the coarser fabrics of the western

Mediterranean and Europe envied easterners their linens and finer wools. The wealthy were avid for silk but sometimes settled for cotton imported from India.

The rich were different, of course. They lived in stone more often than mud and wood, and in finer stone or even marble more often than rough granite. They used leather, wool, fur, and fabric coverings and hangings to make their upscale stone less cold and hard. The elegant Sidonius describes a dining couch covered with fabric depicting hunted beasts with their dripping blood picked out in scarlet thread.[14] At the same dinner, snowy linen draped the table, and bouquets and garlands of flowers flooded the room with color and fragrance.

The rich could be surrounded by glittering mosaics, in which glasswork of remarkable quality supplemented genuine cut stones. Gold and silver were treasures of choice, with silver also serving for tableware. Jewelry and tableware made excellent repositories of wealth because they were so easily hidden or sold in emergencies. So about twenty-five years ago a dazzling treasure dating from around 400 was discovered, perhaps in Hungary. It consists of exquisite silver tableware—cups, bowls, spoons, plates, all in a copper kettle that had protected them, evidence of a lavishness that few rival even today.[15] Ivory was easier to come by than the precious metals, and from about 400 to 700 we have remarkable examples of decorative objects in ivory of every kind. Remains of ambitious ivory workshops have been discovered on the Palatine hill in Rome and outside Alexandria in Egypt.

If you were rich, your hands were smooth, most likely manicured, and you perspired only when you chose to exert yourself in some fasionable way. Public bathing was fading from fashion, however, and the old bath complexes fell into disuse in the fifth and sixth centuries. (Ancient public bathing, a custom that survives in the hammams of Near Eastern souks today, was thought decadent and too likely to tempt bathers from the sexual straight and narrow, and so Christians turned away from the practice.) Thus people generally smelled a little riper than they do nowadays.

For one rich man who died in the mid-sixth century, we have an inventory of his household property taken before it was knocked down on the auction block. He had clothing, tapestries, a particularly valuable shirt of silk and cotton colored red and green, and a trunk to put such things in, with a lock on it. He had cooking equipment, a small amount of furniture (chairs and a table), a saddle—and a slave named Proiectus. The goods of a freedman in his household—perhaps also recently deceased—were being sold at the same time. The freedman had fewer clothes but more utensils: tools and implements for the kitchen in particular.[16]

It was just as well if you didn't travel much, unless you were rich enough to be taken in by other rich people, for roads were dangerous and inns were usually associated with lowlifes and criminals and specialized in pandering and prostitution. A typical inn excavated in Syria had stables on its ground level and a floor or two of cubicles above for guests. Prosperous merchants might have enjoyed a slightly higher grade of guesthouse. Gradually the practice of charging travelers began to be acceptable even among the noncriminal class, squeezing out the more hospitable but dangerous impulses of earlier, more welcoming times.[17]

The peace and prosperity of the Roman world had to do with what we would now call economies of scale. The government could tax a vast and prosperous empire to support an idle professional army on its frontiers and a government that sat in one or two capital cities. Augustus had declared at the outset that Rome should expand its borders no farther and had undertaken the demilitarization of the Roman heartlands away from the frontiers, a prudent step designed to avoid civil war. As long as the outer shell held firm, this was a fine strategy, but if it cracked, then the settled and prosperous countryside was at risk. The rich grew richer while soldiers got only uniforms, bonuses, and small allotments of land at retirement—if they were lucky. Generals might become wealthy on retirement, but the aristocracy of the Roman world had always been civilian. When the great civilians were dispossessed or disappeared, leaving only military men wealthy enough to own land, as began to happen in Italy after the awful wars of the mid-sixth century, we can see the beginnings of feudalism.

Wherever you went, new forms of old religion were part of the air you breathed. One Christian hermit found himself in a town without much Christianity, so he set himself up in trade buying and selling walnuts. Not long after, a tax collector came to town and demanded payments that would have strained many purses. The hermit wisely arranged a loan from friends in a bigger town not far away to help out his new neighbors, and so from that time forward, he made more of his religious authority and was given new respect. In another town (the same church historian reports), little children played monks and demons, and one little girl exorcised her playmates among shrieks and giggles.[18]

The urban landscape of the Greco-Roman world had traditionally emphasized the public and the monumental. By the sixth century, cities in the west were shrinking dramatically—they would eventually recover their commercial legs only when merchants set up shop outside the walls of the tiny communities that survived or replaced those cities. Old monumentality at the city center was threatened everywhere. At Rome in the 530s, in its most ancient heart along the Via Sacra, a few yards from the house where the vestal virgins had lived and tended the eternal flame, two bronze elephants were tottering to ruin. A short-lived ruler signed a letter about the elephants' peril, dilating on the poignancy of how animals thought to live 1,000 years should be nearing ruination in the urban jungle.[19] He offered advice on bolting them together and propping them up, cautioning that even live elephants often need help standing again when they have fallen. No sign remains of those elephants; most likely they were destroyed in the two decades of terrible warfare that were about to pound the ancient capital to a pulp.

The poor lived in huts, the rich in great houses: no surprise there. The old traditional Roman house had featured the atrium in front, and you walked through that to a courtyard. Now it was the courtyard that welcomed you first; the reception and living rooms stretched beyond in no uniform pattern. In the secure city, you slept and dined on the ground floor, but out of town you more often chose to stay on the floor above, perhaps keeping your workshop or the like down below, with strong gates at the entrance.

When the sun went down, you went home and stayed there, mainly in the dark, unless you were rich enough to afford oil to burn. Carthage and Antioch were probably the best cities for nocturnal lighting, because they were close to the olive-growing uplands of Numidia in Africa and Syria in the east. When we hear of an emperor or a philosopher who spent half the night reading and writing, what we should observe is not the studious one's diligence but his prosperity.

For diversion you might play some of the games of dice that were popular, but if you were well brought up you did not snort when the dice went against you, as snorting was the conventional mark of the unmannerly dicer.[20] Many gaming boards survive, including a famous one found in the forum in Timgad, 100 miles south of the Mediterranean on the plains of modern Algeria, with this inscription:

venari lavare
ludere ridere
occest vivere

Hunting, bathing,
playing, laughing
— THAT's living!

Even the poor could agree with that.

LIVING IN THE SOCIAL WORLD

Every page of our story assumes a society of huge chasms with wealth and status running among people who lived with each other every day. All our modern studies of the splendors of ancient civilizations emphasize the similarities between the ancients and ourselves. But the similarities we are fond of invoking connect the rich and socially advantaged ancients and moderns to one another.

It is pleasant to think that Thucydides (for the realists), Cicero (for the optimists), or Boethius (for the intellectuals) have something in common with our own modern interests, predilections, and pastimes. We should remember, however, that their world and they themselves were very unlike what we know in our world today. If a time machine plunked us down in an ancient city, at the door of the house of a great writer or statesman whose name we know, the thrill of recognition would quickly be replaced by shock and dismay.

First, people took ill more often, lingered longer in sickness, were crippled for life by trivial accidents, aged rapidly, and died young. The people themselves were shorter than moderns and took for granted that they lived amid the effluvia, to choose a nice word for it, of human beings and their household and serving animals. Ancient cities stank. The people who bathed to remove some of their own odors then covered themselves with strong ointments and perfumes designed to counteract the smells of social living, and those remedies probably made the original problem worse (to a sensitive modern nose) rather than better. But those facts are physical.

Second, the privileged rich were few in number: a few dozen in a small city, a few hundred in a larger one, perhaps 1,000 or slightly more in Constantinople at its most glorious. Somewhat larger was the group of moderately protected, successful urban dwellers—merchants, artisans, government officers, people who managed the business of the comfortable world in which the rich could live. The poor, on the other hand, were many. Those with connections to the rich might derive some benefit— the well-dressed slave, for example—but might equally be abused by their overlords. By late antiquity the prevalence of slavery had subsided, but not for a particularly good reason. Great landlords didn't need so many slaves (as southern plantation owners discovered after the Civil War) if they had tenants and sharecroppers for whom they had even less responsibility than they had for slaves. The urban poor similarly had no social safety net and were free to starve unimpeded.

Third, the social gradations of wealth and standing were sharp and carried with them the privileges of abuse. A clear hierarchy of secular dignities grew increasingly rigid in the empire after the time of Diocletian (who died about 316), softened only by the emergence of the parallel hierarchy of churchmen, who were not aristocrats but had protections. (Escaping from a lower social status into holy orders was an attractive form of social mobility.) In law there was a distinction between *honestiores* (the more honorable) and *humiliores* (the more humble), but it only codified the great fault line of society, between those who could be beaten and tortured readily and those theoretically immune to judicial violence. The more humble were always far more abundant. Not every poor man was beaten every day or every year, but every poor man knew that he could be.

Fourth, the privilege of the wealthy was reflected in some extraordinary vulnerabilities among the rest of society. A little girl growing up on the serving side of a great house could rarely imagine a bright future. To become, at or before puberty, a sexual instrument for the lord of the house or his sons—not even a plaything, just an instrument, an object—was not unlikely. Marriage of a sort offered some protection (but not from the lord of the manor, as long as a young woman preserved her sexual attractiveness), but was hardly a warm or sheltering life. Demographers calculate for such women of childbearing years (starting in the early teens) one pregnancy every two years, each one a potential death sentence for mother and infant, each one a hammer blow to the mother's health and prospects of longevity.

The rich took it for granted that this society, which coddled them and crushed the many, was natural, orderly, inevitable, and acceptable. Christian kindness for the poor made some difference in late Roman times, but the poor who benefited were usually not the most downcast—the slaves, sharecroppers, hewers of wood, and drawers of water—but people with some social standing, whom we might think of as the lower middle class. Christian love of neighbor and Christian charity were focused mainly—some scholars think exclusively—on other Christians.

Soldiers were different and always had been. In classical Roman times, they could not marry or own property until they were given land at retirement—if they lived that long. We will see the ways that military forces were reshaped into mobile communities of families, acquiring ethnic identities to reinforce group solidarity. Compared with the poorest of the poor, a soldier had many advantages, but only a few soldiers advanced to high rank and opportunity, a few more became junior officers, and most lived hard but modestly protected lives—except when actual warfare exposed them to the ultimate risks.

Few readers of these pages will have any direct way of experiencing the world of the ancient (or for that matter modern) peasant. These lines by Rebecca West, from her luminous and sympathetic account of Yugoslavia in the 1930s, can open a window for at least a glimpse:

> It was a poor day for the market. A storm had been ranging over the mountains all night, and as the year was still early and the crops light, most of the peasants had not thought it worth while to get up at dawn and walk the seven or eight miles to Trebinye. There were a few handsome women standing with some vegetables before them, soberly handsome in the same vein as their plain round caps and their dark gathered dresses, gripped by plain belts. We saw a tourist level a camera at two of these. They turned away without haste, without interrupting their grave gossip, and showed the lens their backs. These were very definitely country women. They wore the typical peasant shoes of plaited thongs, and by their movements it could be seen that

they were used to walking many miles and they bore themselves as if
each wore a heavy invisible crown, which meant, I think, an unending
burden of responsibility and fatigue. Yet there were women among
them who were to these as they were to town ladies, country women
from a remoter country. The eyes of these others were mild yet wild,
like the eyes of yoked cattle, their skin rougher with worse weather
than the others had seen and harsher struggles with it; and their bodies
were ignorant not only of elegance but of neatness, in thick serge coats
which were embroidered in designs of great beauty but were coarse in
execution, if coarse is used not in the sense of vulgarity but to suggest
the archaic, not to say the prehistoric. There was a difference among
the men also. Some seemed sturdy and steadfast as the rock, others
seemed the rock itself, insensitive, except to the weathering power of
the frost and sun.[21]

For such people, the most miserable or abject, the world's delights are
few and measured. They could be matched in accounts from many places
and times, for they are the mass of humanity in all periods. We forget
them often, always to our moral weakness, and often enough with greater
peril still.

WHAT BECOMES OF THE ROMAN-HEARTED?

The long, long shadow of a short, fat man darkens our understanding of
the Roman world, and of our own. Edward Gibbon was an astonishing
figure, for his erudition, for his energy, for his mastery of two languages
of composition (French and English), and for his dachshund-like ability to
pursue his prey to ground and hang on for dear life. The first volume of
his *History of the Decline and Fall of the Roman Empire* was published
in 1776, when he was thirty-nine, and the last twelve years later. Between
first and last, his vision of the Roman empire broadened and expanded.
What might have ended with a conventional explanation, however splendidly developed, of how emperors ceased to rule in the Latin west in the
fifth century unfolded instead into a broad canvas reaching the steppes of
central Asia, with a narrative introducing Tamerlane and Genghis Khan
and culminating with the capture of Constantinople by Sultan Mehmed II

in 1453. No page of Gibbon is not worth reading; few of his footnotes are not worth considering carefully.[22]

Few pages of historical works are as famous as the one where he describes himself conceiving the ambition to write *The Decline and Fall* while sitting on the Capitoline Hill in Rome, contrasting in imagination the mixture of ruins and churchly power before him ("as I sat musing in the church of the Zoccolanti or Franciscan friars, while they were singing vespers in the temple of Jupiter on the ruins of the capitol"[23]), drawing on his classical education to make vivid the glories of the past to his mind's eye. It is almost irrelevant that the pretty scene on the Capitoline probably never happened in quite the way he reports. His themes and biases were evident—"the triumph of barbarism and religion," as he put it—and they had immense interpretive power in the eighteenth century, but his main lines of interpretation have been undermined and rewritten since. His blindnesses, moreover, were significant, not least his inability—for he published his first volumes in the same year Adam Smith published *The Wealth of Nations*—to grasp the main lines of economic argument that need to be spun around these societies in order to understand their development. In his own time, his scapegoating of Christianity led to outrage, but his scholarship defeated objections. Not until the last two generations did scholars rehabilitate priests and barbarians alike, not to whitewash, but to recognize that simplistic solutions always mislead. "They were, those people, a kind of solution," the poet Cavafy said ruefully of barbarians who failed to materialize and could not play the role of scapegoat assigned them.

The myth has two things wrong with it. First, this expansive multiethnic and long-lived community of nations had little do with anything Roman. The most prominent citizens of the Roman empire in its most prosperous times lived far from Italy (mainly in the cities of the east) and owed their wealth to many factors, of which the brutal imposition of the Roman peace was only one, and not indispensable. To make sense of the economic, social, cultural, religious, and even political history of, for example, Asia Minor in the second century CE requires various kinds of competence and broad specific knowledge. It's narrow and limiting to connect the urbane people and societies of that period and place with a community that had its base in a trading post at a crossing of the Tiber River 900 years earlier. But because men and women in the second century believed the story of Romulus and Remus and how that trading post became a great city and founded a great empire, they made it true and relevant—at least to some extent.

Second, the traditional story offers a single narrative point of view, one focus, and a sole omniscient narrator who identifies with an empire seen at the scale of empire itself. The historian who chooses the Roman empire for his topic will inevitably under-imagine the distinctiveness of local cultures and places in that world. Even worse, looking at the history of the Roman empire makes it easy to neglect points of view beyond the ken of the Roman elite. We lose the perspective of provincials, soldiers, women, slaves, businessmen—everyone who lived outside the Beltway, so to speak. Much of the best and most exciting scholarly investigation of our time has plunged with relish into Rome's provinces and sought out its many and various peoples.

Here's an example: in the late fifth century, the Isaurians at last fell under Constantinople's political control. But to judge by the brightly colored maps we post on classroom walls, Isauria, in southern Asia Minor, had long been part of the empire. Because it was mountainous, sparsely populated, and off the beaten track, and so had long been a marginal outpost from which a few soldiers or adventurers might occasionally emerge, there couldn't have been much "Roman" about it. Isaurians first show up in the Roman empire's lore more than sporadically when they are the stereotypical heavies in narratives of the fourth and fifth centuries—"barbarian" in every way except that they found their homes inside rather than outside the empire's borders. Then suddenly their chieftain, Tarasicodissa, famous for having no kneecaps and thus being able to run faster than ordinary men, ascended the imperial throne. By promptly taking the reassuringly and traditionally Greek name of Zeno, he guaranteed that he would disappear into the imperial lists unremarked, as he wished. Within a generation, Isauria was quietly paying taxes and we hear no more of Isaurian bandits and brigands. The Roman empire had just gotten there a few centuries late.

No empire is an island, least of all one in a dead-end corner of the Eurasian landmass. The forested, mountainous, but well-watered and fertile land of the remote western peninsula that trapped all the migrating peoples who moved into it was only a small part of a great stage on which many others interacted. Travel east from Rome's Rhine through land progressively less promising, skirting your way through the marshes of Poland, shying away from the northern winter toward the plains of Scythia not yet turned into farmland, and go on into the steppes of western and central Asia, and you'll have seen a little of the neighborhood that Rome lived in.

Rome, to be sure, still holds our imaginations. The ancient Greeks appeal easily to lovers of beauty and tragedy, but also to flinty-eyed political hawks who prefer to relive Persian, Peloponnesian, and Alexandrian wars. The traditional middle ages call to sentimentalists who admire virtuous primitives, and the Renaissance endures for Whigs of all generations with their self-glorifying provincialism.

Huns and Persians draw few modern enthusiasts. Meanwhile, the allegiance that several generations of nineteenth- and twentieth-century German scholars expressed to the "Germanic" invaders of the Roman empire (the Goths, Vandals, and Lombards, above all) has largely collapsed, toppling under the weighty disgrace of German nationalism following World War II, and undone by more keenly skeptical scholarship. But classical Rome lives for moralists, those people who always know exactly what other people should be doing.

In the Roman world, as one might expect, the books that survive side with the Romans. Even the few narratives that seem to reflect a "barbarian" pride were written in Greek or Latin. Jordanes, a man on the make in Justinian's Constantinople, wrote his book *Getica* ("Gothics") in Latin, inventing a glorious past for the Goths, trying to make sense of contemporary history from the capital's perspective. Goths, Persians, and Huns very likely had tales of their own, to say nothing of their documents, but the Romans were far and away more documentary and textual, and therefore more like us, and therefore capable of making their voices and personalities more vividly known to us. The "glory that was Greece and the grandeur that was Rome" (in the words of Poe) still enchant many who know little about the realities of ancient life.

If you seek the last day of the Roman empire, you'll have many choices. Never mind that the Roman historian Sallust, Augustine of Hippo in his *City of God*, and the modern historian Arnold J. Toynbee all date the downfall of Rome from its victory in the second Punic War in 202 BCE. Almost all historians agree that creating an empire to succeed a republic (which is how we conventionally describe the successful putsch by Caesar's nephew Octavian and his self-remaking under the name Augustus Caesar) merely exalted the Roman past, while abandoning many of its excellences. Dissolution often threatened the hold of the imperial regime over its far-flung realms. Between 235 and 284 dissolution very nearly prevailed, when the longest-reigning emperor of that period was a usurper too marginal for more serious but shorter-lived contenders to bother taking time to ex-terminate. The remaking of empire in 284 and after, first by the emperor Diocletian and then by Constantine, was intended then and is accepted now as an expression of continuity, though much had to change in order to create a stable new regime. Many historians have long been persuaded that at some time in the fifth century, something decisive occurred. The date of 476 was chosen in the sixth century, for political reasons explored below, and has crept into textbooks repeatedly, down to the present day. But there is no good reason to accept it.

So if Rome did not fall in 202 BCE or 476 CE, when did it fall? In 800 CE the Frankish king Karl, Carolus, or Charles—that is, Charlemagne—concluded that the empire had finally lost its way when the eastern throne fell into the hands of a woman, the empress Irene, and so he had him-self crowned emperor by the pope in Rome on Christmas day. Shall we call his dominion—that medieval avatar of empire in the west—a *Roman* empire? It did business under that name for 1,000 years, until Voltaire waggishly commented that it was neither holy, nor Roman, nor an empire. True enough, but at about the same time, in his autobiography, the young Goethe described the impressive ceremonies he had seen himself in Frank-furt for the election of the Roman emperor. That version of Rome finally disappeared in 1806, when Napoleon dispensed with old imperial tradi-tion in order to create his own imperial edifice, however short-lived.

Other dates offer themselves: we have already seen Gibbon's choice, at the sack of Constantinople in 1453, but that was the whimper, not the bang. The balance of power in medieval Asia Minor had tilted strongly toward the Turks 200 years earlier, when the *other* Roman empire and its allies and friends, the crusaders, overthrew the Christian empire of Constantinople. Constantine's fundamental idea, that he could maintain hegemony over the Balkans, Asia Minor, and the eastern lands beyond from a perch in the Bosporus and the Golden Horn, is exactly the idea that Mehmed the Conqueror accepted when he put Constantinople out of its misery and made it his capital. Dismantling the dilapidated city's pathetic rump of an empire in 1453 secured Turkish domination more by securing continuity than by changing anything fundamental. (Some western powers even welcomed the new partner.) Mehmed saw himself as the successor to the Roman emperor, and thus in an important way Constantine's fundamental vision was sustained intact not merely till 1453, but till 1924—the last gasp of the Ottoman empire and its suppression in favor of a more modest and modern republic of Turkey.

If we ask what became of the Roman-hearted (who had power that's now departed), looking for a single date at which a switch was thrown and an empire ceased to exist never makes real sense. Instead, we'll first have to reframe the question as one that can be answered, and answered on a human scale. Human beings live in a moving window of time that remembers a generation or two of the past reasonably well and that imagines a future best measured in decades, not centuries or millennia. The century or so from 476 to 604 CE reflects human plans and wishes with their successes and failures, showing how rulers who could not understand their world as existing on a continuum much older than themselves squandered countless opportunities.

WHEN DID IT HAPPEN?

I will identify the dates of events using the western convention BCE and CE, corresponding to BC and AD. No one alive in the time of this story used that dating system regularly, and only a few were aware of it, but many would have understood it if you had described it to them. To the best of our knowledge, the scheme was devised in the 520s by Dionysius Exiguus ("Denis the Short" or perhaps merely "Denis the Humble"), who calculated that Jesus had been incarnated at the Annunciation—the moment when Mary met the angel and became pregnant, which he dated to March 25 in the year 754 of the city of Rome: that is, 1 CE or AD 1. (The first Christmas, by that reckoning, fell on December 25 of the year 1.)

Fortunately for us, Dionysius had the year wrong. Jesus was born no later than 4 BCE and perhaps as early as 8 BCE. If Dionysius had been correct, then the second millennium would have arrived between 1992 and 1996 and a generation of computer programmers would have had even less time than they did to forestall the confusion of Y2K. We hear of Dionysius's work first in his own time in another writer's treatise on the mechanism for fixing the date of Easter, and at least one seventh-century chronicler reckoned dates that way, but it was not until the eighth century that the Anglo-Saxon historian Bede employed it consistently and found a relatively wide readership. The scholar Alcuin took the idea to the continent, where it caught on and flourished under the influence of Charlemagne.

In the sixth century, in other words, there was no sixth century. People were generally aware of how long it had been since Christ was born (in the late fourth century some surmised that the 365th year after the crucifixion would see the second coming of Jesus), but public documents and official records, even church documents, used more ancient ways of counting. The commonest and most venerable were still consular years, and until 541 CE one or two consuls were appointed in each year and the year bore their names—"in the consulship of X and Y"—and the roster of names going back to 509 BCE was a source of pride for the families who found ancestors on it. When consuls were no longer named, counting and naming years from the beginning of the current emperor's reign was more common.

Meanwhile, a separate reckoning flourished in imperial offices, the so-called indiction, which is effectively the name for a tax year on a fifteen-year cycle. Hence men would speak of the "first indiction" or "the twelfth indiction" and the first would follow again the year after the fifteenth. This system had begun under the reforming emperor Diocletian in 297 and had run for almost fifteen full cycles when our story begins. The practice reminds us that for many purposes, even something so inefficient was serviceable. Periods longer than fifteen years didn't come to mind very often, not as requiring exact dating, but the tax man came every year and defined economic reality for many. People did not much talk about how old they were until their relatives needed to write their age on the tombstone—and often not even then. The people in this story lived in the bright light of the present, with far less sense of an accurately accounted history—short or long—than even poorly educated moderns have.

PART I

THEODERIC'S WORLD

The Empire That Hadn't Fallen
(476–527 CE)

Our story unfolds in three acts. First, here, an account of the empire that hadn't fallen; then the empire that thought it was at risk of falling and partly already had; then what was left in the rubble after good intentions, bad planning, and bad luck had their way. Each act has its protagonist. The curtain rises on Theoderic, who saw that innovation is the best path to stewardship of tradition.

1

Rome in 500:
Looking Backward

OME DIDN'T SEE many emperors in the fifth century. Nero's death let fall a diadem, and in the year 69 CE, Galba, Otho, Vitellius, and finally Vespasian grasped at it. Tacitus drily observed that the success of such provincial generals revealed the "secret of empire"—that emperors could be created somewhere other than at Rome. From Augustus to Nero, Rome had been the only obvious dwelling for an *imperator*, and Tiberius's self-exile to Capri brought scorn and salacious gossip about what he was up to while swimming with slave boys. After 69, emperors spent more and more time with their armies and on the frontiers. Hadrian in the early second century and the Severan emperors around 200 were away almost as much as they were home. The succession of disasters during the third century had kept emperors far from the capital, fighting each other and managing the frontiers. After Diocletian imposed his military order, he and his successors established a string of imperial cities that followed the frontier: Trier to survey the Rhine; Milan, Aquileia, and Sirmium (modern Sremska Mitrovica on the Save River in Serbia) to watch the Danube without abandoning the Rhine; Constantinople between the Balkans and the eastern provinces; and Antioch in Syria.

Rome was a nice place to visit, but a military backwater. Even many successful emperors never saw it during their reigns. Constantinople, on the other hand, was a palace town, almost constantly aware of the presence of an emperor after Theodosius's death in 395. The military cities in the west lost their prestige when in 402 the emperor Honorius retreated to the swamp-protected Italian city of Ravenna, with its Adriatic port offering ready sea communication to Constantinople. He and his brother Arcadius in Constantinople stood at the head of a long line of emperors who were mostly figureheads, dwelling in the capital and delegating military leadership to the able.

Through all this, Rome's emperors cosseted and cared for the city when they had time enough to pay it attention, but dramatic losses befell the city as well. The senate still met, traditional offices were filled, and the old families clung to wealth and position, but their numbers were greatly diminished. By the sixth century, there may have been only a very few dozen active senators, linked together in fewer than a dozen families. The pedigrees by which these people claimed "ancient nobility" were often sketchy as well, for Constantine's revolution and the army he built two centuries earlier produced many rough-bred military husbands willing to marry into distinguished but impoverished families grateful for the protection and sometimes ill-gotten wealth of their new sons.[1] As long as these old families were certain of their prerogatives, they were content to surrender their power to the new men. The city needed the subsidies rich families could provide and clung as well to its ancient self-esteem, but power was another matter.

And Rome's numbers dwindled. The city achieved a population of 1 million or so in the second century, but an estimate by Richard Krautheimer, a scholar who knew that late antique city as no other, brought it down to 800,000 by 400, when Constantinople and Ravenna eclipsed Rome's real function as a capital. Rome lost half of that in the next fifty years, marked by Alaric's brief sack of the city in 410, and it lost another half or three-quarters by the late 400s, when the Vandal raid of 455 was only the worst of a half century of indignities. There may have been only 100,000 or so people left by 500. The fortunate followed power to other capitals, while others died, failed to reproduce, or fled to the countryside.

Emperors had lived from time to time in Rome as late as the 470s, when Romulus was briefly on the throne, but in 500 there came a grand visit like nothing seen since Theodosius more than a century before. Only twice after that date would empire revisit its cradle, for consular games in 519 and for a brief stopover in 663. When Charlemagne arrived to have himself crowned emperor in 800, his business was inventing the new while pretending to cherish the old, and the medieval emperors who followed knew they were foreigners and usurpers in the city of Romulus and Augustus.

To the naked eye, Rome was Rome as it had always been; to the historical eye, change was everywhere, and continual. The Rome of Augustus had acquired, in the third and fourth centuries, sturdy new perimeter defense walls towering forty or fifty feet over everyone from imperial dignitaries seeking a grand entrance to farmers bringing produce to market. Fourth-century sources let us count the visible monuments of the city: twenty-eight libraries, six obelisks, eight bridges, eleven forums, ten basilicas, eleven public baths, eighteen aqueducts, nine circuses and theaters, two triumphal columns, fifteen fountains, twenty-two equestrian statues, eighty golden statues, twenty-four ivory statues, thirty-six triumphal arches, and the more pedestrian necessities as well: 290 granaries and warehouses, 856 private baths, 254 bakeries, and 46 brothels.

Even when Constantine took to Christianity after 312 CE, Christians and traditionalists alike were reluctant to introduce church architecture into the city's historic core. Traditionalists feared the intrusion, Christians the contamination of proximity to the ancient gods. So the great early Christian basilicas stood guard around the core: for example, Saint Peter's shrine on the Vatican hill across the Tiber from the walled city proper; or the church of the Holy Cross, just inside city gates on the east side of town; or the basilica of Saint Paul, some little way outside the walls to the south. In 391, Theodosius had solidified seventy-five years of increasing suppression of the old religious rites by banning sacrifice and public performance of religious cult activities. With that, the great temples in the forums and on the Capitoline and Palatine hills fell silent, protected only by the superstitions of new and old believers alike who prudently feared offending the old gods gratuitously. Churches began to edge closer to the center of the city during the fifth century. The basilica of Santa Sabina took high ground on the Aventine to the south, where Juno, Isis, and Diana had once prevailed; and Great Saint Mary's (Santa Maria Maggiore) stood on the Esquiline north of the forums. Closer to the center the churching of Rome

Rome.

would come, with Pope Felix IV in the 520s transforming the city prefect's great audience hall on the Via Sacra, a few dozen yards from the original forum, into a church honoring saints Cosmas and Damian. Eventually, in the 630s, Pope Honorius consecrated the senate house itself as a church in honor of a martyr who bore an emperor's name—Saint Hadrian, of the early fourth century. By 500, the bishop of Rome had his own church of Saint John Lateran, inside the city but nearly against the walls, at the end of the Caelian on the southeast side. By the time of Pope Gregory's reign in the 590s, at least half a dozen smaller churches had been erected.

Just what condition the city was in around 500 is harder to say. We have, from the early years of the sixth century, a small spate of texts deploring dilapidation at Rome and elsewhere, and directing renovations and repairs. Rome's most imperial symbol, the imperial palace on the Palatine hill, was restored; the senate house and, as we will see, the theater of Pompey were repaired; and walls, aqueducts, and granaries were all variously attended to. Within the city, the population's decline probably revealed itself in the way people contracted together to live in some areas, leaving others to become the so-called *disabitato* of the middle ages, those tracts of the ancient city that became cattle pastures. Maintaining the aqueducts that brought fresh water from the hills was expensive and difficult, especially as demand fell. When we hear a sixth-century ruler's outrage that farmers were diverting some of the aqueduct water for mills and irrigation, the outrage is mainly for show; the water was more useful in the fields by now.

Similarly, Rome could no longer count on the grain supply that had traditionally flooded the city at the tax collector's command every year. No more was there the anxiety of old, when the wary eyes of citizens would watch the weather and the seas, hoping that the grain freighters would arrive before the onset of winter rains closed the Mediterranean until spring. Now there were fewer mouths to feed and they had to rely on local supplies or a freer market. The government in Africa, no longer acknowledging the emperor's authority, kept its grain in Africa, or sold it at market prices. People got by, somehow. The city was by turns both gloomy and grand, still a marvel to the eye of any traveler, but a sad shadow of its former self.

One great monument tells a bit of its own story in this period: the Colosseum, the great amphitheater built at the center of the city in the late first century by the emperors Vespasian and Titus.[2] Holding, at a conservative estimate, 50,000 spectators, it dominated the cityscape and made possible many assorted and often gruesome entertainments. Situated at the crossroads of empire, it witnessed every spectacle and every visitor. A nineteenth-century investigation team found more than 400 species of plant life in the ruins, many of them entirely alien to the Tiber valley and the surrounding country; their seeds had been carried on the feet of animals, gladiators, and soldiers from all over the world. Gladiatorial contests had ended under mainly Christian emperors, though probably not for any puritanical reason—they may simply have lost popularity. Other forms of spectacle, particularly wild beast hunts, lasted into the sixth century.

Inscriptions demonstrate that in the 470s, while Odoacer held power at Rome and made and unmade emperors, the old amphitheater had undergone at least some renovation and upgrades. Where once the seating was rigidly defined by class (senators here, knights there, vestal virgins over there, etc.), now individual senators and families would have their names carved on their own particular seats. Not skyboxes in the modern fashion, but rather down low, more like courtside seats—designed to provide the best views, the richest smells, and even the thrill of an occasional spatter of sweat or blood. So an official letter of around 510 orders the city prefect to make certain that the two sons of a deceased senator should be assured that particular places at the circus and the amphitheater were theirs alone.

As late as the year 522, the incoming consul for 523 was granted permission to stage the great hunting games known as the *venationes*, forerunners of the modern bullfight. An official letter from that occasion captures the flavor of the events and the excitement that surrounded them, while fairly wallowing in anticipated blood. The hunter earns special praise, because he of all performers puts his life on the line to dazzle the audience. When victory eludes him he forfeits even the chance of a proper burial, for he is devoured by his would-be prey. Diana the huntress of Scythia is named as the goddess in whose honor the Romans organized this cult. She reigned first in the sky in the guise of the moon, then in the forests as the huntress, and at last under the earth as Proserpina, but then in Christian disdain the letter writer quickly acknowledges that only Proserpina captures her true character as a demon luring men to hell. Self-satisfied virtue regrets the miserable enthusiasm that would seek pleasure in the destruction of human beings and pronounces this all a cruel game, a bloody pleasure, an impious religion, human beastliness.

But then the event still has to be described: performers bait the creature by charging and taunting it, then the hunter circles his prey as his prey circles him, and at last the hunter leaps in the air as the beast charges, suspending himself almost miraculously in midair as it passes beneath. Various skilled hunters then taunt and divert the animal in different ways.

Sometimes one hunter hid inside a reed basket for protection, while another astonishingly was strapped to a wheel and spun before the creature to put the hunter in reach and then snatch him out of harm's way in a moment. This last stunt was considered the most comically dangerous; the audience enjoyed and accepted such risks because all hunters were expendable, even in an empire that had now called itself Christian for more than 200 years. The official letter from court that tells us all this ends on a primly moral note by comparing it (in the language of Vergil's poetry rather than that of the Bible) to the torments of the underworld, but then it also grants full permission in the name of the ruler to carry on the ancient tradition.

This blood-infused letter is the last surviving document to tell us of traditional uses for the Colosseum, and the last *venatio* at Constantinople occurred in 537. The edifice stood empty till the eleventh century, when it fell into the possession of the Frangipani family, who turned it into a fort.

Why did the spectacles end and the amphitheater fall silent? A disdainful ruler may have been one reason, but competition from the chariot racing at the nearby circus is more likely; that was now Rome's true great passion. And Constantinople, we will see later, had the circus bug even worse than Rome. Chariots may seem proverbially Roman to us as a means of travel, but they were long obsolete as anything but public toys used for racing, which was nearly a blood sport.

Pompous architecture, thrilling spectacles, and ancient prestige: all offered strong enough reasons for a ruler to visit the city. After the death in 498 of Pope Anastasius II, a man who had tried to mediate the religious quarrels between Rome and Constantinople, there was political opportunity as well.

For the church of Rome soon found itself with two popes, Symmachus and Laurentius, elected by different factions on the same day. Symmachus won his title in the official church of Saint John Lateran. A countervote a few hours later, not far away at Great Saint Mary's, gave Laurentius the nod. Symmachus was arguably the hard-liner, Laurentius the compromiser, but it's not clear how far large issues of policy went in dictating these choices, and how much was the result of more mundane local squabbles, such as control of church property. Quite reasonably, the two claimants submitted their dispute in short order to the throne in Ravenna to settle, and Symmachus prevailed. (Ravenna had already shown itself careful in dealing with popes not many years before, when Gelasius I complained that clergy from Nola had wrongly taken a case to the court at Ravenna, and Ravenna rightly and promptly waived jurisdiction, sending the clergymen right back to the pope.)

A few months after the contested papal election, on March 1, 499, Symmachus presided over a grand synod of his clergy and granted Laurentius the bishopric of Nocera, south of Rome between Naples and Salerno, a healthy distance from the city and its troubles. Peace was restored, for a while.

Then came the grand celebrations. King Theoderic came to Rome and went to visit Blessed Peter as devoutly as if he were Catholic—that's how a historian of the next generation described it,[3] when there were many alive who remembered that day of spectacle. Odd things are going on. Theoderic is not "emperor" (*imperator* or *Augustus*) but "king" (*rex*), and his name sounds oddly un-Latinate. He gets to have his churchly cake and eat it too—as somehow not a member of the Catholic community at Rome, yet permitted and quite willing to participate in it. Everything important about the sixth century is in that one sentence, and this visit is worth watching closely for that reason.

Let us start from the moment of Theoderic's grand arrival from Ravenna. What crowds the diminished city could muster were there to greet him. The old phrase SPQR (*senatus populusque romanus*, "senate and people of Rome") still described the city's unity, however paltry and factional the crowd actually was. Pope Symmachus waited with the crowd to meet Theoderic outside the walls. Peter's tomb was on the northwest side of the walled city on the Vatican hill and the procession from Ravenna could well have visited there before it made its way down the Via Cornelia, past Hadrian's tomb and across the Aelian bridge into the city proper. Crossing that bridge, the procession would recall Christian emperors of old, as it passed the arch of those late-fourth-century colleagues Valentinian and Theodosius, and then the arch of the sons of Theodosius: Honorius and Arcadius. Swelling now, the procession entered the *campus Martius*, the "field of Mars," formerly an open expanse that had seemed almost suburban in earlier Roman times, but that was now the clotted heart of the remaining city. The most reasonable route from there wound past the Pantheon, the monument to "all the gods" built originally by Augustus's son-in-law Agrippa in the earliest days of the principate, then destroyed in a fire 100 years later, and finally rebuilt in the form that survives today by Hadrian around 125 CE, with various later repairs.

We would love to know how the Pantheon appeared at this moment. The astonishing dome had protected an imperial audience hall that honored traditional planetary gods such as Mercury and Venus, while offering a literal microcosm of the spherical universe, with earth at the center. After official neglect and then suppression of the old religious rites, this building once full of gods had probably already suffered depredations and neglect, but surely at the same time its magnificence would draw to it some of that past respect. I imagine it as a slightly spooky place back then, quieter than it had ever been, unsure of its future. Not until fully a century later did an emperor deed it over to a pope and have it turned into the church it still is.

A little farther along, the procession passed the porticoed courtyard and theater of Pompey, the great building that initiated urban development on this side of the city and demonstrated the power and presence of its builder. (Pompey indeed might have been Rome's savior if a Gaulish ax had found Julius Caesar's skull before the two great men fell into the ruinous civil war of 49 BCE.) Finally, Theoderic would have enjoyed his first view of the Roman forum coming from the riverside, up between the Capitoline and Palatine hills, by just the route that Vergil said the old Greek colonist Evander used to show the rustic future site of Rome to Aeneas long before in legendary memory. From there, after a brief visit to the senate house, Theoderic made a public address to the people in which the king promised that he would unfailingly preserve what all the *principes* of Rome before him had ordained.

What did the audience see when they looked on their ruler for the first time? He was a man of nearly fifty, fair-haired, and probably beardless, as emperors now usually were. His clothing was doubtless also in the current vein, with the slightly raffish and dangerous look of frontier military wear that had been in fashion among leaders for the last century, but he affected the imperial purple as well. There was a lot of mixing of styles and fashions in Italy in those days, so we should be careful about assuming that we could tell who was who in Theoderic's court just by costume or hairstyle. One hostile source tells us that Theoderic was illiterate, requiring a stencil to trace the word LEGI ("I have read it") onto documents, a story we begin not to believe when we come on it again in a different hostile source, which says the emperor Justin I used the same device to sign *his* name. There is reason to think that Theoderic at least was considerably better educated than this.

The culmination of Theoderic's grand arrival was the formal celebration of thirty years of rule, a ceremony our historian somewhat inaccurately calls a triumph. Claiming thirty years at this moment was a bit of a stretch: Theoderic had now been the uncontested ruler in Italy for only seven years. For far more than half of the previous thirty years he had governed a much smaller, arguably non-Roman population, far from the city he now visited. Thirty years was a pretext for a better party, however, for the feast called *tricennalia* was a particularly dignified event, with a point nobody could miss in its echo of the celebration of imperial longevity from the career of the first Christian emperor, Constantine, almost two centuries earlier. Emperors rarely lasted so long.

An African named Fulgentius, who would end his life as the fiercely orthodox bishop of Ruspe in his homeland, visited Rome when Theoderic was in residence. We have a biographer's version of the story Fulgentius told back home in Africa, of the dazzling pomp and ritual, and of his own resistance to the seductive spectacle. "Brethren," he said to his fellow monks,

> how beautiful must the heavenly Jerusalem be, if the earthly Rome shines like this! And if in this world such honor is paid to worthy men by those who love nothing but vanity, what must it be like, the honor and glory and peace that is bestowed on the saints in contemplation of truth above?

He may have been the last visitor for many centuries who could gaze upon the pomp and glory of Rome and disdain it so firmly, for there would soon be much less to disdain.

From ceremony, then, to palace: that is, to the original and ultimate home of Roman emperors on the Palatine hill itself. Much remade over five centuries, the house of Augustus was once again to be properly occupied. Not all agreed that things were fully as they should be, but skepticism abided for now in discreet silence.

Decrees followed, including generous food rations for the populace, ambitious renovations for the palace, and much-needed repairs for the city's walls and buildings. Diplomacy had its place in Theoderic's lofty thoughts, as he announced the marriage of his sister Amalafrida to Transimund, the king of the Vandals and ruler in Carthage, across the traditionally contentious waters that had once been the marine battlefield of the Punic Wars. Marriage was such an important part of his diplomatic policy that a few months later, on return to Ravenna, he would marry off another sister to the king of the Thuringians along the Rhine to the north.

And finally, administration: a distinguished Roman senator, a man of about forty years, Liberius by name, with a long future still in front of him, stepped down as praetorian prefect (roughly, prime minister) with full honors, replaced by Theodore, a senator from an even more distinguished family. All these acts, deeds, and promises were publicly inscribed on bronze tablets for everyone to see.

Not all was easy and well, though. A colonel named Odoin was found—or alleged—to be plotting against Theoderic, and so Theoderic had him beheaded in the Sessorian basilica, a setting of almost operatic rightness that today forms the core of the elaborate basilica of Santa Croce in Gerusalemme. This was the place where Constantine had built a shrine for the relics of Jesus's cross his mother brought back from Jerusalem. Thus human and divine justice came together with an execution in the presence of the physical evidence of Christ's own crucifixion.

Theoderic stayed in Rome for six months, but we know too little of what it was like to have such a living, bustling court back in residence on the Palatine after so long a time. One source, not terribly friendly otherwise, confides that the shows Theoderic put on in the Colosseum caused the locals to compare him to Trajan or Valentinian, which is no mean flattery. The message to the Romans, however, was unambiguous: this was a grand imperial visit, marked by magnanimity, respect for tradition, and Theoderic's clear assertion of every power. Some contemporaries and most moderns might think him not Catholic and hence not a true emperor, but for these months he played the part of devout *princeps* (the title Augustus preferred) in the grand style. He also succeeded well enough to rule for another twenty-six years, untroubled until almost the end by internal dissatisfaction.

THE BORDERMAN BROUGHT UP
IN A PALACE

Who was this Theoderic and how did he come to this apogee of his career?

He was the son of a powerful Arian general, Theodemer, and a Catholic mother, Erelieva. From early childhood he was brought up at the imperial court in Constantinople, learning to see the world from a palace. The magnificence of monuments, the pomp of ceremonies, and the prerogatives of absolute power were for him home, education, and something to strive for. He was in Constantinople because of guarded mutual respect and careful negotiation between his own father and the imperial court. We would have to call him a hostage, because we have no word in English for this kind of honored, pampered, yet mistrusted guest—a child held to ensure his father's good behavior—but the arrangement was perfectly understood at that time. A few years later, the Persian king would offer his own son for adoption by the Roman emperor as a way of sealing relations between the two thrones and powers.

Theoderic's father, a leader of men in the central Balkans, was not equal to the Persian king in scale or claims, but he already had a serious history as a power to be reckoned with. The men who followed him had fought a few years before Theoderic's birth against Roman armies at a great battle in northern Gaul, suffered defeat, regrouped, and made a place for themselves in the Roman world. To have Theodemer's eldest son at court was insurance and a precaution. On balance the bargain worked well.

In about 471, at age eighteen, Theoderic went back to his father's people, who were then settled in the Pannonian plain of modern Hungary. To explain the thirty-year celebration of 500, scholars are in the habit of treating this event as his first exaltation to rule. He must have seemed an odd arrival in the north, marked by his years in Constantinople in many ways, and even bringing back with him a retinue of associates and servants of a kind not usually seen on Rome's northern reaches. He knew he had to be his father's son, and he learned well from military men what that meant. He married first a woman of low status, with whom he had two daughters; later he married a princess—Audefleda, the sister of Clovis, who was the ruler in northern and central Gaul—and with her had a daughter, Amalasuntha. He had no sons.

In Pannonia he shortly proved himself a leader in his own right, taking a raiding party across the Danube to attack the Sarmatians, who had been harassing the Romans from there. Theoderic returned successful and with plunder, having seized control of the city of Singidunum (modern Belgrade). By 476, in what was then called Moesia, Theodemer had died, and Theoderic succeeded him. Theodemer's people were poor and hungry in Pannonia, and so in the mid-470s, Theoderic led them south to Thessalonica on the Aegean; then they made their way back to the northern part of what is now Bulgaria, where they stayed for several years.

Theoderic and his people moved the way ancient armies moved, with their families and camp followers of various kinds in attendance. Old Roman soldiers had been officially forbidden to marry for as long as they served, and they fought in units that their leaders could move from one end of the known world to another in a matter of weeks or a few months. Theoderic's modern Roman army, by contrast, had grown bulkier and less mobile in later generations, while gaining in return the stability of kinship and family. When these people moved, they moved heavy, and unhappy residents of the places they went would liken those movements to an invasion. For the army, moreover, there were gains and losses as they went. Some members of the group would prefer not to move, or would abandon the community en route; others would join opportunistically along the way.

Groups gathering around and following generals like Theoderic had become contract armies, willing to serve Rome for the right pay, but equally willing to choose independence and look out for themselves. They took their identity from the leader's family, while embracing a broad mixture of backgrounds and ethnicities. The community Theodemer and then Theoderic inspired could easily tell a story about its history in the Balkans going back almost a century. Given half an excuse, its historians would embroider that account with other, more edifying but less relevant anecdotes about more distant pasts and places, stories that none then thought to disbelieve.

In the 470s, when Theoderic went back to his father, the armies like his that worked and lived in the Balkans were often at odds with the home office in Constantinople, which eyed them warily. Emperors gave commands and sent along gifts, which weren't quite bribes, to ensure that the commands would be obeyed. But meanwhile, Zeno, the emperor formerly known as Tarasicodissa, was fending off rebellion closer to home from a general, Basiliscus, who sought the throne for himself. Basiliscus was probably the uncle of Odoacer, the strongman then busy making and un-making emperors in Italy with an army of his own, which Zeno also inter-preted as a threat to his power.

Zeno was immediately successful against Basiliscus, and he rewarded those who supported him, including Theoderic. Still young, probably not yet thirty, Theoderic was named "patrician" and "master of soldiers in the imperial presence," the highest, if honorary, military ranks of the empire, and Zeno declared him to be his own son at arms and comrade as well. In the way of such compacts among strong leaders, tension continued, and by 478, Theoderic had made peace and an alliance with another leader in the Balkans, another Theoderic, usually called Theoderic Strabo—that is, "Theoderic the cross-eyed"—to distinguish him from his more famous neighbor. Together they demanded support for their troops, for this was a world in which emperors had learned to outsource or privatize defense, accepting the idea that in large areas, protection would come by contract with independent leaders like Theoderic rather than by regular stipends paid to directly subordinated soldiers and officers. Pressed for a better deal by his contractors, an emperor would bob and weave and temporize, looking for the best deal he could get. Zeno might offer Theoderic money, but in this case he also proffered the hand of Anicia Juliana, the daugh-ter of a well-born but short-lived western emperor of the last generation, Olybrius. Theoderic declined that offer, but one wonders what this strong-willed woman—whom we will meet again—might have done in alliance with an equally resourceful man.

Zeno was not out of the woods yet, for another rebel, Illus, preoc-cupied him well into the late 480s. Illus holed up in Zeno's native Isau-ria, where he was eventually hunted down and killed. During those years, Theoderic and his forces remained mainly on the southern shores of the Danube, in modern Bulgaria, between the river and the Haemus moun-tains. They guarded the border well enough, but ranged south from time to time, making unwelcome visits down into Macedonia and as far as Thessalonica, or ranging west along the ancient Roman highway, the Eg-natian Way, as far as Dyrrachium (Durazzo) on the Adriatic shore. At one point, Zeno suggested that Theoderic retire to the vicinity of Skopje in northern Macedonia, to protect Thessalonica and Roman interests in the southwestern Balkans, but Theoderic continually returned to the east and the Danube country.

Theoderic's actions were, by now, perfectly normal—but as recently as 100 years earlier they would have been taken as an unprecedented invasion by outsiders. At this moment in the late fifth century, the Balkans had become, uniquely among the old Roman lands, a wild west frontier society. By 500, the zone between the Egnatian Way and the Danube, which had never been as fully romanized as the other provinces, was a borderland between other more coherently unified, governed, and pacified states and communities. If we stand back and take a long view, the decay of the good order of the Balkans from the late fourth century to the late fifth century marks a retreat from the iron-handed enforcement of occupation that the Roman army had once been able to muster. Rome had never managed to get beyond military occupation to a hearts and minds transformation of the countryside and the establishment of a genuinely flourishing Roman city life in these provinces. When Roman resources were overextended, the provincialized and outsourced defense that someone like Theoderic could offer was the best emperors could do. If we regret this transition and mark it as a sign of decline, we must remember to blame the first four centuries of empire for not doing a better—harsher—job of making this corner of the realm fully Roman, prosperous, and secure.

What warlords like Theoderic did in the Balkans was an inherent part of the calculus of power and strategy in Constantinople. Theoderic knew he could roam at will, periodically attacking and plundering vulnerable cities, but he also knew that he could still make peace with the emperor again almost at will, as he did again with Zeno in 483, so successfully that he was now advanced to the very substantial rank of "master of soldiers for the Balkans" and, most exaltedly, given the title of consul for the year 484.

The first consuls had taken power in 509 BCE, and for more than 400 years the supreme magistracy of Rome remained fixed in the annual appointment of two men, who shared power for one year and then let others have their turn. The oligarchy that emerged arose from its members' deep-rooted suspicion of monarchy and of continuing individual power. Over and over, consuls came from the same few families, whose rivalry was tempered by a recognition of mutual interest and common profit. We must not idealize the Roman republic, but it deserves wary respect as the functioning and long-lived rule of the few over the many, achieving unprecedented power through ruthlessness and discipline.

Success swamps oligarchies. The late Roman republic was too successful and had to deal with too many foes and (more threatening still) too many friends both within and without its military sphere of influence to survive unchanged. The consulship diminished in influence during the age of Marius, Sulla, Pompey, Caesar, Antony, and Octavian and became instead one piece of a larger puzzle, with the strongmen of the moment manipulating the key. By the time Octavian allowed himself to be called Augustus, in 27 BCE, the consulship was an emblem of tradition, not a source of power. He destroyed the consulship's power once and for all but lived to dominate its 500th anniversary celebration. He could not have imagined that the office would survive with its outward forms intact for more than another 500 years.

Year in and year out, the emperor nominated candidates, whose hearts rose but whose finances quailed at such an opportunity. They gave their names to a year on the calendar and incurred the obligation to sponsor and pay for ceremonial games as lavish as they could possibly afford. One estimate from the sixth century suggests that a successful consular bash might cost nearly as much as the entire budget for running a reasonably sized province for a year.[4] Justinian's own consulship in 521—paid for out of an imperial treasury, to be sure—cost 4,000 pounds of gold and featured twenty lions and thirty leopards to go with the chariot races, the parades, and the public feasts. When emperors began to find themselves dividing their time between Rome and Constantinople in the fourth century, they commonly appointed one consul from each capital, thereby dividing the financial burden while providing celebrations in both cities.

We have no report of how Theoderic played the role of consul or who paid for his consular games. He must have been feted at Constantinople, and Zeno himself probably underwrote some games in honor of his ally. The one hint we get is a report that a statue of Theoderic on horseback was erected in front of the imperial palace in Constantinople, and his people were rewarded with grants of lands in the northern Balkans. As it happened, Zeno was still facing Illus's rebellion, so Theoderic's exaltation undoubtedly had the effect of buying his support against the rebel. There was even talk, never fulfilled, that Theoderic would go to Isauria to fight on behalf of Zeno. Theoderic had become an integral part of the Roman empire and its plans.

The relationship between Theoderic and his emperor soured one more time, however, and soon we see Theoderic back with his army in 486–487, marching to Constantinople to make threatening demands. The bias of our sources, who were based in Constantinople, generally reflects badly on Balkan generals at such moments, but their restiveness usually grew out of real grievances. The confrontation of 487 ended to Theoderic's advantage, as he brought back from Constantinople a sister of his, who had been at court there as just the kind of elegant hostage he himself had been.

A flow of messages and ambassadors continued back and forth from the Danube to Constantinople during the months that followed, and a remarkable strategic vision took shape. Theoderic had emerged, over his fifteen years in the Balkans, as a pragmatic, effective, and strong leader of his forces. He had given the emperor his share of grief, but had in the main been a collaborator and a force for stability. The Balkans had, on balance, the best government and the most prosperity they had seen in decades. What next? Theoderic's forces were restless because the Balkan mountains and valleys offered little scope for them to settle and expand. What if Theoderic and his forces went to Italy?

The idea was compelling. Odoacer was the latest, most original, and most successful of a series of generals who had grasped the reins of control in the western provinces during turbulent times. He never had any advantage except his talent—no tribe of followers, no official recognition, no wealthy supporters—but he brought stability in hard times. He would not have been human without ambitions, and, as we have seen, he may even have been related to Zeno's recent opponent Basiliscus. He had, surely, few reasons to pay much attention to what an uncomprehending and unhelpful Constantinople might want of him and every reason to think that with the right partner in the east he could achieve great things. But he was alone, and Theoderic, general and former consul, was the perfect leader to send west to seize Italy from him, and settle there to rule as the emperor's viceroy. In 488, Theoderic agreed to do just this.

Ennodius of Pavia was a clergyman with ambitions that he never realized, but we owe to his ambitions various books, pamphlets, and letters that are precious historical sources for this turbulent period. Ennodius may have been a flatterer, but he can still spin us a good yarn. In the account of Theoderic's rise that he once declaimed at court in Ravenna, the arrival of Theoderic in Italy came as a long procession— made up of people whose homes were now in carts, with baggage, livestock, and families all together— crawled its way westward. A generous estimate would put the number at 20,000, including a secretary with a Greek name, Phocas. The trek covered some 600 miles from its start in Moesia along the Danube to the vicinity of Trieste and Venice, where the travelers first entered the north Italian plain, itself stretching another 200 miles before them. Along the way, Theoderic's forces fought a pitched battle in the vicinity of the Save River with a people called Gepids, destroying them and killing their leader. Ennodius tells the story prettily: how Theoderic gave a rousing speech, accepted a cup of wine for luck, then took up his reins and led his men into battle "like a river raging in flood through the fields, or like a lion in the midst of a herd."[5] By now, Theoderic had spent almost twenty years in this warrior role, earning his followers' respect as no palace-bound emperor ever did.

On August 28, 489, Theoderic's community appeared on the Isonzo or Soča River, then as now more or less the northeastern boundary of Italy. Odoacer, who must have heard a rumor of the approach, took his forces in retreat to Verona on the Adige River, in the center of the north Italian plain, at the beginning of the foothills of the Alps, within equal reach for defensive purposes of Milan, Ravenna, and the northeastern frontier across which Theoderic was arriving. On September 28, there was a battle here, recorded as a victory for Theoderic. Odoacer retreated southeast to Ravenna, while Theoderic moved west to consolidate his position. One of Odoacer's generals, Tufa, turned coat and handed over Pavia, just south of Milan, to Theoderic, giving him a secure base. Tufa then wavered again, and so Theoderic and his people spent the winter of 489–490 in Pavia under some pressure, while eyeing Odoacer in his capital at a distance.

Theoderic now proved himself astute, resourceful, and traditional in ways that had never emerged in the Balkans. He made immediate contact with the leading dignitaries of the city of Rome, with some representatives and spokesmen probably traveling to and fro all winter. The great senator Festus, the most senior former consul still living, agreed to go to Constantinople to seek official recognition for Theoderic as imperial ruler in Italy. At about the same time, Theoderic began to issue coins in Milan in the name of Zeno—just what the emperor's designate would be expected to do.

Through 490, he remained in the vicinity of Pavia, engaged in diplomacy in several directions, notably with a government in southern Gaul under the control of some of his distant relatives. In August of that year, Odoacer advanced from Ravenna, and the forces fought a second battle near Milan. Theoderic prevailed again; and this time, when Odoacer retreated to Ravenna, Theoderic pursued him, effectively trapping him in his own capital.

Ravenna is a tough town to attack, surrounded by water and swamp, on land boggy enough to grow asparagus. This hemmed-in quality had recommended the site to the timorous emperor Honorius almost a century before when he moved his own court from Milan to Ravenna, looking for a place easy both to defend and to flee.

The winter passed in stalemate, and the spring of 491 saw the siege continue. In July, Odoacer made an attempt to break out of Ravenna, but failed. This long standoff was an uncertain time for the rest of the peninsula. If Theoderic had men to spare, they were out working to gain control of the tax revenues and machinery of government, while Odoacer had to suffer a slow suffocation of power in Ravenna.

A few years later we hear the story of an astute local potentate in the south. Cassiodorus, the father of a more famous writer of the same name, had served in high government office at the court of Odoacer, holding both of the senior finance portfolios: "count of the sacred generosity" and "count of the private estates." Now he was governor of Sicily. His grandfather had come west with the child emperor Valentinian III in the 420s, when Constantinople made its last serious attempt to shape the political destiny of the west, and evidently received the gift of land in southernmost Italy as a reward. Such rewards also brought protection and support for the regime that gave them, as the Cassiodori went native. Their loyalty shifted with the political fortunes of emperors and warlords, but they remained ever after tied to land they praised all the more enthusiastically for having been immigrants there.

As the long siege progressed, Cassiodorus the elder was one of those leaders elsewhere in Italy who reasoned that support for Theoderic was the wisest course, and Theoderic's eventual success proved him right. Fifteen years after the siege of Ravenna, when all was clear, the son of this Cassiodorus wrote the script for Theoderic to use in praising the father as a staunch supporter from the earliest days of his reign. Cassiodorus the father became governor of his own home province as a result, then praetorian prefect soon after, and he retired at the point when his son was beginning an equally illustrious career as Theoderic's loyal servant. Other provincial leaders were making similar choices to give their support to Theoderic and the future while Odoacer languished in Ravenna.

The winter of 491–492 dragged on with no change in the military situation. In 492 Theoderic consolidated his position by seizing control of Ariminum (Rimini) about thirty miles south of Ravenna on the Adriatic. There was little military use of the sea in those days, but we can imagine at least some harassment and interdiction of shipping in and out of the Ravenna harbor from this new base.

Still another winter arrived, Theoderic's fourth in Italy, and the siege continued. In February 493, just when the food supply in the surrounded city would be at its lowest level, John, the aged and widely venerated bishop of the city, emerged from its walls under a flag of truce, leading a procession of churchmen bearing crosses, incense-burning thuribles, and gospel books. John threw himself to the ground before Theoderic, singing psalms and begging for peace, welcoming the king "who had come from the east."[6] Theoderic welcomed the approach and agreed to share his rule with Odoacer, an improbable arrangement between bloody rivals, but also a promise that broke the deadlock. On March 5, the gates were opened and Theoderic entered the city amid the urgent bustle that accompanied restoration of normal life.

Ten days later, on March 15, Theoderic invited Odoacer to be his guest at a banquet to cement amity and partnership in the palace Valentinian III had built half a century earlier. The appearance was false: in mid-banquet (our sources here are late and unreliable as to details, but the main fact is beyond dispute), Theoderic drew his sword and moved toward Odoacer.

"Where is God?" Odoacer cried.

"This is what you did to mine," replied Theoderic, and murdered his rival on the spot. Loyalists and defenders of Theoderic claim that Odoacer had murdered Theoderic's relatives (there's one way this might have been true), but we cannot overlook the calm, premeditated treachery of Theoderic's act in a nearly theatrical setting. Odoacer's most loyal followers were promptly massacred, hacked down in palace or camp, and their bodies left unburied long enough to make sure the deed was known and feared. Odoacer's brother took refuge in a church but was dragged out and killed;

his wife starved to death in prison; and his son fled but was hounded, cap-tured, brought back to Theoderic, and massacred. This was how regimes changed in those days.

Odoacer's regime had dried up and begun to scatter before the propi-tious winds of Theoderic's power. The new ruler was able to establish his own authority broadly and easily in north Italy and south Italy and down through Sicily. He himself almost never ventured south of the Po valley—that grand visit to Rome was a great exception—and he depended on the willing cooperation and the taxpaying of the whole peninsula and its breadbasket island beyond for his authority.

Liberius, serving Theoderic as praetorian prefect, supervised an impor-tant first piece of business: the settling of Theoderic's followers on avail-able land in Italy. At least half a dozen times in the fifth century across the Latin provinces of empire, such settlements were negotiated and imposed, all bringing with them both disruption and relief. Just how much disrup-tion is a matter of controversy, for no case is really well documented and, clearly, property was seized and reassigned in different ways in different cases.[7] From early times, gifts of land had been Rome's way of rewarding loyal armies.

Here in the 490s, Theoderic's overthrow of Odoacer and the expulsion of his loyalists created one set of opportunities for settlement—probably rather good opportunities, assuming that each regime had feathered its own nest properly. Loyalists of Odoacer's regime may very well have lit out for another province when their protector fell, while others were certainly evicted or murdered. Even if we take all that as normal postwar conduct, acceptable in its time, it is still difficult to determine how many innocents were additionally dislodged. There would, at any time in this period, have also been land and houses that were owned but not actively occupied, and it was always easier to detach vacant property from a larger set of holdings and reassign it than to seize owner-occupied assets.

In principle, the government had the right to seize as much as one-third of any given property, but the total number of Theoderic's followers who might have benefited from that privilege was nowhere near capable of digesting one-third of the property of Italy, and no historian now tries to claim such a thing. The most plausible explanation is that all property holders in Italy saw one-third of their tax revenues redirected to support the army and followers of the new regime—and so, in principle, they suffered no material disadvantage, while Theoderic's men profited handsomely. In practice, the new regime's motivated reinvigoration of tax collecting probably cast heavy burdens on the unwary, but those burdens were alleviated by the knowledge that traditionally resourceful methods of tax evasion would soon restore economic affairs to something like their normal, pre-overthrow condition. Corruption has a way of simultaneously exacerbating and mitigating tyranny.

Making room for a new regime was not without costs and brutalities, but by 493 Italy must also have been reasonably relieved to find itself under consistent and predictable rule. The new power, patient, persistent, and resourceful in diplomacy, supported by Constantinople as no ruler in Italy had been for at least a quarter century, could be expected to prevail for a good long while. Those hopes were not to be disappointed.

While Theoderic had been conducting his barricade of Odoacer in Ravenna, the emperor Zeno had died in Constantinople. His successor, Anastasius I, the most capable and effective emperor in at least a century, was a cautious man who revealed only slowly his opinion of Italy's new state of affairs. Festus had returned from Zeno's court at Constantinople in 490 without the signal success of official recognition that Theoderic had hoped for.

For a few years, Theoderic was careful to settle affairs in Italy, but then in 497 he sent Festus to Constantinople again as the head of a delegation. By now, Theoderic could make a very good case that he had brought peace, order, and good Roman government to the Italian peninsula, and he could profess himself a loyal and faithful colleague of the emperor in Constantinople. The forms of empire were carefully observed, and Festus could and did speak for the senate and its traditions and authority— without mentioning that the senate was a shadow of its former self. Anastasius was persuaded to recognize Theoderic's position.

Festus returned bearing the official ornaments and regalia of the western empire, the same ones that Odoacer had sent back to Constantinople twenty years earlier in a hollow show of fealty after he dispensed with resident puppet emperors in the ancient capital. Their return was a sign to those who would read it that Theoderic had acceded, if not to the throne itself, at least to the very highest and most official Roman status next to the throne.

The Theoderic who appeared in Rome on his grand visit not long afterward was a man of power and authority, but also a man of ambiguity. He would never claim to be emperor of the Romans—never. He would always, for all the thirty-seven years he spent in Italy, give a performance of the most senior and most official imperial presence he could muster. If that role brought with it imperial charisma and imperial respect, so much the better. Theoderic was ever careful to surround himself with advisers and ministers of the first water, recruited from among the Italian aristocracy and skilled in all the arts of culture and diplomacy. His regime clearly and consistently proclaimed itself dedicated to the promotion of *civilitas*, which means something like "civility" and something like "law and order." The traditional forms of imperial government and the traditional roles of the native population were meticulously observed and respected.

At the same time, Theoderic managed his diplomatic correspondence deftly and with finesse. In 507, his best experts drafted a careful letter to Constantinople declaring that his regime was an exact imitation and copy of Constantinople—imitation and copy, yes, but far excelling any other regime in the known world.[8] He behaved in every way, he assured Anastasius, as the emperor would, loving the senate, respecting the laws of empire, and working diligently to sustain the peace and order of Italy. He made a good case.

His arrival in Rome in 500, then, let him play the role of "almost emperor" down to the last detail. To appear in Rome in the grand style, to wear the purple, to reside in the ancient palace of the emperors on the Palatine hill, to address the senate, to confirm the laws of empire, and even to be seen to administer the brutal justice of judicial murder: all this was what emperors did. These acts would assure (or he meant them to assure) the populace of the city, and those beyond who heard about them, that both the order and the governance of Italy were exactly what they had always been and always should be. For the moment—a long moment that lasted most of thirty years—his performance was a success, and many people were the better for it.

The road before him had potholes. The question of the disputed election for bishop of Rome refused to go away. Fresh quarrels about the appropriate date to celebrate Easter and Symmachus's personal suitability for the papacy broke out in 501, when Theoderic was safely back in Ravenna. Laurentius's supporters accused Symmachus of squandering church property and of inappropriate relations with women. The property issue actually may have been the heart of the dispute over the bishopric, representing a struggle for control of the largest fortune in Italy except that of the ruling monarch. Theoderic could not ignore these renewed charges, pressed by high-ranking supporters of Laurentius, and he summoned Symmachus to Ravenna to defend himself.

After the mountain journey north up the Flaminian Way, Symmachus paused for a while at Rimini for refreshment and preparation before making his way the last few miles to Ravenna. While he was there, walking at the seaside one day, he saw a carriage pass containing the women he was accused of consorting with back in Rome. One of them, Conditaria, had a name that is only too easy to translate, quite correctly, as "Spice Girl." Seeing the deck stacked against him even before a sympathetic ruler, Symmachus fled back to Rome and the immunity and sanctuary of his church. For the next five years, he lived precariously, retreating to the church at Saint Peter's grave on the Vatican hill outside the city walls, built as a shrine in a grand style by the emperor Constantine and rebuilt and refurbished since, but not yet the official church of Rome. His rival Laurentius never settled for his exile as bishop far south in Nocera and now brazenly neglected his duties there. He and his followers had seized and held the Lateran and could make a good case that they represented the real, traditional church of Rome.

For the next few years we have official documents, but only glimmers of what city life was like. There was street violence at times, and something not quite short of gangster rivalry between supporters of the two claimants to the papacy. This split divided the senate itself; grave, dignified leaders of important families sided with one churchman or the other, offering financial support and their visible presence. In 502, Symmachus felt strong enough to call together the local clergy for a series of synods at various churches in the city, playing the chess required to reassert his authority. Early in the year, at the church of Saint Mary in Trastevere, just across the river from the heart of the city, Symmachus convoked an assembly to remonstrate with the king for support. None was forthcoming: the pope had overplayed his hand.

Months later, at the basilica of Santa Croce in Gerusalemme, on the eastern edge of the city, a second synod was held, one which Symmachus barely survived, after being attacked by partisans on the streets as he made his way home. We cannot at this distance tell whether it felt like a victory,

because he showed that he could make his way through the city and survive; or like a defeat, because he was so brazenly attacked. Two more such
sessions were held in October and November, and Symmachus eventually
had his way with his own churchmen at least. He took the opportunity to
replace the city prefect's decree of twenty years earlier regulating the management of church property and installed his own law on the subject—one
doubtless designed to justify his own controversial practices.

Success was only partial. For another four years, Symmachus reigned
from Saint Peter's, Laurentius from the Lateran. Supporters of Symmachus
"discovered" (that is to say, fabricated) precedent documents to support
his cause, such as ecclesiastical acts and martyr stories supposedly from
two centuries earlier supporting aspects of his legal and religious claims.
One told a colorful but quite fictional story of Pope Xystus, who was accused in the time of the emperor Valentinian of misappropriating property
and misbehaving with a nun. The Roman clergy held a synod to debate
Xystus's case in the Sessorian basilica, and the matter was resolved when
a distinguished ex-consul observed that popes are immune to the condem-
nations of synods. If you believed that this document was authentic, then
you also had precedent for what to think about Symmachus.

Both sides also published their official versions of history in something
called the *Book of Pontiffs—Liber Pontificalis.* That book, and its later
editions through the middle ages, listed the names and short biographies of
all the bishops of Rome from Peter forward (with a new biography added
on the death of each pontiff). Bishops of Rome for fifty years before the
crisis between Symmachus and Laurentius had been promoting themselves
in various ways as successors of Peter with authority that ran far beyond
the city where he was martyred. The word *papa,* long used affectionately
of the paternal authority of bishops in several major cities of the emperor,
was now increasingly limited in application to the Roman bishop—and
gives us the word "pope," in consequence. We have, then, versions of the
pontifical book from both parties in the first years of the sixth century,
showing how each presented its candidate as Peter's official successor.

Symmachus struggled at Rome but did a good job of brokering the
support of dignitaries up and down Italy. The ambitious Ennodius, however, was embarrassed when he had to submit a bill to the papal court
to recover funds he had "advanced" for defending Symmachus's cause at
court in Ravenna.[9] ("Bribery" is such an ugly word, as I'm sure Ennodius

would have agreed.) There's no sign Ennodius ever got his money back, but Symmachus did prevail, and in 506 Theoderic finally came out with a reaffirmation of his earlier support for Symmachus and put the force of law and the law of force behind his claims. He took only measured steps, however, and Laurentius continued with at least some of his pretensions until Symmachus's death in 514. The election then of Pope Hormisdas marked the final reunification of the church.

This ecclesiastical power struggle resembles many others, but we should pay close attention to Theoderic's role. The reader who knows something—anything—of this history will have been puzzled until now at the omission of some important words regarding him and his followers: Goths, Ostrogoths, barbarians, invasion, tribes, even hordes, Arians, heretics. Theoderic's life conventionally takes up part of the history of the barbarian invasions of Europe, the *Völkerwanderung* or "migration of peoples." This standard tale has as its centerpiece a group of insensate, unfeeling brutes who insidiously overthrew civilization, little understanding what they had done. We must learn to do without that story.

Theoderic was ever remarkable. The story you have just read of him, whatever labels you might wish to put on various people and their deeds, is as exact as I can make it, carefully adjusted (I hope) for the exaggerations and prettifications with which loyal and disloyal narrators over time varnished their accounts. Theoderic's truth at the moment I have tried to capture him, robed in imperial splendor in 500, is complex and not to be reduced to stereotypes, labels, or slogans. He was brought up in the imperial court, and that exposure to monument and ceremony strongly shaped his ambitions for the Italian cities he made his own, including Rome itself. He had to be fluent in Latin, probably knew a fair amount of Greek, and also knew the Germanic language his troops shared. For the first fifty years through which we can trace him, beginning with his return to the Balkans from Constantinople in the early 470s, when he was in his late teens, until the 520s, his self-presentation and his performances were consistently Roman, citizenly, imperial, and respectful of the old ways of the lands where he dwelled. The few and mild military adventures that made his reputation among his people were exactly comparable to the exploits of generals with impeccably Roman pedigrees who came both before and after him.

He was Christian by birth. His father was brought up in the Christian religious traditions of the Danube armies, whom missionaries from Constantinople had converted 150 years earlier. Those armies were faithful to the Christianity they had been taught, but in the meantime doctrinal fashion had changed at Constantinople. The dominant orthodox clergy at court now condemned what had been orthodox under Constantine, calling it Arianism. Theoderic's followers had a Bible that Ulfilas, a bishop trained in Constantinople, translated into Gothic[10] in the fourth century under the influence of Constantine's version of orthodoxy. But this Bible translation was barely intelligible, although it was probably the first serious attempt ever to render Greek into a language with almost no written tradition. That official Christianity and this Bible quickly became the possession of peoples deeply integrated in the Latin Roman world, even when they found themselves rebuked as Arian heretics by followers of contemporary doctrinal fashion at court.[11] Rome's military leaders from 459 onward were all Arians of that kind, and they built and maintained half a dozen churches at Ravenna and at least one in Rome. We have a collection of Latin sermons copied in 500 that comes to us from an Arian preacher in Verona. A little after that date, a monk at Naples—Eugippius, whom we will meet again—wrote to a colleague with a theological question for an ongoing debate with a "count of the Goths" who was pressing Arian points of view on him. That debate captures a relationship between two communities marked simultaneously by disagreement and civility. No one in Theoderic's Italy thought of burning anyone else at the stake.

Theoderic's father's family was Arian, but his mother, Erelieva, was orthodox, taking the name Eusebia (meaning "pious") in baptism, and Theoderic's own experience of Christianity when he was a youngster in Constantinople must have been mainly if not exclusively orthodox. He and his army stayed faithful to the creed and clergy that they brought with them to Italy, and so on Sunday found themselves in different church buildings from most of the native population. Theoderic, though, was repeatedly called on to arbitrate the business of the orthodox church of Rome during his reign. Some of his authority came with his role as the legitimate imperial ruler of the province, and some came easily owing to the religious amphibiousness of his childhood and youth.

What that amphibiousness entailed needs a moment's further reflection.[12] Theological handbooks can tell us the distinction between Arian and Nicene doctrines of Christ, but not many of the military men on the frontier could have explained how their creed differed from Rome's. The distinction was important, because religion had become integrated with the community in a manner casting long shadows into the future. Modern people may identify with a religious tradition even when, often, they do not practice it; by contrast, traditionalist ancient men and women all practiced religion, but they did not personally identify with it. As late antique religions gradually became part of people's identities, those identities themselves began to be portable.

So if you let your religion mark you completely, then you were no longer defined by your birthplace, your family, or any other social status. You could pack up, move, and still be who you were before you moved. Social mobility was possible in the ancient world; but if you moved from Antioch on the Orontes to Rome on the Tiber, you didn't just learn a new language: you probably also changed your religious practices. Judaism first, then Christianity, and then, especially, Islam capitalized on this emerging form of religion-based identity to enable believers to live more independent and mobile lives, and not incidentally this had the effect of making the religions themselves more powerful, cohesive, and influential. The Arians of the frontier would vanish into the Catholic community of the Latin church eventually, but not for decades or centuries after they began living among the Catholics. In the meantime, their presence would anticipate and rehearse our modern confrontations between cult, creed, and identity.

Think of Theoderic as Othello. Shakespeare's Moor appears in his first scenes very much like the Theoderic we have met. Othello is the best of generals, but a gentleman withal, keenly intelligent, articulate, soft-spoken, patient, and magnanimous: the best of the Venetians, yet for all that, men call him "Moor" to claim superiority over him. Imagine Othello, only moderately darker of skin than the Venetians, rather better dressed, rather better spoken, and considerably more intelligent than those who surround him. The tragedy of that Othello lay in others' ascribing to him the Moor's stereotyped traits, traits entirely alien to him. In the course of the play, the people around him tell the story of Othello the Moor so convincingly that eventually the man becomes what people fear him to be. Desdemona's killer is the man whom such fear and ignorance have created, and his tragedy is the betrayal of his true self. A fate not unlike Othello's awaited Theoderic at the end of his life.

A BAD HALF CENTURY

Ordinary bad times in the Roman empire had brought hunger and disease to this city or that province, but worse lay in store when the heavy hand of distant government grew unsteady or unpredictable, and the years from the 420s to the 470s accustomed dwellers in the Latin west to an enduring, dispiriting sense of crisis. People who live through such times are seldom rational or farsighted in their interpretation of events around them.

The Latin provinces of the empire, from the western Balkans through the upper Danube and the Rhine valleys to Britain, then down through Gaul, the Iberian peninsula, around to Africa, and back to Italy and the islands between, exemplified old Roman characteristics, yet did so on the periphery of the Mediterranean. How was that west different from the Greek, Syriac, and Egyptian lands to the east? First and most simply, Rome had gone from obscurity to empire by picking the right enemies and learning from them. Its best models were the seagoing, prosperous Carthaginians, who challenged Rome and lost, leaving the Romans suddenly masters of far more than they had ever dreamed possible .

But Rome and much of what it had conquered were unready for empire. Though Greek and Carthaginian outposts boasted some history and culture, the romanization of the west came about through the establishment of colonies of retired soldiers and the extension of institutions of Roman government and taxation to the new countries. A little emperor worship and a lot of taxpaying were enough to satisfy the government, and Latin was the language of prestige among elites—unless you had the pride of knowing Greek. The cities the Romans built all had a bit of modern-day planned cities like Brasilia or Canberra about them, and not much of the commercial vigor and sprawl of Mumbai or Chicago. They were official constructions, with economies that depended heavily on a government far away. Carthage, destroyed in 146 BCE, then reborn from the ruins, might claim to be the second city of the west, but there was never a serious candidate for third. The natural condition of the countryside, moreover, was villa rather than village: the home of large landowners and their tenants rather than the autonomous community generating its own prosperity. (Rome itself was the unruliest Roman city of all, the one that hadn't been planned and embraced a nearly constant flow of immigrants.)

Much of the countryside of Gaul and Spain, in particular, as you moved farther from the Mediterranean, was still underdeveloped, despite pockets of Roman presence and prosperity here and there. Bordeaux and Tours marked the rough limits of real urbanization and romanization in Gaul, and their rivers, like most of those in the Iberian peninsula to the south, drained naturally westward, away from the Mediterranean, and so they were not good trading partners for the rest of the empire. Once past the Rhone valley in Gaul and the Ebro in Iberia, you knew you were very far from Rome. Southernmost Iberia had been an outpost for the Carthaginians and was still and ever after a center for Romans, Moors, and Spaniards.

The frontier societies on the Rhine and Danube were different. These were the liveliest places in the Roman west. There you found a thriving military Keynesianism: military leaders spent tax revenues they gathered elsewhere in the empire to support soldiers and officials who were in many respects as economically idle and useless as the perfumed grandees of the city of Rome who complained when the lavish, heavy rings they wore made their hands sweat. Soldiers may not have worn perfume or rings, but idle hands with money to spend are good for economic and social development, as long as tax revenues remain plentiful. The prosperity of the Mediterranean lands, especially Africa, was redirected north to the frontiers. Far north on Hadrian's wall, where defenders looked warily north into Scotland, soldiers' letters found thirty years ago reveal a busy economy with not a rich man in sight, but plenty of preoccupation with consumer goods and family affairs. From the time of Julius Caesar and for 500 years, the tax man did his job to maintain Roman frontier socialism. Whether by trial and error, by luck, or by strategy, Rome had struck a balance between what could be extracted from the land and what spending was needed to make frontiers stable. No one understood how fragile that balance was.

Those frontier societies had a military look. Encamped Roman armies protected towns and citizens against raids and harassment from across the river, the wall, or the desert. The frontiers as a whole were messy, sometimes ill-defined spaces. On our maps, we mark the Rhine and Danube as Rome's northern boundaries, but they never worked that way. Rivers make fine tactical boundaries—if you give a general a river for his base of operations, he will mount a fine defense—but they are impossible as strategic frontiers. This impossibility regularly escapes the makers of treaties,

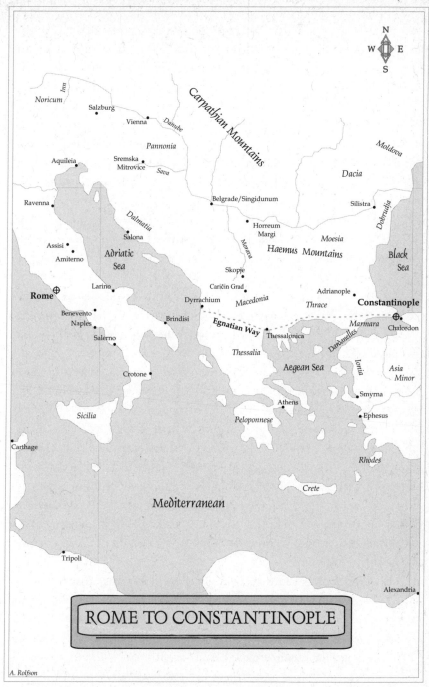

From Rome to Constantinople.

and if you go to El Paso or Laredo, you see in a minute that the Rio Grande is a natural magnet, not a dividing line. People from both sides of the river establish transborder economic communities that make perfect sense. At the same time police officials of every kind try vainly to make the Rio Grande an impenetrable barrier against illicit crossing. Such efforts are always crippled, for rivers make crossing and boating easy, encouraging the movement of goods and people, and thus the flourishing of society.

So if you crossed the Roman Rhine or Danube from the empire side and looked about for the "natives," you'd find a population much like the one you had just left: a mix of some soldiers, many farmers, and tradesmen buying and selling among them all. You would still hear Latin spoken, no better but not much worse than in Roman territory. From outside the border, the frontier felt and looked very Roman, but if you came from the Mediterranean, it all seemed terribly alien. Every border culture is like that.

The Roman Danube and especially the Rhine served their river communities well. The people north and east of the rivers lived nominally outside the reach of Roman law, but in practice they were part of the Roman riverine world. Because they were technically "across the river," their immunity from Roman taxation provided a powerful economic advantage. There are stretches of the upper and middle Danube that resemble the Rhine for making movement back and forth across the river and up and down from one shore to another quite easy, and some stretches of the middle and lower Danube through Serbia that resist, and then the last few hundred miles (the boundary between modern Bulgaria and Romania) once again invite collaboration and community. As Rome's rule endured, moreover, population growth and economic stability meant more soldiers—and thus more tax revenues being spent—on the frontier. This flourishing also attracted more migrants from the other side everywhere fertile valleys beckoned.

The people across these rivers mimicked the Romans' life as they understood it, and as much as they could afford it. Climate imposed some differences. They drank beer more than wine, and they raised livestock as well as grain. Their natural habit of moving to find more or better land in a loosely populated landscape alarmed the Romans, who, anticipating and fearing unrest, tried to teach them stability. The result was that the Romans created what they feared, for the river people also learned organization from Rome, and thus warfare. "The Germanic world was perhaps the greatest and most enduring creation of Roman political and military genius," says one modern historian.[13] One of his ancient predecessors saw it happening in the third century:

> The barbarians were adapting themselves to the Roman world. They were setting up markets and peaceful meetings, although they had not forgotten their ancestral habits, their tribal customs, their independent life, and the freedom that came from weapons. As long as they learned these different habits gradually and under some sort of supervision, however, they did not find it difficult to change their life, and they were becoming different without realizing it.[14]

North of the Danube, in modern Moravia and Slovakia, where old textbook maps show us the names of the Marcomanni and Quadi barbarian tribes, archaeology reveals numerous villas in the Roman style, some with bathhouses, some decorated with the kind of tiles seen in Roman army camps, and all yielding up through excavation bits of Roman military equipment, clothing, and jewelry.

For Rome, it turns out, had no theory of its own empire. As long as Rome expanded, it had a sort of idea of its future, pushing frontiers to the horizons while conquering additional peoples. For all intents and purposes it reached the limits of empire well before Nero ever fiddled in the first century CE. The Rhine and the Danube were too inviting. Each was navigable, and Rome could easily reach either one overland from its central territories. The two originate a few miles from each other, forming a nearly continuous line between them from the North Sea to the Black Sea, from the Netherlands to Moldova.[15] Augustus famously called back his forces from advancing toward the Elbe, and many reproached him for timorousness after a ghastly defeat in the Teutoburg Forest not far past the Rhine in northern Germany. He demonstrated good strategic sense, though, in seeing that the Elbe would be harder to supply and defend from the Mediterranean than from the Rhine.[16]

So Rome thought it could stand still. The establishment of Roman rule in Britain and its moderate advance there were both accomplished in the first century. Then Tacitus's father-in-law Agricola thought longingly that if he had one summer and one legion he could add Ireland to the empire.

In 106 CE, Trajan, easily one of the three or four best emperors,[17] succeeded in bringing Dacia (roughly Romania up to the Carpathian Mountains) into the Roman fold in the early second century, but it slipped from
the Romans' grasp during the bad years of the third century and never
tempted Rome again. Romanization lightly tinted its landscape for a very
long time, however, in the presence of the Roman soldiers' god Mithras,
who remained a fixture in Dacia well after Rome departed. We even find
Mithras in the Crimea, where no Roman army ever dreamed of going.

Eventually the Romans' imagination failed, and failed decisively. No
Roman writer, no Roman ruler, no Roman adventurer (Trajan alone perhaps excepted) seems ever to have had a coherent notion of what would
become of the world beyond Rome's northern frontiers. None of the other
frontiers presented even this problem. To the east, Persia seemed eternally
present; to the southeast, the Arabs seemed eternally negligible; on the
southern flank of the African provinces, border skirmishes and management were necessary, but the Sahara made a satisfactory defensive barrier
and Egypt had a long history of being able to control its relations with the
people closer to the source of the Nile, none of whom were a military threat.
Rome settled for stasis and imagined that stasis could be permanent.

By establishing its frontiers along the Rhine and Danube, Rome remade
European geography forever. Groups attracted to the border areas then
squabbled with each other and occasionally raided across the lines. Rome
had every opportunity to incorporate and rule its neighbors gradually. It
would have been able to establish economic relations, form a friendly alliance, send troops to join its allies against attacks from beyond, and finally
assimilate and consolidate new holdings. At this distance, it is impossible
to tell how feasible such a strategy would have been, but Trajan's work in
Dacia suggests that he at least saw a possibility there. Absent his vision,
Rome chose instead to be the captive spectator and passive victim of events
across its frontiers that it neither controlled nor influenced nor understood.
Every emperor from Augustus forward shares the blame for that passivity.

Nothing stays the same, least of all a great empire standing still. The
change in Rome's scale over time is important, but easy to miss. The first
200 years of the principate were an age of amateurs, when a small army
and a small bureaucracy managed to hold sway over a vast expanse from
the rising to the setting of the sun. As late as 193 CE, such amateurism had
its pretensions, when the elderly senator Didius Julianus bought the impe-

rial throne at auction, standing outside the camp of the praetorian guards offering a higher and higher price for their support until they consented to give it. He lasted only a few months, and the third-century emperors that followed were generals only. The senate, for complicated reasons, had failed to grow and internationalize itself and so was happy enough to subsist as a rich men's club based in Rome.

The third century CE was a far worse time than the fifth would ever be, a time when emperors could hardly stay in the saddle for a few months, let alone years, and when the empire's porous borders gaped open in all directions. Finally, main force of will and disciplined military organization brought the terrors and depredations of the mid–third century firmly to a close.

After he took the throne in 284, the emperor Diocletian and his successors were able to restore Roman borders and Roman order, chiefly by multiplying the number of soldiers and bureaucrats by a factor of five or ten. Diocletian brought the army to about 400,000, and it was later thought to have peaked at around 650,000. By the sixth century, the provincial governor of Africa had a professional staff of 400, and the Augustal prefect in Egypt could count 600 bureaucrats reporting to him. These swarms of functionaries created the real Roman empire as a successor to the thinly staffed, decentralized principate—rather as government functionaries in Washington did after the American Civil War, when they established a new, reunited United States that depended heavily on migrating and immigrant populations to support and sustain its growth. It should not come as a surprise to American readers that outsiders—those diverse groups lumped together as barbarians—played an instrumental role in Diocletian's new empire. In the fourth century, the western provinces particularly experienced a sharp increase in the militarization and bureaucratization, that is to say the barbarization, of daily life. Taxes rose, and the economy of the empire sustained the new burden. The economic bounty of a surplus harvest increasingly supported imperial military administration rather than privileged local elites, particularly bypassing the privileged local elites of the Roman senate.

Diocletian's success affected every part of the empire. On the frontiers, it meant that more tax revenue flowed in. If you could plot as a tiny lightbulb on a map every Roman coin expended from tax revenues in the fourth century, you would see a bright, hard line running the lengths of the Rhine and the Danube, with glowing points in the frontier capital cities like Trier, Milan, Belgrade, and Constantinople, and a secondary sparkling scattered from Antioch east to the Persian frontier. In many important respects, these bright bits are the real Roman empire, where emperors and bureaucrats lived and worked, and where the government heard petitioners' claims. The farther from the army, the fewer the light-bulbs, and by comparison Africa, Iberia, most of Gaul away from the Rhine, and certainly Italy south of the Apennines were left to molder in provincial dignity.

ROME'S CRISIS OF ILLEGAL IMMIGRATION

Mere facts cannot suppress the narrative that we're all certain we know about the period of the barbarian invasions of the Roman empire, the time depicted on those confident maps with large colored arrows pressing southward. Understanding the truth is central to a grasp of ancient history and to any attempt to learn from the lessons of the past. One thing is clear beyond any controversy: the Roman empire was not invaded in the fifth century CE by a series of brightly colored arrows swooping down from the north—or by anything like them.

It all started with a refugee crisis.

Look first at the map of Eurasia and see the superhighway that stretches from the Dnieper River in Ukraine to the Great Wall of China, passing north of the Black and Caspian seas. This route was the natural home of those who flourished on the spreading grasslands of the steppes. Nowhere else in the world is there a landscape like it, so empty and vast, so forbidding, and still navigable by people on horseback. Men of the steppes moved across the map at speeds unimaginable for human transport anywhere else in the world. At both ends of that superhighway, moreover, settled farming country lay just within reach, from the northern plain of China to the beginning of the wooded farmland of southeastern Europe. The horsemen didn't seek to destroy such farming societies; but a little raiding, some desultory pillaging, and the odd season spent elbowing locals aside and living off the fat of the land—a competent nomad would know how to do all those things.

Various groups on horseback, variously aware of each other and variously cooperative, moved west in the mid-fourth century, finding the pickings attractive as they went along. They numbered a few thousand at most and were spread out over an irregular stretch of grassland, joined from time to time by hangers-on of one kind or another, looking for opportunities to prey on settled communities. We hear about them when they attack; then they disappear from our view until the next raid. Their western enemies called them Huns and sometimes depicted them as sons of witches whom the Goths had banished into the steppes of central Asia, there to be impregnated by the unclean spirits who roam those vast, empty spaces.

In the year 373, the Huns began to move into lands where the Romans would hear of them. They came upon peoples called Greuthungi and Tervingi, loose confederations across the Danube, in the real outposts of settled civilization, where the first assaults of the marauders were felt. Fifty years earlier, the emperor Constantine struck a bargain with the Tervingi, encouraging them to move westward up the Danube a bit to buttress the frontier against the Sarmatians, people related to the Persians residing in modern Hungary. Constantine sent the Tervingi food and money, encouraged them to trade with Rome, and enlisted some of their men directly into the Roman army. Gradually, such people felt themselves more and more part of the Roman world even if they lived outside its boundaries.

When the Huns appeared, Ermanaric, king of the Greuthungi, farther downriver, was so disgraced by the losses his people suffered that he committed suicide in the grand way, impaling himself on his sword for the god who protected his people. A large group of Tervingi lost faith in their own leader, Athanaric, at the same time. Younger, more energetic men, Fritigern and Alavivus, emerged to lead these peoples and exhort them to move south and seek refuge across the Danube inside the Roman empire, where surely—so civilized a land was it, protected by so noble an army—they would be safe. Athanaric is regularly called king, and Fritigern and Alavivus generals, but those terms are anachronistic and overstated. A royal leader in such a community embodied a variety of qualities, some religious, some having the do with the prestige of age and family position, and so "king" may not indicate what would be expected of him. These men were simply younger leaders who emerged when thoughts turned to migration and refuge.

The emperor Valens welcomed the Tervingi into the empire. He approved their entry, rightly seeing them as new taxpayers and fine prospects for military recruits. Romans saw them as part of a broad group of peoples called Goths, and so from this time on the border crossers are called Visigoths. Repeatedly, we will see that groups acquire identity and names not from ancestors and time immemorial, but from the circumstances of coming into contact with Rome and the Romans' need to name what they barely understood.

All would have been well, but over the next two years a series of bureaucratic and military blunders by local generals and then by Valens himself turned this refugee resettlement program into a military and strategic tragedy. No one was to blame for this except the Romans. Promises were made and broken; bad luck followed; Roman soldiers overreached while keeping the refugees in line; tempers flared; and finally, Valens himself, rushing to the scene from Antioch, decided to put the visitors in their place without waiting for adequate forces to come and join him from the western provinces.

Disaster followed. The Roman army set out to make an example of the visitors and fell into a pitched battle with them at Adrianople,[18] and the Visigoths did not merely defeat the Romans but thrashed them and sent them fleeing. Valens disappeared in the fray. Rumor and legend about his end abounded, but all we know is that it was the rarest of days, when the Roman empire marched arrogantly into battle, then crawled out leaderless and confused. Did Valens's killers recognize him and recall the days a decade earlier when he had roamed freely across the Danube himself, looting at will? Would they have agreed that Romans were morally superior to barbarians or thought that the barbarians were overstepping some line of civility? The Visigoths were now angered and emboldened by their success, and henceforth determined to set the terms of their residence for themselves.

A shrewder emperor would have welcomed the Visigoths and made homes for them, with a land policy designed to take advantage of their strengths. He could have extended this policy across the Danube to create mutually strengthening relationships with the communities there. As it was, the Visigoths inside the empire now felt no particular loyalty to the hand that had first failed to feed them and then tried to smite them, only to finally prove itself both weak and vacillating. These years set the pattern we have already seen with Theoderic a century later, of independent generals with their followers alternately serving and attacking the empire up and down the Balkans.

The gravest result of Valens's bungled welcome of the Visigoths was that the expanse beyond the river turned into a no-man's-land. Never again would the Romans have a sense that anything but threat lay beyond the river, and experience would repeatedly confirm this fear. Rome would fight the rest of its wars on the northern frontier inside its own boundaries.

The Visigoths were never, until they settled in Gaul and Spain decades later, a numerical threat of any magnitude, but they now had every reason to think of themselves as an encapsulated community, safer if they stayed together, confident in their leaders. Their success and their resentment of Roman highhandedness—not any shared ethnic identity—made them Visigoths.

For the next thirty years, Roman strategy was an inconsistent mixture of blunder and cunning. The best days came when the Roman general Stilicho mixed negotiation and strategy to keep the Visigoths satisfied and relatively settled. He was himself from a barbarian family, and he worked hand in hand with the experienced general turned emperor Theodosius, continuing alone after Theodosius died in 395 leaving only underage sons for heirs. The general Alaric, whose whole career played itself out on Roman territory and who held a Roman military appointment, emerged to lead the Visigoths.

All hell broke loose when the court of the young emperor Honorius engineered the murder of Stilicho in 408, ostensibly because he was suspected of collusion with the Visigoths. Within two years, Alaric sent his forces into Italy itself, the first outside invader in almost 600 years. After a series of negotiations with the Roman senate collapsed, he made an example of the city. On August 24, 410, Alaric and his people entered Rome and indulged in a three-day orgy of violence. Some went for plunder, others for pleasure, but much of the carnage was simply to show off what they could do.

Just what happened in those three days cannot be said with any great clarity. Contemporaries both exaggerated and minimized the carnage and destruction, but there is little reason to think that the physical depredations in particular were on a large scale. Did the invaders really spare the lives of those who took shelter in Christian churches—even escorting prisoners there willingly? Were Christian women who had pledged themselves to lifelong virginity really driven to suicide when their chastity was violated by brutes? The facts in the end are less relevant than what people made of them.

The world stood still—or at least the chattering classes did. The symbolic role of the city of Rome and the legendary histories surrounding Romanness itself made it difficult for many, even those who had never laid eyes on the city, to bear the thought that it had been so flagrantly violated and humiliated. Augustine made heavy weather of some of the complaints he heard in Africa, turning them into an opportunity to write his *City of God*, a book explaining how Christians should interpret the disasters of the present day. He spoke supremely wise words, but they were not quite relevant to the policy debates and choices of the time. He urged people to take a long view, to consider the whole history of the human race, and he argued that Rome's success had nothing to do with Rome but everything to do with the Christian god's need for a nursery in which to plant and propagate a global religion.

Augustine could not see or say that the fundamental error lay in deciding that Rome needed defending against outsiders. Taking them in, making them over in your own image, using their undoubted skills while neutralizing their threat—Roman rulers who missed that promising strategy were doomed to play a defensive game with ever fewer resources. Not for the last time in this book, we can see Rome fail simply because it had no clear idea of what success might look like.

While Roman generals remained preoccupied with the Visigoths, a second irruption of refugee outsiders appeared inside the traditional boundaries of empire. On the last day of the year 405, a full generation after the Visigoths' arrival, a disparate group—comprising various people who called themselves Vandals, Alans, Sueves, and others—made its way west across the Rhine. The invaders took advantage of a brief lapse in official Rome's attention to the Rhine frontier, when troops were distracted fending off a usurper from Britain and blocking Alaric's movements in Italy. Once again, Rome reacted to the symptom rather than the cause. Historians used to theorize that the Huns on the lower Danube pressured this group to move, but that has proved to be not a very good guess. Opportunity, ambition, and chance are probably enough to explain this arrival.

These immigrants seem to have bottled themselves up quickly in northern Gaul, and they settled quietly enough for a while. Then a few years

later, pressed by Roman forces, they made a successful break for the Pyr-
enees and Spain beyond, where they gradually made themselves at home.
They had discovered the *true* secret of empire: that once they breached the
perimeter, there were few internal protections for people, cities, or farms.
A mobile and resourceful group like theirs could do quite well for itself,
without being in any hurry to settle. Of the Alans and Sueves we hear little
more, but the ones who went by the name of Vandals had quite a future
ahead of them.

Visigoths and Vandals had much in common. Both peoples pursued
a line of least resistance, while proving to themselves that the long, long
history of Roman strategy amounted to little more than frontier defense
combined with ignorance and lack of interest in what lay beyond. What
the Romans had perfected was really just elaborate preparation to fail in
handling invasions. The very Roman society that was terrified of outsiders had earlier nurtured them and paradoxically given them their identity.
Bands of refugees were by nature poorly organized, so they made up no
functioning polity. Once inside Roman boundaries, once they sniffed their
own power, and once they were demonized by those they passed among,
they became what the empire feared they were: better organized, more in-
ternally self-conscious, with an ideology about themselves that didn't have
to be true to be convincing.

A minimalist reading of history could argue that the Visigoths were the
first and the Vandals the last peoples normally resident outside the boundaries of the Roman empire to make their way across the northern frontier
and settle permanently inside. The other moments marked as "invasions"
of the Roman empire—notably those of Theoderic in the fifth century
and the Lombards in the sixth century in Italy—are better understood as
resettlements from one Roman region to another. There are some small
exceptions to this minimalist generalization, and there are many complicated scholarly debates, but the point to take away is that the total number
of invasions and invaders, at the most generous count, is still triflingly
small compared with the wealth and military force that Rome had at its
disposal.

As these groups passed across the Roman landscape for two or three
decades on their way to final settlements, moreover, they were still in
flux. Some fell away by attrition, as individuals and small groups found
places to settle while permitting the larger community to move on. Ac-

cretion brought others to join the migration and soldiers acquired wives and fathered children along the way. If you traveled with the group, you absorbed the name and the identity that went along with it, and perhaps you took it seriously.

In the late 410s, a Spanish churchman visiting Bethlehem picked up and eagerly reported a story about the king of the Visigoths.[19] Alaric had died not long after his terror strike on Rome, and his successor, Athaulf (Ataulphus), had been heard to say that when he was a young man, he had imagined he could overthrow "Romania," replacing it with "Gothia," but that now he understood that his Goths were too undisciplined and needed Roman excellence to form an orderly society. The story is most likely a rumor of the kind we would now find in a tabloid, voicing a popular sentiment that anxious Romans needed to think an invader general might say. If it is true, though, we have to remember that this man was speaking almost forty years after the Visigoths came into the empire. That ambition to outdo "Romania" was an ambition, in other words, almost certainly formed inside the Roman empire by a man who was in many ways indistinguishable from many other Romans and Roman soldiers. Most important, it is a vote in favor of civilization. The barbarians who settled in the Roman empire by choice were always attracted to its virtues and prosperity and were in no way interested in destroying them.

This king Athaulf had made himself a good Roman marriage along the way. His bride, Galla Placidia, was a daughter of the emperor Theodosius, and sister of the Honorius and Arcadius who divided the empire after their father's death in 395. She was living in Rome when Alaric sacked it in 410, and she threw in her lot with the Visigoths, traveling with them as something between a hostage and a guest. In 414, she married Athaulf in a perfectly ordinary Roman wedding ceremony in the city of Narbonne. She bore him a son with the imperial name of Theodosius, but he died in infancy. Galla Placidia traveled on with Athaulf as he led his people into the Iberian peninsula. When Athaulf died in 416, she married another general, Constantius, leader of Roman forces in Gaul, and with him had two more children. Constantius claimed the Roman throne briefly in the 420s, received no encouragement from Constantinople, and died shortly thereafter. Galla Placidia then traveled to Constantinople with her children and lived in the court of her nephew, the emperor Theodosius II. In 425, on the long-awaited death of his uncle Honorius, Theodosius sent Galla Placidia and one little son (by Constantius), Valentinian, to Rome to claim the throne for the family, which they did, at the expense of a claimant already on-site, named Johannes.

For twelve years, Galla Placidia reigned through her son's authority, sometime queen of the Visigoths, now de facto empress of Rome. She allied herself carefully with the cantankerous general Boniface, who controlled Africa for Rome, but their relations were always strained. When the Vandals, now in Spain, moved into Africa in the 420s, it was said (probably untruthfully) that Boniface had invited them, but invited or no, they increasingly became a threat to African cities. Augustine died in Hippo in 430 with the Vandals literally at the gates and besieging his city, leaving advice for his clergy about how best to respond to devastating invasions. Boniface soon made his peace with Galla Placidia and went to Italy, leaving Africa to fall to the Vandals soon after. In Italy, Boniface fell afoul of Galla Placidia's other favorite general, Aetius, defeating him in battle not far from Rimini. Boniface himself died of wounds, leaving Aetius in the 430s to become the strongest hand in the western empire. Aetius edged Galla Placidia aside, and the emperor Valentinian remained a weakling figurehead all his life.

Galla Placidia's story shows us the spirit of that historical moment: collaboration with invaders, collaboration with strong generals, and a powerful sense that dynastic legitimacy was the necessary thread of Roman rule in the western Mediterranean. Each of these principles mixed pragmatism and folly.

THE MAN OF THE HOUR

The real history of this time, however, is the story of Aetius. His talent, energy, and ability to seize the moment defined Roman success and opportunities in the Latin west from the 430s to the 450s. He was indispensable—always a bad thing in a general, for generals die, and the most important thing they can give their employers is reasonable confidence in a viable succession. Aetius managed everything but that.

Aetius was a typical Roman general of his time; that is to say, his ancestry was mixed. He was born far to the east of Rome, in Moesia, in a place called Durostorum (modern Silistra, in Bulgaria), the last important crossing of the Danube, just where it turns north from the Bulgarian border to divide into a long stretch of delta that eventually opens into the Black Sea. His mother was Roman and his father barbarian. In his youth, he spent some time among Alaric's people, and more time living outside the Roman borders in the camps of Rugila, king of the Huns. It would be hard not to call him a barbarian, pure and simple.

Aetius made his important military debut as the leader of an army said to consist of 60,000 Huns who entered Italy to support Johannes's claim to the imperial throne. Arriving in Ravenna a few days late and finding Galla Placidia, Valentinian, and their forces in control, he turned coat in a twinkling, declaring his allegiance to the new regime, and he was rewarded with an appointment as master of the horse for the provinces of Gaul. He flourished in Roman high politics by remaining constantly and astutely aware of the possibilities and threats of the Huns he had known so well when young. And so the worst of the barbarians became the real power base for one of the best Roman generals.[20]

In a sequence of campaigns, usually with Hunnish mercenaries at his disposal—that is to say, Huns learning to be Romans in the way new arrivals traditionally learned to be Roman—Aetius introduced order and regularity to various frontiers that had been challenged in recent years. He made good judgments, and also questionable ones.

Africa he had written off to the Vandals, who were left in command at Boniface's departure. Whether Rome could have more firmly defended Africa against the Vandals is an open question. The closer the African provinces were to Carthage, the more thickly populated and defended they were, and Rome had organized the main defensive force in the provinces to manage southern frontiers while controlling relations with backcountry Berbers and Saharan nomads. Farther west, toward and somewhat west of modern Algiers, the Roman presence thinned out and kept its defense focused on protecting the southern border. No one ever thought that a significant threat could come from the west, crossing the Strait of Gibraltar. Then the Vandals appeared.

Once established in Africa, once able to draw on local restlessness while very likely enlisting some rootless border rats along the way, the Vandals could outwait and on occasion outfight the limited Roman garrisons. When the emperors proved reluctant to send reinforcements and when some of the local forces left Africa to go with Boniface, there was not much to do except wait for the inevitable. Even so, the inevitable can take a while. The Vandals crossed to Africa in 429, they besieged Hippo in 430, and they had the upper hand in the whole series of provinces west of Carthage by 435. They did not actually take Carthage itself until 439, but then their regime remained in control for almost a prosperous century. Constantinople at first resisted the new regime and opposed it, but by the 470s made peace. What followed over the next half century was a sharp upturn in commerce between Constantinople and Carthage. Some people say wars are good for business, but apparently, in this case, so was peace.

Vandals and Visigoths were faithful to the borderland Arian Christianity that had crossed the frontier with them. They followed their fathers' tradition, which they could truthfully say descended directly from the apostles: a very old and deeply Roman religion. The Vandals, under the extraordinary Gaiseric, who ruled them from 428 to 477 (and thus can scarcely have remembered any life outside Rome's borders), exercised iron-fisted church management in favor of the orthodoxy the Vandals brought with them, to the disadvantage of the Christian factions they found already there. Many African Christians were still resentful of the forced unification of churches in 411, when the Caecilianist faction won the support of the emperor against the majority Donatist faction.[21] With Augustine and a few of his longtime collaborators gone from the scene at the end of the 420s, the imperfectly unified African church was without strong leaders. Some natives welcomed the Vandals and attended their churches, while others resisted fiercely. The Vandals' suppression of dissent was effective but not total, and the imperial church survived to reappear when the Vandals were ejected. In all this, the Vandals appear to have been the most intolerant, that is to say the most modern, of the Arians who took power in western provinces in the fifth and sixth centuries. All the others—Franks, Burgundians, Visigoths, Ostrogoths, Lombards—were more inclined to make peace with the other versions Christianity they encountered.

What made loss of control of Africa dangerous for Rome was the imperial government's inability to demand the abundant grain that had become Africa's prosperous tribute to backward and overpopulated Italy.[22] In the short run, the decline in Rome's population made the shortfalls manageable, but in the long run this would prove to be the moment when the complex interlocking economic system that sustained Roman rule tipped beyond recall toward regional autonomy and away from central authority.

With Africa essentially independent, the Roman Mediterranean would be at best a confederation and never again a unified empire.

Africa apart, Aetius dominated the west from 433 to 450. He demonstrated what central leadership could accomplish, especially when he suborned the Huns, supposedly the empire's greatest enemy, to his own support. He checked the Visigoths and kept them bottled up in southwestern Gaul, while settling and securing the Rhine and upper Danube frontiers as far east as Austria. Away from the frontier, Gaul had been more unsettled than perhaps he anticipated, with bands of fighters called Bagaudae flourishing at various locations in west central Gaul. The Bagaudae challenge our modern interpretations no end, with every choice of words betraying some overinterpretation. Were they brigands, rebels, freedom fighters, terrorists? The fairest assessment is that they represented the emergence of ill-defined groups of upstarts, differently configured in various places, who filled the vacuum created when the sweep of disruption revealed the weakness of Roman governance and left some of the usual controls of Roman society broken and lax and certain people dispossessed and rootless. Another gang called themselves Burgundians; their leaders appear to have come across the Rhine and settled in eastern Gaul in the two decades following the Vandals. Aetius, summoning Huns as allies, took a firm position. Contemporary sources said he massacred 20,000 Burgundians, before forcing those remaining to settle in modern Savoy in southeastern Gaul. When our historical maps break out the colored arrows to show them settled there, this looks like the result of just another successful barbarian invasion, but any real Burgundian was relieved to be alive and would surely be aware of just how strong the Roman state still was.

Aetius's greatest achievement came in 451 with the defeat of his patrons and partners, the Huns. Few historical names are as familiar yet, oddly, as unimportant as that of Attila the Hun. He is envied and admired by history buffs and business-management writers who conveniently forget that as a leader, he was a catastrophic failure. From the 370s to the 450s, the Huns bobbed and weaved and feinted just outside Rome's reach. From a series of camps and headquarters far enough from the Danube to stay out of range of Roman raids, they counterraided and terrorized Roman and non-Roman populations. Attila was one of several opportunists who flourished in the late 440s. He was lucky enough to entertain a Roman, Priscus, who visited his camp and wrote of what he saw there. Priscus's whole history has not survived, but one fragment is like a precious video clip of life in Attila's circle. When we read it in a moment, we should avoid the modern mistake of believing Priscus's portrayal of a powerful, dominating bogeyman. We'd do better to envision Attila as the bad cop and Aetius as the good cop, and then wonder who used whom in the pathological relationship that emerged.

The Attila whom Priscus visited made forays close to the Danube with his troops, but his real base was safely far behind that line. When Priscus and his party reached Attila, they found numerous Romans visitors ahead of them, including the governor of Noricum. They also observed a man whom Aetius had sent to Attila to serve as secretary—or minder, or spy, or a little of all three. So far from Rome, but in a way not so very far after all. The royal approach was hypnotically attractive. Here is part of Priscus's clip:

> When Attila entered the village he was met by girls advancing in rows, under thin white canopies of linen, which were held up by women who stood under them, and were so large that seven or more girls walked beneath each. Many lines of these damsels came singing Scythian songs under their canopies. When he came near the house of Onegesius, which was along his way, Onegesius's wife came out, with a number of servants, bearing meat and wine, to greet him and beg him to accept her hospitality. This is the highest honor that can be shown among the Scythians. To gratify the wife of his friend, he ate, just as he sat on his horse, his attendants raising the tray to his saddlebow. He tasted the wine and went on to the palace, which was taller than the other houses and built on an elevated site.[23]

In the mix of languages and peoples at this court, most readers have focused on one man, whom Priscus himself reports as an anomaly: a Greek happily living among the Huns. After years as a merchant on the Danube he fell in among the Huns and decided to stay, with a perfectly coherent rationale:

> After war, the Scythians live in idleness, enjoying their plunder and left almost entirely to themselves. The Romans, on the other hand, are first of all likely to die in war, since they depend for their safety on

soldiers and their tyrants do not allow them to bear arms in their own defense. . . . But Roman subjects in peacetime suffer worse than the evils of war, for the tax collectors are brutal and unforgiving and un-principled men who inflict injuries on others, because the laws are not fairly applied to all classes. An offender who belongs to the wealthy classes is not punished for his crime, while a poor man, who does not understand how business is done, suffers the full force of the law—that is, if he does not die before trial—for lawsuits are drawn out forever and cost the parties immense amounts of money.

We recognize in this voice the spirit of an American living among revolutionaries in central Asia or religious enthusiasts in Jerusalem: an irresistible story and part of the natural diversity of fates in a civilized world. This story says not that Hunnic splendor was somehow superior to Roman splendor, but that it offered enough civilities to provide an alternative world for malcontents.

Priscus caps his tale with an account of a banquet in the great hall of Attila's palace. The meal was served on silver plates, but Attila had the wit to confine himself to a wooden trencher, to drink from a wooden cup, and to keep to Scythian (that is, barbarian) clothes and shoes. Priscus gives us the barbarian chieftain's manners as a piece of performance art, letting himself be entertained by native singers when a Moorish dwarf, Aetius's gift to Attila, comes in gabbling in Latin, Hunnic, and Gothic. Everyone except Attila laughed to exhaustion, but Attila showed himself calmly above such silliness, smiling only at the arrival of a son on whom he doted. Attila played his part of humble nomad achieving great dignity with aplomb.

The luck that Aetius and Attila depended on for their partnership was about to run out. Attila had till now navigated adroitly the fault line between the eastern and western empires. The effective spheres of interest of the two domains blurred and sometimes separated in the Balkans. Constantinople cared a lot about the lower Danube; Rome and Ravenna cared about the upper Danube through the Hungarian plain and down to about Belgrade. Each had an interest in the lands between those two zones, roughly from Belgrade to Sofia, but neither a compelling presence there, for the country was more remote, the profits were fewer, and the threat to one or another capital was less direct. After the death of Theodosius II in 450 in Constantinople, emperors began to pay more attention to their northwestern frontier. Theodosius was succeeded first by one of his generals, Marcian, who took the late emperor's sister Pulcheria in marriage after agreeing to respect her religious devotion by allowing her to remain a virgin. He supported the religious politics of Pulcheria and her circle, which would culminate in the next year in the grand church council of Chalcedon, of which we will hear much more later. On the Balkan frontier, Marcian favored a hard line with the Huns and began by canceling payments of tribute that had flowed north with regularity.

Next came a question for Attila and Aetius. Pressed from the east, Attila began to move west, looking for an easy mark—but where to go? How daring could he be? He must have known there would come a point at which Aetius would need to oppose him, and he must have thought he would prevail. Drifting north, Attila reached and crossed the Rhine. We will never know with what enterprise, treachery, and anxiety Aetius began massing forces to meet him. The Visigoths now chose to ally themselves with their old oppressor Aetius; but after the battle was over, some of Attila's allies claimed to be the Visigoths' long-lost cousins and called themselves Ostrogoths. They were under the leadership of Theoderic's father. (Theoderic himself was born about two years later.)

This dance of forces across northern Gaul ended in July 451 on the Catalaunian Fields in northern Gaul. In the sixth century this was already incorrectly considered one of the great battles of the western world, and historians imagined an impeccable Latin oration for Attila as he suitably roused his troops at the outset of battle:

> After victories over such great nations, after bringing the world to its knees if only you would stop to receive it, I would think it foolish to try to sharpen your spirits with words as if you were novices. Let the new general or the untried army try such things. It is not right for me to say anything trite here, nor should you have to listen to such.[24]

The massed armies—probably indistinguishable from one another to the observer[25]—clashed that day and the Huns came off second best, retreating across the Rhine.

The next year, weakened by defeat and perhaps also by disease among his people, Attila confined himself to raiding north of the Po River in Italy, returning again to his cross-Danube haunts for the winter. There he died suddenly. Gaudy rumor assigned his death to a wedding night, barbaric excess, and a resulting hemorrhage—or was it a knife wielded by his new wife?—but we have no reason to take any such stories at face value. Attila was gone, and so was the threat he represented. The Huns did not disappear, and those bearing similar names and some relationship to the diverse groups that had assembled under Attila would crop up long after; but in that moment, the greatest force outside the empire that had both supported and threatened it crumbled. Aetius had prevailed, by some mixture of luck, stubbornness, and valor.

He was not trusted or loved. The Roman government had come to depend entirely on the leadership of men like him—men who saved them, but whom they repeatedly hunted down and murdered. Stilicho had been killed in 408 at his emperor's order, and perhaps thousands of other "barbarians"—good, assimilated Romans in every respect—were slain at the same time. Aetius faced worse. His emperor, whom he had served and saved for two decades, turned on him and in 454 in Ravenna, when Aetius was making a report on the state of the army's finances, Valentinian murdered him with his own hand—and the help of a few burly soldiers who held the victim for the coup de grâce. Six months later, allies of Aetius murdered Valentinian. They had been put up to it by other members of the court; the good order of Rome was preserved. The dignified senator Petronius Maximus, qualified by his distinguished rank and family and nothing else, became the emperor. He lasted all of two months. Three weeks later, in June 455, the Vandals reached Rome, sacked the city, and carried away (allegedly) precious treasures that Emperor Titus had looted from the Temple of Jerusalem almost 400 years earlier; they also took along an empress and two princesses.

The Romans' murders of Stilicho and Aetius were eerily similar. An imperial regime under pressure gave command to a general who straddled the border dividing Roman from barbarian. Over a few years, the general succeeded in calming a chaotic situation. He used his judgment and diplomacy to negotiate effectively with other generals who could be dangerous. The progress was palpable and of great value, and at the point of greatest success, the ineffective, traditionalist, and uncomprehending emperor became anxious, jealous, and optimistic—in short, he lost touch with reality—and engineered the murder of the general, who had been the making of him. What becomes of the emperor in such a case is of no interest, but the goals of calm and prosperity that were before in reach now receded dramatically from view. The most powerful force working against the Roman empire on such occasions was the ambition, the patriotism, and the stupidity of the empire's leaders themselves.

SIC TRANSIT GLORIA MUNDI

After Aetius's death, twenty years unfold in a sequence of events of little interest except to specialists. The historian Procopius, writing 100 years later, drew the curtain on this page of Roman history: "There were, moreover, still other emperors in the west, but although I know their names well, I shall make no mention of them whatsoever. For it so fell out that they lived only a short time after attaining the office, and as a result of this accomplished nothing worthy of mention."[26] The borders held, one ineffective ruler succeeded another, city populations diminished, and the world seemed to grow colder, the distances greater.

The local ruler in southwestern Gaul in the 450s was a successor of Alaric named Theoderic, who took power by murdering his own brother in 453, not long after they had fought side by side with Aetius against the Huns, and ruled until his own death in 462. Sidonius Apollinaris describes him and his daily round in a famous letter[27] that makes him out to be a paragon of civility, anything but a barbarian. This Theoderic goes to church first thing in the morning, out of habit rather than an excess of piety, then spends the rest of the morning in his audience hall, receiving visitors. He may spend some time in the field hunting, with appropriate royal decorum, for he thinks it unsuitable to carry his own weapons, but he also considers it effeminate to allow anyone else to string the bow for him. He returns from the field to a dignified midday meal, where the food is well prepared, not expensive; the wine is poured with a sparing hand; and the conversation is serious and quiet. His dining hall is Greek in elegance, says Sidonius, Gallic in abundance, Italian in efficiency. After a short siesta, he spends a little time playing at dice, for the fun of it only, trying hard to treat his courtiers as peers. Sidonius slyly admits that he does lose on purpose sometimes, the better to have Theoderic approve his next petition.

Sidonius was equally at pains to show us the calm ordinariness of aristocratic Christian life in that "barbarian" realm. A Sunday afternoon in the Auvergne comes vividly to life in one of his letters:

> It was still almost summer, and the night was so sultry that it suffo-cated us, imprisoned as we were in that steaming atmosphere; only the first freshness of autumn dawn brought some welcome relief. . . . Some of us sat down under an old vine, the stems of which were trained trellis-wise and covered with leaves and drooping fronds; other sat on the grass odorous with the scent of flowers. The talk was enlivened with amusing jests and pleasantries; above all (and what a blessed thing it was!), there was not a word about officials or taxes, not an informer in sight to betray us, but not a syllable we said that would have been worth betraying. Everyone was free to tell any story worth telling as long as it wasn't improper, for a most appreciative audience. The gaiety wasn't allowed to spoil the distinct telling of each tale.
>
> After a time, we felt a little sluggish from sitting still so long, and we voted for some more active amusement. We soon split into two groups, according to our ages. One called for the ball, the other for the board-game, both of which were to be had. I was the leader of the ball-players; you know that book and ball are my twin companions. In the other group, the chief figure was our brother Domnicius, that most engaging and attractive of men. There he was, rattling some dice which he had got hold of, as if he sounded a trumpet-call to play. The rest of us had a great game with a party of students, doing our best at the healthful exercise, even though our sedentary occupations made our limbs too stiff for much running.

Sidonius's friend Filimatius had trouble keeping up in the game and was outrun and outshot by younger men, until he gave up, "out of breath from exercise and suffering sharp pains in the side from the swollen fibers of his liver." So the friends tease each other till Sidonius writes a poem in honor of the towel with which they wipe away the sweat:

> *At dawn or when the steamy bath invites*
> *or when the heat beads the brow*
> *may goodly Filimatius with this cloth pamper his face*
> *till all the perspiration flows into the thirsty fleece.*[28]

Indoors the party had a fine library at its disposal, with the devotional works of religion set aside at the ladies' end of the room, and the older classic works ready to hand for the men.

The landscape was not without alarms and overreactions, betraying the tension in the air. In a poem of praise for the emperor Majorian, whose reign was short, Sidonius tells the story of a brave Roman war band that attacked Frankish invaders who had settled at Arras in northern Gaul. But his description of the battle sounds unpleasantly familiar to readers of modern reports of mistaken identity in wartime. What the Romans broke up turned out to be a marriage party, where "amid Scythian dance and chorus a yellow-haired bridegroom was wedding a young bride of like coloring and the enemy was forced to flee. Then you could see the jumbled wedding trappings heaped in the wagons and captured food and crockery were pitched in together." The wedding guests surely didn't interpret this brutality by mistake as a civilized response to barbarism![29]

Sidonius, still a young man in the 450s, hitched his own wagon to the short-lived emperor Avitus, who failed quickly and thoroughly. Even so, Sidonius's traditional and lightly Christianized world was left in many ways undisturbed. He simply praised other emperors and generals, maintained his dignity and his lifestyle, and was eventually made bishop of what is now Clermont-Ferrand.

After Avitus's try at the throne, a new general, Ricimer, emerged as the real power in Italy. He in turn found other puppets to set on a precarious imperial throne, including Libius Severus, from the southernmost provinces of Italy. This is the period, once Valentinian III was gone, when Constantinople paid steadily less attention to the west and such affairs, even when a highly qualified and professional savior like Ricimer appeared. At the same time, another claimant to the throne, Marcellinus, ruled from Diocletian's massive 150-year-old retirement palace near Salona (the remains of the palace form the core of Split, Croatia), and sent out a general with the oddly classical name Orestes to see what power he could claim in Gaul.

But Ricimer failed to achieve even what his predecessors did. Too many cats had been let out of the bag when Aetius died. The Huns, to be sure, had faded into the east, but the Vandals controlled the Medtierranean, the descendants of Alaric controlled southern Gaul and effectively Spain, there was no direct and sustaining control of northern Gaul, and Italy was too much of a backwater to be an effective base of operations. To be master of the city of Rome had become a small and perilous thing. The Balkans, refuge for a smorgasbord of people, remained hanging over Italy, ready to threaten any regime's attempt at stability. When Ricimer failed, Orestes succeeded him and he in turn ended by putting up as emperor a puppet of his own, Romulus, a young man whose insignificance led some people in the next generation to call him—as now he is regularly known— Augustulus, "little Augustus": a cheap shot.

Men like Aetius, Ricimer, and Orestes are usually called warlords or generalissimos, wheras Alaric, Theoderic, and Clovis (we will meet him soon) are called kings. The most successful of these figures ruled in their own names and built personal political bases, but the generalissimos were the ones who had too little personal support to counteract completely the influence of the old order. To declare yourself independent of that order was to transform yourself into a barbarian king—or get yourself killed.

With such prospects, talented men still found power worth grasping for, and so Odoacer came to the fore and made the most of his opportunity. In the fifth century, he is a worthy third to Stilicho and Aetius, and fortunate to have been succeeded, if unfortunate to have been murdered, by Theoderic. He gets too little respect from historians.

The pattern Odoacer represents will be familiar by now. He is marked as a barbarian even though his success was entirely Roman. His father, Edeco, was a Hun; his mother, we are told, was most likely of Scirian ancestry. Scirians never amounted to much and their very name has a floating, variable meaning. So we are variously told that Odoacer was reared as a Scirian, as a Rugian, or as a Goth; that he had a brother or half brother who had a Thuringian father; and that he was brought up in the court of Attila the Hun. In other words, he was typical of the new Roman military aristocracy from the frontier. Born in about 433, he first appears in our sources in 463, at the head of a band of Saxons, fighting the Franks in far western Gaul, near modern Angers—as we have seen, part of the real wild west of the fifth-century empire. At this time and in this place, Odoacer fought on behalf of the Roman empire against a population now imagined to be external and barbarian. What is characteristically fifth century about this engagement, however, or characteristically "wild west," is that he was next seen, probably quite shortly afterward, linked with the Frankish king Childeric attacking a force described as comprising

Alamanni in Italy—though it is unlikely that the two of them actually got to Italy at that stage. More likely, their short-lived partnership began and ended in Gaul.

Around 469, we glimpse Odoacer again, this time just south of the Danube in modern Austria, the province then called Noricum. He has abandoned his Saxons and leads a small group off to seek their fortune. Short of stature and modestly dressed, he is still unquestionably the head.

We have to be careful about this story, because it was written two generations after the fact, in a comfortable monastery at Naples in 511, at the height of the safety and complacency of Theoderic's rule. The author was one of the most learned Christian scholars in Theoderic's Italy, Eugippius, who compiled rules for managing monasteries, copied and corrected Augustine's major works, and produced an anthology of Augustine's writing that fills 1,000 pages in modern printings. This bookish man wrote the story of the wild, wild west we will now follow, and we need to bear his authorship in mind. Neapolitan readers were astonished to hear of the Danube freezing in winter so hard that carts could cross it and of how a bear came out of hibernation to lead good Christians to their destinations. The writer knew other books of the same kind, including the standard life of Saint Ambrose and the *Dialogues* of Sulpicius Severus, bursting with miracle stories of an earlier generation of Gaulish Christians.

Odoacer has only a walk-on part in this story, but despite that it's the best personal picture we ever get of him. The hero is a mysterious stranger, Severinus, who rode out of the east, dressed in black, never quite coming clean about his past.[30] He sometimes suggested that he had traveled far and faced much danger in eastern cities, and he attracted the honor and attention of the failed emperor Glycerius (r. 473–474), enough to make some wonder if he had been a soldier or a government official. His Latin, at any rate, was excellent.

Severinus arrived in Noricum in about 453; he died there in 482 with the words of Psalm 150 on his lips: "Praise the lord in his saints, let every spirit praise the lord." This one holy man filled up a lot of map, according to his biographer, traveling the Danube from Vienna west, up the river Inn to Salzburg, and sending his reputation in his lifetime as far afield as Milan. His asceticism and life of prayer attracted attention, for he ate only once a day (during Lent, once a *week*) and was ever at prayer in or out of church.

His world was full of good barbarians and bad barbarians. Roman forces—or, to be more precise, the forces that Rome *paid*—were fading away, leaving flourishing towns to struggle just to maintain law and order. When the story ended and the people who loved Severinus fled to Italy in 488, they did not flee barbarian invasion but left behind a breakdown of law and order. Before that happened, a group of good soldiers went off to Italy to retrieve their pay and their colleagues, but they were ambushed and lost along the way—unbeknownst to anyone except Severinus, who broke off reading one day in his cell to weep for them. His followers rushed to the river to see it running with blood, and then to see the bodies of the soldiers washed ashore. They hadn't gotten far.

In this world of fading power, Severinus became the new figure of authority—an authority that earthly disasters could not undermine. He encouraged people and they were cured; he chastised people and they changed their ways; he knew things at a distance and people were left in awe. Every story of a holy man needs a miracle here and there, but his miracles are paltry. For example, at one point he asked everyone to bring a candle to church, and then revealed that the ones whose candles wouldn't light worshipped false gods. Followers gradually clustered around him and he built a monastery, but he kept a private hermitage as well.

The good barbarian king Flaccitheus, leader of the Rugi people across the Danube, maintained warm relations with the holy man until his daughter-in-law tried to rebaptize catholic Christians—for she was probably an Arian—and Severinus raised his voice to get her to cease, as she apparently did, at least for a time. Odoacer's appearance introduces his followers to this account, from a people called the Heruls who liked to serve in the Roman army. Other Heruls would wind up fighting for Constantinople's generals Belisarius and Narses inside Rome's world; still others fought for Rome against barbarians in Hungary and were destroyed for their pains; the last of them faded to the north and disappeared from history not long after.

Rescuing captives, everyday business when you live among warlords, was part of the holy man's job. After rescuing one man, Severinus sent him back across the Danube on market day to look for another particular man, whom Severinus described in detail, even his clothing and where in the market to find him. When found, the second man beseeched his new friend to take him to the man of God, offering any price for the favor. He turned out to be carrying relics of saints Gervasius and Protasius, the same saints whose bodies Ambrose had discovered in a conveniently anti-Arian moment in Milan 100 years earlier.[31] Severinus was happy to receive saints who had confounded Arians, and he put them in his basilica along with the relics of many others. Relics of John the Baptist, no less, would join them not long after, coming not from the Holy Land far to the east but from across the Danube—barbarian territory, but not without its powerful saints.

Severinus's most impressive miracle has the weakest attestation, and the beneficiary rejected it. He successfully prayed to bring a priest who had died back to life, only to have the priest complain: "By the Lord I beg you, don't hold me here longer or cheat me of the eternal rest I had begun to enjoy." And he then fell asleep again in death. The subdeacon Marcus and the doorkeeper Maternus kept this story secret until after Severinus's death, for they had sworn to the holy man that they would not reveal it while he was alive; they then passed it along to Eugippius.

Severinus's death left the community at the mercy of brutes. A bad barbarian (a son of the good king we just heard of) sacked the monastery, but then his own nephew Fredericus quickly killed him in turn. Odoacer, now ruling in Italy, made war on the rebels, but Fredericus, now the new king in his own right, fled to join Theoderic's forces in the southeastern Balkans. No one reading Eugippius's book when it was written in Italy in 511 failed to notice the future ruler of Italy playing this bit part, but for now Odoacer's general immediately ordered the remaining Romani to migrate to Italy if they wanted protection. "Then all the inhabitants of that place went out as from the house of servitude in Egypt."

Eugippius, our source, was there on the day when they opened Severinus's grave, six years after his death, and the odor of sanctity was very sweet in the surrounding air. The wooden coffin was loaded onto a horse-drawn carriage, and the procession wended its way south to Italy—and not only to the safety of Italy, but well south, to Naples, passing across the plains to Ravenna and Rimini, settling for a time at Montefeltro near modern San Marino. While the members of the straggly group were there, they received a message from a woman named Barbara (the name means "barbarian woman" but her rank was *illustris*, which bespeaks the highest stratum of Roman society) inviting them to come and place the saint in a mausoleum she would establish at the Lucullan Castle at Naples. There he

was interred by the holy bishop Victor himself and with what we are assured is the approval and encouragement of Gelasius, bishop of Rome. In
that comfortable resting place, far from the frontiers, the story of the holy
man could be told and refreshed for the edification of many. It dramatized
the now safely abandoned past, a period of disarray on the frontiers; it
heartened its hearers with holiness; and it underscored the legitimacy of
Odoacer's rule and thus, a fortiori, of Theoderic's as well.

Those days were still in the future in the early 470s, when Odoacer
stopped off to see Severinus on his way to Italy. In Italy he joined the imperial bodyguard, now, finally, an officer on the rise in the heart of the
establishment. He cast his lot with Ricimer, when that general was at odds
with and in a virtual civil war against the short-term emperor Anthemius;
but when Ricimer fell, Odoacer found himself increasingly visible under
Orestes. Opportunity came when a group of soldiers, Scirians, Heruls,
and Torcilingi—in other words, a typical Roman mix—demanded land
from Orestes, as generals expected their soldiers to do. Orestes did not respond as well as they would have liked, whether because he hadn't enough
to offer or because he wanted more support and service from the troops
than they had yet given him. The restless soldiers turned to Odoacer and
offered him their loyalty if he would deal on their terms. He seized the
opportunity.

Soldiers raised Odoacer up on a shield, in the military way of declaring rulership, and then he led his troops through northern Italy against
Orestes. Seen through Italian eyes, he comes across as a revolutionary,
grasping at power by any means, seizing Pavia and inspiring all the usual
poetry about a city under assault, clichés as old as Homer. Once Orestes
retreated and Odoacer's men hounded him down and killed him south of
Pavia at Piacenza, the violence ended quickly. Within two weeks of Odoacer's coup, Orestes was dead and his brother Paulus had been similarly
killed in Ravenna. The emperor that Orestes had advanced, Romulus, was
deposed and placed under elegant house arrest near Naples, where he lived
unharmed for decades, probably in close proximity to Eugippius and the
monks who venerated Severinus.

Odoacer went on to behave in as natural and Roman a way as one
could expect. He sent ambassadors to Constantinople with the traditional
insignia and badges of office that had been, in some form, in the city of

Rome since the founding of the empire. "You are," he argued to Zeno, "emperor enough for me." By returning the insignia, he made the case that he was a loyal servant of empire—but not one who would put up with any emperors in *his* vicinity.

Zeno saw opportunity, as he would see it again a few years later when he sent Theoderic to supplant Odoacer, and so for now he accepted the offer. Zeno conferred on Odoacer the highest title in his gift, *patricius*, and henceforth Odoacer seems to have added the imperial prefix Flavius to his name (we have coins minted for "Fl. Odoacer"). Zeno encouraged Odoacer to direct his nominal allegiance to another imperial claimant, Julius Nepos, then still hanging on by his fingernails to a scrap of authority in the Balkans. No one recorded Odoacer's response, but when Nepos died shortly afterward, Zeno was the only emperor in all the Roman realms.

What was Odoacer? In Roman governmental eyes, he was *patricius* (patrician) and representative of the emperor. In military eyes he was *rex* (king), but we shouldn't make him a barbarian king without clearly understanding the different kinds of lordship he exercised: *rex Torcilingorum, rex Torcilingorum Rogorumque, rex Gothorum*—all names of groups of soldiers and their families that offered allegiance to this Roman ruler. In one way or another, Odoacer managed to be associated with or claimed by at least half a dozen such groups in his career, but from the time he came to Italy, the Roman ones predominated.

Odoacer ruled from Rome and from Ravenna and, setting a pattern followed and exceeded by Theoderic, paid careful attention to the senatorial class in Rome, by now a shrinking number of families with an inflated sense of their own preeiminence. Odoacer's restoration of the Colosseum and his assignment of seats to senatorial dignitaries, as we saw, were probably the most visible of his tactics to consolidate power and aggrandize himself as a Roman of Rome. There isn't much eventful narrative of Odoacer's reign left to us, and so we tend to minimize his achievements, but he did win back Sicily from the Vandals and extended his control into Noricum and Dalmatia north and east of the Italian peninsula. For the first time since Aetius twenty years earlier, a resident of the peninsula could feel that control, dignity, and Roman prosperity were in the land again.

And then Theoderic. Theoderic's successes were greater than Odoacer's, his reign lasted twice as long, and (most important and most misleading for history) he appears in abundant documents of many kinds. He made sure we had the wherewithal to tell his story, as I have already been telling it, and in this he was very shrewd and very Roman.

We have returned now to the year 500, a midpoint in a rare and privileged moment of history, when two strong, successful rulers, neither of them a saint but neither more vicious than most, ruled in succession for a combined fifty years between them. The long fourth century that lasted from the accession of Diocletian in 284 to the murder of Stilicho in 408 represented a better time, but that epoch followed a short third century (from the death of Alexander Severus in 235 to Diocletian's accession) that had been every bit as abysmal as the fifth century. After Theoderic's death in 526 and the murder of his daughter in 535, Italy as a whole would know no comparable unity, prosperity, and freedom from warfare until the 1950s. We concentrate, inevitably, on Theoderic's years, but Odoacer deserves praise as well, and our remembrance as one of the noblest Romans.

What differentiated Theoderic from Odoacer—other than good luck and a long life—was his identification with the people on whose military loyalty he depended. The creation of Ostrogothic identity—or, if he did not create it, the exploitation and orchestration—is Theoderic's most audacious and impressive achievement. We will see Clovis, his contemporary, follow a similar path, creating the Franks at about the same time, when it was impossible to predict which of these new groups would have the longer future. Odoacer was too Roman and too naive to take the precaution of cooking up an identity for his followers; that loyalty to old ways undermined him in the end.

In shaping the clay from which Ostrogoths emerged, Theoderic was at a disadvantage, as well, for he needed the collaboration of the native population to reinforce, or reinvent, an older artificial notion of a unified native people—the so-called Romans. In ruling those two peoples, Theoderic was the author of an extraordinarily successful constitutional novelty. Seeing his world hidden behind the scrims of performance and masquerade that he created has challenged the best historians, and none has escaped unenthralled. We must now step into his theater ourselves.

2

The World That Might
Have Been

E MUST ENTER Theoderic's theater with appropriate reverence for the stately performance he will stage for us, and with keen-eyed skepticism, determined, as if we were at a magic show, *not* to let our attention be distracted. Surely, we will be smart enough not to let anticipated misdirection and legerdemain fool us into believing in magic, won't we?

ROMANS AND ROMANS

Uncontested in power from 493, triumphant at Rome in 500, Theoderic would reign until 526. Of all the rulers who held sway in the Italian peninsula from Romulus to his own day, only the original Caesar Augustus enjoyed a longer reign, and in the eastern empire Theodosius II (r. 408–450) and Justinian (r. 527–565) outdid him, but then no comparably long-reigned rival would appear until Basil II in the late tenth century in Constantinople. To this day, Theoderic has no rival on the Italian peninsula, unless we allow popes into the contest, and even then Pius IX's nearly thirty-two years fall short. It was an age when Italy was divided between Romans—and Romans.

Italy.

Contemporaries made the era out to be a golden age, when you could leave your money lying outdoors at night, confident that none would steal it, and when cities never closed their gates. The peninsula was secure from serious military attack, disturbed only by skirmishes on the margins and news of one brief but substantial conflict in southern Gaul. Land tenure was certain; law was consistent, predictable, and enforced; and public officers served in a regular order, almost all with titles long familiar in local history and use. People could grow up, marry, raise families, and die exactly as their forebears had. The stability of empire had returned. Given how needy and overbuilt the region was—long accustomed to being propped up by tax revenues, living on imports—Odoacer's and Theoderic's achievements are unexpected and striking.

As in all of classical antiquity, however, too much of what we hear about this age is filtered through the experience of aristocratic families, the kind who still hung the smoke-stained ancestral death masks in what they probably still called the atrium of their family home, whatever architectural form it took. Those ancestors foreshadowed the ones that Gilbert and Sullivan's Major-General found in the chapel on his estate in *The Pirates of Penzance*:

> FREDERIC: But you forget, sir, you only bought the property a year ago, and the stucco on your baronial castle is scarcely dry.
> MAJOR-GENERAL: Frederic, in this chapel are ancestors: you cannot deny that. With the estate, I bought the chapel and its contents. I don't know whose ancestors they were, but I know whose ancestors they are.

The legends of Roman families took a particularly sharp turn in the fourth century under and after Constantine, when many old families found themselves rather taken over and brought under new management by the freshly minted aristocrats—usually military men—of the regimes of Diocletian and Constantine. The children and grandchildren of a colonel who made a good marriage to an impoverished blue blood deferred to no one in their ostentatious reverence for ancient lineage. Undoubtedly, genealogists might trace some twig of marriage and descent on even the shakiest family trees back to olden times. The Decii, the Anicii, and the Basilii of the fifth and sixth centuries in Rome—those were the families that loomed largest in Theoderic's Rome—were far removed from the worthies of old whose names they bore. Any members of the Decii of the sixth century could tell the story of their heroic ancestor in the Samnite wars of the fourth century BCE, the one who made an offering of himself and the enemy's soldiers to the gods above and below before riding into battle in order to ensure victory for the Romans during his consulship. And that was usually enough for family pride dozens of generations later.

Some of these families we know well enough to strike up an acquaintance, as the generations lead one into another for at least one or two turns of fortune's wheel. Even when we fasten our gazes on the leading families, though, we see arrivistes as often as we see those who could claim long ancestry. Liberius, for example, we have met already, flourishing in Theoderic's early days, from a family of no special repute. Still only about thirty years old at the change of regimes, from somewhere in northern Italy and of unremarkable family, he had served Odoacer, had switched allegiance nimbly to Theoderic, and made no pretense of hating his former master while matter-of-factly offering his services to the new. Theoderic admired and accepted the offer, and he advanced Liberius directly to the highest office he had to give, that of praetorian prefect.

In all Theoderic's years, only traditional candidates like Liberius or the Cassiodori held the traditional offices of praetorian prefect, count of the sacred generosity, quaestor, master of offices, and the like, the jobs elaborately laid out in the law codes and bureaucratic documents of the evolving late empire. Since the fourth century the praetorian prefect had effectively become the prime minister and highest civil officer of government, drawing his title from notional supervision of the praetorian guard, but now he was responsible for that most important of government functions: survival. In other words, the praetorian prefect was the tax man: rate setter and collector of the money that supported the military, i.e., the real government. The official calendar was managed by the tax years, the indictions we spoke of, running from September to September, the period in which the summer's harvest was collected and distributed to those who would consume it. Liberius earned enough praise for raising revenues without raising rates to make us think he was efficient, but his efficiency was probably due as much to the support the new ruler gave his prefect, and the power he could wield. The effectiveness of Roman government depended on appropriate fear in the governed.

Liberius was the one who settled Theoderic's followers on their land with almost no disruption that we hear of. Those who had followed Theoderic into Italy or materialized out of the ground to ally themselves with him during the several years of his fight with Odoacer numbered in the low tens of thousands. Over the sixty years of his and his successors' regimes, we get a good picture of the strikingly limited settlement patterns of those followers. Italy north of the Po and mainly east of Milan and Pavia is their heartland; a much smaller community appears at Rome itself. There are sightings in Tuscany, but also indications that their concentration was small, wealthy, and situated not far from the city of Rome itself. Because of their wealth, on one occasion Theoderic sent tax collectors to dun his Tuscan followers for their arrears, just as traditional Roman tax collectors had dunned senators there for centuries. In what seem to be smaller numbers, others settled down the coasts of southern Italy, in modern Calabria and Apulia.

Those strategic few remind us of the central place of military power in the Roman empire at all periods. The Roman word that becomes "emperor" is *imperator*, general; and from the death of Nero to the death of Theodosius in 395, every emperor had generalship and soldiery about him (with one or two near-exceptions, like the religion-obsessed Heliogabalus). In the fifth century the retirement of delicate young emperors to palaces brought forward the real generals, stern men from the northern marches, to do the emperors' dirty work for them.

For a very long time, the dirtiest of that work had gone on far from the Mediterranean, its cities, and its settled populations. Roman soldiers, coming to the end of their service, expected to be looked after, and the customary form of care was a gift of land. Viewed from inside the empire, they could seem like Zionists in Palestine during the early twentieth century. Looked at from far enough away, with the right spyglass, it could seem that the land they were given was empty. For centuries, soldiers had been given other people's land like that, and Italy was secure. Now Italy had to get used to compensating its own protectors. And some land in Italy was empty. The arrangement we have seen Liberius make was very clever, very Roman, and very ingenious. The most settled and wealthy of Roman landlords, the great senators, who held property mainly from Rome south through Campania to the bay of Naples and then in other advantageous areas from Tuscany down to Calabria and—some of them again, or still—into Sicily, would have felt little impact from the supposed invasion. It was the ones without connections, the ones who could be ignored, who suffered. No surprise.

Liberius served as praetorian prefect until Theoderic's visit to Rome in 500, when he stepped down, but even then he always stayed in touch with the court at Ravenna, ready to take on a delicate commission for Theoderic if need be. This happened in 506, when he went to Aquileia to supervise the election of a new bishop there and make sure the right man won. Getting things right was important in Aquileia, the city that guarded the northeastern land frontier of Italy from any incursions from the Balkans or from Constantinople. As one of many rewards for his good service, Liberius was allowed to see his own son Venantius inaugurated as consul in 507—which would have made Liberius responsible for presenting the grand consular games at Rome. Liberius was never a member of one of the first families of Rome, and the games were expensive, so perhaps he had a little help from on high in ensuring a memorable show that demonstrated how loyalty was rewarded in Theoderic's world. Venantius served as consul jointly with the eastern emperor Anastasius himself, a high honor and an important gesture from Theoderic.

Liberius still had a long run in front of him. In 508, Theoderic found himself tested on two fronts. There were raids first in the Adriatic from seaborne forces of Anastasius, puzzling encounters that even one contemporary in Constantinople called "more an act of piracy than an act of war"[1] and they came to nothing, but they reminded Theoderic that he could not count unthinkingly on sustained good relations with Constantinople, where envious and covetous eyes would always gaze in his direction. Affairs in Gaul were more serious and not irrelevant to the eastern concerns.

Clovis had made himself master of the Roman forces in northern Gaul. He now sought to extend his authority to the south as he attacked and defeated the forces of the young Alaric II, who prided himself on being Theoderic's distant cousin. Clovis was devastatingly successful, defeating and killing Alaric himself, and broadly extending his power through central and southern Gaul. The defeated armies regrouped in Spain, leaving behind most of their claim to Gaulish rule.

Theoderic seized the moment to enter that stage, ostensibly to support the young Alaric, and he succeeded in establishing himself in Provence. He also took advantage of the opportunity to extend his protection to the cousinly regime in Spain, and Clovis was smart enough to pull up short and respect the new arrangement. Just then we get a hint that Anastasius extended an olive branch from Constantinople to Clovis over Theoderic's head, sending him the papers making him an honorary consul. Theoderic was right to sense conspiracy in the air, but strong enough to stand his ground without provoking or being provoked. He succeeded in deferring real risk until beyond the end of his own life, when Clovis's successors more than once allied themselves with Constantinople against Italian regimes.

Theoderic now needed a presence in Gaul. He had gone as far west as Milan himself during the campaigns across the Alps, but as far as we know he never left Italy after he arrived in 489. The man he selected to be his face and hand in Gaul was Liberius: tested, tough, and true. Clovis had at some point—most likely just at the moment of his conquests in southern Gaul—declared his allegiance to the approved official Christianity of the time, the kind that comes down to us as Catholicism, in contrast to the old-fashioned imperial religion, Theoderic's Arianism. Theoderic's position in Italy had taught him survival and toleration, and Alaric II, though himself similarly old-fashioned, had made his peace with the Catholic fashion in Gaul and let that church flourish under his rule.

Theoderic had the sense early on to invite the leading Catholic Christian clergyman of Provence, bishop Caesarius of Arles, to visit him in Ravenna. Even Caesarius's biographers a few decades later, suspicious of Theoderic (now long dead) and claiming that Caesarius had been virtually arrested and brought to Italy to face accusations, nevertheless describe how Theoderic greeted the visitor graciously, laying aside his crown and interviewing him patiently about affairs in Gaul. Theoderic said he saw an angel in this bishop and showered him with gifts—only to be mildly rebuffed when Caesarius used the gifts to redeem captives from the late war who were being held in Italy. It was more likely that Theoderic invited Caesarius to Italy to honor and thus tame him, rather than attack him, but if Caesarius had been unwilling to be wooed, things might have gone badly for him. Caesarius went on to Rome, where Pope Symmachus, by now secure in his office, welcomed him with all dignity and confirmed his status as first bishop of Gaul. By the time Liberius was installed in Arles as Theoderic's plenipotentiary, governor, and general, Theoderic, whatever his religious views, had made clear that he would enthusiastically support the Catholic churches of Gaul and thus deny Clovis any opportunity for subversion. So Theoderic wrote to one of his own generals, ordering him to restore property to the churches of Narbonne, west of the Rhone, that they had lost in the war.

This was Liberius's world for the next quarter century. He represented the Roman empire (Theoderic's branch of it, that is), commanded its military forces, showered generosity on the Christian church and so made it feel indebted to the regime, and was in every way the loyal supporter of the ruler who sent him there. In Provence, the old aristocracy had regrouped and reinvented itself, its churchmen were flourishing, and what passed as normality prevailed. When Bishop Apollinaris of Valence, from well within Clovis's domains, paid a visit to Arles, the holy and distinguished lord bishop Caesarius greeted him and his companions. The prefect Liberius joined in along with his whole prefectural retinue, welcoming Apollinaris with festive speeches. They were certain, they said, that divine mercy had sent him. Apollinaris returned the welcome in equally kind phrases. On such a day in such a place, the Roman empire seemed to be what it had been for centuries.

Liberius's post was still military in its importance, and flare-ups occurred from time to time. The life of Caesarius written by three of his disciples gives us a moment in 527 when Liberius was personally in command of forces that had crossed the Durance River on patrol. Wounded by a lance in a minor skirmish, he fell from his horse and lay unconscious while the bishop was summoned. Liberius regained consciousness and began to kiss his bishop's hand and then, by what he took to be a godly inspiration, grasped the bishop's hooded cape, the *birrus*, and pressed it to his wound. At that moment the blood stopped flowing, and he was so restored, not just to health but to strength, that he swore he would have climbed back into the saddle and ridden on if the others had let him. The story goes on to tell how Liberius's wife, Agretia, was similarly cured of illness when Caesarius laid hands on her. Even if we are skeptical about the bishop's magical powers, these stories offer a snapshot of the role and presence of this pious power couple in southern Gaul for a quarter century. Liberius was viceregal in authority and reputation and provided the essential link between Theoderic's Italy and the protectorate in Spain. The last time we see Liberius in action in Gaul he is the patron and partner of Caesarius again, signing the acts of a church council held at Orange in 529. That council quietly rewrote the doctrines of Augustine—dead then 100 years—to make them palatable to the Gaulish church by deflating some of Augustine's predestinarian ideas while continuing to praise the man himself. Without this deft act of homage and revision, Augustine's chances of being reviled for heresy at some later date were perilously high.[2] We needn't imagine Liberius rootling around in the theological issues himself, but the secular guarantor of ecclesiastical authority was a very Roman role for a high official now, going back two centuries.

This viceroy was not done yet. We will see him again in later chapters more than once in military and civilian roles spanning the Mediterranean. Liberius is the authentic Theoderician man in many ways: Roman, pragmatic, tough, loyal up to a point, churchly enough to get by, and effective in establishing and maintaining Roman order in any setting.

Consider, by contrast, Boethius—Anicius Manlius Severinus Boethius— a man with a fine name and a family, the Anicii, almost as fine. Though we have no trace of anyone who read it in his century, Boethius wrote what later became the best-selling book, other than the Bible, throughout the Latin middle ages, the *Consolation of Philosophy*. That book, with its apologia for a life well lived that ended badly, is a precious source, corroborated and supplemented by other views, for the place of one man and his family in the Italy of his time.

Boethius began well and soon improved his lot. His father was consul in 487, when Boethius was a small boy, but died not long afterward, and so Boethius was brought up in the household of the greatest senator of the age, his kinsman Symmachus, who had been consul in 485. Quintus Aurelius Memmius Symmachus (the claim to antiquity here is in the name Memmius, which recalls the wealthy patron the poet Lucretius had flattered 500 years earlier) was a man too lofty to spend much time in public office, preferring to devote himself to writing the history of Rome. We cannot follow the money in Boethius's life as closely as we might wish, but by the time he had married Symmachus's daughter, he was as wealthy as any man could be who was not emperor.

To the advantages of wealth, Boethius added real talent and an education unmatched by any native Latin-speaker in at least a century, and unmatched by anyone in Italy or the west for hundreds of years afterward. "You attended the schools of Athens from afar,"[3] one contemporary wrote to him, leading scholars to debate whether this means he never left Italy or, on a more sophistic reading, that he actually pursued his studies in Alexandria, where the Platonism had a Christian flair. But philosophy was his métier; a comprehensive interpretation of all ancient Platonic and Aristotelian thought was his goal. This was the last age that could easily believe Plato and Aristotle had really been of one mind, and Boethius attempted—in a series of books that are now not much or easily read—to persuade his contemporaries of this truth and give it full expression. A handful of his short theological treatises, written in the 510s, survive as well. In these he took definite and intellectually sophisticated positions on the church controversies of his time, seeking peaceful solutions to the quarrels that separated Constantinople from Rome.

By now Theoderic was the self-assured and supreme master of the Roman empire's Italian domains, with secure control of the approaches to Italy from all land directions—from the Balkans, from across the Alps to the north, and from Gaul. He had to watch for threats from Clovis in Gaul and from the Vandals in Africa, but neither truly unsettled him, and Theoderic had the diplomacy to manage both. Constantinople was still the 900-pound gorilla of the Roman world. Occasional brushes with the empire's raiders and hints of rapprochement between Anastasius and Clovis would hold Theoderic's attention, but he was at least certain of the loyalty of his own citizens—mostly.

He earned that loyalty by governing well, by settling his forces in Italy without gross disruption, and by convincing both the senatorial classes and the high churchmen that order and tradition were on his side. Could anyone else have persuaded them that perhaps another way existed to ensure their dignity and future? Perhaps, but from the time of his arrival in Italy, Theoderic had one particular assurance that Italy's aristocracy would not be looking eastward for such persuasion: ecclesiastical animosity. In 484, the bishop of Rome formally broke off relations with the bishops of Constantinople over points of theology and imperial interference. A sympathetic member of the community of "sleepless monks" in Constantinople pinned the decree of excommunication from Rome to the back of the patriarch Acacius's vestments while Acacius celebrated the Eucharist. The Acacian schism gave the Roman church the serene confidence that it knew the true religion and that Constantinople fell short. Constantinople might again come to its senses, but for the moment, Romans who traveled there were instructed not to share communion with any of those so-called Christians.

If Theoderic's own old-fashioned Arian religion separated him in principle from Italy's Catholics, he could modulate that division by generosity, as we have seen him do in both Italy and Gaul. As long as the Christians of the first families of Rome and their allies in the church hierarchy were supercilious and judgmental about the Christians of Constantinople, the western détente would hold. If Rome and Constantinople began to speak of reconciliation and harmony, then Theoderic's religion, shaky enough in any case, would be the anomaly. Then the notion of ecclesiastical harmony between Rome and Constantinople might open Romans to persuasion that they should listen to Constantinople on other grounds. And for Theoderic, that was the real threat.

So for all his reign, Theoderic was careful to cultivate and support the senatorial dignitaries, as much as Odoacer did. Boethius's father and his father-in-law Symmachus had won the consulship under Odoacer. If the highest offices sometimes were given to reward the loyalty of arrivistes like Liberius, at least as often they graced the old and wealthy families. Boethius was not to be disappointed. In the year 510, at a moment of Theoderic's highest confidence, Boethius, age thirty or so, acceded to the consulship without a colleague, and gave his name to the year, and Boethius had the satisfaction of knowing that men would always remember 510 in their annals by his name.

Grander rewards awaited. In 522, Boethius had the honor—unheard of for more than a century among Roman citizens not of the imperial family—of seeing his two sons share the consulship in the same year. He must have found this triumph gaspingly expensive, but no one would have been in a better position to bear the burden of proclaiming by ostentatious expenditure just how glorious his family was.

At the same time, Theoderic invited Boethius to stand next to the throne. In 522–523, he was called to Ravenna to serve as *magister officiorum*, master of the offices. In this role, he supervised the civil bureaucracy and also the coming and going of ambassadors and missions to and from Constantinople and to and from the courts of other rulers in the western Mediterranean. One might think of him as minister of foreign affairs.

This Boethius, the successful Boethius, who had the ear of the ruler and was the object of his flattering attentions, we see mainly through the eyes of the official letters from Theoderic, written by his longtime associate Cassiodorus. Theoderic addressed Boethius consistently as the master of the arts called liberal: the technical disciplines that a true philosopher thought would cleanse his mind of confusion and prepare him for deeper understanding, yet disciplines that a worldly monarch might find more utilitarian than mystical. So when embezzlers clipped metal from coins, threatening the reliability of the currency, Boethius was the expert to consult. When Theoderic needed to impress another western ruler with his elegance and good taste, Boethius supplied ingenious gifts—water clocks and sundials for the Burgundian king Gundobad, or a musician for Clovis in Gaul. All these requests came during the years surrounding Boethius's consulship, when his learning and his philosophical works were already objects of high praise, and he was still in his thirties.

If we want to balance this high praise and remember that even famous philosophers have neighbors who aren't fond of them, we might look at his contemporary Maximian, a Latin poet down to his fingertips, even if a purist might quibble that these were no longer the fingertips of, say, Horace or Propertius. Maximian crafted light verse depicting Boethius as more of a libertine than we might have guessed. The grasping cleric Ennodius in Pavia, always on the make and looking for the right Roman patrons, attempted several times to buy a house from Boethius but never quite made the transaction work, leaving a sense that he thought Boethius was a little too snooty to deal with provincial clerics. Boethius's critics were few, and they were the critics of a man secure in wealth and power.

Boethius knew many years of untroubled days in opulent surroundings. There, tranquil but for those few whispers of jealousy, we will leave Boethius content for now. Later his end and Theoderic's will be bound up together in the unhappiest story of the age. For now we must look past his celebrity to see the rest of the Romans. There were, for example, Faustus, Faustus, and Festus, bearing the kind of names that the lower classes mock as indistinguishable, when everyone who was anyone could tell them apart instantly. They were of the old families, and the first two of the three were as dissimilar as their nicknames: Faustus the Black and Faustus the White.

Faustus the Black claimed descent from the ancient Messala Corvinus and was known for his books, both those he owned and those he wrote. His distant and moderately poor relation Ennodius wrote poems about both, hoping Faustus the Black would think well of him. Faustus was consul in 490 and later master of the offices and quaestor at court, positions reserved for the elegant and loyal. He was a leading supporter of Pope Symmachus in the quarrels of these years, and so we last see him in office as praetorian prefect from 508 to 512, years when Theoderic was at the peak of his power.

Faustus the White had been prefect of the city—that is to say, governor of Rome itself—in the early 480s. He had his own seat inscribed at the Colosseum, and he would be prefect again in the 500s. A gentleman through and through, he demonstrated grace by having a statue of Minerva, that fine and not too toxic goddess of the old order, restored after it fell from a roof during a civil uprising. The 470s before Odoacer came to power were rough days, so Faustus's restoration would have been an emblem of Odoacer's and Theoderic's long campaign to polish up the city.

The third grandee, Festus, we have seen already, the most senior of the ex-consuls in all these years, having given the year his name in 472 and won his seat in the Colosseum afterward. By 490, he was already the senior surviving consul, when Theoderic sent him to Constantinople to represent his claims as the legitimate Roman ruler in Italy. Although Festus was unsuccessful then, he returned to Constantinople more successfully on the same mission in 497. He was loyal to Theoderic by choice rather than necessity, securely independent in his seniority. When he returned to Italy, he became the moving force behind the election of the alternative pope Laurentius. Rumor had it that Festus promised the emperor an end to schism. Emperor Zeno signed a decree of church union called the *Henotikon* in 584, but that only made the divided parties dig in their heels, confirming the break between Rome and Constantinople. Pope Anastasius II (r. 496–498) was a promising candidate for leading a rapprochement and signing the *Henotikon*, but he died too soon, and so (the most common interpretation goes) Festus scattered bribes to ensure Laurentius's election and did everything in his power to advance the Laurentian cause, to the point of giving Laurentius lifetime asylum on his estates when the tide went against them in the end. Festus managed this intrigue without losing Theoderic's favor, and he is last seen as an object of worthy praise in 513, having by then become a man of very advanced years by Roman standards.

We should not think that these men were representative of their class. To an important extent, they *were* their class, that is, they were the undoubted leaders of a shrunken and diminished senate. Could there have been as few as thirty or fifty real senators by now, bravely meeting in the traditional senate house and keeping up the order among the echoes? At Rome in those days, genealogists of taste and learning could tell you the fates of old families, as many disappeared and some merely degraded into obscurity. Without them, it became a little lonelier at the top.

There were other Italies. Even the richest of these men had to have their roots somewhere, their power and their lands in some province. Liberius came from Liguria and was buried in Rimini, but the more traditional senators had at least a foot in the city of Rome, and land between there and Naples. Theodahad, a relative of Theoderic's whom we will meet later, settled in Tuscany, where he became a local tyrant, more than once rebuked publicly by Theoderic and forced (or at least Theoderic ordered that he be forced) to give up property that he and his private army had illegally seized. Meanwhile, Sicily, long a bastion of senatorial wealth and land, only latterly came back under Italian control when Odoacer retrieved it from Vandal rule. The days of great estates spreading across the African highlands and sending produce to Rome and wealth to a few Romans were now long gone.

So where were the Goths? They are the invisible men of Theoderic's Italy. We have seen that their numbers fell far short of a horde, and that they settled mainly in the north and down to Rome. They and all their predecessors and all their successors among the barbarians who supposedly invaded poor, defenseless Italy ended by disappearing, and the language spoken in Milan, Rome, and Palermo to this day is a direct and astonishingly uncontaminated descendant of Latin. Where did the supposedly mighty Goths and Lombards go?

We must give some credit to the powerful urge to go native—to romanize—that newcomers in Italy felt for many centuries. The priest-poet Ennodius made fun of a contemporary, Jovinian, who couldn't decide what part he wanted to play, for he wore a Goth's beard and a Roman's winter cloak. Was he Goth or Roman? Or was Jovinian the sort that Cassiodorus had in mind when he observed drily that it was poor Romans who imitated the Goths, just as rich Goths imitated the Romans? Imitation is the first step toward assimilation.

Or were the Goths even ever there? Numbers and time tell the story. The invasions of Italy of which we know consist of four distinct events, two still to come in our story. The arrival of Alaric and his troops in the early 400s brought outsiders, and most of that group moved on in the 410s. Through the fifth century, other frights and fights, notably with the Huns, came and went, each leaving behind a few new settlers—and time passed. Theoderic appeared in the late 480s with the largest force ever until then to think of settling in Italy, and those soldiers and families spent the next fifty years, two generations, nestling into their homes. Italy was then to be attacked from Constantinople and the ruling government eventually, after a long and bloody battle we will have to steel ourselves to watch, overthrown. Theoderic's regime had little effect on the ethnic makeup of the population, or its tendency to coalesce into one people. The last two invasions were equally barbaric. Justinian sent troops in the 530s and 540s in an act that was notionally Roman, but the troops themselves came from the same wellspring of Roman military force in the Balkans as Theoderic and his men. When, in the 560s, the Lombards arrived, they came as creatures of empire themselves, with no less obvious roots in all the obvious places, but we will see them settle mainly away from the cities, in numbers that cannot have been large. Of those four invasions, Justinian's left the greatest demonstrable number of "barbarians" resident in Italy.

Of the northern people who came to the Mediterranean, whether we call them Vandals, Visigoths, Ostrogoths, Franks, Lombards, or eventually Slavs, all had more in common with one another *and* with the Romans than traditional narratives ever suggest. If there were any primeval forest dwellers in those communities, they were the ones their smarter, more acquisitive, and more ambitious cousins left behind. Immigrants are always like this, especially those who push across borders that resist them. By the time people like Theoderic's followers find themselves in Italy, they were there not as barbarians but as Roman soldiers, bearers of the distinctive frontier culture of the north, to be sure, with styles of dress, religion, and speech that differentiated them from the settled southerners, but that made them nonetheless part of the same imperial community. They had their own officers, their own bureaucrats, and their own jargon.

If some of them did not speak Latin (though there is little or no evidence for Latinless Goths in this period), and if there was a Gothic language that they did speak, it was a heavy creole, with German roots but abundant romanization, and with ritual literary presence. The most splendid document of that Gothic tongue is the *Codex Argenteus,* the silver codex preserved today in the library of Uppsala University. Only a fragment of what it was, the manuscript contains passages of the four gospels written on purple-stained vellum in letters—quite beautifully and regularly inscribed—of silver and gold.[4] It was written in Ravenna as a treasure that handsomely displayed the splendor of Gothic civilization, but absolutely nothing about its physical form owed anything to any source other than

The Codex Argenteus: *gospels in Gothic.*

the Mediterranean. The manuscript may have come from the workshop of a man with a Gothic name, Wiliarit, known to have produced handsome Latin manuscripts in Ravenna as late as the dreary war year of 551. One of his products was a copy of Orosius's *History against the Pagans*—a seemingly authorized Christian version of all of Roman history as seen by a disciple of Augustine in the early fifth century. Gothic culture in this period was not a counterculture but a badge of pride and belonging, deriving all its meaning from its Roman setting.

Many who know nothing of the facts of the matter still deeply and instinctively believe an alternative view—that these people represented an

irreducible and uncivilizable injection of barbarism into Rome, for good
or ill. Nineteenth-century nationalism nurtured this confidence, as did
the pride of German scholars who saw in these figures their own cultural
ancestors. We should be wary of such psychological projection and self-
aggrandizement. Sober and reasonable scholars took the perfumed sixth-
century Latin texts of Ennodius, Cassiodorus, and Avitus and published
them in the "more ancient authors" series of the *Historical Monuments
of Germany* (*Monumenta Germaniae Historica*), a huge collection of impeccable scholarship. Felix Dahn, one of the most serious scholars of this
period, known for a long series of volumes, *Kings of the Germans*, also
produced one of the most successful historical novels of the time, *A Fight
for Rome* (*Ein Kampf um Rom*), which was later known to be a favorite of
the emperor Wilhelm at the time of World War I. Its title evokes both the
Kulturkampf of nineteenth-century Prussia and the better-known *Kampf*
of a later German tyrant. In it, the confident nationalism and racism of
the nineteenth century proclaim themselves through the voice of a Gothic
leader: "So where is this 'mankind' you speak of? I don't see it. I see only
Goths, Romans, Byzantines! A 'mankind' over and above these peoples,
somewhere in the air, that I don't recognize. I serve mankind when I love
my own people (*Volk*). I cannot do otherwise!"[5]

No surprise, but such words come in a novel that contrasts the bravery
and intelligence of fair-haired northerners with the weakness and treachery of darker-hued southerners. Dahn's book survived to be made cheaply
into a two-part movie, filmed in Romania with German dialogue, in the
late 1960s. Justinian was played by Orson Welles; Amalasuntha, daughter of Theoderic and regent of Italy, by Honor Blackman, who had attracted more attention a couple of years earlier in the arms of James Bond
in *Goldfinger*. This faux-Hollywood trifle was the kind of production such
unhistorical rubbish deserved. Yet it is extraordinary to note how much
modern scholarship has still tended to agree that there must be something
to all this racist nonsense.

But surely, a reader might reasonably object, all that smoke about barbarians must point to some fire. There must have been true-blue, ethnically pure tribesmen who followed their leaders ever since they strode,
blond and blue-eyed, out of Scandinavia centuries earlier. To get beyond
such thinking, look at Mundo, a man of Theoderic's time in every way, as
good a candidate for the description "barbarian" as they came. Mundo

was the son of a leader of the Gepids who died young. His uncle Tapstila snatched the leadership away from Mundo, and stood at the head of forces that Theoderic defeated on his way to Italy in 488. When Tapstila was killed in that battle, Mundo's cousin Traseric succeeded his fallen father and patched together a life in the Balkans serving as one of Theoderic's tributaries. Around 500, Mundo himself fled his family as he came of age, setting up in business as a leader of fighters (shall we call them bandits, insurgents, mercenaries, or militants?) in what is now Hungary. Constantinople sent out a general to bring Mundo to heel, but just then Pitzia, one of Theoderic's generals, advanced toward Sirmium, where he and Mundo joined forces, defeating the intended Byzantine police action at Horreum Margi on the Morava River. Twenty years later, Mundo turned up leading Gepids and Heruls, now accepting a command from Constantinople to fight *for* empire, against Slavs and Bulgars, in 529. He did so well that he was briefly general in chief of all the Balkans, taking the emperor's side to put down an incipient revolt in Constantinople itself. Not long afterward, in the mid-530s, he led Constantinople's forces to Split, on the eastern shore of the Adriatic, asserting control in a vacuum when Theoderic's successors were hard pressed just to stay alive in Italy. When Mundo's son was killed in battle, the father lost both judgment and control and pursued his Gothic opponents so recklessly that they killed him. Mundo lived and died a Roman of his times, whoever his ancestors were.

And bear in mind the passage of time. When adult men and women who made their way from the Balkans into Italy with Theoderic saw his last years in the 520s, they also watched their grandchildren come of age, grandchildren who had never known another home. Those grandchildren and their children faced the sudden shock of a nominally Roman invasion in the 530s and a long war fought to overthrow Theoderic's heirs and replace them with a puppet regime managed from Constantinople. To place this in perspective, the Goths of the 540s stood at the same remove from the founding moment of Theoderic's invasion—with a shorter life expectancy and a more rapid perceived change of generations—as the Israelis of today from the kibbutzniks and founders of 1948. Whatever one makes of the politics of the Middle East, the Israelis of today really are Israelis, with no other home and no other culture. Theoderic's followers, fewer in number proportionally, more assimilated, and more welcomed (even if force made them welcome) than the

Zionists of 1948, were if anything more fully at home in that Italian world. They belonged.

The great curiosity of Theoderic's reign in Italy is not that there were Goths, but that thirty years after his rule began, then (and then only) he began to look to his Gothic roots and tell a Gothic story about himself. Some of this had to do with planning for the succession.

Despite all his successes, Theoderic had one failure; he never had a son. Pious hopes for a successor from his seed appear in occasional texts of the time, but there was none.

Theoderic did have that daughter, Amalasuntha, and she was his opportunity. Having taken effective control of the Visigothic regime in Spain and looking to consolidate his rule throughout the northern coast of the Mediterranean west, he imagined unity by dynasty. Theoderic summoned from Spain a man my Irish ancestors would have called "some kind of cousin," Eutharic. Once married to Amalasuntha, Eutharic could produce an heir, and did: Athalaric, born in 518. Theoderic, by now well into his sixties, could breathe a sigh of relief. The moment was propitious for celebration, and a celebration was arranged.

Eutharic was named consul for the year 519, under the proud eye of Theoderic and notionally alongside the new emperor, Justin, as fellow consul, though of course they never laid eyes on each other. More dramatically, Justin proclaimed Eutharic his "son in arms" by an honorary adoption conferring recognition and acceptance of the highest kind. The aged Anastasius, who had been emperor since 491, had always been suspicious of Theoderic, but left him alone for the last decade, preoccupied in part by worries closer to home. Justin, more a barbarian than Theoderic ever was, came down out of the Balkans to make his way in the imperial army, and then followed talent to the top—we'll watch him make the final leap. Theoderic clearly thought that he could now proclaim his own heritage more grandly, without imperiling the position he had succeeded in obtaining, and using this renewed statement of his Gothic identity to improve his standing both at home and in Visigothic Iberia. Whether this was entirely Theoderic's idea, or whether Eutharic—known also to have been more zealous in promoting the Arian religion—was behind this invention of family pride, we cannot tell.

So the realm celebrated Eutharic's consulship in 519 with all the Roman pomp of which it was capable. In that year, the contemporary account tells us, every performance of the games and shows had unimagined marvels to offer. The official representative of the eastern emperor was astonished (we are told) to see the extraordinary wealth handed out to soldier and civilian, that is, to both Goth and Roman. The wild beast shows in the Colosseum were like nothing anyone then alive had ever seen, with rare animals from Africa, their acquisition no doubt the result of good diplomacy with the Vandals. Eutharic could scarcely tear himself away from the Romans' love and admiration to return to Ravenna and the court of his father-in-law, where the chariot races began once again, with such immense largess shown to Goths and Romans alike that it surpassed even what he had just seen at Rome.

The spectacle hit every note of Roman splendor, but the message was deliberately Gothic and dynastic. At the same time, Theoderic's house historian wrote books just to capture this splendor. This was Flavius Magnus Aurelius Cassiodorus Senator, the son of the man who secured Sicily and Calabria for Theoderic. He wrote a chronicle of all of human history, from Adam forward, through all the consuls of Rome, from the first in 509 BCE down to the exaltation of Eutharic himself, and then turned to a formal history of the Gothic people in twelve books, emphasizing the obvious, which was truer than the author or his patron knew: that the Goths had been forever part of the Roman world. His chronicle took every opportunity to mention the turning points in the history of Gothic-Roman relations and, where necessary, smooth over awkwardness. The larger work was marked throughout by the legend of Theoderic's own family, the Amals, outlining seventeen generations of kings that culminated in the year he wrote: 519.[6] Cassiodorus delivered a formal Latin oration in honor of Eutharic as well.

With three such magnificent books—chronicle of Romans, history of Goths, and prose poem praise of the ruler—the Roman enthronement of Eutharic, consul and heir, was complete. His ancestry was validated and approved, and at the same time firmly grafted onto the Roman family tree. The audiences for the games may have been seduced by the generosity that they received, but they also went away with a very clear message. The Roman empire was alive, well, and doing business in Italy, on pompous display in both Rome and Ravenna, with a regime that had deep roots in the history of the Mediterranean world, and with a long lineage. This consulship and the great visit of the year 500 were the two grandest spectacles at Rome in at least a century, and not until papal Rome of the Renaissance would there be anything to match them.

When we hear such a thunderous assertion, we should listen for corresponding small voices that might say something else. What were they saying in 519? They suggested that this regime was illegitimate, that there were other families of long standing, that true religion might provide a reason for failing to assent to the regime's perpetuity. The people who said this were the ones who saw a comet in the sky for two weeks that summer and interpreted it as a sign of dynastic change. Few if any voices were raised against the regime's putative barbarianism, for ambitions of the kind that were in the air needed few excuses and plenty were at hand. The irrelevance of modern ideas about Goth barbarianism is proved when we see that a mighty empire was overthrown without anyone's needing to use barbarians as an excuse or pretext. Theoderic's great achievement was the coexistence of Romans with Romans and Romans of many different kinds, and even a suggestion of dissolving that unity would have baleful consequences.

These whispers were far from Theoderic's mind in 519. All was in order and all was prepared for an orderly succession and a long and glorious future.

Then Eutharic died unexpectedly in 522 or 523, and without the crucial certainty of succession, the world Theoderic had brought together began to come undone.

CIVILITY AND TOLERATION

Civility and toleration were the hallmarks of Theoderic's rule in Italy— he said as much himself. If they were the civility and toleration we find in strong-armed imperial orders, they were still real, but they were not the whole of his regime, nor was his regime the whole of life in Italy. To do justice to him and to understand what was lost when his successors destroyed what he had built, we have to slow down and marvel at how life went on in his land and time.

Theoderic was not merely lucky. A good reputation follows those who are well spoken of by their contemporaries, especially when they make sure to have contemporaries speak well of them. Then a measure of luck takes over. People wrote books by hand on papyrus or animal skins, and they were copied a few dozen times at most, passed from hand to hand, and preserved in households of the wealthy and powerful—and therefore of the doomed. From no age of antiquity do more than a tiny fraction of the books written survive to us in even one medieval copy.

Yet we have nearly 150 letters from Theoderic's time that profess to be from his own hand, and come at least from the hands of those who served his will and heeded it most closely; we have transcripts of synods of the church that met under his direction; we have almost 300 letters from Ennodius of Pavia, the churchman with ambitions, who also wrote a grandiose panegyric oration in Theoderic's honor, to sing his praises to his face and the faces of his court, and poems and other documents besides; we have letters from every pope who reigned in his time; we have the *Book of Pontiffs* recounting the deeds of those popes in short compass (and also the crucial part of the variant edition of that book done by the followers of the would-be pope Laurentius); we have the philosophical, theological, and autobiographical writings of Boethius; we have other fragments of panegyric orations in honor of his court, the chronicle of all the years of Rome made in honor of Eutharic, and a history of the Goths that was put together in Constantinople twenty-five years after he died but that depended somehow on the propaganda and learning of Theoderic's last years. Considering the devastation that would strike his Italy in the decades after his death, and the long history of political disunity and disarray that would follow, the survival of so many books and artifacts of his time is a testimony to the ambitions of the man and to his posthumous good fortune.

Other books survive to represent his court and its tastes: the Uppsala Gothic Bible has an obvious claim to our attention, but no less impressive is the elaborate and expensive manuscript, also coming from Ravenna and perhaps from the same book-producing house, of the *Corpus Agrimensorum*—the *Collection of Surveyors*. Magnificently illustrated, this manuscript brought together the technical treatises of the men who made possible Roman property management and Roman imperialism, the surveyors who put names and measures on the land and regulated a world of agricultural property for the benefit of the imperialists and their favorites. At approximately the same time, scholars at Theoderic's court wrote about geography as well, and in the seventh century an anonymous writer admired Latin writers of this period for their learning, authors with the seemingly Gothic names Athanarid, Eldevald, and Marcomir.

Theoderic once had to settle a property dispute that called on the surveyors' skills. The Chaldeans, he reminded his subjects, had discovered geometry, but it was the Egyptians who put it to practical use by marking out the lands that the Nile flooded each year. Augustus himself had, after all, ordered that the whole Roman world be surveyed and recorded in a census. "Today," Theoderic said, "the surveyor's art is far more popular than the other numerical sciences. Arithmetic has empty classrooms, geometry is for specialists only, astronomy and music offer knowledge for knowledge's sake only. But the surveyors are the wizards who bring peace among men. You might think them crazed when you see them prowling the woodland in search of boundary markers, for the road is their book and they read it well."[7] Theoderic was every bit the Roman ruler in his patronage of these books and related arts.

His buildings speak to us of him as well. Some we know indirectly from contemporary reports: palace buildings in Ravenna, Pavia, and Verona, with great sculptures of the triumphant monarch outside. In thirty years, Theoderic never finished the great palace he undertook in Ravenna, but every successor regime there used it until it fell to ruin long after. The pat-

Theoderic's tomb at Ravenna.

tern was entirely imperial, complete with a connection to the circus where the ruler could watch the horse races. You could see Theoderic on horseback in a portrait in the "Seaview dining room" (*triclinium ad mare*), and also standing between figures representing the cities of Rome and Ravenna over the grand entrance to the palace. At Ravenna, he also restored an aqueduct built in Trajan's reign, to ensure the water supply. Some of his work there survives more or less intact; one example is the church of San Apollinare Nuovo, which was Theoderic's palace church. The original decoration included mosaic portraits of Theoderic and his court at one end of the south wall, by the entrance. They appeared at the head of a procession of saints, martyrs, and biblical figures, with an image of Christ at the altar end of the wall. (In later years, when Constantinople had seized control of Ravenna, clumsy mosaicists effaced Theoderic's own image and others of his court, leaving just enough traces, including a ghostly shadow of the man himself, to let us see what they meant to destroy.) His buildings follow others equally impressive—like the mausoleum of Galla Placidia, the doughty princess and empress regent of the fifth century—and precede others, as we shall see. We can hardly differentiate Theoderic's Ravenna from what went before or came after in its magnificence.

And then there is Theoderic's tomb. Built just outside the city walls of Ravenna, close to the harbor where ships from Constantinople and elsewhere in the Mediterranean docked, this looming structure astonishes visitors to this day. Today it stands alone, set apart from the built-up area of the modern city that serves European tourists and beachgoers. Theoderic finds rest in a surprising white decagon, two stories and thirty-three feet high, a shrine for the lavish porphyry sarcophagus in which his body rested. Over all, the dome or cap is made of a single piece of marble weighing many tons; it was brought down from Istria at the head of the Adriatic. Every attempt to discern barbarian influences and tastes in it has failed. We are left with a relic that stands second only to Hadrian's mighty tomb in Rome as a statement of imperial grandeur. Augustus's own tomb in Rome, grandiose enough in its day, fades from memory in this contest.

TOLERANCE IS EASY to applaud, and Theoderic has always been applauded, if often patronizingly. Something like "not bad for a barbarian" has been the subtext of many favorable judgments about him over the years. Two sentences from his various public statements have repeatedly attracted such praise, so let us listen to them:

"We cannot impose religion, because no one can be forced to believe against his will." (*Religionem imperare non possumus, quia nemo cogitur ut credat invitus.*)

"Obeying the law is the mark of civility." (*Custodia legum civilitatis est indicium.*)

For any Christian Roman of this period, these are admirable sentiments. To know what to make of them, we have to go to Genoa.

First, bear in mind the map of Italy. Genoa was important to Theoderic. His center of power and presence stretched from Milan east to Ravenna in northern Italy, with important taproots south to Rome. The western front along the Ligurian coast toward Gaul was sensitive territory. When hostilities broke out in Gaul and the Franks were active and suspected of being in cahoots with Constantinople, Genoese support was important to Theoderic. On two occasions around 510, we can tune in to hear his public voice addressing the Jewish community there. At about the same time, we see him taking particular care to make sure that the grain supply and other expected benefactions were well looked after in that area and in the provinces of Gaul beyond, for he was aware that soldiers, in their passing to and fro, needed to find supplies locally. Even a friendly army passing through your neighborhood could have a devastating effect if the governing regime was not as careful as Theoderic tried to be.

Those Jews of Genoa had addressed their ruler, as they would have done a century or two earlier no less frankly, to ask for permission to renovate and extend their religious property. Theoderic was cautious in his response.[8]

TO ALL THE JEWS WHO LIVE IN GENOA:
When we are the object of requests, we always wish to give our assent to what is just. Equally, however, we want to make sure that our generosity does not give rise to fraud and trickery carried out under cover of law—especially in matters of religion.

Roman emperors always had to worry about the way they were being used. Most lawmaking consisted of responses to requests from interested parties, who did not always make the fullest and most frank representation of the facts that underlay these requests, and often the imperial blessing appeared to many as a support for the grasping, the greedy, and the well connected.

> So we do not want people who are devoid of God's grace to become too full of themselves and lord it over others.

No Jew was surprised to hear this. The fundamental fact of religious life in the later empire was the absolute authority of Christianity. The question is not whether the Romans disadvantaged Judaism, but how much. This is still far from anti-Semitism in its modern sense, for Christian condemnation focused on religious belief and practice, not nationality, ancestry, or antiscientific notions of race. A Jew who converted to Christianity lost any taint of his former belief almost immediately, and gained all the advantages of converting.

> So we are approving here by these presents that it is permitted to replace the roof on the walls of your synagogue, and we grant approval to your petition insofar as it conforms with imperial legislation. But there must be no adding of adornments or expansion of the structures. And you should know that you will not escape the stringency of the law. Even in the renovations we have approved, know that we only grant authority if the thirty years prescription does not prevent it. Why do you ask for what you should be avoiding? We grant permission, but we are right to refuse to approve the prayers of those who are in error.

That "thirty years prescription": if any property claim could be shown to have remained unchallenged for that long (in practical terms at this moment, it meant since before Odoacer's rise to power), it would be left untouched. This was Roman conservatism enshrined at the center of Theoderic's lawmaking and law-managing, for it put in place a strong bias in favor of the past.

The community that received this message—elaborately engrossed, very likely on purple-dyed vellum, ceremoniously handed over by elaborately robed and attended officials in the local hall of government—will not have mistaken its purport: very limited approval for a basic request, with stern and clear limitations. But the letter has a concluding sentence, the one we already quoted:

"We cannot impose religion, because no one can be forced to believe against his will."

We should hear the diplomatic restraint: assertion of principle hedged with cautious enactment. This ruler leans slightly away from the most intolerant of emperors and stands in the middle of the road for traditional Roman government—that is, the government of Christian emperors of the fourth and fifth centuries.

So when, not long after this, Theoderic wrote to the Genoese Jewish community again, beginning this time with the other platitude I quoted above ("Obeying the law is the mark of civility"), he renewed the theme of civility as the core of city life, civility that distinguishes people from rude rustic life and from the life of beasts. Whatever protections the law allowed—those they could have.

Tolerance was not universal, and on another day the Jews of Rome were the victims of a very modern-sounding hate crime: arson. Theoderic was again generous and restrained, insisting on punishment for the criminals, but cautioning that if there were any charges to be leveled against the Jews themselves, those charges were also to be the object of formal legal attention. The Jews of Rome would not have been unreasonable to think this response a mixed blessing, but it is impeccably fair in form and apparent content.[9]

We, of course, would like to see Theoderic more enlightened still. Then by a familiar rhetorical ploy he could be the idealized barbarian with his fresh ideas from outside the gray world of civilization. He was enlightened only up to a point: refusing to impose belief, and refusing to transgress the laws. He resembles Hadrian more than an American president—stern in modesty, but stern nonetheless. His gentleness was an ancient trait, soon to be rendered obsolete by Justinian's more modern integration of religion and politics. Toleration has had to be relearned by many modern generations, and religious exclusion roars back repeatedly without much invitation.

Everything Theoderic did as monarch, I am tempted to say, embodied this Hadrianic moderation and calm. What if you did not know he was supposed to be different, supposed to be a "barbarian"? What if you knew he was born inside Roman boundaries (he probably was), and if you knew he had changed his name to Hadrianus? I venture that most students would comment first on how Roman his regime was, and then on what a wonderfully abundant cultural heritage this Roman regime left behind, far richer than anything since the late fourth century. Theoderic would be remembered as the great restorer of the Roman order.

For Theoderic belongs to an old, conservative tradition, and if the *Edict of Theoderic* that comes down to us in 154 short chapters—virtually every one a quotation from earlier law—is his (as in some form it may well be), it is in the tradition of the praetor's edict of old: "If anyone bury a dead body inside the city of Rome, he will be forced to hand over a fourth of his property to the treasury. If he has nothing, then he will be beaten and expelled from the city."[10] Romantic fancy about falling Rome might lead one to imagine that the city was less thickly settled inside its walls than before and that the old and healthy idea of taking bodies outside the walls for burial was giving way to more practical use of space, but we needn't let ourselves be fanciful. This prescription asserts both the authority of tradition and the traditionalism of authority. Even the Christian-influenced precepts of the edict are phrased in ways that make it clear how Roman this Christianity had become. The right of sanctuary is phrased thus: "If anyone should drag people out of churches, that is to say, places of religion, or think that anything can be taken away from there violently, let him be subject to capital punishment." That is the voice of an ancient Roman magistrate.

Theoderic's working court—the administration in Ravenna—was Roman at every level as well, with officers like the praetorian prefects and masters of offices we have met on other pages. Throughout the time of Theoderic, the traditional titles of office were attested, respected, and held by one or another of the Romans of Rome—the old senatorial families or, at best, some of the arrivistes who were ready, willing, and able to become an old senatorial family at the earliest opportunity. (Theoderic's death challenged these boundaries. During the regency of his infant grandson, the rank of patrician fell in turn to both a Roman civilian, Liberius; and Tuluin, a career soldier in Theoderic's retinue.) The emperor at Constantinople managed an essentially identical cabinet, though the complexity and intrigues of the large imperial palace gave rise to a further apparatus of guards and chamberlains.

Theoderic continued to appoint not only the supreme officers of the realm, but even the lesser ones: managers of arms factories and mints (Theoderic continued a very Roman coinage), governors of provinces, and the prefect of the night watch of the city of Ravenna. Of particular interest are the "defenders of cities" (*defensores civitatis*) appointed from the court since the fourth century and still under Theoderic in at least some places. Roman society had rooted itself in a core of elites based in communities from Arabia to Britain. Wealthy and wellborn citizens would lead their cities, and in exchange they were obligated to pay for their communities' infrastructure and ostentation. Membership in the local senate may have been an onerous honor, but in the classical age these leaders welcomed it. Prosperity and pride led men to accept the opportunity and to build an empire of a grandeur that could not have been imagined without their resources and generosity.

After Constantine, the burdens grew more onerous and the honors less satisfying. A spate of laws in the fourth century attempted famously (and quite unsuccessfully, by all evidence) to deter local senators (*decurions*, they were called) from fleeing their offices for opportunities elsewhere. For us, the obvious message of these laws is that people *were* fleeing. Augustine of Hippo, the great Christian, was one such refugee, abandoning his ancestral home of Tagaste and the duties his father had bequeathed him in favor of an ecclesiastical career. The townspeople of Tagaste lost Augustine's talent, but the citizens of Hippo found in him a leader with a new kind of community spirit and offering a new kind of public service.

The old model was fading. In the later empire, more and more of the *euergetism* (one might render that Greek word as do-goodism) came from on high, from the emperor himself, with money that had flowed up to the throne coming back down to cities and local communities. The individual community had less ability to control, manage, and protect itself, and so this imperially appointed commissioner, the *defensor*, emerged as the de facto leader of the local society and a point of connection to the imperial government and its taxing authority. Many would feel themselves better off and few would notice the loss of effective self-government.

Somewhere at the bottom of the hierarchical pyramid of government, we find one officer whose role may still inspire some skepticism: the "tribune of pleasures" (*tribunus voluptatum*). Let's call him the minister of public entertainment. The office was perhaps less than a century old, created when local generosity did not suffice to keep up a suitable standard of public diversion. The shows and games of the ancient city had once been outsourced to the private sector, that is, to those wealthy and ambitious families who rivaled each other in ostentation; but now, in the late empire, these diversions were treated as a more routine kind of imperial business. Since baptized Christians were not allowed to perform onstage, the tribune himself walked a delicate line, supervising the impure while remaining uncorrupted. With grave and reverent caution, Theoderic's words catch the ambiguity—"be sure you love chastity, sir, you to whom the prostitutes are subject."[11] We see this officer at Rome under Theoderic, but also at Milan, where a senator of advancing years was granted the title for life.

One rank and title in Theoderic's Italy is new: *saio*, a kind of man-of-all-work for the ruler. The older empire had "case agents" (*agentes in rebus*), combining the roles of spies, the secret police, and inspector generals. The name *saio* is exceptional for its Gothic sound, but the role is the same. We see such agents only through the eyes of the ruler's public relations apparatus, and there must have been times, places, and people who did not welcome their arrival—but that, in the end, is as it should be. On one occasion the *saiones* were checked in a letter from Theoderic for excessive and presumptuous use of the public post-horse system, which supplied relays of horses at regular intervals along the great Roman highways for officials of a certain rank. Theoderic ordered one *saio*, Gudisal, to ensure that the service was reserved for appropriate representatives of the praetorian prefect and the master of offices, and that other *saiones* be allowed to use the service strictly on business assignments.

How might imperial attention have seemed excessive? Let's take a case of high visibility and sensitivity—the magician magnates of Rome.

Sometime during the years 507 to 511, dark suspicions about high-ranking men began to be heard—from their highborn rivals? from envious servants or tradesmen? We don't know. Basilius and Praetextatus were from the very best families of sixth-century Rome. The charge against them was "magic arts," a phrase that covers a multitude of virtues. They were probably found performing secret acts connected to the old traditions of Roman religion, rituals for which some might claim the power to influence divine behavior and material reality. The usually moderate Theoderic was sufficiently pompous now: "It is not to be tolerated for people to go so far as to defile the heavenly majesty with their assaults and follow the cruel paths of error, forgetting true piety. . . . There shall be no dabbling in magic arts in Christian times."[12] Theoderic ordered the distinguished senator Argolicus, prefect of the city, to turn the case over to the *iudicium quinquevirale*, the "court of five," an ad hoc body, dating to the late fourth century, that reviewed capital charges against senators. The names of the men Theoderic appointed to this jury are no less distinguished than those of the accused: Symmachus, Decius, Volusianus, Caelianus, and Maximianus. Theoderic authorized his senior military officer Arigern, general of the garrison at Rome, to use force to bring the suspects to trial if need be.

If all we had were Theoderic's letters about this case, we would be left thinking only that he had made a grand show of forwarding the accusations and appointing the judges. As it happens, a page of the *Dialogues* of Pope Gregory I, written in the 590s, lets us follow more of the story. Basilius, he tells us, was caught in the act of supposed magic. He disguised himself as a Christian monk and fled to the hills east of Rome. Coming to Amiternum in the Abruzzi, he asked the bishop to help him take refuge in a neighboring monastery. Deceived, the bishop complied, but Equitius, the abbot of the monastery, immediately recognized Basilius as a devil in the guise of a monk. The still credulous bishop prevailed on the abbot to accept him. Then an attractive member of a religious house of women nearby fell ill and cried out that unless the monk Basilius should come to her, she would die. Basilius's own reluctant abbot was derisive and assured the messenger that the woman would recover immediately—and she did. Outraged by what they took to be the scheming of evil spirits, Equitius's monks expelled Basilius from their number. Pope Gregory concludes, "When he had been sent away, he claimed that he had often caused the cell of abbot Equitius to levitate in the air by his magic arts, and said that no one could harm him. Not long after at Rome, thanks to the blazing zeal of the Christian people, he was put to death by fire."[13]

Many aspects of that story pull us into the world of Roman late antiquity: clashing religious practices, legal interference in religion, the brutality of the laws, and the willingness of all parties to believe a very great many impossible things before breakfast. Since Christians believed that there were in the world demons happy to help bad men perform wondrous deeds, the right response was to punish the bad men accordingly. Theoderic's role in this case can retain our attention for this much: in passing the case to the appropriate civil authorities at Rome, he did what an emperor was supposed to do. Whatever Basilius and Praetextatus really did or thought, no one at Rome would think that Theoderic displayed high-handedness, heresy, or a failure to maintain standards.

The Rome that produced these magicians and their judges was, in the minds of those who lived there, the Rome of old. The senate met, poets read, young men went away to school in the traditional ways. Those who lived in Theoderic's Rome could not have known that they were but two generations away from the sudden disappearance of many of these traditions and practices. Theirs was the Christian Rome of late antiquity, to be sure, where a few well-advised families had become leaders in the new aristocracy of the church, and so bishops of Rome by now tended to be chosen from families who had already held the office, just the way the republic used to produce its consuls. Theoderic, through his ghostwriter Cassiodorus, praised the consul Felix, on his appointment to office for the year 511, as the "Cato of our time": "Devoted to literary studies, he spends his whole life in learned pursuits. His eloquence did not come from merely touching his lips to the Aeonian fountain but by drinking deeply there. His books are full of strenuous argument, his tales are told with gentle pleasure, and he sows his words so well that he is the equal of the authors he had read so often . . . He had investigated the depths of natural science as well, stuffing himself on the Attic honey of Cecrops' teachings"[14]—the audience was expected to remember that Cecrops had been the founder of Athens and lay buried on the Acropolis in the Erechtheion.

Though Rome had been a Christian city for 200 years, Cassiodorus was troubled by the traditionalism that kept the secular schools open and by the absence of any comparable schools with Christian content. Only after Theoderic's death did Pope Agapetus I, in 535–536, bestir himself to establish some kind of formal institution for Christian biblical and doctrinal studies—and the effort, tellingly, came to naught, ostensibly because of warfare and political distractions, but at least in part because it was an idea whose time had not yet come. As long as the old schooling was available, it was the surest indication of the culture, the leisure, and the wealth of the urban aristocrats who took advantage of it and used it to define their own places in the world.

Theoderic the builder and restorer put his support behind big projects, but he also appointed auditors to supervise job sites and expenses and to ensure the best use of funds, and in at least one case he directed the city prefect to recover funds from fraudulent contractors. His letters about reconstruction and renovation often suggest that contractors reclaim building materials from ruins and derelict buildings, for use on signature monuments. This is a sure sign that some of the air had gone out of the bubble of preposterous wealth that protected Italy for centuries, when it and especially Rome were filled with the riches of the whole Roman world. Archaeologists are not so sure about Theoderic's supposed habit of reusing materials, finding evidence at least in Ravenna that he went out of his way to build afresh.

When the right combination of patron and project came together, Theoderic could be very grand. He selected Symmachus, Boethius's father-in-law and patron, to take in hand the restoration of the Theater of Pompey in the Campus Martius. Built in 55 BCE at the height of Pompey's power, while his junior partner Julius Caesar made his name and power in Gaul, this building had been the wonder of the city in its time. Said to seat 40,000 people (10,000 may be nearer the mark), it imitated the theaters of the Greek world and introduced ancient grandeur into a city that was still an upstart in those days. It had devilish connotations by now, because it had fit the familiar Roman pattern of a theater-temple, with a shrine to Venus the Victorious at the top of the central section, and forming the rows of seats to appear as stairs leading to a temple. The shows in such a theater were part of religion, and religion was part of what Romans went to any theater to find, in the stories of the gods and heroes.

A centerpiece for the pomp of empire, it housed meetings of the senate and consequently Julius Caesar was murdered there. Renewed and glorified under Augustus, it boasted a statue of Pompey that had been in the senate house. Nero added his distinctive taste to the decoration, incorporating lots of purple and gold—never a subtle fellow, that Nero. The theater was burned and restored repeatedly, and among the emperors who could claim the dignity of being its patrons were Diocletian and Maximian around 300 and Honorius around 400, at a time when there were collapsed sections inside.

Theoderic, writing to Symmachus to begin the project, pulled out all the stops. "We could easily dismiss the stories about this theater if we had not had a chance to see the place: the great space of the seating area hollowed out with overhanging rock so invisibly joined into beautiful forms that you would think you were seeing great caves in a lofty mountain rather than anything made by the hand of man. The ancients made this place large enough for such vast crowds that the people who had seized dominion of the world could come together for a single spectacle."[15] He went on to praise the muses and the talents of pantomime dancers ("their eloquent hands, their loquacious fingers, their roaring silence, their silent story-telling") and ended by saying that this is truly what made Pompey worthy of the title "the Great" that followed him to civil war and death a few years after this achievement. Since the population's energy and enthusiasm had migrated largely to the open-air spectacle of the horse races in Theoderic's time, this reconstruction was as much for the ostentation of imperial dignity alone as anything else. Symmachus's work may be the last known example of Roman private funding of a secular public building (i.e., not a church). The benefactions of the rich had once filled Roman cities with mighty halls and temples and baths, but now and for a very long time to come it would be the government or nothing.

In these times, the circus was the public heart of city life. The public enthusiasm that the circus races roused, in comparison to anything in modern times, cannot be exaggerated. The World Cup may come close, but only somewhat, to the mania for the ancient races that went on year in, year out, and intensified within the cities where the famous charioteers attracted their fans. From earliest imperial times, we can see the teams forming: the Reds, the Whites, the Greens, the Blues—and those four sets of racing colors (evoking autumn, winter, spring, and summer, respectively) attracted fans until the history of the ancient circus came to an end. The Greens and the Blues were the nearly perpetual champions, the Yankees and Dodgers as it were. In Constantinople, we will see the circus at the center of imperial life, but in Rome, there was rarely an emperor at hand, so the life of the circus went on, unchecked and—for all appearances—apolitical.

Theoderic discovered just how volatile his city of racing fans could be during the riot of 509. Quarrels among the factions led to murder in the streets. In response, Theoderic evoked the most famously prim and proper Roman of them all: "You don't find Catos going to the circus."[16] The Greens complained to Theoderic that the patrician Theodorus and the consul Inportunus were behind the violence. Theoderic represented himself as shocked that the seat of all civility should be so disrupted, and he ordered that judges hear the charges against the two—but with all dignity, and all protection of the accused. It was to everyone's advantage to consider the fray just a riot by a rabble, not a proxy battle between great families.

There is more here than meets the eye. As they shifted alliances, the circus factions clustered and cheered for one cause or another. Sometimes they appeared to have political motivations, sometimes religious ones; and sometimes the simple brute force of factions and allegiance to one or another powerful patron or family drove them. In 509, Rome's aristocrats were still at odds with each other in many ways, and the disagreement over the papal election of a decade earlier still festered. Which came first—the people, the politics, or the churchly argument—is hard to say. Most likely, the answer is old rivalries and envy extending down to the level of marriages, dowries, and the intense jealousy that animated the Verona of Shakespeare's *Romeo and Juliet*. If the most recent argument is right, then the Blues clustered around the venerable Decii family, imitating the would-be Pope Laurentius, while the Anicii, the Greens, and the Sardinian-born pope Symmachus joined in mutual admiration and support on the city's other piazzas. The Decii had been Theoderic's oldest open supporters, from the days when Festus traveled to Constantinople repeatedly on behalf of Theoderic's regime. The Anicii would become his opponents. Theoderic himself never showed his hand, however, by taking sides in Roman family wars, and so he calmly supported Pope Symmachus at most periods to a greater or lesser degree. One reason many previous scholars have thought the fundamental fault lines of the time were religious is simply that Theoderic did not tip his hand otherwise.

At any rate, Theoderic barely slapped Inportunus and Theodorus on the wrists, and in 525 the two of them went on a mission from him to the court at Constantinople, side by side with Pope John I, pleading the case for the regime and its legitimacy in the bumptious and threatening days of Justin and his nephew Justinian.

On another day, not long afterward, the circus recruited a superstar charioteer named Thomas from one of the cities of the east, to the citizens' delight. Theoderic paid close attention, assuring everyone that the new arrival would be appropriately compensated for his talents. "Carried along by public applause as much as by his chariot," writes Cassiodorus, he continued a tradition to which Augustus and Nero had given full Roman glory in the days when the emperor dined overlooking the racecourse and tossed his napkin out a window to indicate that it was time for the race to begin. Ever since those early gestures, the throwing of the napkin continued to mark the start of the racing. The mobs were delighted.[17]

Rome was not the only city seized with chariot madness. At Milan, that same "Cato of our times" we met earlier, the consul Felix, decided to cut corners with regard to the magnificence of his consular games. Charioteers from Milan, whom Felix cut out from their expected contract for these games, complained to Theoderic, who wrote to the consul, firmly. Standards of generosity must be kept up, for "precedent demands the traditional gift as if it were really a debt," he said,[18] offering just the right tone of noblesse oblige that still controlled such events. The *appearance* was of a gift that the rich and powerful freely gave, but the fact was an ingrained social obligation, in the eyes of the public, of performers, and of the prince as well.

Theoderic played the senate well for thirty years, then lost his touch near the end of his life. Moderns who study the period usually find themselves taking sides with the senators they like and cherish in this autumnal moment, the century that would see the last of the senate. What survived was not all good. More than once in Roman history, the *bravi* of powerful families had terrorized the city streets. Pope Gregory asks, "Were not its leaders and chieftains like lions who run throughout the provinces and seize their prey, pitiless and deadly?"[19] Roman grandeur always exacted such a price.

Beyond the great cities, Theoderic's vigilance and ceaseless, self-congratulatory care were constantly on display. We see him worrying about new baths for Spoleto, tax collection in the cities along the eastern side of the Adriatic in Dalmatia, and the selection of a new governor for the province of Pannonia (modern Hungary) at the extremes of his domains on the Danube, while responding closer to home to the damage done by a substantial eruption of Vesuvius, assuring those whose property was affected that they would receive tax relief.

What is hardest to see in any ancient society—it is known to us by hints and guesses—is the progress of something we now blithely call "the economy." Emperors, senators, churchmen, and businessmen alike in antiquity had, by modern standards, an astonishingly feeble grasp of what it took to make a society prosper. We have seen how in the western realms of the empire, the great landed estates and the colonies and cities founded by Rome had never cohered to create self-sustaining, enduring prosperity. Divine beneficence would send crops in abundance, taxes would flow from great realms into mighty cities, and the cities' ostentation would demonstrate the flourishing of all.

When it worked, it worked. When it did not work, no one could understand why, beyond the most obvious causes—failure of crops, episodes of plague, autocratic and grasping rulers, or interruption of ordinary business by military events. Theoderic brought to Italy a settled regime that preserved the existing legal and social order, ensured peace, and offered a balanced measure of ostentation—enough to please, not enough to bleed dry. For the most part, he was fortunate, and so he had a reputation as a good ruler.

The signs of the future were not invisible. The people of a fortified hill site called Verruca, probably in the south of Italy (modern Calabria), came to Theoderic's attention. He wrote to them to offer support—sending one of his lieutenants to supervise and probably to finance construction of homes for them in the *castellum*, the fortification on the hill itself. The Verrucans were ahead of their time. Theoderic's letter tells us that in "the middle of spreading fields, a circular and rocky hilltop rises, with steep sides stripped of trees, making the whole mount effectively a single tower. The lower slopes are easier but the top is like the cap of a mushroom. No adversary will dare come there and no one who lives there needs to fear anything."[20]

Not, Theoderic assures the Verrucans, that they need to be so cautious "in our times"—but it's always good to prepare for storms in times of calm, for winter in mild weather. A charming riff on birds and fishes makes the point. All true, no doubt, but the strategic point remains that this is the age in which those fortified hill towns begin to take on their individual identity, as the unity and peacefulness of the Italian peninsula, brought about by Roman cruelty and assertiveness centuries before, began to dissipate. Rome itself had begun on the tops of the seven hills, and the descent into the forum and the Campus Martius was the symbol of a community gaining in confidence. The movement now began to go the other way.

All in all, shall we still say, "Not bad for a barbarian"? Every account of Theoderic's career has that sniffing, patronizing judgment somewhere in the background, spoken or unspoken. His praise for *civilitas* is universally noted as a theme of his regime, then discounted as something imposed on him, spin from his spin doctors—as if such ideas had come *naturally* to the hard men who had been emperors 100 or 400 years before. Civility and toleration are not nothing, and a regime that seeks to promote them will earn a reputation for generosity and justice. They are a necessary though not a sufficient condition for human dignity. After the bad half century that preceded Odoacer, the two men who ruled Italy from the 470s to the 520s deserve high marks for making it an ordinary, civilized place again. And that was a very Roman accomplishment.

So we must ask: was Theoderic actually an emperor? His constitutional position is a subject that has repeatedly exercised scholars, and in practice all agree to speak of Theoderic as "king of the Goths," with the occasional addition of "patrician" (*patricius*) to suggest the Roman military rank that went along with his rude barbaric kingship. But such a view does him, and the Roman society of his age, a great injustice.

The reader, of course, may have noticed how gingerly I have named his office in my account, dodging "king" and "emperor" as best I can, emphasizing the naturalness and Romanness of his rule over his domains. My goal was to show the man and his world and not allow a label to get in the way of the larger picture. Our surviving sources help us in many ways. From time to time we get little pictures of him, taking his exercise by riding horseback with one of his finance ministers, or interrogating his quaestor on matters of science and history, in ways that remind us of Sidonius's description of that other Theoderic half a century earlier. It is partly because of our sources' bias, but surely also because of something about the man himself and the regime he created, that in this case we see only the civilized Theoderic.

To give his age back its voice, we should heed the words carved on a stone on the Appian Way south of Rome:[21]

Dominus noster gloriosissimus adque inclytus rex Theodericus,
victor ac triumfator,
semper Augustus,
bono rei publicae natus,
custos libertatis et propagator Romani nominis,
domitor gentium . . .

> Our Lord, the most glorious and celebrated King Theoderic,
> victor in triumph,
> ever Augustus,
> born for the good of the state,
> guardian of freedom and propagator of the Roman name,
> who has tamed the nations,

has successfully, with God's help, restored to public use and the security of travelers the route and area of the Appian Way's Nineteen-Mile stretch [i.e. from Tripontium to Terracina, which had been inundated by the surrounding marshes under all previous *principes*]. The honorable and illustrious Caecina Mavortius Basilius Decius, of the Decian family, ex–City Prefect, ex–Praetorian Prefect, ex–Ordinary Consul, Patrician, zealously perspiring in the task enjoined him and happily devoted to the proclamations of the most clement *princeps*, has restored them to a most ancient dryness quite unknown to our forefathers by means of many new channels which drain the water into the sea—for the perpetuation of the glory of such a lord.

Augustus, *princeps*—those are the most solemn titles of empire. The Latin voice here belongs to the grandee in charge of draining the swamps, who was rewarded with real estate from the reclaimed land.[22] When passersby here, not far from Rome, read to themselves or aloud to their fellow travelers Theoderic's name, and saw the titles with which he was graced, they felt at home in a flourishing Roman empire. Theoderic did not, as far as we know, put any such words on a document himself, certainly not one that would make its way to the court of Constantinople, but the author of these lines was not overstepping the bounds of flattery. In coldest prose, Theoderic was never emperor of the Romans, but in word, deed, habit, culture, and impact on his world, he was one of the very best of them and deserves praise—even when that praise is mitigated by recognition of his capacity for brutality and of the blunders that he made in his last years, which undermined his own accomplishments. And why shouldn't it be so?—for the Roman imperial tradition itself was no stranger to blunder and brutality.

Theoderic at his peak, Theoderic at that moment in 519 when he thought he had it all arranged and could gaze on his son-in-law, the consul

Eutharic, and his grandson Athalaric, and see the future of dynasty and empire, was no fool. If he believed, as I surmise he did, that the emperor would soon recognize him or Eutharic as legitimate emperor in the west, then everything else about his policies and career makes sense. His confidence may have been misplaced, but many other emperors, some of them equally happy with their offspring and prospects, were equally wrong.

The possibility that lay before him then was an unbroken continuation of Roman imperial civilization in its homeland. The bad days were over. There were, of course, dangers to be deterred—as there had always been—but order had returned. (Ironically, in his own failure to think beyond the borders, Theoderic became the most Roman of them all—the *Roman* world was enough for him.) Within the traditional domains of Rome, order and empire were reestablishing themselves. The Vandals in Africa and the Visigoths in Spain held independent, geographically coherent, reasonable kingdoms, and administered them as well as at least some previous Roman emperors could claim to have done, though the growth of cities and building seems to have ended in much of Spain about the time the Visigoths arrived. The Franks in Gaul were at this moment the least defined players on this stage, but in the long run, as we will see, the most Roman. Theoderic died with Liberius in command in Gaul of his own province, very likely historically aware that the territory he held was not so unlike the original Roman *provincia* in southern Gaul (whence the name Provence today) that had sufficed until Julius Caesar's ambitions drove him north to the Low Countries, the English Channel, and beyond.

There was work to be done—no question about that—but much had been done, and the west was in far better shape than at any time since the death of Stilicho over a century earlier.

By comparison, Constantinople was a wild card in Theoderic's calculations. For most of his reign, Anastasius was at the helm. He was a sane, rational man, a man much like Theoderic—his military upbringing had started in the Balkans but took him early to Constantinople and the court; his own religious views were at the margins of what his society would accept, and he therefore had learned to navigate with skill shoals that others would not encounter. But in 519, Anastasius died at the great age of eighty-eight after a twenty-seven-year reign (people were already calling him elderly when he took the throne), and Justin, a very different kind of man, succeeded him. Another soldier from the Balkans, but one without polish or presence, Justin had none of Anastasius's tact. If Roman civilization was at risk in the early 520s, the threat its leaders had most to watch was one that came from the capital city itself.

CHRISTIANS AND CHRISTIANS

Many modern readers know at least something about barbarians and the fall of the Roman empire, but many more readers will know a fair amount about early Christianity. To such readers I must now say, Would you please leave everything you think you know about Christianity at the door? We really must start over.

A Roman historian writing about the reign of Trajan or Marcus Aurelius, 100 years or so after the lifetime of Jesus, will customarily dismiss the early Christians with a few paragraphs at most. Church historians can and will tell you much more, much of it grounded in hard evidence, about the fate of the Christian religions in that period, but those stories were played out well away from the narrative center of historical attention, in places where Jews and Christians, and their friends and neighbors, were sometimes not all that easy to distinguish from one another, and where not many of the rich and privileged people who wrote the books that survived even bothered to try to distinguish them.

By the fourth century, historians must pay much more attention to Christians of various stripes and their doings. No reader has to search very far to find stories about the triumph of Christianity after Constantine, and it is common to speak of the Christian Roman empire from the fourth century forward. Such expressions have made it harder to see how transformative and revolutionary were the reigns of Clovis and Justinian in the sixth century, for it was they who invented Christian empires.

Until the sixth century and Justinian's interventions, official Christianity was much more modest than what it became. It was intrusive and bizarre by our modern standards, but still a far cry from the integrated church-states that followed. If we have not spoken more of religion in Theoderic's world it is because he was the last of the old Roman Christian rulers, remarkably traditional in beliefs and practices.

Before any attempt to describe the religious landscape of Theoderic's time and the changes to come, it will help to state explicitly what the triumph of Christianity consisted of, for the truth is mildly surprising.

The Christian communities of the first three centuries were what a modern reader should expect them to be. There were active and successful communities, achieving some size and scale in places like Alexandria and Carthage, and at the other extreme forming many small pockets and outposts, seeded by missionary enthusiasm and watered by zeal over the years, but not always surviving. A map of the Roman world showing Christian presence during the years before Constantine would have dots sprinkled like a rash, clustered in Egypt, around Carthage, and in Asia Minor and Syria, with odd clusters here and there elsewhere, and a lighter sprinkling of dots in places like Gaul and Spain. Christianities were everywhere, but a force to be reckoned with nowhere.

I use the surprising plural "Christianities" to speak of this religious movement for good reason. Even in Paul's letters, the tension between homogeneity and diversity is evident, as when he insists that he speaks of the creed of *Christ*, not that of Apollo or Paul. This implies that the *idea* of a unified, coherent Christian community was already powerful, but far from fully realized. Within a very short time, different flavors of preaching about Jesus were growing and spreading. Even those communities expressing friendship and solidarity for others might be found on close examination to be quite different in their beliefs and practices.

People speaking of Christ originated in the midst of Jewish communities and continued to use the Jewish scriptures, so we should not be surprised that it was not always obvious just where Jewishness left off and Christianity began, nor was it always important to everyone concerned to make the line obvious. Though both Jewish and Christian communities emphasized tokens and deeds identifying fully committed members, well-wishing, curious, semi-affiliated people also surrounded them in many or most cases. Though both Jewish and Christian teachers preached a single supreme deity, not all of the well-wishers—and sometimes not all of the circumcised or baptized believers—were fastidious about staying away from other religious festivals and communities. Some Christians surrounded themselves with bright, sharp doctrinal lines to keep out all manner of outsiders. Many famous preachers regularly inveighed against lukewarm Christians, pagans, and even Jews in the midst of their flocks: that is to say, people who showed up in church without being quite as zealous about it as others expected them to be. Reality was not so tidy or clear as preachers wished.

This messiness of boundaries in belief and practice was entirely normal. Everyone in the Roman world was religious. On examination, even the most cynical skeptics lived securely within the realm of ancient religious practices. Some worshippers manifested their beliefs in a manner that moderns might call superstitious. But were they really? In our world, is a baseball player who crosses himself before stepping up to the plate devout or just superstitious?

Religion, moreover, was at bottom a technique, sometimes rising to the level of a technology. In a threatening and dangerous world, religious acts provided a measure of control over unseen powers. Only a fool outright refused to participate. The Hebrew scriptures said as much: "The fool has said in his heart, 'There is no god.'"[23] No one at all would disagree. The old Epicureans, believing in a divine force, thought it so lofty and imperturbable that attempts at appeasement were pointless, but they were a tiny minority. Everyone else was doing something to keep divine forces at bay.

The word moderns most commonly use for these practices was in origin a stinging Christian insult: *paganus*, roughly, "hick" or "rube." A high- or narrow-minded Christian, holding that all religious expressions except the most orthodox were at best folly and at worst demonic, would lump together all those practices (except the Jewish) as pagan, expressing a sniffy social superiority. We would do better to avoid that polemical word entirely. Instead we should speak of old practices, either particular (such as Mithraism, a cult popular among soldiers for some centuries) or general (traditional rites). Doing so makes it easier to see what is distinctive about Christianity—innovation and cantankerousness.

The latter quality derived from the more stiff-necked qualities of Judaism. Judaism takes its name from a place, Judaea, and the ancient word for a member of the cult, Judaeus, meaning "person from Judaea." Judaean pride convinced itself that the one and only true god visited his temple on a hilltop just at the boundary between cultivated land and the desert, in Jerusalem. Anyone would agree that a provincial god might do such a thing, but to claim that this one local god was uniquely true and powerful—such self-assurance would strike almost everyone as bizarre.

At the heart of Judaism, however, was the Judaeans' assurance that their god was still local, and therefore that only they should worship him. They made certain that joining his cult—through circumcision—involved a high degree of commitment and difficulty. They argued that Yahweh was the one and only god; yet, ironically, it also did not matter if most of the world owed him no allegiance and went on about their many-godded ways. Yahweh was the highest and the greatest, but he was not the only, god.

Real Judaism in the Hellenistic world after Alexander and under the Roman emperors moved away from some of its original particularism, as its identity and some of its practices followed many real Judaeans who lived far from their homeland. When the general Titus destroyed the Jerusalem temple in 70 CE, much of what it meant to be Jewish was uprooted and ravaged, and still the community lived on and even thrived. Judaism in the later Roman world underwent the most wrenching change in its history, adjusting to the absence of the temple, while retaining its particularity and disinclination to pursue new converts. We will return to the Jewish story on a later page.

Christianity, born and bred in the Jewish matrix, made the rest of the world what it called pagan by detaching the Jewish assertion of uniqueness from place of origin, and opening membership to all humankind. "Go and teach *all* nations," Jesus was said to have taught,[24] and Christians most often took this teaching quite seriously, even if it didn't move most of them to relocate and teach in strange lands. They followed in this regard not only Jesus but Paul, for it was Paul's reading of Christianity—as something far more ambitious than the revival or fulfillment of traditional Judaism—that prevailed in the end.

Forcing a message of uniqueness and exclusivity allowed Christians to make themselves satisfyingly unpopular. Persecution became their badge of success. Popular imagination probably still thinks of a long period of time in which hard-nosed Roman governors regularly pulled brave, dewy-eyed, idealistic Christians off the streets, tortured them, and then fed them to the lions. The facts are less glamorous, but the influential church historian Eusebius, a fourth-century contemporary and supporter of Constantine, imbued this idea with long life in his account of ten waves of persecution that mirrored Egypt's ten plagues in the time of Moses. What really happened was episodic, local, and highly inconsistent. The young Christian wife and mother Perpetua suffered such a fate at Carthage around 200, leaving behind a document that would be influential far beyond its time and place (and would have been perfect for Hollywood): *The Acts of Perpetua and Felicity,* some parts of which she may have written herself.

Occasionally in the third century such things did happen, but most Christians lived and died like their fellow Romans, undisturbed by government, quarreling now and then with some of their neighbors. In the 250s, the emperor Decius ordered the suppression of Christianity, and in the early 300s, the emperor Galerius launched the most systematic attempt ever to deter and uproot Christian practice. In such times, suspect Chrstians were required to perform some minimal public religious act and get a certificate to prove they had done so. There is no sign that such fits of suppression and persecution had any lasting effect.

Christians resisted persecution well—both the ordinary spasmodic kind and the infrequent broader campaign—because their communities were many-headed, did not have substantial real property, and lived so fully intermingled with Roman society that they could not simply be carved out and attacked. A century after Galerius, when Christian emperors set out to—we might as well use the word—persecute "pagan" communities and practices, they were far more devastatingly effective. They halted the supply of state funds for traditional practices, crippling much of what had been long familiar. Then they seized buildings and banned ritual in them, sweeping the landscape nearly clean of the old ways. What survived—and much did—was personal, small-scale, or highly localized. Over a relatively short time, the new bludgeoned the old into submission and eventually supplanted it.[25] That's what real persecution could do, unafraid to use violence but not needing to use very much of it. But Christianity never faced anything like what it would later visit on the traditional cults.

That last Galerian persecution backfired completely. The young general Constantine (son of Constantius, who had ruled Britain for Diocletian and himself briefly succeeded to an unsteady throne) saw a chance to grasp for power. Diocletian had created a college of imperial leaders and put in motion a complicated system of succession and promotion that collapsed as soon as it was implemented in 305. In a welter of emperors and would-be emperors, Constantine emerged from the pack, establishing himself first in the west, and eventually in all of the empire. He was the victor of a critical battle in 312 for control of the Milvian bridge, just upriver on the Tiber where it protected the approaches to the city of Rome. Constantine told a story afterward of a vision he had before the battle and how he and his men had fought under Christ's protection. For the rest of his life—he lived and reigned until 337—he was consistently the best Christian emperor he could be. This is not to say that he was a particularly devout man or even well informed about the distinctive features of his new religious enthusiasm. In many ways, he was perfectly pre-Christian, expecting his new god to support him on the battlefield and in return doing that god favors. If he also showed a brave neglect of other gods, he did so without quite subscribing to the high Christian view that all the others were frauds and worse.

Constantine postponed baptism until he was on his deathbed to assure himself of heaven without risking post-baptismal relapse. The half century that followed saw a sequence of emperors who mostly favored Christ, but who also did not do much to graft this new god onto old traditions of culture and politics.

The great exception in that line of Christ followers was the emperor Julian (ruled 361–363), whom Christians called "the Apostate" because he had been brought up in their midst but devoted himself on the throne to advancing traditional religious ideas and practices under the label of "Hellenism," using Christianity as his template for what a good "pagan" cult might be. If anybody in the ancient world was ever a "pagan," Julian the ex-Christian was, but he won few followers. When he died, even the traditionalists in his retinue were willing to see a Christian succeed him on the throne. That successor lasted mere months, but Valentinian I, the general from Pannonia who succeeded him in turn, was an effective and at least nominally Christian monarch. In the years afterward, clergymen competed for the emperor's attention, eventually persuading the adolescent emperor Gratian to take his own religious professions seriously enough to reject some of the traditional garb and rituals of empire.

Gratian and his brother Valentinian II were children when they ascended the throne, and in 378 they found themselves alone, when their uncle Valens was killed in battle at Adrianople in the botched refugee resettlement we recounted. They summoned Theodosius, a senior general officer who had distinguished himself under Valentinian, from retirement on his estates in Spain to take the title of emperor alongside them. Theodosius quickly took the lead in military and civil affairs, and when, over the next years, Gratian and Valentinian II themselves were killed in struggles with usurpers, he reigned alone till his death in 395.

Theodosius I was a Christian, from a part of the empire where a conservative, determined, and committed Christianity had taken root. Within two years of his accession, he was actively involved in regulating Christians' internal doctrinal differences and supervising a meeting of bishops at Constantinople designed to declare and ratify a formal theological statement of central doctrines. Constantine had tried to do the same thing at Nicaea in 325, but its position came under attack, remaining in the minority for fifty years. Constantine himself had given his own council's solution lukewarm support at best. Athanasius, bishop of Alexandria, frequently in exile and always in conflict, fought to sustain the Nicene position, and at the council held at Constantinople in 381 his ideas prevailed; what is today recited in churches as the Nicene Creed is the product of that council.

The fundamental point of the Nicene-Athanasian-Theodosian settlement at Constantinople was outwardly straightforward: Jesus was God. A commonsense ancient view of a figure like Jesus held that he was too limited and too small to be divine, confined for years in a human body and a provincial place, working a few minor miracles, and favored by a powerful god, but no more than that. To declare him God had the merits and demerits of simplicity. The next two centuries would fight out the implications of this fundamental assertion.

After a decade as emperor, with doctrinal disputes put to rest, Theodosius felt he was in a position to crack down. In 391, he issued the formal imperial edict banning traditional sacrifice and religious ritual. The mandate was enforced by imperial troops, by social fear, and, here and there, by the partially approved thuggery of Christian zealots. Theodosius died in 395, and it was only in 399 that real temple busting came to Roman Africa, for example; and when it did come, it was quick and decisive. Not since Caracalla, who conferred full Roman citizenship on all free inhabitants of the empire in the early third century, had a single emperor done so much to affect so many lives, irreversibly. Ramsay MacMullen has noted the supreme confidence of the Christians at that time, leading to a nearly complete cessation of serious efforts to proselytize for their religion.[26] Henceforth, Christianity was a matter of requirement, and persuasion was irrelevant. Pope Gregory's mission to convert the English in the 590s was a surprising innovation, but it reached beyond the lands where imperial requirements could go.

Theodosius I suffered from a common weakness of monarchs: love of his children. When he died in 395, he left two sons, Arcadius in Constantinople and Honorius in Ravenna, to inherit his throne. Neither was of age, neither was up to the job, but no one was ready to let them fail. Honorius was in the hands of Theodosius's general Stilicho, and for as long as Stilicho flourished, Honorius's regime performed respectably, but it foundered in the wake of Stilicho's murder until, as we have seen, Aetius brought his steady hand to the high command. In Constantinople, what emerged was not a general, but a court, a corporate regime that managed civil and military affairs, with no single power behind the throne and no emperor more than an imperial front for this court, at least until Zeno and Anastasius nearly 100 years later.

What Theodosius left behind, more important than his sons, was a religious landscape denuded of the familiar and the emergence, by encouragement and by default, of an empire-wide leadership class of Christian bishops and their wealthy supporters and associates. This was an empire with traditional religion forbidden and Christianity allowed to run amok, but it was not a Christian empire.

Christianity flourished, was privileged, and did its business. Emperors and many if not most courtiers and senior officers attended Christian services. When (rarely) it snowed in Constantinople, as it did one day in the reign of Theodosius II, the emperor would lead the crowd in the circus in Christian hymns in hope of better weather.[27] The military officers recruited from the margins of empire, the ones often thought of as barbarian, were themselves predominantly Christian, of their old-fashioned Arian kind to be sure, but their advance into positions of leadership in the western empire had its own effect, over time, in favor of Christianization. They took Christianity for granted and had no interest in or sympathy for traditional Mediterranean religions.

In cities all over the empire, bishops and wealthy Christians took decisive control. They acted as though persecution could return at any moment and concentrated on controlling what they could control around themselves. If you were not a Christian, or if your views of Christianity were not those of the ruling elite in your neighborhood or in the great cities, you might encounter various nuisances, but for the most part you could go about your business as before—just so long as you did not insist on engaging in sacrifices or other forbidden rituals.

Remarkably little testimony survives from the first generation of those accustomed to the old rites about how they coped with the ban they now faced. Many of them found their way quite directly into Christian churches, and not always skeptically. They reasoned that the Christian god must be mighty indeed if he could suppress the worship of all others, and this was a strong reason to spend time in his churches, if only as a way of making sure that this new and powerful deity would look kindly on those who paid proper attention to him. Others appeared in church simply out of prudence, and some were heard to murmur skeptical thoughts, especially at moments when the world's misfortunes let them suggest that the new god was not so powerful as his promoters had promised.

In a few cities, the more authoritarian and centralized future began to be enacted. The great cities of the east—Alexandria, Antioch, and Constantinople, and to a lesser extent Jerusalem—were the focus of religious discontent and contention. They had passed the tipping point, now having active Christian majorities, and they were large enough and diverse enough to discover that "Christianity" was not something obvious or simple on which all followers of Jesus could agree. When those cities were restless, emperors noticed and acted: first to contain, eventually to control.

Surely Jesus preached a message of love and peace? Perhaps, but, as is only too obvious, love and peace are not the only leading characteristics of Christian communities or their relationships with non-Christians. A community of followers of a teacher from one place and one time naturally tends to diverge in beliefs and practices as the community spreads over space and time, especially when it crosses language boundaries. Christianity always had as a countervailing, centripetal force its deep-rooted belief in the unity and homogeneity of its various expressions throughout the known world. This noble but impractical ideal meant that people with divergent ideas who lived side by side could not tolerate their divergence but were compelled to mistrust one another and to seek to persuade their neighbors of the error of their ways.

The fundamental puzzle went back to the texts that Christians relied on.[28] Those texts told the story of a distinctly human, circumscribed being, a man who had a family, a job, a hometown, a career, and then a death. His only really unusual characteristic was that he also had a resurrection, even if the several accounts of his life were oddly at variance about that defining event. (The gospels agreed that he came back to life, and mostly agreed that shortly thereafter he departed from among his followers without a second death, but they varied on the details. One—the gospel of Mark—contained traces of two or three different versions, and only Luke 24:51 tells the story of the miraculous bodily ascension into heaven.)

Jesus and his first followers, moreover, offered a variety of assertions about his relationship with the supreme divine being, evidently the god of the Jews. On any reading of his story, he was a privileged representative, a spokesman, even an empowered plenipotentiary. Some of the most provocative language connected him to Jewish traditions about a messiah, an anointed, kinglike successor to Israel's ancient rulers, restoring something of its former glory and independence, whereas other language referred to his sonship and his personal, intimate relationship with the divine. The task of interpreting what he said and what was said about him is made dramatically more difficult by the decision to treat the scriptures of the Jews as themselves inspired truth. There is simply too much scripture for it all to make sense.

Reducing these various stories and assertions to a single set of dialectically defensible assertions that all can agree on has proved, over two millennia, to be entirely impossible. The boundary between the human and the divine is impossible to define. There are three main lines of possible definition about Jesus's role: mostly to entirely human; mostly to entirely divine; or human, then divine. The last of these was the most comfortable for ancient religious practice to accept, for there were ample cases of mortals raised to divinity—not least visibly in the case of the Roman emperors from Julius Caesar onward. On his deathbed, the emperor Vespasian is said to have expired with the line, "I think I'm becoming a god." The philosopher Seneca had already mocked the late emperor Claudius by describing in a little satirical pamphlet how he became at his death not a god, but a pumpkin.

The holy transformation may have been a commonplace model, but it was never widely accepted. Despite some language in the holy books that lent itself to an "adoptionist" position—Jesus was a human being adopted as son by his god and thus transformed—the fault line or rift in these debates regularly fell between the human and the divine, the central theological issue of the fourth century. The position we now call Arian insisted on distinguishing Jesus from his god, whereas the Nicene position insisted on identifying the two with each other, absolutely and without reservation. "Of identical substance," *homo-ousios* in Greek, was the wording of that creed. Proponents of the alternative position occasionally went so far as to say "of similar substance," *homoi-ousios* in Greek, distinguished from the other Greek term by only a single iota. But even when two positions came that close, they proved incompatible. Either Jesus was divine or he was not.

Theodosius's intervention in support of the long guerrilla war that Athanasius of Alexandria fought on behalf of Jesus the god ensured that the hard deifying position would prevail, and within the main lines of Christianity, eastern and western, it has prevailed ever since: no small achievement for a lone Spanish general.

Though the issue of divinity was apparently settled after 381, however, it still refused to go away. Theologians now framed that old issue in the form of new questions. If Jesus was divine, then *how* was he divine? Where and how did the human and the divine mix, meet, match, and mingle in him? Three sets of answers to these questions were possible, and theologians advanced them, and to this day all three continue to have living traditions upholding them in the orthodox, Nestorian, and Jacobite churches.

Did the human and the divine remain clearly distinguished in Jesus (as logic would insist they should), the human attached to his mortal, fleshly, fallible qualities, the divine marking his spirit and mind? Is it impious to suggest that the transcendent excellence of the divine can be tainted by contact with flesh, food, sex, and death? Would you be shocked, in other words, to hear Jesus's mother, Mary, spoken of as the "mother of God" (*theotokos*)—because you would believe that no woman of flesh could aspire to such a title? That position is named Nestorian, after a patriarch of Constantinople, Nestorius, who misspoke and found himself condemned at a church council in Ephesus in 431, blamed for positions that he did not particularly hold, but that others after him would hold. The traditions of Antioch, the most Jewish or at least most Semitic of the Christian churches of the east, held most to this view, and from there the doctrine crossed Asia to greet European missionaries to China in the sixteenth century.

Or did the human and the divine come together in Jesus in a unique way, mixed or rather fused and transmogrified into a unique new being, a single being of single nature? If you think that is the case, theologians will call you monophysite or—the more fashionable term for such believers today—miaphysite. In the Jacobite churches of the Near East, especially the Coptic church, which preserves the tradition of Egyptian Christianity in an unbroken line, this position is strongly represented, and uses the technical Greek term as a sign of respect. Like the Nestorians, members of this group will insist that their respect for divine majesty is at the heart of their faith and argument. In the fifth and sixth centuries, this view sprang from Alexandria, the most philosophical of the churches, and the one most imbued with Greek philosophical traditions.

Both positions face challenges. Scriptural language speaks unmistakably on one page of Jesus's divine qualities, and on another page of his human ones. Numerous objections on one side or another counterbalance both monophysite and Nestorian views, making neither fully capable of carrying the day.

And so a third position emerged, insisting on a "both-and" solution, asserting both the godhead and the manhood of Jesus at the same time. Jesus was divine and human, of two natures, conjoined, indissoluble; but the divine and the human never mixed, never changed, in him. The western church, the church of the less theologically sophisticated and engaged Latins preferred this position, and found support in the imperial capital of Constantinople. This doctrine arose among theologians rather than believers, and without the bishops of Rome and emperors in Constantinople to support it, it would never have been more than a theological footnote. Instead, in 451 CE, at a meeting of bishops whom the emperor Marcian—he of the pious virgin wife, Pulcheria—called to Chalcedon, a city within sight of Constantinople across the Bosporus, this formula fatefully won the day after heated debate. Approval was a compromise and only a compromise, with too few real supporters and too many others accepting it only because their enemies would not.

Each of the three positions was distinct. The Nestorians imagined Christ's divinity as a kind of benign possession, a god's mind in a mortal's body; the monophysites envisioned a magical new kind of being; the Chalcedonians put forth a logical construct, yet still quite difficult to grasp and comprehend, and they made this incomprehensibility into a virtue, at least as far as they could. If the scriptures were contradictory and confusing, they represented not conflict, but rather a lofty, divine logic that mortals could not grasp, and became evidence of the truth of a logically paradoxical doctrine. The figure of Jesus was smothered by these different representations of Christ, and the gospels dropped back to second place in such attempts to resolve the discordances of scripture into a philosophically satisfactory doctrine.[29]

Paradox and irony do not easily win a mass audience away from confident assertion and certainty. Churches that call themselves orthodox or catholic today accept Chalcedon, but in every age since 451 Chaldedon's position has been challenged. Often in the early decades and centuries, the Chalcedonian position was that of only a minority of those with any capacity for understanding what was at stake. No sooner was the council over than strong forces attempted to subvert it, and the emperor Marcian did not last long enough to sustain the position he supported. By 457, a mob lynched the orthodox Chalcedonian patriarch of Alexandria, Proterius, making it clear that leaders could not impose official orthodoxy from above.

Emperors in the fifth century could still be pragmatic and thoughtful about religion. Few were as effective as the emperor Zeno. He must have been a novice in matters of religion, but he saw the threat to imperial government implied in religious disagreement and moved—with good theological advice—to close a widening gap between those who accepted the Chalcedonian position and those who insisted on the high majesty of the divine and the single nature of the Christ. The "unity document" (*Henotikon*) that Zeno disseminated is a masterpiece of diplomacy and judgment. If no theologians and only statesmen had been involved in such a thing, it would have been acclaimed.

Theologians responded to the *Henotikon*, and politics intervened. Not only were there hard partisans, in Zeno's own domains, of the two positions he sought to bridge (more single-nature believers in Egypt, more Chalcedonians at that point in Syria and Palestine and the areas around Constantinople), but the west lay tantalizingly beyond his grasp. The bishop of Rome—Leo I, who in later history came to be called, for his pains, Leo the Great—had been the strongest partisan of the Chalcedonian "both-and" position at the time of the council, and his successors invested heavily in loyalty to that position. Zeno could not expect much help from Odoacer, who was in command in Italy at the time of the *Henotikon*, perhaps implicated in the revolts against Zeno, and with plenty of other more urgent business at hand, including a desire not to aggravate relations with the dignitaries of Rome and especially their bishops. We have seen how from 484, the bishops of Rome and the Chalcedonian loyalists behind them refused to share communion with those who were at peace with Zeno's church patriarch Acacius, and from then until 519, eastern and western churches were officially in a state of schism.

Even though would-be moderates controlled both Rome and Constantinople, their respective definitions of moderation fell on different parts of the spectrum. As long as they could not agree, the emperor of Constantinople and his patriarch could not use the west as a balancing force against the one-nature zealots, who proceeded to make hay in the east. From the 480s to the 510s, these zealots were assiduous and faithful to their belief and saw their influence expand. The emperor Anastasius I, who succeeded Zeno in 491 and reigned until 518, belonged to the monophysites in all but name. In 511, he banished the patriarch of Constantinople, Macedonius, for supposedly Nestorian but in fact Chalcedonian sympathies. Macedonius's successor, Timothy, was imprudent enough to introduce an explicitly monophysite proclamation into the liturgy in the great church, however, and riots broke out. Anastasius weathered this crisis, and the threat of a coup, which he put down brutally; we will shortly meet one of the victims of that suppression.

By the time Anastasius died, his successors Justin I (r. 518–527) and Justinian I (r. 527–565), devout Balkan westerners that they were and deep enthusiasts (particularly Justinian) for the Chalcedonian position, were too far behind to win the day for their creed. Justinian's frustrated zeal will mark much of our story.

THE END OF THEODERIC

Theoderic ended badly, and this was partly his fault. Think of him again as Othello—for his end shows his virtues as well as his defects, and the corrosive effect expectations can have on the best of intentions. Starting about 519, we have seen him reach back into his past, a past that was only myth, to bring forth stories of family and dynasty. In those stories, seventeen generations of his family, the Amals, through history, chronicle, and panegyric proclaimed Theoderic king of the Goths, on a Roman throne. Now the Gothic story began to be heard more clearly. No good came of it.

Meanwhile, Theoderic greeted the accession of Justin in Constantinople with a mixture of optimism and complacency. With hindsight, we can see that Justin's regime was more of a threat than an opportunity for Theoderic, but Theoderic could not have known that. As the situation frayed around the edges of his regime, he may have been slow to see the coming dangers.

For one thing, churches were beginning to matter in the west in ways they hadn't mattered before. With Rome and Constantinople (not to mention Clovis's church to the northwest) all now in peace and harmony, Theoderic's religious position began to make him seem strange and vulnerable.

And one most promising force was in eclipse. Vitalian, the best general in the east, could have been a friend for Theoderic and could have been a bridge between Ravenna and Constantinople, but things went badly for him and he left the scene a failure.

Vitalian was born in Zaldapa, just south of the Danube and not far from the Black Sea, in what is now northeastern Bulgaria or Dobrudja, to a family long at home there. His sons had names that sound barbarian, but his father was Patriciolus, and he had religiously enthusiastic relatives with the Greek names Stephanus and Leontius. Leontius was a distinguished theologian in the community of Scythian monks at Constantinople, a party that ferociously pursued compromise in matters of doctrine but could never quite succeed in propagating the compromises it reached. Vitalian may also have had an uncle who became Chalcedonian patriarch of Constantinople, only to be thrown out in 511 when the emperor Anastasius placated the monophysites.

Many scholars try to gothicize Vitalian and make him part of the families of Goths who chose not to go with Theoderic into Italy, but we need not accept the ethnic distinction to see the underlying fact. He was of an established family in the Balkans, the kind of family that produced generals and statesmen, and he was more like Theoderic than like the foot soldier Justin, who went to Constantinople to flee a life and likely death in the ranks of a general like Theoderic or Vitalian. Vitalian was short and he stammered, but he had spirit, and he became one of history's great might-have-beens.

Under Anastasius in the 510s, Vitalian was the bulwark of empire on the Danube, but little respected by his monarch. He was an officer of moderate rank in 513 when—from Constantinople's point of view—he led a revolt. He clamored for adequate supplies for his troops, known as *foede-rati* (allies)—sworn recruits either from across the river or from among peoples not yet habituated to Roman military service—but he quickly persuaded regular troops to join him. In short order, he found himself master of Thrace, lower Moesia, and Scythia—essentially all of modern Bulgaria and European Turkey.

He saw his moment and sought to take it, but in the end was never ruthless enough and never successful enough. He approached Constantinople with a large force spread out to fill the peninsula from the Sea of Marmara to the Black Sea, and rode unopposed to the city's great Golden Gate. He presented himself as committed to supporting the Thracian army and the orthodox church (by which he meant the Chalcedonian one), and he made a credible case. After eight days of standoff, he allowed Anastasius to buy him off with reassurances.

No sooner had Vitalian and his troops withdrawn than Anastasius reneged, sending out a general named Cyril to oppose him. This was a mistake. If we believe our sources, Vitalian bribed his way into the opposing general's camp and killed him with his own hands, seizing control of his forces. Anastasius's nephew Hypatius led another force that Vitalian defeated in its turn. Vitalian's men captured Hypatius, and when ambassadors went out to ransom him with 1,100 pounds of gold, they too were captured and the gold along with them. Many in Thrace and beyond cheered these victories and could see that a new emperor was in the making, no trivial thing when the reigning emperor was in his eighties.

Now triply empowered, Vitalian marched on Constantinople again, and this time was more classically successful. He liberated his captives in return for ransom and for the title of master of soldiers for Thrace. There was religious rapprochement as well, as Vitalian and Anastasius both wrote letters to Pope Hormisdas in Italy encouraging him to call a council of reconciliation in church matters, but nothing came of it. When that disappointment sank in, Vitalian marched on Constantinople—third time unlucky—and saw his fleet destroyed and his army defeated and so fled back to Thrace. The betting that had gone in his favor paused. Some sources had it that the future emperor Justin was involved, paying the philosopher Proclus of Athens 400 pounds of gold for a sulfur compound that could be thrown a distance and catch fire, devastating the wooden ships.[30] Though several sources tell the story, and no one quite believes it, it marks the importance of Vitalian's defeat. Had Vitalian prevailed on that ap-proach, his imperial dreams might have been fulfilled.

What would have happened then? A man much like Theoderic would have been in power in Constantinople, able to ensure ecclesiastical peace at least with the west, and military harmony as well. The history of the sixth century might then have been one of restored Roman imperial do-mains, stretching from Italy to Constantinople, unified in purpose and able to offer support from each capital when fighting was necessary on the northern frontier against Franks or the eastern frontier against Persians. The religious unity would very likely have brought together all forces west of the Bosporus, and their eventual ability to prevail over eastern belief would have been strong. If division had finally come, the boundary would have run through Asia Minor, not the Balkans. Most important, that uni-fication of Constantinople and Italy would presumably have made the Bal-kans a heartland, not a borderland.

For just a moment, Vitalian brought into play the possibility of a dif-ferent geopolitical future. His failure casts a long shadow over the coming years.

Now tamed, Vitalian still potentially remained a power. From 515 to 518 he was still in the field, though with no official position. From the last days of Anastasius, Justinian, as the power behind Justin's throne, seems to have thought it better to keep Vitalian inside the tent than outside, and so honored him at Constantinople, making him "master of soldiers in the imperial presence" and supporting his Chalcedonianism by sending him to represent the true faith in councils at Tyre, on the Palestinian coast; and at Apamea, inland in Syria, in 518 and 519. He gave his approval and thus lent credence to Constantinople's reunification with Rome that Justin and Hormisdas brokered in 519, and he supported the Scythian monks in their struggle for Chalcedonian orthodoxy. In 520, he was honored with the consulship, but in the year that was named after him, he was murdered in the imperial palace along with two of his aides. Justinian was, at last, without a serious rival, and feared or despised by those who assumed, rightly or wrongly, that he had done in the better man himself.

Theoderic was a distant spectator of Vitalian's career, forced to depend on scattered and belated reports of his progress and ambitions. As that hope faded and then ended with Vitalian's death, Theoderic soon found himself with suspicions and rivalry of his own closer to home.

Boethius, the philosopher, was proud of his family, ostentatious in his learning, and ambitious in every way. Entering his forties in the 420s, about to see his sons' grand joint consulship, he had made his name through his education, as we have seen. That learning makes him hard to observe clearly, because he fits so neatly into the roles of both public intellectual and man of letters that our historians of philosophy and literature take him over and take him for granted. But he came to a bad end, and an important story that doesn't belong exclusively to philosophy *or* literature sits in plain sight, yet despite its obviousness remains easy to overlook.

Our chief sources for the story of Boethius's end are two. The first is the *Anonymus Valesianus,* a chronicle of Theoderic's years in power. It gives Theoderic's story as an Othello-like tale—virtue and success coming to a tragic end as bad blood wins out over good intentions. The unnamed author, who was an eyewitness to at least some of Theoderic's story, was already the source for our account of Theoderic's grand visit to Rome in 500 and was at that point still making Theoderic wise, humane, benevolent, and just. With the rise of Eutharic—this is also the source that makes him a zealot for Arian religion—things begin to sour for this chronicler, consistent with Theoderic's reactions to events he saw unfolding in the world around him.

The other source is far better known: Boethius's *Consolation of Philosophy,* one of the gems of western literature by any standard, pervasively influential in much late medieval philosophical and religious understanding. It is a gorgeous book, deserving wide readership: "A golden volume, not unworthy of the leisure of Plato or Tully [Cicero]," said Gibbon. "To acquire a taste for it is almost to become naturalised in the middle ages," added C. S. Lewis. To write so beautiful, wise, and resigned a book assures you of the goodwill of all the later generations of scholars, fitting you comfortably into the pigeonhole reserved for sages and scholars.

But the *Consolation* is also a disingenuous book, and it has deceived many. What story can we piece together from these texts and the brief mentions of a few other sources? Why did Boethius have to die?

In the early 520s, Theoderic became more and more suspicious of those around him, and with good reason. His planned succession—a son-in-law and a grandson—failed when Eutharic died by about 523. Theoderic realized he would leave behind an infant grandson, Athalaric, in the care of a strong-willed daughter, Amalasuntha. Who would accept his regime?

The military could well want a stronger hand in command; and the old Romans of Rome, believing what Theoderic had long wanted them to believe—that nothing had really changed and that they were still citizens of a civilized Roman empire—would have their own ideas about an appropriate successor.

Boethius, meanwhile, was in the ascendant. As we have seen, he had been consul in 510, and in 522 saw his own two sons share the consulship—an almost unheard-of achievement for men who were not emperors or kin of emperors. In Ravenna to serve as master of offices under Theoderic, he was the second-ranking civil dignitary of the imperial government. In his forties at this point, he was the most prominent citizen in Theoderic's realm. Liberius might have come closest, but was far less rich, had never been consul, and was away across the Alps in Gaul, far from the court.

Then the suspicions began.

To hear Boethius tell it, he was surrounded by enemies even though he himself embodied selfless honor and justice. He had repeatedly thwarted the barbarous greed of royal officials with the grating names Cunigast and Triguilla, while persuading the king to prevent his praetorian prefect from imposing draconian measures to remedy a threat of famine in Campania. He protected the virtuous, such as the former consuls Paulinus and Albinus, from those who would ruin them. Even so, he made more enemies, and Basilius, desperate for relief from loan sharks, filed accusations against Boethius, while two other shady characters, Opilio and Gaudentius, on the verge of exile for their crimes, took refuge in a church to avoid deportation. Then on the day when they would have been branded and driven out of Ravenna, they bargained for their immunity, as we would say nowadays, by making their own string of accusations against Boethius.

And what did they accuse him of? I do not see that anyone has ever thought to be puzzled by Boethius's somewhat unhelpful answer: "We are said to have wished that the senate be safe."[31] And just how did he attempt to ensure the senate's safety? "We were accused of having stopped an informer from producing evidence that would convict the senate of the crime of *maiestas*"—that is, of attacking the intrinsic authority of the throne. He passed over, without deigning to comment (an old rhetorical trick), "the counterfeited letters that made it look as if I were daring to hope for liberty for Rome." And just how does he deal with *that* accusation? "As if there were any liberty left to hope for!"

Boethius's presentation requires the historian-detective to offer several observations. First, wanting the senate to be safe and hoping for Rome's liberty are either meaningless platitudes or else specific political crimes in a context about which we know too little. Second, Boethius does not deny them. Third, the expostulation about the preposterousness of hoping for liberty at this moment in its own way confirms rather than confutes suspicion—for surely the offense lay in suggesting that Theoderic's regime was deprived of liberty at all.

Boethius then sets a dramatic stage for us to contemplate. "You recall" (he tells the allegorical woman called Philosophy, his personification for wisdom itself visiting him in prison to hear and sanctify his lament) "the time the king was at Verona, hell-bent on destroying us all, and how he tried to take the accusation of a crime of *maiestas* leveled against Albinus and make it encompass the whole senate. And then you recall how I defended the innocence of the whole senate at great risk to myself."

Apparently *that* is what has landed him, without trial, in prison, 500 miles from Rome and home, where he wrote his lament. The king suspected treason in his court and Boethius forthrightly defended the suspects—too forthrightly, too persuasively for his own good.

Worse is yet to come. Those who seek to destroy Boethius added a charge of sacrilege—that is, of having defiled himself with black magic "out of ambition for high office." The simple meaning to his contemporaries would be that he had engaged in secret religious rites of the old order (as we saw some of his contemporaries in the senate doing a few years earlier) to advance his own career. Preposterous, he huffs; impossible to imagine the likes of me doing the likes of that!

What can be going on here? The answer is straightforward and not hard to see in Boethius's own *Consolation*, although most readers pass right over it. "But you, [Philosophy], approved this remark from the mouth of Plato:[32] 'Republics would be happy if either the philosophers ruled them or if their rulers came to study philosophy.'" Boethius goes on to represent that precept as what led him to public life, and I think most readers assume that it justifies a modest entry into upper bureaucracy. The true meaning is too obvious.

Theoderic was not merely paranoid: he had a real enemy. Boethius wanted to be emperor himself—or, more precisely, he wanted to be Plato's philosopher king.

Think of it this way. If you were Boethius, if you were a senior minister at the imperial court of Italy, if you had an impeccable pedigree and the very highest imaginable social standing, and if you saw that the reigning ruler (emperor or would-be emperor) was nearing his end without a satisfactory heir in place, what would you think *should* be done or *could* be done? Who was there that a Roman of this period would think better qualified or better positioned to succeed Theoderic?

And if your neighbors thought you were using black magic to advance your ambitions, what did they think you were aiming for? A one-step promotion to the highest civil office of praetorian prefect? Nonsense: patience and good behavior could get him that. Wouldn't they assume he was looking at the big step, up to the throne itself?

If it then happened that this man and his colleagues were in correspondence with leading figures in Constantinople and if they were known to have supported reconciliation with Constantinople going back to the years of the Laurentian schism and then the years of bringing the Acacian schism to a halt, and if they had relatives and colleagues at court—then anything might be possible.

To be fair, there is no direct evidence that either Theoderic or Boethius saw things this way, but we do have every reason to believe that this idea must have been in the air. It would not take much in the way of suspicion for what might now seem to be—might then have *been*—only a pipe dream to take the shape of a real possibility and threat. In that setting, Boethius's remarks reported in the *Consolation* were at the very least astonishingly indiscreet and risky, and may have dug the hole deeper, especially once the accusations were abroad and Boethius himself was imprisoned. Whether or not the charges had merit, Theoderic would be a fool not to take them seriously by this point. When Pope Hormisdas—the pope who had made peace with Constantinople—died in August 523 and Pope John I, a friend of Boethius and a collaborator with him in theological debates, replaced Hormisdas, Theoderic had to react.

Boethius paid for his indiscretion—or his ambition—with his life. With Theoderic in residence at his palace in Pavia and Boethius there as court official, he was held in custody with his accused coconspirator Albinus in a baptistery. Theoderic summoned the prefect of the city of Rome, Eusebius, to Pavia and there condemned Boethius to death in absentia. Then they took him out for execution. The *Anonymus Valesianus* has it that a rope was tied so tightly around his head that his eyes bulged in their sockets, and then he was beaten to death.[33] His sons, the child consuls of 522, were allowed to live.

Theoderic, seeing his regime still at risk, immediately sent a delegation from Ravenna to Constantinople, led by Pope John himself, to confirm that assurances of religious peace would be observed and that Arianism would be respected. Theoderic particularly asked that people who had been forced to convert from Arianism to orthodoxy be restored to their original state—but for an emperor eager to be seen as devout, this request was impossible to accept. Pope John refused to carry the message at first, but Theoderic forced him and his delegation of bishops and senators to board ship and make their way to Constantinople.

Once there, the emperor Justin came out to greet them with all respect, welcoming the pope "as if he were blessed Peter himself" and confirming that those who had left Arianism were safe forever and could not be restored to their original error. While they were away, if the *Anonymus Valesianus* has the sequence right, Theoderic summoned Boethius's father-in-law, Symmachus, from Rome to Ravenna; tried him on trumped-up charges; and put him to death lest he take any subversive steps out of grief for his dead son-in-law. When the pope returned to Ravenna, the king made his disfavor clear, and within a few days John was dead. No one says there was foul play, but it was at least a foul moment. When a man possessed by a demon attended Pope John's funeral, he was miraculously and suddenly released from his torment. The crowd saw this as a sign of the pope's holiness and took him out to burial while making wonder-working relics out of the papal clothes.

There is much debate over the dates of these events, but it is safe to put them all in the years 524–525. If a coup had indeed been in the making, Theoderic had succeeded in putting it down. The line of succession continued in his own family.

Theoderic came to his own end in 526, and by then the author of the *Anonymus Valesianus* is fully against him. So maddened was Theoderic, the story goes, that he issued an edict that the Arians would seize the orthodox basilicas on the very next Sunday. This could not have been more than a token gesture—perhaps a single basilica—a symbolic gesture to protest what Theoderic saw as Justin's comparable interference. Then Theoderic fell victim to the same power that had destroyed Arius, the teacher for whom Arianism was named. Following the traditional story, just as Arius had died of dysentery, so too Theoderic fell ill of it and died on the third day, the very day he had intended to seize the holy basilicas. He was in his early seventies.

We needn't believe more than that Theoderic died with rumor and hostility in the air and at least some of his legacy in question. The summer after he died, there appears to have been a fear of a sea invasion from the east, and our source praises Cassiodorus as one of the new king's ministers for swift action designed to keep a sharp watch on the seafront and protect Italy from invasion. He even paid troops out of his own pocket to ensure obedience.

Athalaric, the grandchild of Theoderic by Eutharic and Amalasuntha, was the new king in all but fact. His widowed mother was the effective regent of the state, relying on a cadre of civilian and military officials already at court. We are less well equipped with any narrative of affairs during her regency than for adjacent periods, but it appears to have been mainly stable and a continuation of what had been known under Theoderic. From 526 to 534, the Theoderician era continued without the man who had made it. The terminology of *civilitas* returned to the royal documents after a few years in abeyance, but was addressed only to civilians, not the army. A Gothic name, Tuluin, appears on the list of senators, while in roughly the same years the Roman name Cyprian belongs to a father whose children were educated to the language and ways of the army.

Disaster loomed. We should not trust the standard story about Amalasuntha's son and his end, yet we must tell it. Amalasuntha, we are told, put the boy in the care of three grave, prudent older Goths, but others were unhappy and "because of their eagerness to wrong their subjects, they wished to be ruled by him more after the barbarian fashion." A dialogue, surely made up long after, recounts how Amalasuntha defended her style of educating her son against Gothic critics, who succeeded in taking control of the boy and giving him over to companions who "as soon as he came of age, enticed him to drunkenness and to intercourse with women, making him an exceptionally depraved youth, and of such stupid folly that he was disinclined to follow his mother's advice."[34] He plunged in short order into the depths of a wasting disease and died on October 10, 534, still a teenager.

This moralizing reading appears twenty years later, from the skeptical historian Procopius of Constantinople, and he burdens it with several overlays. It shows the Italian regime to disadvantage while preparing us for the claim that the barbarian regime was deteriorating and thus appropriately an object of military intervention from outside. The cartoonish barbarians who sent Athalaric to his grave with wine, women, and song are what one would expect in such a story, but these caricatures bear no resemblance to any Italian reality we know of. There were surely differences of opinion within the Italian court, and the young king could well have been a political football between factions, with his death an opportunity for blaming and posturing on all sides. The division is unlikely to have been between Roman and Goth; rather, it would have been between civilian and military, with the advocates of a strong defense seizing control of the young man's future.

ONE SHORT NOTE: What should we think of Boethius? The fame of his popularized version of Plato in the *Consolation* in later centuries is real and his book stands on its merits. Its encouragement of quiet withdrawal from public life is in tune with a culture that would eschew ambition and wealth—at least in principle—but the message is at the very least controversial and worth controverting. Boethius's actions and his career make sense in their place and time. If he grasped at the brass ring, missed, and then paid for his attempt with his life, he was no more and no less than a typical Roman aristocrat of any age and can scarcely be judged otherwise than as having misjudged his moment. Would Justinian have been happier to have Boethius in command in Italy than Theoderic's heirs? Would Italy and later history have been spared some of Justinian's mad restorationism? The effort Boethius made, if it makes him out to be less an otherworldly philosopher than we have thought, might not have been so ill-advised as first appears.

THEODERIC'S DEATH OFFERS an opportunity to take a deep breath and look around the Mediterranean at the state of the Roman empire in the year 526. This is arguably the last moment of genuinely ancient history when it makes sense to take collective stock like this, when the totality of what Rome created could still be thought of as one community.

The government that had begun doing business on seven hills in the Tiber valley in 753 BCE (the legendary date of Romulus's founding of the city) or 509 BCE (the traditional date of the founding of the republic) was still fully alive and well and collecting taxes. It had moved its corporate headquarters to Constantinople almost exactly 200 years earlier, and flourished as a result. Two hundred years is a long time. At a distance of 1,500 years, many people, places, and events seem crowded close together by a foreshortening of the historical time line, but Constantine and his epochal changes (founding Constantinople, privileging Christianity) were as far in the past then as Napoléon and Thomas Jefferson are from us today.

This empire's sway at the outermost boundaries of territory changed little in the eastern provinces. Though there had been military alarms and excursions in the Balkan provinces during the fifth century, at this moment the Danube frontier was no more and no less unsettled than at many other times since it had begun to be taken seriously as a boundary 500 years earlier. East of Constantinople, its boundaries with Persia were, if occasionally tested, mainly stable. South of Syria and around through Egypt and Cyrene, the long past of Roman dominion, which in turn continued Alexander's heritage, now represented some 800 years of continual inclusion in the Mediterranean world.

The world of people who spoke Latin had seen some changes, but those changes must not be overstated. The traditional cities dominated the traditional landscapes. The economic bases of these societies had not visibly changed—the same crops were being grown in the same places; the same markets were doing the same business. Cross-Mediterranean traffic from Carthage to Rome had fallen off—a fundamental fact of the age, but invisible to many. The Africans actually saw this as good news, for it meant that more wealth stayed home, untouched by taxation. Populations shrank and the world was not so prosperous as it once had been, but it was recognizably the same.

In governmental terms, a conservative observer would say that the provincial lines had been redrawn a bit, and new chief local rulers were in place in Africa, Spain, Italy-Provence, and northern Gaul. Since Diocletian around 300, the empire had been officiously divided into a series of larger and smaller units of organization, where the more than 100 provinces were aggregated into dioceses of a dozen or so provinces, and those in turn into four or more prefectures whose alignment would shift with political and military needs. The arrangement under the rulers of the late fifth century and the early sixth century looked more like a rearrangement than a revolution. More authority had devolved on leaders such as Theoderic and Clovis, but they in turn had recentralized at least some control from the multitude of smaller bureaucratic units of two centuries before. The chief variations from the imperial past were Italy's power in southern Gaul and Rome's abandonment of Britain.

In all respects, however, the provinces of the Roman empire from Gaul to Arabia, from Mauritania to Armenia, were in a better and more peaceful order than they had been for almost 100 years. What had changed was the scope, or scale, of Roman pretension and control. Theoderic, we have seen, praised the idea of empire but kept a firm grip on his own part of it. Had he been expressly offered an imperial crown by the soldiers, the senate, or Constantinople, he surely would have taken it, and he probably expected that either for himself or for his heirs.

In practical terms, if you sat in the palace in Constantinople in the fifth century, you had less western tax revenue at your disposal than before, but you also had less responsibility for defending wide swaths of territory that had long been a plague to maintain. Reasonable observers in Constantinople would probably have had interesting discussions and disagreements as to whether the trade-off was positive.

It is true that something had been lost. The advantages of scale were real. The coherence of a culture and the freedom of movement and interaction of peoples were powerful by-products of the Roman Mediterranean hegemony. The world paid a real price for the violence that brought subjugation and discipline to peoples to secure that hegemony, but the victims of this imperialism had died 500 years ago and their suffering could reasonably if cold-bloodedly be written off against the benefits of empire. Whether the new world order of 526 could have, with different strategic choices, coalesced again into a more coherent Mediterranean community of nations is a question that cannot be answered.

MARKET DAY IN CALABRIA

Can we grasp a little of what life in the Italy Theoderic created was like away from cities and palaces? Here is a story from a letter that Cassiodorus wrote in the name of Theoderic's grandson.

At a place called Consolinum, on the inland road from Naples south to Reggio di Calabria, the locals took over a spring that had been the site of an ancient religious festival—the Leucothea—to use as the site for a Christian baptistery.[35] Or at least that was the official version of what happened. We cannot know for sure whether the residents set great store by such a transformation or whether they continued to think of and frequent the site much as their ancestors had done for centuries. But the natural springs on the site gave abundant pure water, fish boldly frolicking in them unaware that hungry fishermen would soon capture them. Leucothea, the white goddess and aunt of Dionysus, was a patron of initiations into religious cults long before anyone heard of Christianity.

A market festival occurred there every year in mid-September for the feast of Cyprian, the martyred Christian bishop of Africa in the third century. This was the greatest market of the year, drawing merchants and buyers from Campania to Calabria and over to Apulia, virtually all of southern Italy. Some sellers erected stands and tents throughout the spreading meadows to display and protect their merchandise, while others cobbled together a temporary camp of shelters from tree branches to provide hospitality for all the visitors. It was a veritable city without buildings. Elegant clothes and handsome livestock, to say nothing of agricultural produce (it was harvest time, after all), were the great sellers, but the royal letter writer from whom we know of the event takes pains as well to describe and prettify something horrific: a brisk trade in children whose impoverished parents sold them into slavery. People could think it was better for children to be slaves in town than to live without food on their parents' farms.

On the climactic night of the festival, we are told, when the priest or bishop began his prayers, the water in the baptismal spring sensed what was about to happen and rose exultantly to meet the prayers from above. A course of man-made steps led down into the spring, with the water regularly covering five of them, but the two higher steps remained dry, except when the prayers began and the water welled up spontaneously—miraculously—to facilitate the baptism.

And in the evening, songs were sung in the tents and shelters, songs we shall never hear, for the real life of ancient times always escapes us. This corner of the ancient world had changed little with the coming of Christianity or with the coming of Theoderic and saw little reason to change. People took prosperity and social order for granted. The only cloud in this sunny scene was the king's concern at reports that such a throng with goods and money might also attract marauders. He commanded the senator to whom the letter is addressed to convene the local landowners and farmers to ensure the security and tranquillity of the event. In this moment, they succeeded, and the Roman empire still lived.

PART II

JUSTINIAN'S WORLD

The Empire That Couldn't Help Itself
(527–565)

Act two: In which, at a time of relative peace and prosperity, we meet a young, ambitious emperor who began life on the Balkan frontier, not far from modern Skopje in Macedonia, following a path to power paved by his enterprising uncle. When his uncle died, he took the throne and revealed ambitions for his capital and his empire on a scale that had not been seen since Constantine 200 years earlier. He won many battles and built many monuments—but that was not enough, for such zeal to preserve civilization can also prove unimaginably destructive.

3

Being Justinian

USTINIAN COMES INTO history from out of shadows. We know how his uncle Justin came to Constantinople on foot to seek a military career and ended on the imperial throne. Justinian was the nephew who was the son Justin never had. Already in his thirties when we see him slipping into position next to his uncle's new throne, he is a mystery to us until that time. At some point, he came down out of the Macedonian hinterlands to make his fortune, at some point he changed his name to emphasize his connection to the throne, and he acquired some of the skills of a prince. And he found himself a wife, Theodora.

Theodora haunts all the stories of Justinian, as virago, whore, mother superior, and great lady all at once. Hers is a character part, not a leading role, but she deserves an introduction separate from her husband. She was nothing by birth, in a world where birth was usually destiny. Her father kept bears in the circus at Constantinople, a world where shadows were dark enough to conceal a life of humiliation and sexual slavery for many a young woman. A prudent telling of her story has her use proximity to power as opportunity, leading her into a series of liaisons with powerful men, one of whom turned into an emperor. But the stinging portrait of her in Procopius's *Anecdota* ("Secret History") goes far beyond the facts we can confirm otherwise to tell of her rise to power as a fallen woman, so to speak, ascending from common prostitute to pop celebrity to great courtesan to domineering empress. Her reportedly lurid sexual practices are so vividly reported in Procopius that Edward Gibbon congratulated himself on respecting his reader's modesty by quoting them only in "the obscurity of a learned language"—the original Greek. The reader who wants to know the truth should read Procopius—did she really use geese to nibble the grains of wheat her handlers sprinkled over her nude body in her strip shows? Precisely what anatomical improbability did she imagine to expand her sexual pleasure? And there's more. The *effect* of the public reputation of Theodora in Justinian's lifetime and since is to give this humorless and indeed almost lifeless emperor a colorful and plausible counselor for his best and worst decisions. Her role is that of Nancy Reagan with a lurid past.

We know him best from one portrait, made when he was in his sixties and shimmering in colored mosaic stone on the walls of the church of San Vitale in Ravenna, a building he never saw in a city he never visited. Middle height, ordinary-looking, round-faced, brown-eyed—without the purple cloak and diadem, he could be like any other soldier turned courtier. He

Justinian and retinue at San Vitale.

Theodora and retinue at San Vitale.

faces across the altar in San Vitale an equally famous portrait of Theodora. He has a bishop, clerics, and soldiers with him; she has attendants and great ladies, much more purple, and a cascade of jewels. Together they are bringing the bread and wine for the liturgy to unfold among the living on the altar below. The portraits capture them at a moment of high ceremonial drama, atypical in a way, but not so far from the truth—for the trappings and ceremony of empire meant that few people ever saw them except on display, self-consciously dramatic and seeking to make a great impression.

Everything we know about Justinian similarly veils him in his robes of state and hides him in his palace. The scandalous stories that circulated about Theodora (we'll whisper about them shortly) all point back to her forgotten early life, not to the palace days, when she was equally invisible—that is to say, equally on untouchable public display. They wanted to be known by the display. To know them as they were, we will have to circle around the palace and creep up on them unawares.

His city is easier to grasp first. Constantinople demands superlatives, and usually gets them. We'll start there.

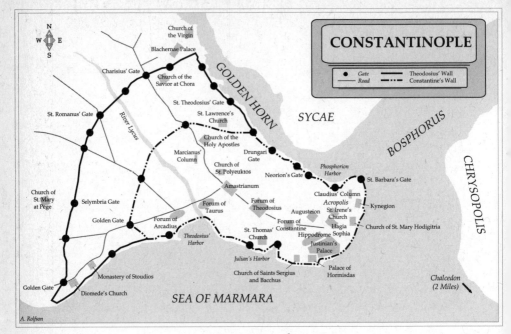

Constantinople.

In 658 BCE, the legends said, a Greek colony, led by a man named Byzas, was sent out by the city fathers of Megara, a city a few miles west of Athens along the coast road toward Corinth. Its mission was to establish a settlement on a peninsula about 350 miles northeast of Athens, on the sea highway to the remote, chilling coasts of the Black Sea. Byzas already knew the legend of Jason and his Argonauts, who went that way on their quest for the Golden Fleece, venturing on a little-traveled sea, and then to the trackless and unimaginable waste of the lands beyond it. Some less legendary travelers doubtless had reported back about a unique site that Byzas now prospected along that route. From the water, it looked like a city made by the sea.

From the many-isled Aegean, Greek sailors entered the Dardanelles, a narrow passage separating Thrace and the Balkans on the left from Asia Minor on the right. Fifty miles on, the waters broadened into the Sea of Marmara, wide and daunting enough to compel ancient sailors to cling to the shore for 100 miles or so, until currents and winds brought them in sight of a modest hilltop jutting into the sea on the left. Creature as he was of the winds and the water, the typical sailor would approach the site at first gingerly, but then, once he knew the place, with delight. For the peninsula stood at the mouth of another narrows, a thirty-five-mile passage broad enough for the most ambitious shipping but narrow enough today to be crossed, twice, with suspension bridges. That passage, the Bosporus, if you sailed up its course, led to the Black Sea, or, as the ancients called it with polite irony, the Euxine Sea: "the sea that is kindly to visitors" (its cold and currents were anything but kindly). Right here, where this hill rose on the left, a channel of water ran behind its peninsula. It was a few hundred yards wide and a couple of miles long, providing a weather-safe deepwater harbor that sailors welcomed. They called this route the Golden Horn, and it made the city from that day onward.

In recognition of Byzas's efforts, the city established there was called Byzantium. It claimed all customs duties travelers paid up and down the Bosporus, and thus had a steady prosperity during all the centuries when Greeks opened up the Black Sea and planted flourishing colonies around it—colonies that stayed in touch with their mother cities. Byzantium knew almost 1,000 years of that prosperity. Now and again it was drawn into the margins of Mediterranean political and military conflict.

Constantine, the first Christian emperor, saw the possibilities in the place. He was brilliant in both his plan for the city and its execution. In 324, when he was the newly unchallenged ruler over the eastern provinces of empire after a twenty-year struggle, he declared the city his own and laid out its ambitions. Unlike modern, fabricated capitals such as Brasília and Canberra, this one already had a reason for being, but it manifested all the artificiality of a city built quickly on overweening ambition and tax money. On May 11, 330, with his namesake city still for the most part a bustling construction site, Constantine was ready to host a grand inaugural celebration for it. In his not quite Christian way, the rituals mixed Christian and traditional elements, deliberately evoking the old Rome in a new place. With some effort he identified seven hills, naming them to ensure a resemblance to the old capital. (Whatever Constantine's beliefs, the city was determinedly traditional in form and decoration, with statues of the ancient gods and heroes lining its streets; Christianity was visibly present in only about a dozen churches.[1]) He offered land grants in nearby provinces, encouraging the ambitious recipients to build city houses as well for themselves. In 332, he established the free handouts of grain, long familiar to Romans, to feed Constantinople's poor.

Emperors kept Constantinople at the center of imperial ambition for 1,600 years. In the fifth century, Theodosius II surrounded it with walls worthy of a mighty realm. They ran in two lines (mostly still standing), nearly four miles long, the inner one about sixteen feet thick at the base and forty feet high. Ninety-six towers averaging sixty-six feet high stood along that wall, about 200 feet apart. Outside the inner wall was a broad terrace about sixteen feet above ground level. Then the outer walls were about seven feet thick and thirty feet high, with another ninety-six towers staggered for location with the towers on the inner wall. And then the moat lay beyond, a ditch originally thirty feet deep and sixty feet wide, ready to be flooded when the city was threatened. Ten gates pierced the wall, but five were reserved for military use only. They held—in the main—for over 1,000 years.[2] (Late in the fifth century, Anastasius built another rampart about forty miles west of Constantinople, a wall with a ditch outside it. That wall was never meant to be guarded the whole length; it was intended to slow invaders and facilitate defense.)

In late 1453 there was an abrupt—and some would say overdue—change in management and a substitution of new rituals for old ones. The Turkish sultan Mehmed II the Conqueror finally put the surviving stump of the Greek empire out of its misery by capturing the city. Mehmed was the son of a slave woman who was either Christian or Jewish, and some people thought he could count at least one Byzantine emperor among his ancestors. Many loyal contemporaries, including the remarkable Kritovoulos of Imbros, praised Mehmed's achievements, imitating the Greek masters of old. We have a copy of Kritovoulos's history, meant to be in the style of Thucydides, on the same kind of paper and in the same format as a copy of Arrian's ancient life of Alexander. Mehmed liked to compare himself to Alexander, spreading a story that he had a courtier read to him from the ancient and medieval historians of Greece, Rome, and Europe.

Mehmed's revival of Constantine's vision kept Constantinople (now known as Istanbul) the inescapable capital of empire for as long as the Ottomans ruled. It took World War I and its aftermath finally to beleaguer the region into mere nationhood and civility. The swarming mix of cultures that influenced Constantinople from its earliest days remained in evidence until the last days of the Ottomans. The city's more homogeneous Turkish culture that travelers observe now is mainly the result of a narrow-minded and often violent twentieth-century belief in making nation-states ethnically pure.

That city with a very long future, no longer now just a boomtown with more construction sites than buildings, came into its own in the fifth century as a result of two developments we have already traced. First was de-westernization. The empire that Augustus solidified was headquartered in the Latin west, but the bulk of its population and wealth lay in the Greek east, and this imbalance continued for as long as Augustus's creation lasted. If he ruled long enough, every emperor down to Theodosius in the 380s moved back and forth, up and down the Roman roads of the Balkans, or took ship on the Mediterranean, balancing his western obligations—often administered from the northern Balkans, northern Italy, or the Rhine frontier—with his eastern ones. Before Constantine, emperors usually managed the eastern provinces from Antioch or other points along the way. They rarely visited long-secured provinces such as Africa or Egypt, although they depended on tax revenues from these provinces as the richest supports of empire. When western emperors lost African tax revenues in the fifth century after the capture of Carthage, their position became more precarious. Constantinople's last serious attempt to unite the empire ended with the reign of Valentinian III, a boy whom the Romans sent out to serve as a figurehead ruler in the 420s.

Constantinople's other great advantage was the de-imperialization, so to speak, of emperors. The word we use in English, "emperor," derives through French from the Latin *imperator*—loosely, "commander," the man endowed with the state power, the *imperium*. From Augustus to Theodosius, a few individuals who held the highest power were disinclined to the warlike arts and more at home in palaces than camps. Yet they were all in principle generals, and leaders of warlike men. Theodosius's sons, Arcadius in the east and Honorius in the west, learned to let others do their fighting for them, and emperors ever after imitated them as much as possible. Honorius was comfortable in the narrow splendor of Ravenna, but Arcadius made his home in the seven hills of the new Rome, and he also enjoyed other splendors. By Theodosius's time, that enthronement or, shall we say, empalacement of emperors had been in preparation for a century. Rulers from Diocletian's reign (284–305) forward surrounded themselves with more and more ceremonial encrustations and ever-larger palaces. Diocletian's retirement home was a vast palace complex in Salonae on the Dalmatian coast of what is now Croatia. His retinue of courtiers and slaves numbered in the thousands, all for a ruler who had already relinquished ultimate power.

Constantinople's rulers still saw the riches of worlds flow into their hands, and Constantinople grew and flourished in consequence. The supreme urban achievement in antiquity was the life of a parasite, drawing wealth from landholdings tilled by peasants or, for the courtier, from taxes. With few cities and many peasants, this model could last a surprisingly long time. Ancient cities, moreover, were created in ignorance and maintained in wasteful ostentation.

The city of Rome, for example, gained no special economic advantages in imperial times from its location.[3] Although it lay close by the naturally flourishing port city of Ostia a few miles away, it mainly grew and thrived by collecting taxes, while attracting the empire's richest landowners to live there as senators and citizens. The spectacular monuments of Roman greatness depend on coercing and seducing the outside wealth of its vast empire. As a vivid symbol of this dependence, witness the steady flow of grain ships across the Mediterranean year after year, feeding the populace of Rome on the produce of Africa. A tiny oligarchy like Rome and a vast peasantry like Africa can survive and go on that way for a long time.

So from the beginning Constantinople replicated the Roman model. Alexandria supplied much of Constantinople's grain—and Egypt was naturally rich enough to be able to spare the surplus. Two or three times a year, whole fleets of grain ships arrived, filling a seemingly endless stretch of wharves with urgently welcomed cargo. Water was a different story—it was piped in from fifty miles and more away in Thrace. City fathers followed the example of the first Rome in constructing aqueducts, with only a meager local water supply (no helpful Tiber here), and they could look for help only northward into Thrace. For 500,000 people, there was usually enough, but such dependency was still often a source of deep anxiety. (One innovative answer to the problem still greets visitors today. After the great riot of 532, Justinian took advantage of the subsequent urban renewal to build a huge underground cistern 460 feet long and 230 feet wide, its roof supported by 336 columns 26 feet high. A sixteenth-century Swiss traveler claimed credit for rediscovering it when residents had forgotten it was there. It still amazes tourists.)

There were other anxieties. Slaves, soldiers, and the poor were there in abundance, living in cheaply constructed buildings too close together, easy prey to fire. One count has noted seven major fires in Justinian's city, most notably after the great Nika uprising that defined the reign. There is no adequate count of the number of earthquakes Constantinople endured, including those severe enough to damage the greatest monuments.[4] An ancient city like this was a spectacle bought at a high price and trembled on the edge of disaster every moment. Eventually, as we shall see, the worst did come: the plague of the 540s.

This new Rome on the Bosporus had the great advantage of having been built from scratch. Old Rome had to undergo considerable urban renewal to shoehorn onto its central hills ostentatious new dwellings for its rulers, most notably the Golden House of Nero. But it was always crowded, and even the greatest houses were only a reflection of senators' spectacular rural villas. They built their best properties in Campania and down around the Bay of Naples, with others—including some astonishing displays of wealth—in Sicily and even Africa. Rome's wealth and power stemmed from those squires and gentlemen, short on talent but awash in abundance. What ability there was in the later empire went to the army and the court. Rome was very, very rich but could not be called a city with a future.

Constantinople, on the other hand, was all power and future. It was built for its rulers, and its rulers were men of that city: government officials, lawyers, bankers, careerists. Some heirs of great fortunes moved to town to pursue power, arriving as refugees from other cities and political events, both western and eastern. One sprig of the ancient Anicii of Rome, Olybrius, had ruled as emperor briefly in the west in 472 after Anthemius, with nominal support from Constantinople. He married Placidia, daughter of the emperor Valentinian III. Olybrius had a family tree that crossed and recrossed the house of Theodosius at several points. A detour through empire was a step down for him in some ways, so perhaps unsurprisingly it all came to naught. Ricimer and Odoacer were at that point the future in the west. In the next years, Olybrius's beautiful and extraordinarily wealthy daughter Anicia Juliana emerged in Constantinople as a woman to be reckoned with.

Juliana and her mother had never gone west during Olybrius's brief reign, when she was only about ten years old, or after, and so were entirely creatures of Constantinople. Juliana's beauty, ancestry, and connections were all to be envied. At one point the emperor Zeno offered her hand in marriage to Theoderic, accompanied with the promise of a substantial dowry, in order to persuade him to remain loyal to the eastern throne. She escaped that marriage but accepted another man of even greater promise, Areobindus.

Areobindus's family was not old, but of the first rank. His grandfather, Flavius Areobindus, had been consul in 434 and general in chief in Roman service from 434 to 449 and held the ultimate rank of patrician. His father, Dagalaiphus, was a consul in 467 and had married the daughter and granddaughter of other consuls, Aspar of 434 and Ardabur of 447. This would have been an absolutely stellar lineage in terms of power, except that the names were all of the wrong sort, stubbornly barbarian in flavor. Areobindus managed to smooth away these rough genealogical edges, however, by marrying Juliana, the premier heiress in Constantinople.

Portrait bust of Anicia Juliana.

Areobindus and Juliana begat between them a baby consul of their own, Flavius Anicius Olybrius, whose celebration they funded in 491. He went on to marry Eirene, the daughter of the emperor Anastasius. Areobindus took a modest part in military affairs, appearing as a general on the Persian front in 503–504, but soon ascended to the more comfortable dignity of consul in 506. We happen to have a copy of the ivory diptych—a two-leaved, hinged tablet—that memorialized his year. These exquisitely carved party favors were as elaborate as any later scrimshaw and typically showed the honoree in all his dignity. A foot or more high—the size that would now look good on a mantelpiece or coffee table—they were handed out to a few well-chosen recipients for each consular year and represented the acme of tasteful self-advertisement.

In a capital where the monarch was an emperor without an heir, no family was better positioned to face the future. But Areobindus and Juliana's son was a cipher and not taken seriously, so it fell to Areobindus himself to carry the family's hopes. Anastasius was too intelligent and effective an emperor to be popular, so when the monophysitism of his puppet patriarch Timothy outraged the people in 512, he saw his own statues thrown down in the streets and a flurry of insurrection. Courtiers promoting church orthodoxy, or at least their own futures, offered Areobindus the throne, but Areobindus fled in fear and the streets calmed down as Anastasius prevailed. We do not hear of Areobindus again, though Juliana remained rich and prominent, corresponding with Pope Hormisdas, to praise his loyalty to Chalcedon, around the time of the reunion of the churches in 519.

And she built a church—a vast construction, like nothing anyone had ever seen in any city of Christendom. Honoring the martyr Polyeuctos, it stood on a rise of ground along the main processional street of Constantinople that stretched west from the palace and then turned northwest through the heart of the city. Juliana planted her own church just past the turning, forcing it onto the most public stage set of empire in a central role, advertising her wealth and her piety equally. In the tenth century, the emperor Constantine Porphyrogenitus knew the church well and described the processions he took part in that went past the bakers' quarter, and how he paused by Polyeuctos's and Juliana's church to get a fresh candle to light his pious way to the church of the holy apostles at the top of the rise a little farther out on the main avenue. Juliana's church building collapsed in the twelfth century and was all but forgotten.

Roughly square in form with a domed central space, it measured about 175 feet on a side—approximately the size of Saint Patrick's Cathedral on Fifth Avenue or Saint Bartholomew's on Park Avenue in New York. The dimensions of the building are important, because they closely match those of Solomon's temple in Jerusalem as reported in the Christian Bible.[5]

Juliana's pride and piety echo for us in the text of a forty-one-line inscription that ran around the basilica's central space and glorified both the builder and her aims. Fragments of that inscription, which were long known from manuscript copies taken down by an admirer, made it possible to identify the remains of her church when excavators found them during an urban construction project in 1960. The great inscription ran around the church in letters four inches high, a line each on a series of arches, surrounded by elaborate vine leaves and each arch itself filled with an ornate, elaborate carved peacock's tail; several of those arches, each about nine feet across, survive. The inscription begins:

> Eudocia the empress, eager to give honor to God, first built a temple of Polyeuctos the servant of God: but not one like this, not one so huge. It was not that she was ungenerous or lacking in wealth—what can a queen lack?—but she was endowed with a prophetic spirit, to know she would leave offspring who would know well how to fit it out better.

It showed no impiety to outdo one's ancestors in this manner, especially while outdoing one's contemporaries to advance the family name.

> From among them Juliana, shining light of God-blessed parents, fourth in the line of that royal blood, did not belie the hopes of the queen who left such splendid children. She raised up a small temple to the great and glorious one here, augmenting the glory of her many-sceptered forebears, bearing the orthodox faith of a zealous lover of Christ. Who hasn't heard of Juliana, how she made her parents glorious by her well-made works, pious as she was?

By the time this church was built, of course, no one could fail to know the name. And not only in Constantinople:

You alone built countless churches in every land, ever fearing the servants of the God of the sky.

The apse arching over the altar was decorated with human figures on a gold background, and there were mosaics and sculpture everywhere, including busts of Christ, the Virgin, and the apostles. Later in the sixth century, the bishop of Tours in Gaul, Gregory, wrote in one of his histories how Justinian envied Juliana's riches and her gold, so she promised him that he could take what he liked—but then she had it melted down to decorate her church before he could take possession and he was too embarrassed to complain. She gave him a small ring as consolation. Although Justinian eventually built bigger churches, the sting of the snub lingered.

Building well was Juliana's best revenge for her husband's downfall.

Portrait of Anicia Juliana from the Dioscorides manuscript.

For ten years, Polyeuctos's church was the biggest and best ever seen, and Juliana died in 528 before she saw her church outstripped in grandeur. When she died, her eunuchs left Constantinople to become monks at the monastery of Saint Sabas in Jerusalem, a notorious hotbed of her Chalcedonian religious views.

Juliana herself is memorialized and pictured in one of the most dazzling surviving late antique manuscript books, the *Materia Medica* of Dioscorides, in a copy now in Vienna, written for and dedicated to Juliana as patron. This lavish book is a copy of the handbook of drugs and remedies that Dioscorides—an intrepid traveler in the Greek world—originally wrote around 65 CE. Nearly 400 color illustrations show us plants in loving detail, each one facing a page of text describing its medical powers,

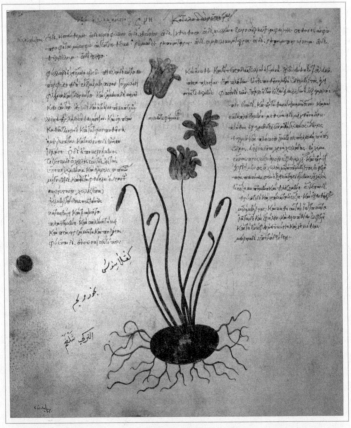

Illustration of a medicinal plant (the sow cyclamen) in the Vienna Dioscorides.

with the original material from Dioscorides supplemented, rearranged, and revised. An illustrated handbook of Mediterranean birds is also included. *Materia Medica* was still in Constantinople when the city fell to the Turks in 1453 and eventually came into the possession of Suleiman the Magnificent's Jewish physician. Emperor Maximilian II purchased it at a vast price and brought it to his library in Vienna, where the book remains to this day, having resided for 1,500 years in only the two imperial cities.

Four years after Juliana died, Justinian accused her son Olybrius of plotting against him and sent him into exile, confiscating his wealth. Although he was eventually restored to favor, Olybrius vanishes from history. A son or nephew, another Areobindus, married Justinian's niece Praeiecta and went out to fight the Moors in Africa in the 540s, a decade after Justinian thought he had successfully recaptured that province. This Areobindus played a double game in Africa, recruiting and then betraying different Moorish leaders. Seeking refuge in the bishop's monastery in Carthage, he was received with all state and assured of his safety, then murdered in his bed there the same night. That is the last trace of the family except for the church Juliana built.

The city was full of churches, and getting fuller. In the mid-fifth century, near the head of the Golden Horn and thus outside the original Constantinian city, a church dedicated to the Virgin had been built at Blachernae. During the reign of Emperor Leo I (457–474), it was privileged to become the place of repose for an astonishing relic, the robe of the Virgin herself, and so by about 500 the court had built there a subsidiary palace for emperors and their families. Such a gesture is religious in many ways, not least for the statement it made about the Virgin's lofty dignity in a period when, as we have seen, some people thought her a mere woman and unworthy of the title "God's mother."[6] On the way out to this palace, the church of the Apostles that Justinian built in 550 became the resting place for emperors and a regular site of suitably deferential worship of them: Theodora and then Justinian would both come to lie there—Justinian's funeral being the occasion of a vast congregation along the main street and the subject of part of an epic poem in honor of Justin II.

There were few like Juliana in Constantinople. At Rome, such wealth and ostentation had once been commonplace, and the dwindling senate there acted as if traditional wealth and the privilege of wealth were still in the ascendancy. Constantinople had no such vast fortunes. Gradually the city's economic position would bring commerce to supplement what empire could do, but until the final collapse of the Ottomans after World War I, this was a city of empire—or rather, a theme park of empire, a place where parts were played, opportunities were seized, and privilege was exercised quite independently of merit. The circus and its factions, the palace with its eunuchs, the churches and their zealot monks and pillar sitters were all part of a never-ending Vanity Fair, a spectacle that enraptured visitors then and enraptures scholars now.

The center of the city stood along the ridge of land that seamen saw as they came up the Sea of Marmara, just before they rounded the Golden Horn to anchorage: the circus, the palace, and the church all appeared there. If the circus had fired the passions of the Romans, it was the center of urban life here at Constantinople. The Reds, the Whites, the Blues, and the Greens were the teams here as well, and the Blues and the Greens dominated, their rivalry driving race fans to frenzy. In the best of times, the government paid slightly nervous attention to the factions rather in the way British authorities keep a weather eye on soccer thugs. Racing was mainly a harmless sport, but when it sent mobs into the streets, it could begin to look political. Patrons poured money into the circus largely to protect themselves from its mobs, and that in turn reinforced the need for protection. The business of the factions was applause, but they could also withhold it.

Six times a day (we know from one surviving program found on papyrus in Egypt) the chariots would race, starting with a ceremonial parade. During the time between races, entertainers diverted the crowd with animal acts, mimes, athletes, and, apparently, singing rope dancers.

In the great cities—not just Rome and Constantinople, but at least Antioch, Sirmium, Milan, and Trier—the construction of the circus next to the palace emphasized its importance, with an official imperial box, the *kathisma*, presiding over all. The emperor could come and go discreetly from the palace to the box and back again, and was as reasonably well protected there from the enthusiasm of the factions and fans as architecture and guards could make him.

But at the circus the emperor had to face and deal with his public . He infrequently appeared in public in ceremonial processions, or more often at church, but in the circus he had to both listen and speak. We have the transcript of one wild day when the Greens pleaded for redress of a grievance, accusing a courtier of corrupt influence, and intervening with the herald who spoke for the emperor:

GREENS: It is Calopodius the spatharius [a military rank] who wrongs me, Lord of all.

HERALD: Calopodius is innocent.

G. If he is not, he will share the fate of Judas. God will requite him swiftly for my wrongs.

H. You come, not to watch the games, but to insult your masters.

G. If anyone wrongs me, he will share the fate of Judas.

H. Be silent, Jews, Manicheans, and Samaritans!

G. Do you insult us with the name of Jews and Samaritans? The Mother of God is with us all!

H. How long will you go on bringing down curses on your own head? [At this point the Greens shout and chant under the direction of their leader Antlas.]

G. If anyone denies that our Lord the emperor is orthodox, let him be anathema as Judas.[7]

This easy recourse to abuse based on religion is absolutely typical of the time. With dialogues like this, expectations inevitably rose, and there was an ugly scene in the late sixth century when a mob rebuked a new arrival on the imperial throne, Phocas, for not observing proper ceremonial procedure. "Maurice [your overthrown predecessor] is still alive to teach you [the ceremonies]," they cried, and so Maurice was dead by the next day, on his successor's orders. Eventually the emperors realized that they could make a virtue of necessity by subsidizing and bureaucratizing the factions, and by the seventh century the circus had been tempered to a pale, tamed, ceremonial irrelevance.

In their day the factions could almost unmake an emperor. Anastasius mainly stood above the factions and their enthusiasms, and so was often accused of religious innovation—for mobs like this are deeply conservative in spirit. Justinian surprised many by patronizing the Blues with unusual enthusiasm but found them a troubling handful. Justinian was a man of alternating extremes, and so went from generosity to oppressiveness with his favorites.

And so in 532, when he ordered the execution of two criminals prominent in the factions—one Blue and one Green—he poked the hornet's nest once too often. When the scaffold for their public killing broke under the feet of the condemned men, the mob took it as a sign of the merciful will of God, but Justinian would have none of that. He insisted that the execution proceed. Putting every vacillating foot wrong, the emperor postured and yielded, yielded and postured, and in a few days the city was on fire. "*Nika!*" ("Victory!") cried the mob in the street, and for a time the throne was threatened. We have no real idea what went through Justinian's mind, but all historians have to tell the story of his despair and the way his wife, the (reputedly diminutive) empress Theodora, plucked up his courage with a cry too good to omit and also too good to be true: "An empire makes a fine burial shroud!" And so (the story went) Justinian stuck it out. He may not have had much choice.

Eventually, the mob brought two nephews of the emperor Anastasius—Hypatius and Pompey—to the circus to acclaim them as emperors. Justinian had to respond to such overt provocation and sent troops into the circus to do their worst. One modern reader suspects (for suspicion is always the order of the day in Justinian's Constantinople) collusion between the emperor and one of the apparent pretenders. Justinian intended to crack down on him and then take public credit for showing mercy. In the end, General Belisarius took things in hand, restoring peace by way of massacre; it is said that 30,000 people were killed in the hippodrome that day. In an enclosed space thronged with defenseless people, the number is not impossible.

Ever after, Justinian would be known as the emperor who had not hesitated to kill. Just as the regime of Hafez al-Assad in Syria was known for the day he chose to massacre his enemies in Hama, so Justinian was known, among his many other excellences, as a cold-blooded murderer—or rather, as the master of murderers. Such a reputation has its uses.

On the far side of the palace from the circus stood the church, the other place where the people regularly saw their emperor. Constantinople's earliest decades saw a series of churches built on that site, churches devoted to "holy wisdom"—in Greek *hagia sophia*—a name already intimating that the builders had Solomon's fabled wisdom in mind and that Solomon's temple was their model.

The church that Justinian found on his accession did not survive: during the Nika riot it went down in flames.

Once back in control after the riot, Justinian saw his opportunity, and he raised up a new church, the one that still stands there. If he envied Anicia Juliana her great church of a decade earlier, now was his chance. The new Hagia Sophia was half again as large as Juliana's building. Hers had the artistry of decoration; his had imperial pomp. From its completion in 537, Hagia Sophia has defined the city of Constantinople (now Istanbul) by its massive presence on the central point of the central ridge.

Hagia Sophia never charmed anyone. It shouts at the viewer, roughs him up, and leaves him stunned and inarticulate. From the outside, it is a heavy, graceless pile, despite the addition of graceful Ottoman minarets. Mehmet the Conqueror made it a mosque, and then the modernizing Turks of the twentieth century made it a museum, though some of the devout now grumble at the loss of a visible sign of Muslim triumph. (The Ottoman Blue Mosque a few hundred yards away offers a space to rival Justinian's, a space where even a pope has now whispered words of prayer. It stands on foundations remaining from Justinian's palace.) The architecture of the dome of Hagia Sophia took risks never taken before to achieve an interior space of magnificence if not subtlety. The dome dazzled on-

Justinian's Hagia Sophia.

lookers with its height, its expanse, and the mosaics that adorned it. If it collapsed repeatedly in later years, that only proved the risks were worth taking. "I've outdone you, Solomon!" cried Justinian when he entered the finished building, a claim all the more adolescent and pathetic for being literally true.

The reconstructions (beginning in Justinian's lifetime) confirm the church's iconic status, triumphing over itself at the center of the city's imaginary life. Paul the Silentiary[8] celebrated the church's reopening in 563 after the first collapse in a poem that captures pitch-perfect the song of Justinian's Constantinople: "Justinian is the one who vanquishes the poisons of disease and conspiracy in his city and extends his reign to the ends of the earth. In the great church, Justinian outstrips Rome," he says, "the way God outstrips an idol: the old Capitol saw nothing like this."

When the dome collapsed, Paul tells us, clouds of dust darkened the day, the earth shook, but Christ protected his church and no one was killed: there was no defiling death in the holy place. In the poem, the city of Rome personified as a great woman appears to Justinian to exhort him, and he comforts her in return. The church reopened at the Christmas season to the eyes of the faithful.

Paul goes on to give us our best sixth-century description of the church: the supporting subdomes, then the dome of domes. With a connoisseur's eye, he inventories the colors of all the marbles, the special green from Thessaly, the famous white from the great quarries at Proconnesus in the Sea of Marmara, and many others, from every direction under Justinian's sway. Silver had been brought from all over as well to create four columns for the canopy over the altar. Above and over all, the great mosaic of Christ covered the dome, with Peter on one side and Paul on the other. At night, dazzling illumination flashed forth, with lamps hanging down on chains vast distances from the ceiling, poised at the right height to make the illusion of day. Within that space 60 priests, 100 deacons, 90 subdeacons, 110 readers, 25 singers, and a retinue of 100 doorkeepers brought the building and its services to life.

The great church must be imagined in the fullness of its life, with all the staff and clergy shepherding throngs of people into a space where they were doubly intimidated by architecture and ritual, then keeping them carefully in their places. The processions and hymns in the church occasionally erupted into the streets outside, as when late in the sixth century the emperor Maurice instituted an annual procession of thanks for a victory over the Persians that took a huge retinue through all the city out to the Virgin's church at Blachernae.

The church was often not merely visually but also musically dazzling. Romanos the Melodist came from Syria in the days of Anastasius and flourished as poet of the imperial liturgy until his death sometime after 555. His dozens of surviving hymns speak in great detail to the celebrations of the annual liturgical calendar, turning a saint's day or a church holiday into song with the urgent relevance of modern hip-hop, but with a serene and stately air. Thus Mary addresses the newborn Jesus in prayer:

> *Accept my child, a trinity of gifts,*
> *grant her who bore you three requests:*
> *I pray to you for the seasons*
> *and for the fruits of the earth*
> *and for those who dwell in it.*
> *Be reconciled to all,*
> *Because through me you have been born.*[9]

The pious astonishment of that space lasted 1,000 years, during which emperors of Constantinople would pose, pray, and be enthroned there. The people of the city waited on the emperor's pleasure in the circus, while its god and its clergy greeted him in the church. Some scholars used to call Constantinople's peculiar theocracy Caesaropapism, but the word overstates the fact. Patriarchs sometimes led emperors, emperors often dictated to patriarchs, and they were sometimes at loggerheads, but the sheer physical drama surrounding the divinely approved ruler every time he set foot in this space said more than any doctrinal definition could about the alignment of powers in the city and the empire. Nothing the Ottomans could do with the space quite made it live in the same way.

Between the two great spaces for public display, circus and church, was the emperor's palace: the real heart of the city, the real showplace.

Rome never had room for the likes of this palace. It was far easier to build in the purpose-made imperial city than to try to squeeze such imperial pomp into the historic precincts of the ancient town that had outgrown itself long before. Constantinople and its palace were built from the ground up by people who understood what it was to have an empire to call your own. The palace was the centerpiece of that political statement, and therefore the seed of the eventual failure of the enterprise it embodied. It gave a forbidding appearance to the city and was the home of deep mysteries. It's unlikely that any emperor who ever lived there saw all of its ramifications, dependencies, back rooms, and secret chambers.

The best approach to the palace was from the west, on foot. The great middle street of the city drew together those who arrived from different gates, leading them southeast to city center. The street became a ceremonial stage in its own right, with porticoes on both sides, regularly occupied by successful merchants and professionals. The more pompous and grander Forum of Theodosius came first as you approached; then, closer to the palace, came the older and less overbearing forum of Constantine. Beyond that, the last stretch of the now grand, formal main boulevard entered the Augustaion, the last open square between the circus and the church, where in 543 Justinian would have a huge statue of himself erected on a lofty column, displaying the full military prowess he claimed probably without spending a day of real soldiering in his life. It lasted there until the sultan Suleiman the Magnificent tore it down in the sixteenth century.

From the Augustaion, the highly privileged entered the palace proper through the great bronze gate called the Chalke, where Justinian had covered the ceiling under the arches with mosaics displaying his great vicarious military triumphs (his general Belisarius actually won them for him) over the Vandals first and then eventually the Goths. Nothing was quite permanent in such a place and there was always elaboration, development, redecoration, and the perfecting anew of the proper temple for the residence and veneration of the current ruler.

The rest of the complex cascaded out behind the great gate, sprawling down the hill to the water. Great halls with triple doors and antechambers lay hidden within high walls. In imperial audience rooms, a raised platform stood at the end of the hall, to be approached through an elaborate twisting and turning of corridors, curtained alcoves, and inlaid floor patterns that guided the subject or guest to the emperor's seat. Visitors saw consistories, or meeting halls; and triclinia, or banquet rooms. The greatest of these, the Triclinium of the Nineteen Couches, held 228 guests, but this proved too vast for certain kinds of private splendor, so later in the sixth century the emperor Justin II added the Golden Banquet Hall, octagonal in shape, domed above, with room for a mere 102 select guests in an even more opulent setting. Elaborate mosaics, their tiny tiles carefully pieced together and cemented in place by hand in dazzling patterns, were the decoration of choice, in enormous variety. Mosaic scenes included a tiger hunt, a bear devouring a young stag, a bear chasing a young man, a fight between an elephant and a lion, an eagle biting a snake, a boy feeding his donkey, a monkey attempting to dislodge a bird from a tree, the mythical hero Bellerophon fighting the Chimera, the head of a young man with a bear, the head of a mustachioed youth amid foliage, and a mock chariot race in the Hippodrome with four drivers.[10] Neither the wizard of Oz nor the builders of Caesars Palace in Las Vegas could outdo what the emperor of Constantinople had already mastered to perfection.

The court was now the home of all power. Rome had come full circle and Tacitus was now wrong, for emperors could scarcely be imagined, much less made, anywhere other than in the capital and indeed in the palace. If the emperor set foot outside his palace in the city, it was only for ceremonial and usually religious reasons. From time to time, he might flee the city for another palace at Chalcedon, in sight across the Bosporus, but if he did so he left by water from within the palace grounds, without having to pass through the crowded city streets.

The palace was the place for the wearer of the purple. The technology of ancient dye making had advanced to a point where moderns could envy it. In the days of the republic, Rome had allowed purple or purple-edged garments as a sign of public office and success. From what we know of the dyes involved and from surviving representations in art, the hue was probably closer to that seen on Roman cardinals today than to our Newtonian sense of purple as an equal mix of blue and red. Under the early empire, fashion took over and the color became more common among the rich, and eventually Roman men overcame their disdain for effeminate silk and turned out in fine, glowing fabrics. The greatest dye works were at Tyre in the eastern Mediterranean, where sea creatures were harvested for their durable coloring. The emperor Diocletian took over the works as an imperial possession; his introduction of eastern ways into his court included the creation of a new wardrobe of purple silk to replace the former sturdy, sensible wool. Within a century, only the emperor could wear the special color; anyone else who wore it was guilty of treason. During the fifth and sixth centuries, increasingly agitated emperors legislated ineffectually against such encroachment. One way Theoderic showed himself imperial in demeanor was by wearing purple silk (acquired from a western source), while banning it for all others in his realm.

Deep inside the palace were the private quarters, the bedchamber or *cubiculum* of the emperor and a separate one for the empress—each, of course, a suite of rooms rather than a single chamber. Other officials had their own accommodations, but were rarely allowed to reside in the palace. Each *cubiculum* had its own staff, even its own kitchen, and only the eunuchs, guards, domestic servants, men of medicine, and clerics or monks of great holiness or influence could venture within these most remote precincts.

Bringing emperors back from the frontier and walling them up in a palace gave empresses new opportunities to act like and be seen as serious participants in the imperial drama and ritual. The empress had her own staff and budget and provided many supplicants with access to the throne that they could not achieve any other way. The *Augusta* was often a vehicle of continuity, for a widow or daughter could bring fresh male energy into the imperial house through the convenience of marriage. (If the widow had been married young to a considerably older emperor, as often happened, her influence could long outlast the original marriage contract.) In the fifth and sixth centuries alone, seven of the empresses of the rank of *Augusta* were themselves the daughters of emperors. Although Justinian's Theodora gets all the press, by their standard she was a nobody from nowhere, the exception rather than the rule.

Eunuchs gave the palace at Constantinople a special atmosphere.[11] They were men who had been sexually damaged by disease, accident, or deliberate mutilation. Mutilation, as horrible as it sounds, was not always or only conscious cruelty, inasmuch as eunuchry was a path to power and safety for the marginal or the vulnerable. One source speaks of the Abasgi outside Roman territory at the eastern end of the Black Sea (modern Abkhazia retains the name), whose king sold boys for castration and killed their parents. If the fatality rate on these castrations was about ninety-five percent, few cared, and the survivors might feel themselves lucky in many ways.

So normal a part of the landscape did the eunuchs seem, and so easily was their involuntary sexual isolation compared with religiously approved abstinence, that in later times when exegetes read of the service of the prophet Daniel at Nebuchadnezzar's court, they naturally assumed—

meaning it as a respectful interpretation—that he must have been a eunuch too. On a higher level, the angels and their sexlessness gave sexless males below a kind of respectability. The general Narses, who replaced Belisarius and finally brought grim peace to Italy for Justinian, was a eunuch. By the eighth century, a eunuch could even rise to the patriarchal throne in Constantinople.

At the pinnacle of the household was the grand chamberlain, always a eunuch and thus supposedly without family interest to corrupt his service, responsible for every aspect of management and control. He supervised the silentiaries with their golden wands, who offered discreet guidance and control to ensure that all would be orderly and impressive, and whose influence could thus incidentally mean a great deal. (On retirement they were normally admitted to the senate.)

Ceremony proliferated in the court like kudzu on a Mississippi roadside, and with ceremony came the writing down of rules and procedures. The making of ceremonial books reached its high point with Constantine Porphyrogenitus[12] in the tenth century, when the emperor himself made sure that the records and rites were properly recorded, at immense length. Books like that give us a window to see into the palace at its most brilliant.

On a day of ceremony, the great hall of audience was slowly and quietly filled with the highest dignitaries, who would stand by the emperor. At the appropriate moment, a curtain would rise and a flush of tension would run through the hall as the emperor was seen on his throne, itself on a raised platform, protected by a golden canopy. The master of ceremonies then called the names of the visitors for that day, beginning with the humblest (though none who could make it this far were very humble), and they came in one at a time, throwing themselves on the floor in a rite that all knowing judges recognized as having come from the east. (The Persians, it was widely known, knew how to do these things.) As the silentiaries watched carefully and gestured discreetly, the last and highest-ranking guests would enter and, if specially favored, would be allowed not merely to prostrate themselves but even to bestow a kiss on the imperial slipper.

A proclamation might follow, or the welcoming of an ambassador. At the end, the emperor would rise and leave, and then the dignitaries would leave, now led by the highest-ranking of them. For some, this was routine; for others, it was a thrilling opportunity; but for all it was a clear reaffirmation and declaration of the power of the throne and a definition of the positions of those who came within that space or were kept outside.

In Justinian's time, the entire ceremony was conducted in Latin, but this most Roman of Roman habits was starting to change. Constantinople's rise had gradually allowed Greek to claim equal rights as a legal language in the fourth and fifth centuries. The law codes Justinian created were all in Latin, but he began to issue later laws more and more often in Greek. His successor Tiberius II in the 570s would be spoken of as the first Greek emperor; and by the 580s the man about to become Pope Gregory I noticed that it was becoming harder to find anyone in Constantinople who could translate Greek into Latin.

GAINING THE THRONE

Such was Justinian's Constantinople, the city present in all its possibilities in 527 as he took the throne, but I have gotten a bit ahead of myself. Who was Justinian, and how did he get here?

He was Petrus Sabbatius by birth, taking the name Justinian to declare how closely he followed his uncle Justin's coattails. Legend would have it that Justin and two companions, Zimarchus and Dityvistus, came down out of the Macedonian hills with nothing in their knapsacks but *paximadia*, the twice-baked bread that wouldn't go stale, which within living memory was still the food of shepherds in Crete and beggars in Greece. These were ordinary men out for adventure. They found it in Constantinople.

Justin advanced in the elite corps of 300 palace guards called the excubitors, moving up to the senior rank of count in that service. It was a considerable office, purely military—if there is anything purely military about guarding a monarch. We think he was well on in middle age, around sixty-five, when the emperor Anastasius, after twenty-seven years on the throne, died at age eighty-eight in 518. Five hundred years later, another emperor, Constantine Porphyrogenitus, told the story of what followed in meticulous detail.[13]

When the chamberlains and courtiers allowed Anastasius's death to be announced, the master of offices, Celer (also from the Balkans), and the count Justin were called in, each going back shortly afterward to consult with others—Celer with the civil bureaucracy, Justin with the excubitors. The next morning, the leading citizens (in principle, the senate, but in practice an ad hoc group of potentates) arrived variously dressed, some in gray for dignity, others in the many colors of court style. They heard cheering from the circus, where a throng awaited the news of a new emperor the way people now fill Saint Peter's Square to wait for a new pope. The secular and religious dignitaries were seated in chairs placed for them in the portico outside the great banqueting hall near where the public and private sections of the palace met.

There a bitter argument began. The aptly named Celer ("Swifty") argued that if the inner-circle courtiers were to retain the initiative, a quick decision must be made. Meanwhile, events marched ahead outside. In the circus, the excubitors acclaimed a tribune named John as their candidate and lifted him on their shields. But the Blues would not accept this and began throwing rocks to break up the crowd. Some of the excubitors responded with bows and arrows and killed a few of the Blues. Another body of guards, the *scholares*, seized a patrician who was serving in military office (we don't know who this was) and hauled him off to the great triclinium to propose him for coronation. But the excubitors angrily rushed to the scene, dragging the candidate off in great peril of immediate death. Just then Justinian, still not a most senior figure, intervened to rescue the patrician and have him taken away in protective custody. A ripple of enthusiasm for acclaiming Justinian went through the excubitors, but he would have none of it.

All the while, a mob clamored at the ivory doors of the palace itself, demanding that the chamberlains release the imperial regalia to them so they could enthrone an emperor, but the courtiers within kept stony silence. Eventually Justin's name came to the fore, for reasons that later gave rise to speculation. The historian John Malalas, writing later in the sixth century, reports that one of the senior chamberlains resisting the mob's demands gave money to Justin for his troops in order to buy their support for a candidate named Theocritus. But Justin put the bribe to a more personal use, and the troops chose him instead. This matches a story from another sixth-century historian, the count Marcellinus, that Theocritus and his patron Amantius were put to death (Marcellinus gives no explanation) very early in Justin's reign. Justin was a known quantity, of mature years, who could control the troops at this critical moment— letting them bluster enough to make people fear revolt, then showing them deftly pulled to heel.

Justin was acclaimed in a raucous scene—the new emperor came away with a split lip from a scuffle with the *scholares*—and was carried off to the circus with the enthusiastic support of the senate, the soldiers, and the circus factions. The Blues and Greens acclaimed him, and the chamberlains finally relented and sent out the regalia. Justin entered the royal box, along with the patriarch and the other most prominent men of the city. He was lifted on a shield and received the heavy necklace from the hand of Godila, an officer of the lancers. All around, military units lifted their standards from the ground and brandished them in salute, shouting and clashing their weapons impressively.

At this point custom would have had Justin go in to the triclinium again to be robed, but instead the soldiers surrounded him with a barrier of shields for modesty's sake, and within that protection he donned the imperial clothing. Then the bishop crowned him, he took up the lance and shield, and he ascended to the most visible place in the imperial box, where all could see him. "Justin Augustus, may you conquer!"[14] the crowd cried on all sides. He was handed the pages of his official speech and passed it on to officials who would read it aloud for the public to hear:

Justin: By the decree of almighty God and by your choice and common election and support we take up the supreme authority and call upon divine providence for aid.

The crowd acclaims: May the world be rich in good things! As you have lived, so may you rule! May civil government be rich in good things! Heavenly king, preserve the earthly one! Justinus Augustus, may you conquer! May the years of this younger Constantine be many! We are the slaves of the emperor!

Justin: May your kindness give us strength to accomplish all that you and the republic need.

They exclaim: Son of God, have mercy on him! You chose him, therefore have mercy on him! Justinus Augustus, may you conquer!

Justin: For it is our concern, a thing close to our heart, with the help of divine providence, that we bring you to enjoy every prosperity, and that we preserve each one of you with every kindness and concern and gesture of the most tender love to rest in peace and freedom from care.

They all acclaim: Worthy of the kingship, worthy of the trinity, worthy
of the city! May the emperor have many years! Give us pure and
wise rulers for the world!

Justin: For this birthday of our happy reign, we will give to you five
nummi and one pound of silver.

They acclaim: May God preserve the Christian emperor! These are
the prayers of the whole world!

Justin: God be with you.

And so the deed was done. Power had passed securely (as hindsight
would confirm), but grumbling remained. One distinguished citizen,
briefly holding office under Justin in 519 but not thought to be a partisan
of his, made sure that the emperor's undistinguished youth was remembered by having the story of his origins and then his impoverished arrival
in Constantinople depicted on the walls of a public bath there.

None of this mattered. Justin had security for his legacy in the form of
his two nephews. Germanus remained in relative obscurity with the army
in Thrace, but the other was the emperor-to-be, Justinian. He immediately attained the rank of count, then shortly after replaced Vitalian as
general in charge of the guard and court and entered upon the consulship.
By the time Justinian stepped down as consul at the end of 520, Vitalian
had been carefully murdered, as we saw.

Justin had the signal luck to follow Anastasius, the best financial manager the throne had seen in many years. The currency had been stabilized
with the circulation of large copper coins, which both offered liquidity
to facilitate commerce and at the same time enriched the treasury. (The
Roman emperor's reforms imitated, on a smaller scale, what the supposedly barbarian governments in Africa and Italy had already done.) Anastasius spent money wisely on public works and defense, such as the frontier
outpost of Daraa facing the Persians. He had managed expenditures well
and offered tax relief. With an expanded, effective staff of tax collectors,
he died with 300,000 pounds of gold in the treasury, a blessing that Justin
and Justinian would squander relentlessly away.

Justin remained on the throne for almost nine years, but he was neither
young nor forceful nor well connected nor well educated. The younger
and evidently ambitious Justinian was reasonably assumed to hold the

real power. He used the time of his uncle's reign to consolidate his own power, to learn the ways of court and capital, and to prepare for his own ascendancy. (He made sure, for example, that his unfashionably lowborn spouse, Theodora, would be accepted as empress when his time came, and she too was ready for power.) He was about forty-five when the time came.

The way forward was clear when Justin died in 527.

NEW STATESMEN

The Roman empire had once been dominated by aristocratic families, then later by soldiers. In Justinian's empire, priests and bureaucrats came to the fore. They drew their authority not from ancestry or from prowess, but from books they had mastered, books from which the rules of life could be extracted. Late antiquity's most lasting contribution to western societies was its invention of the culture dominated by books and their interpreters, whether religious or legal. We have already seen the written word organized afresh to shape power in the hands of Rome's bishops, whose claims to papal authority seemed familiar, and even natural, to later generations. To seize the collective imagination, Christianities of every stripe had already used scriptural texts and then the clustering of scriptural texts that we have come to call Bibles.

Roman law tells another story of the power of the written word. In its most archaic form, Rome knew the laws of the Twelve Tables, written down around 450 BCE and still taught to schoolchildren, such as Cicero, who represented the elders he knew as holding up that short text as the key to all legal knowledge. There were legal texts of many kinds in all eras of the late republic and then the empire, and mastery of the techniques those texts depended on was a critical tool for establishing legal authority. That said, legal authority was itself a subsidiary craft in a mainly authoritarian society, a skill the rich drew on in order to protect their claims, but not one they themselves needed to possess. For much of the first centuries of empire, one might expect the legal text to rank second in importance to the judge's goodwill, especially that of the supreme judge, the emperor himself.

Emperors made law their own through the written word. In a wide variety of ways, they controlled the legal destiny of empire, but through remarkably fragile and evanescent instruments. Most of the laws of the Roman empire that later generations depended on were not carefully crafted proclamations, with every contingency considered and a precise ritual of promulgation that made them part of a whole society's legal consciousness. At their worst, they were more like letters from on high. Citizens would write to the emperor protesting over grievances, and the emperor would reply—in a letter, often called a rescript, in which he connected the request to what his staff could tell him of legal principle and practice. Then he adjudicated the case as best he could with the information he had. That letter would be sent back to the people who requested it, and copies would be kept in the imperial archives. Who else might know of that text was highly variable. Well-informed legal scholars in major cities would stay in touch with the emperor's written effusions, but at the geographical extremes of empire even the most privileged men could be quite badly informed. The rule of law had as much weight as it could in a world where any given reader rarely had access to all the laws that might exist.

The defects of such a legal system were widely felt, but only very slowly ameliorated. The first great age of Roman jurisprudence coincided with the bureaucratic development of the empire under the Severan emperors, and came on the brink of an age of disorder and disarray in the third century. The product of this age lay in the work of authoritative canonical jurists, men such as Gaius and Papinian, whose words could be consulted and quoted as long as Roman law held sway. They offered not the actual texts of laws, but digested interpretations and sets of principles for the practical application of, for example, property, torts, and criminal procedure. As indispensable as these works were, they were not themselves the law, and the production of law and the disruption of precedent by living emperors continued.

Between that age and Justinian, a great change came over the Roman world: a change of scale. We have seen how under Diocletian and his successors, the number of government employees grew tenfold, although the empire had added no new territory and had experienced only modest population growth. With the reorganization of the western provinces under new management in the fifth century, the absolute number of people who can be described as government employees of the Roman empire declined somewhat, but over comparable spans of territory in the east, it grew and grew and grew.

Such growth meant that central government could know local affairs, and thus meddle in them, with much greater accuracy and timeliness than ever before. It was possible for the first time not only to imagine but to achieve a consistency of legal authority and practice that had so far eluded every western state. (China's story has parallels to Rome's, and in 587 CE we first hear of the so-called civil service examination system that produced centuries of text-mastering bureaucrats for a long series of imperial dynasties.)

Under the newly intrusive, managerial empire, there had been ambitious attempts at codifying the existing laws. By the early fourth century, two individual jurists, Gregorius and Hermogenes, had put together immense books in the newfangled codex format that Christians favored (bound pages, not an unrolling scroll), in which they gathered what they could find of Roman law and arranged it by topic. The resultant books were expensive and difficult to obtain and copy correctly, but they were as popular among the legally aware as one could imagine. They were reference books, however, not authoritative publications. The imperfections of those codes sharply limited their ability to transform practice, until finally in 438 an emperor, Theodosius II, created the law book that bears his name: the Theodosian Code.

Modest in ambition, it collected and arranged known imperial laws in something like a logical and useful order. The laws in this code preserve for the most part the signs of their creation—often the exact date of promulgation, often enough the place where the particular copy incorporated in the code was published, and enough of the original details of composition to make many of them valuable historical sources for the events of the fourth century and early fifth century.[15] The Theodosian Code was less successful in doing the intellectual work of rationalization. There are exceptions, but far too often, if two different emperors said conflicting things about the same subject, their edicts still find themselves side by side in the law book.

Justinian had grander dreams. He took the project of codification to a logically higher level and produced three mighty works of law whose usefulness remains to this day. If we praise his achievement, we must remember that it also meant a relocation of authority—away from men and into texts, away from the place where people quarreled with each other and off to the emperor in his court, all mediated by lawyers.

The most famous of codifiers, Tribonian the quaestor, rightly deserves to have his name enshrined in the histories of law. In the 530s, just a few years after Justinian's accession, Tribonian and his colleagues succeeded not only in bringing together the texts of Roman law in greater completeness and accuracy than ever before, but also in doing the hard work of making useful sense out of them.

The first step was compiling the Code of Justinian. Carried out on an unprecedentedly ambitious scale, this collection and arrangement of the laws stripped away a certain amount of the original context of dates and addressees, making itself more timeless, less historically rich, than the Theodosian Code. Tribonian paid more attention to the completeness, consistency, and accuracy of his collection than had ever been possible before. Supplemented on a regular basis, for as long as the initiative of Justinian retained its force in the sixth century, by the *Novellae constitutiones* ("New Constitutions," usually called, misleadingly in English, the *Novels*) of Justinian and his immediate successors, this enterprise presented the sum of Roman law. Its reproduction in official copies sent to the main cities of the empire made law more transparent and effective than ever before—and thus strengthened the hand of central authority.

To the code, or *Codex*, already finished in 529, Justinian's men added essential further tools. They made a synthetic interpretation and summary of all the individual laws in the codes in the form of a work called the *Digest*. This was the most ambitious and extensive direct statement of the content of Roman law ever produced. Ostensibly only a restatement and summary, the *Digest*, like the *Codex*, effectively imposed a more centralized, standardized, and inflexible rule of law by virtue of clarity, simplicity, and organized coherence. It was finally possible—and therefore it became necessary—to look in one place to find the direct, authoritative statement of the principles and details of Roman law.

The *Digest* was not the end, however. It was still too large—several bulky and expensive manuscript volumes in any rendition—to be more than a work of reference. So the final astute achievement of Tribonian and the others was the preparation in one compact volume of the *Institutiones* ("Institutes") of Justinian. Following other, less official works of the same name by earlier jurists like Gaius and Ulpian, this was the officially approved textbook of Roman law. Standardized teaching of law means standardization of law practice, and the *Institutiones* had this purpose clearly in mind. The whole task was done in 533, with a slightly revised edition of the *Codex* (to address issues discovered in making the *Digest*) in 534.

This codification was so effective and (mainly) so faithful to the past that when I was an undergraduate and took an introductory course in Roman law, we still read the *Institutiones* in translation, with abundant footnotes, as the best way to enter the whole history of Roman legal thinking from the republic to the end of the empire. This usefulness is a sign of a deep consistency in practice and theory of legal relationships—quite unmodified by any Christian interposition—that was in some ways the most vivid hallmark of what was Roman about Rome. Even the *Institutiones* were a bit much for some, and in the 550s, a teacher produced a still shorter textbook, which survives as the *Epitome by Julian*, to teach the basics, apparently to refugees from Italy. That digest of a digest of a digest would be widely used in the early middle ages.

In the western provinces during the sixth century, remarkable tributes were paid to this consistency in the so-called barbarian law codes—summaries of the law prepared by the local ruler, extracting sometimes too haphazardly the key points that were thought to be needed by local lawyers. One of those we have seen already, the Edict of Theoderic, and similar texts survive in the name of the Burgundians, Visigoths, and Franks—texts in which one feels the tenacity of the Roman tradition even as authority took new forms. There was little that was barbarian about them, for their variations and imperfections were quite naturally those of distant provinces, without the legal expertise of the capital, and paying attention to local customs and preferences.

In the eastern provinces, the prestige of the law progressed in other ways. From later in Justinian's reign, the historian Agathias tells us about a show trial that was staged on orders from Constantinople at the foot of the Caucasus Mountains among the Colchi people there. All the flummery of the law was sent from Constantinople, and no expense was spared. The judge sat on his raised bench in the full robes of court, surrounded by his official stenographers, heralds, bailiffs, and torturers. The local population could not understand a word of the proceedings, but Agathias showed them going along with the prosecution by imitating the sounds and gestures of the speakers they approved of. At the end, of course, the defendants were condemned, paraded through the streets on mules, and beheaded.

Roman legal training had already achieved a high level of consistency and clarity, in the west most notably at Rome itself, but also at Narbonne and Lyon; in the east at Berytus (modern Beirut), where as early as the fourth century Greek men of letters were heard to complain that the young had no taste for the finer studies, instead devoting themselves to the lucrative and pragmatic ways of the law. By the mid-fifth century, Constantinople had caught up and emerged as the main center, and Athens, Alexandria, and Caesarea in Palestine were centers as well for as long as Roman rule obtained. Beirut itself faded from view after an earthquake and fire wreaked wide damage in cities of the east in 551. Agathias reports how "the lovely city of Berytus, the jewel of Phoenicia, was completely ruined and its world-famous architectural treasures were reduced to a heap of rubble, practically nothing but the bare pavements of the buildings being left."[16] John of Ephesus adds an account of a tidal wave that pulled the water back from the land; when people rushed to rescue or plunder ships left high and dry, the rushing return of the water drowned them unawares.

The late Roman legal course of study lasted five years. A first year took you through the *Institutiones* and the first four books of the *Digest*; then three more years were needed to complete the whole of the *Digest*. In the fifth year, the study of the *Codex* itself brought the student up to date with the concerns and constitutions of reigning emperors in and close to his own time.

From 533 on, Justinian banned any teaching of law privately, to make clear that only the official canon, taught in the official way, would be effective. Law, lawyers, and court proceedings now belonged unmistakably to imperial government, not to the empire's citizens. The same years of the codification of law, for example, were accompanied not only by Theodora's antiprostitution campaign, as she built shelters for fallen women (we cannot tell whether those places felt more like shelters or prisons), but also by actions against homosexuals. "In that year [528] some of the bishops from various provinces were accused of living immorally in matters of the flesh and of homosexual practices. Among them was Isaiah, bishop of Rhodes but formerly prefect of police at Constantinople, and Alexander, the bishop of Diospolis in Thrace. They were brought before Victor, the prefect of the city, to be examined, condemned, and punished in conformity to the sacred decree. Victor tortured Isaiah severely and banished him. He had Alexander's genitals cut off and had him carried around on a litter to be mocked. Justinian immediately decreed that those convicted of pederasty should have their genitals cut off. In those days many homosexuals were arrested and died after having their genitals mutilated. From then on there was fear amongst those afflicted with homosexual lust."[17]

Government management under the enhanced rule of law was in the hands of a serious class of professionals now. We know many of them by name, and we have books by some. The influence of the men at court had never been stronger, nor their professional qualities more impressive. A professionalized aristocracy, courtiers, and a standing community of lawyers and businessmen stood at the heart of what from this date forward is more and more often called the Byzantine empire.

John the Lydian (from western Asia Minor) was proud of the historic line of Roman service that he had taken up, and other men like him came from all parts of the empire, trained in a meritocracy and ruling in it with a mixture of authority and indiscretion. John studied philosophy first, then found a job as a shorthand writer when Zoticus, from his home province, was praetorian prefect for a brief time. Under Zoticus, John advanced rapidly, made 1,000 gold coins for himself, and made a good marriage to a woman whose dowry brought 100 pounds of gold. He could have retired with that, but Anastasius invited him back to service and he made a career of it. He served with the court for many years and wrote books embodying his idealized view of imperial service.

Grasping the perspective of these men can help us understand the spirit of the age, and its deformations. Let us linger a bit over one interesting figure, the count Marcellinus.

Like many of the most ambitious people of this time, he was born in the Balkans—not far from modern Skopje, Justinian's own home territory.[18] He was born in uncertain times there, when the two Theoderics vied for position, and stability was slowly returning, but he received a solid education in Latin and Greek. Marcellinus emerged during Justin's reign, when he served as *cancellarius* ("chancellor," something like a chief of staff) to Justinian while the latter held the title of patrician and was the power behind (or alongside) the throne. In that job, Marcellinus would have seen all and known all, and would have come to know Justinian very well indeed.

A man of the new age, he was inflexibly loyal to Justinian and remarkably blind to the virtues of earlier emperors. In the year 519, the same year in which Theoderic set out to have Roman history summarized for Gothic purposes, Marcellinus began to write history, history that survives in his *Chronicle*, twice extended. His voice is one Justinian knew well and his views are the influential ones of a senior courtier in an autocracy.

He began with the year 379, at the point where the earlier authoritative account begun in Greek by the learned Eusebius, bishop and colleague of Constantine, then translated and continued by Jerome in Latin, broke off. The choice of date imposed by that tradition let him tell the story of barbarian invasions and the first generations of palace rule from the reign of Theodosius down to Justin and Justinian. The story Marcellinus tells reads like a first draft of every modern textbook of the period: barbarians, resistance, restoration. There are no good barbarians in Marcellinus; the Huns are the worst. The pragmatic emperor Anastasius was a negligible force in this view, and his achievements were undervalued. The rise and fall of Vitalian is the most interesting personal tale Marcellinus tells, for he overstates Vitalian's successes, makes him out to be violent and arbitrary, and then tells the story of his end deadpan—noting that he died in the palace, along with his retinue, after being stabbed sixteen times, but with no mention of Justinian's role. Justinian's power was so solid that Marcellinus could describe his crimes directly and boldly, without fear.

Roman historical tradition began with the founding of the city by Romulus in 753 BCE, with Vergil's heavily embroidered prequel to that story firmly in everyone's mind. The reign of Augustus drew a bright, sharp line through history, as the story of the man who separated the old world of republican liberty falling into chaos from the new world of imperial repression well-curtained by the appearance of tradition. From that moment forward, the Augusto-Vergilian propaganda of empire (*imperium sine fine,* "a rule that knows no bounds," is how Vergil had Jupiter himself put it) dominated the landscape. Rome mastered the whole of the known Mediterranean world, barbarians lay beyond to the north; deserts lay to the south; and the mysterious, insidious, luxurious, treacherous east sheltered people whose moral failures offset any claims to civilization. Good times kept the barbarians and easterners at bay; bad times let them slip their leashes and go on a rampage.

Marcellinus, a Roman who never went to Rome, could not see the progression and evolution of his own governmental system. The palace-based

rule in Constantinople of the fifth and sixth centuries represents governance radically transformed from anything Rome knew before Diocletian
and resembles any earlier period of Roman history in name only. This
blindness was clearly on display in the book *On Magistracies* of John the
Lydian. Nothing made him prouder than the continuity of offices and traditions from ancient times to the present. He was fooling himself.

Now, nothing about Marcellinus's own way of doing history ensured
it a long readership. The foreground of his story is the city of Constantinople, with its earthquakes, its bread riots, its portents, and the splendid
sight of a tame tiger sent to Theodosius II by the "province of India"—a
gesture from some potentate of the east. But there is not much more than
that kind of vignette to be had at best. Modern taste prefers narrative to
episode and story to chronicle, and the work would be only a documentary of taste and a record of scattered events were it not for one passage
that reports the year 476:

> In the fourteenth indiction, when Basiliscus and Armatus were con-
> suls, the tyrant Basiliscus made his son Marcus Caesar and dared
> to rise up against the catholic faith, swollen full of the monophysite
> treachery. Basiliscus and his son and his wife Zenonida were sent into
> exile, when Zeno returned to his former throne, and in the city which
> is called Leminis in the province of Cappadocia he was thrust away
> and perished of hunger. Odoacer the king of the Goths held Rome;
> Odoacer murdered Orestes there; Odoacer condemned Augustulus
> the son of Orestes with the penalty of exile to the castle of Lucullus in
> Campania.

So far the facts, or one version of them. Then Marcellinus adds a comment atypical for him:

> The western empire of the Roman nation, which in the seven hundred
> ninth year of the founding of the city Octavian Augustus seized as first
> of the Augusti, perished along with this Augustulus, in the 522nd year
> of the succeeding emperors of the realm. From then on, Gothic kings
> held Rome.

All the textbooks that give 476 as the year of the "fall of the Roman empire" base their claim on this paragraph. But what does it really tell us?

The world that Justin now faced was shaped, to a large extent, by how he and others remembered the fifth century. Zeno and Anastasius had taken the wrong tack. Religiously, they sided with the monophysites, Zeno in his *Henotikon*, Anastasius in his sympathies and policies; politically, they had surrendered the west to Theoderic and the other kings beyond. But now, strong men were taking control and their enthusiasm for restoration of the past would dominate policy for a generation. The Acacian schism that had separated Rome and Constantinople since the Romans objected to the *Henotikon* was now being healed, and Chalcedonian Christianity was back in control in Constantinople. Less obviously, the future held a series of vastly overweening military campaigns, staged from Constantinople, each seeking restoration and regeneration of the old models of empire, each doomed to disaster. But history had to be rewritten first.

And so Marcellinus, voice of Justinian's court, chose the moment of illegitimacy: 476. It had its merits, in a keenly perverted way: 476 makes sense as the year when the bad days of the fifth century came to an end and Odoacer's reign marked the beginning of better days, just as Theoderic's reign would mark their flourishing but also, alas, their culmination. The irrelevance of emperors in residence was trivial by comparison to the good that these men did in the west in those decades.

The hard men of Justinian's circle in Constantinople carried with them who knows what resentments, fears, and insecurities from their Balkan homes. These were the men who fled to the safety of the big city, and they could not understand or accept such progress. Instead, they needed to belittle and misread the past, in order to change their present. How better to end the Roman story than with a Romulus, one you could nickname Augustulus? Never mind that there was another western emperor (Julius Nepos) whom Constantinople recognized, and who was still in business as late as 480. Neither historical nor legal accuracy was the point for Marcellinus. Justinian lived, from his earliest days in the palace, in a delusion his own courtiers made for him, a former glory that they clearly imagined, but that had never truly been what they said it was. The past these men created was not real, but a screen on which to vividly project their anxieties from the present.

That is how Justinian came onto the stage. He was a man of limited talents from the provinces, surrounded by gifted men who knew only too well how to reshape their world in the image of delusion about the position of the city and its emperors in this world, about its past, and by implication about its future. We may choose to call them Justinian's best and brightest or, if you prefer, his neoconservatives.

THE BIRTH OF THE CHRISTIAN
ROMAN EMPIRE

This may seem an odd place in our story to speak of the "birth" of the Christian Roman empire. Christianity had long since triumphed, as everyone knows, and Constantine, saint to the Orthodox church, had founded the Christian empire.

But what everyone knows is rarely true. We have seen Constantine and his successors become (mostly) Christians themselves, and we have seen them tilt the advantages of empire in favor of their new creed. Theodosius's ban on traditional religious practices, coupled with the (intermittent) partisanship of emperors in controversies over creed and doctrine, was a dramatic departure from the past, but his interventions still left most of the empire and most of its citizens well enough alone.

As late as Anastasius and even Justin, and certainly in Theoderic's realm, Christianity was the religion of empire in the way traditional practices had been. Not so for Justinian. This son of Balkan peasants sought not only the restoration of Roman glory, but also the perfection of Christian unity. In his pursuit of those twin goals, but unaccompanied by either good judgment or good luck, Justinian managed to ensure that neither would ever be attained. A sad thing it is, to come from a distant province and achieve the heights of power, to devote yourself to such lofty principles and marmoreal ostentation, and to discover that zeal and stupidity are not enough. He was not the last ruler of a mighty realm to be so purblind.

Justinian reacted to the multitude of divergent Christianities in his world as though they were so abnormal as to justify and even require a forceful solution. In so doing he took up again the most ancient and perversely appealing of Christian doctrines: that there must be a single form of Christianity throughout the world, which was resolutely far from unified in any other way. As Christian factions defined their respective doctrines with greater and greater clarity, it was inevitable that different modes of belief would congeal in different regions. But Justinian and the unworldly men around him could never accept this.

They also forgot that their capital city itself was an unnatural place.

In establishing his seat on the Bosporus, Constantine created a third focus of power in the Roman world. If Rome, Carthage, and Ravenna made a natural enough axis for western power, and if Antioch and Alexandria made another axis in the eastern lands, Constantine's intrusion was unwelcome and unnecessary. Left to their own devices, the Latin west and the Syrian and Egyptian east would doubtless have gone separate ways far earlier and far more easily and naturally. But a Mediterranean-wide empire, artificial and fragile though it was, had long since been taken for granted as normal, and so Constantine and his successors could successfully claim that great power emanated from a location halfway between the two main centers of economic and social power whose union created Rome.

The overweening blindness of Constantinople's men arose in part from an accident of the fourth and fifth centuries. Antioch and Alexandria (that is to say, Syria and Egypt) seemed for a good while naturally to be in disharmony with each other and also with Constantinople in religious matters. But Antioch and Alexandria learned in the late fifth century and early sixth century to think more alike than ever before. Constantinople pressed on all its subjects the result of the theological balancing act of the Council of Chalcedon, with very limited success. If there had been no Constantinople for an emperor and if Antioch and Alexandria had evolved as we know they did evolve, toward a common embrace of monophysitism, the eastern provinces of the old empire would have settled down to a more or less harmonious future at a considerable doctrinal distance from Rome and the western churches. Instead, the Chalcedonism fostered at Constantinople and in the colony of similar thinking found in Jerusalem and the Judaean desert monasteries was self-satisfied and unpopular, and would stay that way. The old east, alienated in faith from its own capital, lay ripe for Islam's taking, and left Constantinople in a state of lonely splendor, a milieu that came to be called Byzantine. It was still orthodox Chalcedonian, but quite irrelevant and isolated on history's stage, however long it survived.

The development of Justinian's passion for orthodoxy will follow us through our story of the next decades. With too little schooling, he became an aficionado of theology and theologians. The settling of the Acacian schism marked his uncle Justin's rise, along with the abandonment in Constantinople of Zeno's *Henotikon* of thirty-five years earlier, the document that had almost held together a world of conflicting opinions. Justinian had little real idea what forces he was playing with. (Among other things, he never traveled south and east from his capital to see any of the heart-lands of his empire or to confront its religious traditions face to face.) His backhanded attempts to stifle fashionable Arianism along the northern frontier and in Italy aggravated his falling-out with Theoderic and Theoderic's successors—a situation that probably pleased Justinian perfectly well, though it set Italy on a course that ended in the ruinous wars of the 530s through the 550s.

And meanwhile, grave men were making a future for Christian theology that did not take Constantinople seriously. Severus was patriarch of Antioch in Syria until he was expelled in the Chalcedonian upthrust under Justin. In exile, he became the hero of this generation of one-nature theologians, and most accounts of the period follow the rise of his movement to respectability and power. But there were nastier undercurrents. Michael the Syrian, a much later orthodox chronicler, offers a letter to the emperor, ostensibly from a Jewish community, circulating in the early sixth century but purporting to have been written just after Chalcedon half a century earlier:

> To the merciful Emperor Marcian: from the people of the Hebrews. For a long time we have been regarded as though our fathers had crucified a God and not a man. Since the synod of Chalcedon has assembled and demonstrated that he who was crucified was a man and not a God we request that we should be pardoned this fault and that our synagogues should be returned to us.[19]

The fool who accepted that text as authentic would also believe that the Chalcedonians were nothing but Jews, but there were such fools aplenty by that time.

Meanwhile, heroic examples of saintliness had a disproportionate influence on the public mind. Saints are hard to control. Early in the fifth century, a man named Simeon sat on a six-foot-square platform, atop a sixty-foot pillar high in the Syrian countryside, and remained there for, we are told, thirty-six years, preaching to the crowds that gathered below twice a day. The emperor Zeno shrewdly provided funds to build a great church around the site of Simeon's pillar—the better to benefit from his famous holiness when his tart tongue was no long able to criticize emperors.[20] A more practically opportunistic man, named Daniel, found the suburbs of Constantinople a better location for a pillar and established a reputation so strong that the patriarch of the city came to him to ordain him to the priesthood—patriarch on the ground, Daniel in the air. From his aerie, Daniel cured the sick, foretold disasters and rescues, and even chased demons away from an old temple some distance from his pillar.[21] A contemporary wrote this poem about him:

> *Midway between earth and sky there stands a man*
> *With no fear for the gales that swirl around him.*
> *His name is Daniel; he competes with great Simeon,*
> *preaching the son of the mother who did not know man.*
> *Hunger is the ambrosia he feeds on; thirst is his bloodless drink;*
> *He plants his feet on a twice-strong column.*[22]

By comparison, Severus the Sober embodied a newly serious age. He was born in Sozopolis (near modern Konya) in Asia Minor, where his grandfather had already been a bishop at the time of the first council of Ephesus in 431, one of the 200 who had voted there to depose Nestorius. As a young man, Severus went to Alexandria for his first years of study, and then on to Berytus in 486 to study law. There he fell into the life of a religious enthusiast, associating with anti-Chalcedonian believers and monks and becoming one of the smug pagan-hunting *philoponoi* we met there on an earlier page. His life story, told in the generation after his successes, was full of nearly magical tales of pagan survival and Christian resistance, making sense of the rise of ultra-Christian zealotry. Severus took baptism, abandoned the law, visited Jerusalem, and moved eventually to a monastery of his own not far from Gaza.

At every period, Severus was loyal to the emperor and did his bidding; this remarkable trait was shared by all theological parties in this period. Even though there were great fallings-out over doctrine, the emperor remained the object of civic respect and faithful service. Early in his career,

Severus found his way to Constantinople and under Anastasius from 508 to 512 he was a kind of house chaplain and hound of heresies. He came into his own in a sermon of 516 in Antioch, where he had been consecrated bishop with Anastasius's approval. "We move along the middle of the royal road, turning our face away from the tortuous sins on one side or the other, and knowing that he who lives on the heights and dwells by nature in grandeur is worthy of the God who emptied himself . . . to become author of our salvation."[23]

Severus was seen far and wide as the hero of the anti-Chalcedonians, and so he is remembered, but behind him lurked the more shadowy and more unscrupulous figure of Philoxenus of Mabbug. Mabbug is Syriac for Hierapolis ("Holy City") in Syria, modern Manbij, where the mysterious "Syrian god" of whom Lucian wrote had ruled. Philoxenus made straight the way for Severus's ascent by blessing thugs and inciting hostility, an IRA forerunner to a smooth Sinn Fein politician, as it were. It did not hurt that Antioch was a reputed hotbed of clerical corruption and that Severus soon established a reputation among men of all persuasions by working hard and effectively to restore integrity and good behavior.

In 519, in the swirl of Chalcedonian reunification and harmony with the west that Justin promoted, Severus was marked for deposition, and as Justin and the still flourishing Vitalian marched out to meet the visiting pope, Hormisdas, at the tenth milestone from the city, all might have seemed to be in order and at peace. Even former emperors could be rebuked with aplomb, and so Zeno and Anastasius in their graves heard obloquy heaped on their names. A gaggle of monks from the north called Scythians (though few if any came from as far away as modern Moldova and Ukraine) rapidly rose high in court circles, espousing a hard anti-Nestorian and anti-monophysite line. "One of the trinity suffered for us," they proclaimed, and so they were called Theopaschites for their bold doctrine, shocking those who considered their god—in his perfection and untouchability—immune to suffering. Westerners would perceive this as a soft form of Chalcedonianism, but the monks were zealous in their softness and they played a strong part in keeping the capital on the straight and narrow, and out of sympathy with the rest of the eastern world, at least for the next decade. Severus was anything but one to go quietly and abjure his beliefs; his loyalists in Antioch taunted his successor by calling him "Paul the Jew."

When Justinian became emperor in 527 in his own name, then, he sought unity and faced disagreement. His initial instincts were pacific, and so he sought reconciliation. A precious document catches the moment in 532 when he thought he could make things better.

Written in Syriac, this text transcribes three days of debates held in Constantinople in the spring of 532.[24] The smoking ruins of the fires from the Nika riots were still on the streets, and Justinian must have felt that his regime needed support wherever he could find it. Doctrinal disagreement was a dangerous luxury. The emperor's men brought together half a dozen bishops of the Chalcedonian party and half a dozen enthusiasts of Severus. The bishops who met were not the real leaders of the various factions of the church at the time, but they were respected figures who could still meet and talk with some hope of flexibility. There is a point in the debates when Justinian suggests that Severus, now deposed, be invited to Constantinople to continue the conversations, but nothing came of the idea.

Instead, this session was an attempt to move the discussion forward without histrionics and public posturing, and one must give Justinian full credit for making a remarkable effort. They met at the palace of Hormisdas—not quite part of the grand palace in Constantinople, but for discretion and privacy a good choice, for it lay down the hill behind the circus and toward the water. It offered a discreet semiofficial location for conversations away from the public eye—which would have gazed intently on a meeting held in one of the magnificent churches of the city or in the palace proper. The location may have put the conversation under the particular eye of Theodora. (The empress had a reputation for being the court's friend to one-nature Christians and she seems to have played a careful game, keeping doors open without breaking with her husband's brand of religion.)

In the dialogue, the Chalcedonians were strong on two points: Chalcedon itself, and the support the Roman church gave to it. The latter bears the real mark of Justinian's policy, because he was already meditating the invasion of Africa the next year and the eventual restoration of the western, Roman world to his domains. To unify his political empire, he could not afford a division of his ecclesiastical empire. He overestimated himself.

The Syrians, on the other hand, were interested only in promoting good doctrine and condemning bad teachers. Ibas of Edessa and Theodoret, teachers of the fifth century whom the monophysites thought had wrongly escaped condemnation, were the objects of their attention. Ibas was a relatively minor figure, but the awkwardness lay in the fact that he had quoted the supremely eminent and revered Cyril of Alexandria, the leading light of that generation, in ways that were incompatible with Chalcedon. The critics of Ibas did not condemn the author but claimed instead that he hadn't written the letter in question at all. By that evasion, they could avoid dealing with the quotations from Cyrus and could pretend that these were also inauthentic. In the arguments that followed, the defenders of Ibas had the simpler position of asserting that he was orthodox and that the text was authentic. Justinian never found peace with the Syrians, but twenty years later he promoted the condemnation of Ibas and Theodoret and their senior and more theologically sophisticated colleague Theodore of Mopsuestia at a great global church council, in the hope that such condemnation (which we will see backfire) would encourage the one-nature Christians to support him.

On the first evening and again on the morning of the second day of the meetings, the Chalcedonian bishops saw Justinian on their own. Then on the third day, they sent for the Syrians, who joined their clerical colleagues and the emperor. Justinian tried for compromise: "I don't think you are actually unorthodox, but you have scruples over detail that make you want to avoid communion with us, and you are indignant at the presence of certain names on the official diptychs" (the lists of former orthodox bishops). Justinian suggested that the Severans get out and about and visit Rome and Alexandria to see how much agreement there was in the world, but they demurred. He pushed on with this proposal for a compromise:

Would the following conditions perhaps be acceptable to them: they might anathematize Diodorus, Theodore, Theodoret, Ibas, Nestorius and Eutyches, and accept the Twelve Chapters of the holy Cyril, while anathematizing what had been written against them; they might confess one nature of God the Word incarnate, but they should refrain from anathematizing those who speak of two natures after the inexpressible union, anathematizing instead those who hold Nestorian views and divide up Christ into two natures, while confessing, as a crafty device which they had discovered long ago, together with the other side "the two united and inseparable natures"; they should accept the synod of Chalcedon as far as the expulsion of Eutyches was concerned, but they need not accept the definition of the faith made there; they should cease anathematizing the Tome of Leo; and the *libelli* of the *Romaioi* should not be suspended.

This anticipates Justinian's prescription for the council that he would hold at Constantinople two decades later: sacrifice the reputation of named individuals left and right as a way to agreement. To a connoisseur of the debates of these decades, this is an ingenious, thoughtful, and possible compromise. But it didn't work in 532. And it didn't work two decades later, either.

In the absence of such compromise, Justinian the stubborn amateur theologian was willing to insist on unity. This is the moment at which a Christian emperor can first be seen using his authority effectively, consistently, and deliberately to bring all his followers into one religious tent. The natural effect of such employment of authoritarian power is to encourage and promote disagreement, and that is what happened.

The year 536 was a turning point. In that year, the deposed Severus and Jacob Baraddaeus, the two leaders of the monophysite community, accepted that they would not prevail at court and so began consecrating a hierarchy of bishops of their own. Over the next forty years, traveling relentlessly through all the provinces between Asia Minor and Egypt, Jacob would ordain hundreds of bishops, including a patriarch for Antioch in the 550s. On one occasion, at Tralles in 541, he carried out the consecration of his bishop in the gallery of the cathedral while the Chalcedonians conducted their service downstairs, ignorant of what he was doing. The Jacobite church that survives to this day in the Middle East and elsewhere takes its name from him. Justinian's fellow Chalcedonians had to regret that he let the consecration happen, but in the moment he had few choices.

In 536 Pope Agapetus I visited Constantinople and refused to take communion with Justinian's patriarch, Anthimus I, seeing him as too tolerant of eastern aberrance. Justinian was embarrassed and deposed Anthimus shortly afterward and replaced him with Menas, who turned out to be the hardheaded, outspoken Chalcedonian that monophysitism needed as a pretext for declaring independence. Severus, the hero of a generation of monophysites, died in exile only two years later, but by then the pattern was set. Constantinople remained faithful to Chalcedonian orthodoxy, and could count on support from Jerusalem (grateful that Chalcedon had raised the city's ecclesiastical status), but in the main the sympathies of Syria, Palestine, and Egypt were lost. The insistent formation of a fiercely Christian Roman empire made the unity Justinian most wanted impossible to attain.

So the Christian empire of Justinian and his successors took a particular shape. On the one hand, official ideology prevailed, with an official clergy, heavily subsidized and performing ritual duties in the imperial churches of the capital city. On the other hand, stubborn hostility and resistance grew among those whose religious sentiments were not respected by such practice. Justinian as a religious monarch resembles Stalin, and as a political monarch he favors Milošević: outwardly in control, using ideological purity as a weapon to ensure control, and in the process inadvertently fueling the sympathies and ambitions of all those who simply did not agree.[25]

Justinian's establishment of a Christian empire succeeded in ensuring that its subjects would confess the name of Christ for 900 years, but it did not guarantee that they would do so with one voice. His success and his failure both cast long shadows forward.

HAMLET ON THE THRONE

Hamlet would have made a terrible king. Justinian, intellectually arrogant, priggish, not as well educated as he thought he was, and alternating between indecisiveness and rashness, shows us how Hamlet would have turned out. Thinking about that comparison can help us avoid the most common failing of histories of this period—let me call it Procopianism.

The libraries of Caesarea, on the coast of Palestine, a little more than halfway up from Tel Aviv to Haifa, were among the wonders of late antiquity. They are now lost to us, with the city effaced and left for archaeologists to retrace.[26] Since the third century (and the days of Origen, that most versatile and prolific of early Christian writers, destined to have his own long-posthumous quarrel with Justinian), Caesarea had plied two trades: one of the intellect and the other more mercantile. It had a less grand scale of commerce than Alexandria or Antioch, but it offered a con-

Justinian as general: a spin doctor's fantasy.

venient Mediterranean port for caravans from southern Arabia, and provided a no less distinctive advantage for the scholars who lived and wrote there. Procopius came from Caesarea in the early years of Justinian's reign to make his way in Constantinople.

When Procopius came to write the history of Justinian, he knew exactly the story he wanted to tell. He had a good emperor, a good general, and wars that gave every promise of great success. But the good emperor was not Justinian—it was Khusro I, the Persian—and Justinian's wars of great promise all turned out ill in the end. The good general was Justinian's loyal Belisarius, on whose staff Procopius had served during African and Italian campaigns. Since Procopius was self-interested enough to tell his story as *though* it were in praise of Justinian, most ancient and modern readers have taken for granted that he was a serviceable court historian, doing the best he could with difficult material. If Justinian is Procopius's central figure, however, he comes through these pages silent and sullen, and at one point is even accused of behaving like a barbarian.[27] Whether Procopius revives the spirit of Thucydides or anticipates that of Leo Strauss (both notions have their supporters among scholars today), he is a slippery and ambiguous figure to be the source of so much precious and privileged information.

Procopius of Caesarea wrote the history of Justinian's wars in eight books, and in so doing he accomplished exactly what Justinian wanted, making the regime of the soldier's nephew into a thrilling tale of reconquest and imperial glory: Persians, Vandals, and Goths all fall at the feet of the mighty Roman. But Justinian did not see through the ironies and complexities of Procopius's text, and many readers since have missed them as well. Though Procopius leaves the serious reader with no doubt that his Justinian was anything but a great emperor and hero, his real disdain simmers unmistakably half an inch below the surface, and in his public histories he succeeded in capturing the ambiguous spirit of his age. He could still write an appendix to his histories of the wars, an entire volume devoted to Justinian's buildings, outwardly glorifying the shells of empire that Justinian constructed but leaving the readers to form their own judgment

Procopius then wrote another book, one not published in his lifetime, and one that cannot be ignored in any discussion of the sixth century or of Justinian. The *Anecdota* (literally, "unpublished material," usually rendered in English as *The Secret History*) was first published and read, as near as we can tell, in the seventeenth century. It is the scandal sheet of its times, and no modern writer can resist it. Procopius told his explicit misogynistic stories to shock, but their historical value, at the very most, is to say that well-bred Constantinopolitans were appalled that their emperor had not chosen to perfume himself with an ambitious marriage to a society girl. Instead he reached below his social station for a partner of whom the worst had to be said, whatever the truth might be. If you insist on reading the stories—as most readers certainly will—then you should at least learn their main lesson, that Procopius knew how to manipulate his audience's attention to make a point. Justinian and Theodora on the throne may very well have been the happiest (or sappiest) and most devoted of old marrieds, very nearly the least interesting people in the empire, but Procopius succeeded in making them larger than life.

And that was his greatest disservice to history. Many moderns—I am not one of them—think the exaggerations just that, irresponsible and vengeful "stretchers" (as Huck would say), which distort the history of a serious and successful emperor. Rather, I think the stories clearly intensify rather than falsify the atmosphere of self-absorption and corrupting adherence to principle in a court that had lived too long on its own with too few roots in the society it dominated. There is plenty of evidence for a Justinian at least as dismally arbitrary and unpleasant as Procopius's gossip makes him out to be. (And there is none to suggest that his slanders of Theodora should be credited.)

The Justinian who sat alone in an empty hall of the palace with a few theologians late into the night, and the Theodora of a shady past who said, "An empire makes a fine burial shroud," and thus planted courage in the heart of an emperor quailing before the Nika riots, are figures from what Hollywood would call a high-concept story—the worst kind. Better Hamlet for an analogy, a royal figure not quite connected to his society but always powerful within it—like Justinian. The origins of the prince and the emperor separated them from their peers and colleagues, and they never quite grasped what any of their contemporaries were about. If we map Theodora into the Hamlet story, her part is divided between the two poles of unattainable enticement, Gertrude and Ophelia. Justinian's fate is to be shown as the cat's-paw of a temptress witch, himself a figure of power without potency, energy without production.

Justinian died childless, surrounded by the sexual legends in which he is the invisible and passive partner, a hollow and tottering figure still larger than life after thirty-eight years of sole rule, the longest reign since Augustus. Had he died in the plague in 542 (he sickened of it, we know), he would be remembered as the man of law, the man of buildings, and the man who started wars he did not finish. Someone else would have had to invent the world for his successors. Instead, he lived a long time and carried his own intentions through to their morbid conclusions. So it goes, as Kurt Vonnegut's doomed men and women of Dresden might say, and we should realize that longevity is itself a marker not of success, but only of endurance.

Procopius slanders not only Theodora but also Belisarius, Justinian's most successful general. Belisarius's Antonina could not be accused of low origins, but Procopius blames her for infidelities meant to titillate the reader but even more to show that Belisarius was a compromised man at home. Procopius wanted us to live in a world in which the domestic intrigues of those two men and their wives were the centerpiece of historical drama. That reading is a mistake.

The better to see Justinian clearly, we should bring back another figure of his time, not any of the lesser ones who surrounded him and formed part of his hallucination of empire, but rather the one he got out of his way, Vitalian. We know too little of Vitalian to judge his education and personal capacities, but his family connections to men of learning and religion, combined with the astuteness of his political maneuvering and his successes (not unrelieved, but regular) in military campaigns suggest that here was a worthy successor to Theodosius, Stilicho, Aetius, Odoacer, and Theoderic. We see a man who was first suppressed and then cold-bloodedly murdered in order to let a lesser man have the throne and surround himself with men of talent but no stature. The age that we should most regret losing is the one that Vitalian would have built had Justinian found his more natural destiny in obscurity or an early demise.

4

Opportunities Lost

N THE SIXTH and seventh centuries, Roman emperors were compelled as never before to attend to worlds beyond their frontiers. Never had their attention been so fragmented over such a wide territory.

To follow this story in the age of Justinian, we must go back in time to the fifth century, to see the world as Anastasius I inherited it, and then as he bequeathed it to Justin.

Anastasius wasn't quite a border man himself, but he was no city boy either. He came from Dyracchium, modern Durrës in Albania (the Italians call it Durazzo), the western terminus of the Egnatian Way, the Roman highway that ran from Constantinople to the Adriatic shore, there to connect with shipping back and forth to Brindisi in Italy. The city was and is an important small-time port, never known for culture, never famous, even though it had been a pawn in the opening moves of Thucydides's account of the Peloponnesian War. One account had it that Anastasius's mother was a Manichee, and a brother of hers was an Arian—therefore by some standards a barbarian. Anastasius himself was interested enough in religion to be spoken of for bishop of Antioch not long before he became emperor, and while still a courtier he lectured on his moderately monophysite views.

Anastasius made his way to Constantinople as a young man and became one of the silentiaries at court. When Zeno died, his widow selected Anastasius to be her consort and to rule. At the outset, Anastasius represented the corporate tradition of stability that flourished in the palace of the fifth century. Some hated him, but they were wrong to do so.

Tall and dignified, Anastasius earned a reputation for generosity and intelligence. He was a deft and prudent manager of resources and opportunities. He brought Isauria into the mainstream of imperial life, settled relations with Theoderic in Italy (not without one or two small skirmishes and maneuvers, but nothing to disrupt the underlying arrangement), and kept the Persian front quiet as well except for a brief outburst around 502–503. Vitalian, as we have seen, was Anastasius's biggest challenge, but on balance the emperor handled even that risk well. When Anastasius died, the treasury was full, taxes were being paid, and the Roman world was at peace.

His success makes it all the more interesting and important to understand how people could hate him. A precious document of that hatred is written in the imaginary voice of one of the mysterious prophetesses called sibyls.[1] The legend of these women was already old when Rome could still call itself a republic, and so the story that one of them met Aeneas when he landed at Cumae in Italy and led him to the underworld made perfect sense. At every period of historical Rome, books were in circulation that the sibyls were said to have written. Typically these books offered prophecy after the fact, to validate themselves as tracts for the times in which they were "revealed." Such forgeries were infrequent enough to retain their power to charm and persuade. *The Oracle of Baalbek* earned enough respect to have survived for us to read it.

The oracle was written at or near Heliopolis not long after 502. It certainly predates the death of Anastasius, but it also prophesies that Constantinople would undergo a massive disaster in 510, so it must date from before then—for the actual year passed by with the city untouched. By failing to mention some contemporary events on the Persian frontier, it probably dates itself even more precisely, most likely to 503–504.

The oracle claimed to be that of the sibyl of Tibur, not far from Rome. She told this tale, we are told, four generations before the birth of Christ, sitting in a temple on the Capitoline hill in Rome. The book's afterlife was diverse: a Latin version of it was known in Lombard Italy in the eleventh century, but the Greek text was first discovered in a manuscript on Mount

Athos, in the sprawling monastic community there, with copies found later in the Vatican Library and in the National Library in Athens.

Heliopolis is modern Baalbek, a place still marked by fear and mystery. The northern end of the Bekaa valley of Lebanon is home to a largely Shiite Muslim community, and so it was the temporary residence of a variety of foreign hostages in the 1980s during the worst times in Lebanon; more recently it has been a target of Israeli attacks. It is also the site of astonishing ruins of the ancient temple of the sun, and it has always been a magnet to pilgrims and worshippers from far and wide. Ancient travelers going from Antioch or Aleppo to Damascus or Jerusalem probably went that way, through a valley that saw many such travelers even in dry years, and doubtless paused to marvel at the then undamaged edifices. It remained frankly pagan in many ways long after other places ceased to be, always marginal yet prosperous. The temple prostitution that flourished there offended Constantine's nascent Christian spirit, so he insisted on building a church in the courtyard of the temple of Jupiter. It hardly changed things.

In short, Heliopolis was a good place for a supposed ancient prophetess to be read and taken seriously. The pamphlet, made up to look like an ancient oracle, is the work of a traditionalist in Christian religion, for the religious phenomena of this period often surprise us with such juxtapositions of old and new. In form, it is poetic-prophetic; in substance, political-historical. Here is how it tells of the years during and after Emperor Leo I. Read it as a contemporary counterhistory of the years we have been sketching.

> In the eighth generation there will arise an emperor named after a wild beast [Leo]. The birth pains of the world begin in his times, earthquakes, drownings of cities and countries, and there will be wars and burnings of cities. Thrace will be laid waste, and there will be no one to administer or to manage the Roman Empire. Taurocilicia will lift high her neck. There will arise Scylla, wife of the ruling wild beast, and she will bring forth two wombs, one of which will give birth to a male child; and they will call it by the name of the father. And he too will share the throne with his father of the beastly name and they will have one and the same likeness of earthly kingship. While he is king, an Isaurian will appear, and he will be worshipped by his father. And

then those men will speak blasphemous words against the nature of the Son [Christ]. And because of his saying his father will be brought down powerfully from his throne, but the power and domination of the womb will hold sway for fifty-two years. And after that an Isaurian will become king, and he will hate the inhabitants of his city and will flee to his country. And there will arise another king whose name is that of the trailing beast; the name of the beast begins with the letter beta: it is Basiliscus. And he will speak blasphemy against the highest god, and because of his blasphemy he will be treated scornfully by a woman and will perish, both he and his entire kin. And after that an Isaurian will return to the kingship, except that his kingship is not given to him by heaven. His name stands in Roman letters at the end of the alphabet, but is written in Greek letters beginning with the seventh letter [zeta] and his name is Greco-Latin [Zeno]. And his rule will be powerful and will be pleasing to the entire people; he will love the poor and will humble the powerful and rich.

And after this there will arise another king from the western city of Epidamnos, which is in Latin Dyracchium. The name of the king is hidden from the gentiles, but his name resembles the last day and begins with the eighteenth letter [sigma], but when he seizes the kingship he will be called Anastasius. He is bald, handsome, his forehead like silver, he has a long right arm, he is noble, terrifying, high-souled and free and hates all the beggars. He will ruin many from among the people either lawfully or unlawfully and will unseat those who observe godliness. And the Persians will arise in his times and will overturn with the sword the cities of the east together with the multitudes of the soldiers of the Roman empire. And he will be king for thirty-one years.

Here is where we turn from melodramatized history to grim fantasy of the future:

And after that men will be rapacious, greedy, rebellious, barbarian, they will hate their mothers, and in lieu of virtue and of mildness they will assume the appearance of barbarians. They will raid their own ancestral cities, and there is none to resist their works and deeds. They work their land because of their great avarice. In the ninth generation the years will be shortened like months, and the months like weeks, and the weeks like days, and the days like hours. And two kings will arise from the east and two from Syria, and the Assyrians will be countless like the sand of the sea, and they will take over many lands of the east. . . . And there will be much shedding of blood, so that the blood will reach the chest of horses as it is commingled with the sea. And they will capture and set on fire the cities and despoil the East. . . . And after that there will arise another king who has a changed shape and he will rule thirty years and will rebuild the altars of Egypt. And he will wage war upon the king from the east and will kill him and all his army and will seize children from the age of twelve. And people will seize poisonous asps and suck milk from women with new-born babes and draw blood for the sake of the poison of arrows and the violence of wars. . . . And after that there will arise a woman. She will run from the setting to the rising of the sun and will not see a man; and she will long for the track of a man and will not find it. And she will find a vine and an olive-tree and say, "Where is he who planted these?" And she will embrace these plants and give up her spirit, and wolves will eat her. And after that there will arise another king from Heliopolis and he will wage war against the king from the east and kill him. And he will grant a tax-exemption to entire countries for three years and six months, and the earth will bring forth its fruits, and there is none to eat them. And there will come the ruler of perdition, he who is changed, and will smite and kill him. And he will do signs and wonders on earth. He will turn the sun into darkness and the moon into blood. And after that the springs and rivers will dry up, and the Nile of Egypt will be transformed into blood. And the survivors will dig cisterns and will search for the water of life and will not find it.

The story ends first with the return of Enoch and Elijah, and then with the second coming of Christ. The fear running through these lines is palpable: fear of the forces of the east, but fear of the emperor as well, and fear of the barbarians—in this case, as likely as not the Arabs and bedouin to the south. Hope resides, if anywhere, in apocalyptic redemption (accompanied by tax cuts), for this is the land of the Fertile Crescent where such hopes had long sprung up and taken root. Objectively, this world was in better shape than it had been, and looked forward to better prospects than it had known for a long time; and Heliopolis had not suffered special depredations in living memory, despite isolated raids by Huns 100 years earlier.

But the possibility of disaster turned into fear, which turned into expectation, which shaped the way men and women lived in the world. That kind of fear is corrosive and pervasive, the drop of water on a stone that, if continued long enough, wears away a mountain. We must keep in mind the role of the religious traditions of the eastern provinces in creating and nurturing this skepticism, this fear, and this alienated expectation of magical redemption as we watch men making the sometimes bungled and self-defeating political calculations of their age.

THE MYTHICAL EAST

Ancient history as commonly retold in European and American societies is pervaded by a great and deluding absence. When it suits us, we can easily turn that absence into a bogeyman and we show how easily we can absorb fears like those of the oracle of Baalbek. Understanding the ancient world and ours requires us to notice what is missing and to remember that bogeymen are creatures of children's imaginations.

The mistake lies in thinking that east is east and west is west and never the twain shall meet. Even Kipling, who wrote those famous words in his *Ballad of East and West*, really had it just about right:

> Oh, East is East, and West is West, and never the twain shall meet,
> Till Earth and Sky stand presently at God's great Judgment Seat;
> But there is neither East nor West, Border, nor Breed, nor Birth,
> When two strong men stand face to face, though they come from the
>   ends of the earth!

Start again with the Greeks. The old story is perfectly well known and predictable. For reasons of imperial lust for expansion, the Persians loom up out of the east and seek to conquer the Greeks, who resist them heroically and succeed in defeating them, bravely at Thermopylae, more lastingly at Salamis. Beaten once for all, the Persians slink away. They are next seen in the cameo part of villains in Xenophon's tale of the march of the 10,000—where it is to be noticed that whatever we think of Persians beating up on Greeks, here was a case where Greeks beat up on Persians.

And we approve of Greeks, because they are our ancestors and taught us all we know. "Greeks," however, is a word that was not a natural or easy name for the people who lived, in Plato's words, like frogs around a pond on the shores and islands of the Aegean. The story of Troy let Homeric readers begin to imagine such a category. When the Persians conquered the people of Lydia in western Asia Minor in the fifth century BCE, the people with whom the Lydians shared language and gods began to think of themselves as similarly threatened, and defined themselves back into existence as the un-Persians. Persia always offered Greece the counterimage of itself, and much of Greek thought about religion and politics—down to the present—emerges as a way of declaring independence from powers to the east. (Nothing to the north or west of Greece was of any account, and the Egyptians were just, tantalizingly, too far away to make a real difference.) The reason for the Greeks to prevail against the Persians was not intrinsic excellence, but simply that the Persians came a little too late and found the Greeks a little too far along commercially and militarily, a little too ready to band together to resist them. Out of this accident of history a lasting opposition emerged. But there was an alternative.[2] We must take a detour to understand these Persias and Persians that succeeded one another.

Alexander the Great, a right-minded man even if he did drink too much (according to the common view), sought to conquer all of Persia and succeeded, but he died too soon, and his conquests were lost. Few people spend much time imagining a middle-aged and successful Alexander, a man lucky enough to live as long as Augustus did, let's say. If we knew *that* man, we would know him not as a Greek or Macedonian, but as a Persian emperor. That is what he set out to become, and that is how he appeared in much of the territory he crossed. At his death, his armies were turning rapidly Persian in composition and form, and they would have become much more so with the passage of only a little time. His conquest would have proved what only the Ottomans ever demonstrated—that linking the Aegean basin with Asia Minor and Mesopotamia was possible and, if achieved, could have been a source of great power for the one who accomplished the bravura deed. For Alexander to be Macedonian, from the farthest reaches of territory within Persian ken, was no disqualification:

conquering rulers in many societies come from the margins, at least as often as from the center.

Alexander's Persian empire collapsed after his death and fell into pieces.[3] The Seleucid kings who prevailed in the Asian provinces of Alexander's empire, notional partners to the successor kings who took the name Ptolemy in Egypt and the similar Antigonids in the Aegean basin, proved unable to maintain even the traditional Persian pretensions and range, from Syria to Afghanistan, and were for centuries a limited and dwindling force on the world stage. The Seleucids prevailed for scarcely a century before beginning to give way to the Parthians, based in the Iranian uplands, who went on to dominate central Asia until the third century CE. Landlocked, turned in on itself, never seriously expansive in the west, this Parthia was a great success story in its own right, but the central fact of its existence was its geographic focus, far from the Mediterranean.[4] And that is why the Roman empire could exist. It had no serious Persia to deal with.

The Mediterranean unity that Rome created was artificial, and the most artificial thing about it was that it could make the Mediterranean seem sufficient unto itself, and that Rome could build an empire, most of which lay within a few days' march of that sea. The reasonable and natural course of ancient history would have wedded the Aegean to Asia, with the western Mediterranean left as the outlier. The Roman unity that emerged instead was artificial and destined to be sustainable only as long as there was no Persia to be dealt with—that is, as long as the Persians' attention did not reach the Mediterranean.

Another moment of possibility slipped away when Caesar and then Antony found a base of operations in the Egypt of Cleopatra. History written by the victors has us all heave a sigh of relief when Augustus defeats Antony and Cleopatra at Actium, but their victory might have recentered the emerging emperor far enough east to make a difference. Antony, however, is unlikely to have had Augustus's iron-willed staying power, and disintegration of the world of the Caesars could equally well have ensued.

Persia returned. It was not that Rome did not know Persia was there. The death of the triumvir Crassus and the devastating loss of his forces at Carrhae (Haran) in 53 BCE was a reminder of what was possible when Roman ambition overtook its limitations. Haran remained known, well into Islamic times, as the quintessential border city, preserving its traditional religious practices in the face of many generations of Christian and then Islamic attempts to suppress them. Ingenious reading of the Koran won an exemption for infidelity there based on the great antiquity of Haran's cults. Though the patriarch Abraham had supposedly lived there, none of the three communities that claimed his inheritance could also claim his town.

The arrival of the Sasanian dynasty in the third century in Iran and the gradual shift of its interest and energy westward into Mesopotamia and beyond began to send messages to Rome about a future that Rome never properly understood. In the second century the emperor Valerian was captured in battle on the eastern front, mocked, put to death, and then immortalized in a famous relief sculpture, larger than life-size, looming over Naqsh-e Rustam near Persepolis in southwest Iran. Valerian is shown in abject humiliation: he bows on bended knee at the foot of the triumphant Persian king. A later Christian writer's report that Valerian was skinned at his death and his skin stuffed with straw may take the story a little farther than necessary. Had Rome not been distracted by internal strife and disarray in those years, it might well have recognized the presence of a formidable foe. Of more importance than the misfortunes of one man were the Persians' raids that laid low Carrhae and even Antioch on the Mediterranean coast, and their sporadic raids beyond into Asia Minor itself. From this period came reports of Persian "magi" (learned men of the Zoroastrian religion) living scattered through Cappadocia in Asia Minor, where the Christian bishop Basil would find them in the fourth century. In the late fifth century, the Persian emperor Peroz wrote to Constantinople to complain of oppressive tactics by the now Christian government, which forbade these pious people to keep alight the eternal flame that was the focus of their rituals.

Movement was slow and stability the rule. A century passed after Valerian before the Christian-hating emperor Julian, imagining himself a new Alexander, set out to invade Mesopotamia, against military and religious advice, with too few troops and no exit strategy. He fell in battle himself—a victim of deliberate "friendly fire," some thought—not far from modern Baghdad. And then came another century, for part of which the Sasanians may have been distracted by invaders from the steppes to the northeast, from the direction of modern Kazakhstan.

Early and late, these frontier encounters changed little. The division of the lands remained what it is today: one population in the more mountainous regions of northern Mesopotamia (then Armenians, now Kurds), one population in southern Mesopotamia, most likely with connections to Iran (where we now find Shiite Muslims), and one population in the Syrian desert on both sides of the Euphrates (the land of the Sunni Muslims of Iraq). The Armenians, long independent in the mountainous lands to the north, were really an outlying remnant of an older Persia, on which they had depended, and the Christianity of Armenia was a privilege of aristocrats, who used it to help create an independent identity for themselves and their people. The border between Roman and Persian influence shifted back and forth from the third century onward, but until the age of Justinian, the real effect of these border skirmishes was slight to positive. The infusion of men and resources from outside the area to fortify and defend the borderlands undoubtedly had something to do with the flourishing prosperity of some improbable places. The limestone highlands west of modern Aleppo were one of the most intensely cultivated and densely populated rural zones of the empire, relatively democratic in their small villages and abundant in their agricultural production, especially during the fifth and sixth centuries. In the days of Anastasius, there were rumblings again in those parts, some of the things that frightened the author of the oracle of Baalbek, and the kind of frontier skirmishes that two elaborate empires can afford to undertake against each other.

Persia in those years demanded a demilitarized frontier and sought diplomatic relations through mutual recognition of rights, adoption of one another's imperial children, and a Roman subsidy for defensive works along the western shores of the Caspian near modern Baku in Azerbaijan, from which both empires benefited. That Caspian route was a traditional passage through which Huns and other northerners and steppe men would come marauding into the more fertile and settled lands south of the great Eurasian seas. Kavadh, the Persian ruler who made this proposal, was himself a man of parts, supported by Hephthalite Huns from the north and allied with a fire-breathing religious movement called the Mazdakites. A cynic would say that he saw in Rome a source of cash; a strategist would pause and wonder if we should not take him more seriously.

An ancient or modern student with a western focus could easily conflate and confuse all the regimes, peoples, and movements that have made

Iran their home. This flatters modern Persian nationalism and offers an easy outlet for ancient hostilities, but Persia of the fifth century was no more the Persia of Xerxes than was Rome the Rome of the Scipios. The empire that Rome faced was loosely connected, spread over a wide territory, and a focus of religious controversy between the more traditionalist Zoroastrians—the state religion—and the newfangled Mazdakites. (Mazdak was a Zoroastrian priest and at the same time a social revolutionary fighting against taxes. Kavadh seems to have thought the Mazdakites a useful counterbalance against the decentralized and hereditary nobility.) Kavadh's successor Khusro restored the Zoroastrians firmly to favor, but from that time until the end of the Persian monarchy we observe a gradual permeation of the highest classes of the regime by Christian individuals and ideas. (Khusro II, ruling in the late sixth century, received help from the Romans when he was temporarily ousted by a coup in 590, and once back in power kept peace with Rome until a change of imperial regime ignited hostilities. He had a Christian wife, a Nestorian Christian finance minister, and a Christian general in his closest circle.)

One strength of Persia was its decentralization. The shah (for so the ruler was already called) was a king of kings, and his subsidiary kings, strong local rulers deep-rooted in the land and people, were the strength and weakness of the whole. They were strength in that they kept the empire based in its native peoples and drew support and resources directly from them, but they represented weakness in that the shah's position depended on his ability to herd these royal cats.

Cat-herding empires do not prevail for very long. The more one tries to create a central power, the more one needs a consistent mechanism of taxation. Ancient societies had no reasonable way to measure the amount of local wealth that taxes could draw on to support a central government without draining the life out of the society. Instead they exploited incompetence and corruption to manage the process of trial and error by which they found out whether they could sustain themselves or not. They set tax rates high, and then sent dishonest and amateurish men out to collect the taxes. When revenues were not high enough, they increased the rates and sent more tax collectors out. If they could gather enough revenue in this way, then the regime was a success. If not, it collapsed. In Persia, in the end, the strength of the local magnates prevailed. They survived to reinvent themselves under Islamic rule when Persia itself vanished from the stage of history. The language and people endured and eventually restored the Persian name to the prevailing regime.

WHAT WAS TO BE DONE?

Before setting out to describe the unweaving of the Roman empire in Justinian's stubby fingers, we should pause to think about alternatives. What could one reasonably expect a Roman emperor in the year 527 to think about doing, without the hindsight we enjoy? Could it be that the unfolding of circumstances in Justinian's lifetime was inevitable?

The Roman empire lived with very substantial odds against it at every period. It was much too big to manage, for one thing. The match between its economic resources and governmental needs, depending on the mechanism for taxing the former to support the latter, was as hit-and-miss as it was for the Persians. At its core was a governmental system designed to favor rottenness, arbitrariness, and corruption. The Persian and Chinese empires of antiquity broke regularly and periodically into fragmented remnants of themselves. Rome, remarkably, resisted coming unglued for many centuries, but the more tightly its governors sought to control local life, the harder their jobs became.

In the period long generally acclaimed as Rome's most successful, the time of the Antonine emperors in the second century, one primary mechanism for ensuring a succession of competent monarchs was dumb luck—the dumb luck that kept Nerva, Trajan, Hadrian, and Antoninus Pius childless and thus sent them in search of adopted heirs whom they could conveniently select for demonstrated talent. A secondary mechanism was the good choice of successors that they made. When Marcus Aurelius had the bad judgment to beget Commodus, competent leadership vanished for a decade until another primary mechanism for selecting talented leadership, the coup d'état, brought Septimius Severus to power. (Marcus Aurelius, played by Alec Guinness, and his bloody-minded son are the cinematic embodiments of the end of Rome in *The Fall of the Roman Empire*, toga film of 1964; Richard Harris reprised Marcus Aurelius in *Gladiator* in 2000.) Severus promptly reverted to type, bringing into the palace and succession such clods and twits as Caracalla and Elagabalus, the latter of whom busied himself with service as a priest to a god he had brought from his native Syria, while arranging to have himself worshipped as well. The mid-third century saw a succession of ruinous struggles among those who grasped for the throne, and Diocletian, once settled on it himself, sought to restore a measure of order and choice to the monarchy. Constantine overthrew that scheme and replaced it with the more traditionally effective tool of dynastic murder. One can perhaps argue that Zeno and Anastasius coming to the throne at moments of dynastic interruption show what could be done by selecting for talent; but from the accession of Justin onward, corruption and family feeling balefully reasserted themselves.

Nor was any emperor in this period reliably surrounded by men of substance to offer leadership that might supplement or even rival his own. Some thought Belisarius, Justinian's best general, a candidate for replacing his master, but more remarkably he was the only plausible candidate in all thirty-eight years of Justinian's reign. Instead, those new men of the state of whom we read above were bureaucrats and servants, dignified and skilled, but incapable of ascension. They also offered no useful checks on imperial daffiness.

It did not help that emperors lived in a dark sort of ignorance rivaling that of Plato's cave. They were reasonably well informed about people and events inside their boundaries, but woefully unaware of what lay beyond. I remember the American southwest of the 1960s, when U.S. meteorologists had to labor under the disadvantage of forecasting without having any radar data from across the Mexican border to show them approaching storms. Roman emperors knew even less about the world beyond their borders.

Communication was slow, and borders had settled at points of perceived maximum extension. To go beyond them required resources and efforts that were hard to muster. Voyagers like our old acquaintance Cosmas or the visitor to Attila's camp whose stories we read represented the apogee of the Romans' attempts to penetrate and understand the world beyond their territories. Isolated individuals must have gone farther, but when we hear of merchants reaching the Han empire in China in 166 CE claiming to come from the world of Rome, we cannot be sure if they were telling the truth or merely using an exotic name to impress others.

No wonder, then, that rude surprises lay in store for emperors on more than one occasion, and that in the sixth century even the Balkans, long since domesticated as Roman provinces, had slipped back into semidarkness as a zone of mystery and rumor. This had little to do with the perceived barbarianism of their inhabitants and everything to do with bad communications and low expectations.

Finally, there were matters emperors were incapable of understanding, or understood but rarely. Chief among them were religion and economics. No one—unless we make an exception for the satirist Lucian, who came from the border town of Samosata in Syria in the second century—had a place outside the world of religious experience and practice from which to contemplate the effect on empire of emperors' various religious enthusiasms. Constantine undoubtedly thought the Christian god would help him, and may even have thought that there were already enough Christians to be a political force. After him, emperors too often made their own religious choices for statesmen based on the worst of impulses: their own theological judgments.

In the fifth and sixth centuries, we have seen the sequence of emperors distracted by Christological debates and then, as Justinian loomed, the increasingly strenuous and destructive expectation that the emperor's followers would propagate his faith to the borders of his realm, that loyalty to the state entailed loyalty to a creed. In moments of zealotry, such a tactic might have been a short-term blessing for the monarch. In the long run, adding an unnecessary and irrelevant criterion for the loyalty of one's subjects, a criterion depending on unprovable and deeply suspect beliefs that are an object of controversy on all sides, surely weakens the political consistency and functional loyalty of a society.

Emperors also flunked basic economics. No Roman emperor had a reasonable idea of the prosperity of his realm, or its diminution, except in the most general terms and mainly long after the fact. Reports of annual harvests dominated imperial thinking about economies in a manner proportional to the urgency of feeding a population but disproportional to their role in the aggregation and use of wealth for other purposes. No emperor could say, if asked, what steps he or his government might take to improve or weaken the economic fortunes of a region or of an empire, except that conquest of neighbors might provide plunder and imported wealth, and that tax relief would make the emperor popular.

The backwater western provinces were happy pigs in clover if they had good years, but they were baffled otherwise. Some western regions, notably southern Gaul and much of Africa, were fortunate enough to be blessed more often than not. Salvian of Marseilles in the fifth century wrote a stinging polemic about an empire that "dies and laughs at the same time," with enough remarks about the injustice of landlords to attract the attention of social historians; but on close examination, even Salvian is without a clue about the true forces at work. The emergence of cities, trade, and prosperous populations with a stake in the economic fortunes of their regions and their ablity to do anything—even on a purely personal or local scale—to advance those fortunes simply did not come to mind for anyone. The prosperity of the eastern provinces, moreover, was the legacy of political and social developments favoring self-aware and self-contained city communities going back to the city-state models of ancient Hellas. The best that can be said of Rome in the eastern Mediterranean is that it did not destroy what it stumbled on there.

It is a miracle, therefore, that Rome survived as long as it did as coherently as it did; we need to keep that perspective in mind alongside the more familiar line of interpretation that Rome could have lasted forever.

So where did Justinian go wrong? What should he have done? To the greatest extent possible, I try to take what I say here from examples that were known or knowable in Justinian's world, seeking to minimize the curse of hindsight. Justinian did not have the advantage of calling on John Maynard Keynes, Angelo Roncalli, or Alan Greenspan to bring economic or religious enlightenment to his world. But here are four suggestions he could have heeded.

First, he should have made peace at the eastern frontier on a basis of agreed spheres of influence and a common interest in trade. Greed and pride held Justinian back from this kind of rapprochement, with the result that in all the histories of his own realm, it is Khusro, Persia's ruler, who comes across as the enlightened modern leader. It would not have hurt in the least had Justinian bestirred himself from Constantinople, as emperors used to do, and made his way to the eastern front. Such a dramatic encounter of mutual respect and shared ambition would have shaken the expectations of men across two-thirds of Eurasia. Khusro would have welcomed Justinian, for he was said to have kept three thrones empty and waiting by his own: one for Rome's emperor from the west, one for China's from the east, and one for the king of the Khazars in the north, would they but deign to visit.[5]

For that boundary to remain hostile, armed, and simultaneously attractive and difficult (attractive to merchants, difficult for all) created and perpetuated exactly the weakness that cried out for exploitation by raiders from the north (coming down through the Caucusus) or from the south (coming up from Arabia). Muhammad's heirs heeded that cry in the seventh century, and the world has not been the same since.

Imagine a strengthened Constantinople side by side with a strengthened Persia—more urbanized, more literary, more open Persia, thanks to influences from Rome in the way that Rome had earlier been enlightened by Greece. Such a pairing would have taken the world of late antiquity a good deal farther along the road to precocious globalization than has ever been imagined. The mobility of peoples, whether individuals like Cosmas or outsiders like the Huns, was already greater than it had ever been before. In the end, the traditional powers of late antique Eurasia invited themselves to be defeated by that mobility, and the invitation was accepted.

A Roman-Persian rapprochement, leading to a more open and prosperous society from the Atlantic to the Indus, would in turn have provided opportunities for more systematic and effective contacts with the Indian subcontinent and even eventually with China. What happened instead was fractious and dissipating—one new center of power in the northwest of Europe, culminating in the rise of Charlemagne; one limping Byzantine empire in its odd outpost of Constantinople; and the heart of the Middle East seized by various Islamic powers. Persia and India became outstations of that Islamic empire for many centuries, with some connections down into Africa and southeast Asia. China remained in isolation far longer than was necessary.

Second, if it was venturesome for Justinian to imagine establishing warmer relations with the shah of Persia, it was far less difficult to think of building a diplomatically successful future with the monarchs of the western Mediterranean. By Justinian's time, a rational apportionment of lands had created stable rulers in Spain, Gaul, Italy, and Africa. For them to enter or cement a partnership with Constantinople could, would, and should have linked afresh the old territories of the Roman empire in a unity that would have been far stronger, with its distributed centers, than the overstretched and incoherent territorial unity of classical antiquity. As it was, the only one of those rulers that Justinian approached with any semblance of respect (and then mainly to create mischief for the regimes in Italy and Spain) was the one farthest from him, the king of the Franks. Once the mischief had been well and truly done and Italy was a shambles, Constantinople as good as forgot about the Franks, offering them contempt and occasional patronizing spasms of sniffy respect, until the Franks and their allies repaid the contempt in kind by pausing on their way to the Holy Land to seize Constantinople in 1204, thus reshaping the Mediterranean economy for the benefit of the Venetians. By 1400, the Byzantine empire was merely a fading city and a collection of small towns. The ruin of the Byzantine empire itself in the later middle ages was critically facilitated by its failure to make real peace and good relations with the west.

Third, peacemaking east and west would have left Justinian free for the most critical task facing him, the one he most consistently neglected: the pacification and development of his own homeland in the Balkans. We do not know Justinian's mind well enough to understand how and why he could muster all his resources for conquest and ostentation in places where he had, truth to tell, no grounds for action, while at the same time he so consistently undermanaged, underattended to, and underdeveloped the Balkan lands of his birth. He was content to imitate his predecessors weakly, attempting with far less success than Zeno and Anastasius to play forces off against one another.

Such geopolitical wisdom may have lain beyond Justinian's ken, I admit. Economic wisdom was demonstrably beyond him and his times, as he surveyed a capital pumped up with wealth leached away from lands no Byzantine emperor would ever again visit.

The fourth and last piece of advice that even a contemporary might have given Justinian and that he should have heeded was straightforward—to take his religion a little less seriously. The natural wealth and strength of the oddly configured empire that Justinian inherited lay in the south and east, in the larger Syria behind Antioch and the larger Egypt behind Alexandria. Justinian came to power with one religious idea—support for Chalcedon—and promoted it relentlessly. He managed by the end of his reign to confirm Egypt in its alienation and hostility to the throne and his religion, and to see Syria turned decisively against the metropolis as well; both became hotbeds of monophysitism. On a churchly balance sheet, Justinian could take comfort in the flourishing of Chalcedonian ideas in the heavily subsidized city of Jerusalem and its neighboring monasteries, and he built a huge new church adjacent to the Temple Mount there, again rivaling Solomon. He also had to accept, however, that the other form of Christianity he thought most deviant, Nestorianism, fled across the frontier to Persia and became effectively the official form of Persian Christianity from that time forward. Medieval and early modern travelers to the eastern realms, such as Marco Polo, found Christianity there ahead of them, but mainly in the forms Justinian had banned, for so it was that the gospel reached to those ends of the earth.

In the end, it was his religious obsession more than anything else that enabled Justinian to kick away his opportunities and to leave his successors with few choices except to muddle and manage in the world he had ruined.

Talk about a tough act to follow.

5

Wars Worse Than Civil

HEN WE COME to Justinian's wars, we must be students of Procopius, but we must read him cautiously.

Procopius saw perfectly well that Justinian never fought a war he should have fought and that he was eager to fight the ones he needn't have ventured, rivaling in his ambitions (but not his successes) the emperor Trajan 400 years earlier. Justinian also never finished one war before starting another, and he had an infinite capacity to deny, to himself and to the world at large, the catastrophic failures that followed his adventures. The Persian wars could be made to seem a stalemate, with only a little stretching of the truth; the African wars could be made to seem successful, as long as one ignored a pesky and continuing insurgency; and the Italian wars could be made to seem a triumph of long-suffering and patient government, until the reader realized that a war lasting nineteen years and resulting in no stable regime for the nation, which had given its blood offerings and seen its cities ravaged, was anything but a success.

Read aright, the stories that Procopius tells, and that I will recount as succinctly as possible, are the public chronicle of the flagrant self-inflicted ruin of the Roman empire.

ALL QUIET ON THE EASTERN FRONT

During the fifth century Persia had been preoccupied with affairs on its own eastern front, as the Hephthalites—who made their home between Persia and India, in lands again acutely troubled today—sorely pressed on Persia's most vulnerable approaches much as they did on the Gupta empire of India. The Hephthalites supported implicitly the long reign of Kavadh I (488–531, with interruptions), allowing him to pay more attention to the prosperous western part of his empire. Anastasius was the first emperor in decades to see Persian activity, but he controlled the frontier with a few skirmishes and with an enlightened public works project: building the frontier post—almost a city—of Daraa in 506, and granting it his own name, Anastasiopolis. From that fortified location, Roman troops monitored the border and maintained arm's-length relations with the Persians beyond.

The stories Procopius has to tell of Justinian's Persian wars, by contrast, mainly represent the period of obtuse skirmishing in the late 530s, starting up north in the Caucasus and scattering along the border. A Persian historian of the same period would pay much less attention to these events, and we have to bear in mind that one of Procopius's intentions is to show us the arrival of the Persian king Khusro as the heroic antithesis of Justinian. (Khusro reigned 531–579; thus he and Kavadh controlled Persia for just over ninety years.) The wise and brave emperor who leads his forces to victory offers at every turn an implicit rebuke to Justinian, hiding in his palace.

The skirmishes at the beginning of Khusro's reign concluded with what both sides called the "endless peace" of 532, purchased by Justinian for a mere 11,000 pounds of gold. "Endless peace" lasted eight years.

But when Justinian started sending his main forces west to fight even more foolish battles, Khusro doubtless understood what it meant and so in the late 530s began pressing for tribute. There was an old argument that Persia deserved Roman support for what it did in protecting the Caucasus passes against invaders from the steppes, protection from which both Rome and Persia benefited. Rome never acquiesced, so the Persians took to the field. (They may have been encouraged by an embassy sent to Persia from Witigis, whom we shall see leading the beleaguered forces Justinian was trying to overthrow in Italy, now encouraging the Persians to open a second front.) City by city, Khusro got what he wanted, from Edessa, Hierapolis, and Apamea. In the year 540, he got as far as Antioch, raiding, plundering, and devastating the great city of the Roman east, which would never be the same. It could not have helped if the city's residents heard that when Khusro returned to Ctesiphon, he built (or perhaps merely renamed) a city there "Khusro's City Better than Antioch" to mock them!

A revival of Roman attention in the early 540s led to a truce in 545, which would last, in the main, until Justin II frivolously returned to warmongering in the 570s, leading to another twenty years of intermittent conflict, and then again to twenty more years in the early seventh century. Because Procopius gives us a detailed account of the skirmishes of the late 520s and again some coverage of the 540s, it is customary to take these hostilities more seriously than they deserve to be taken in themselves, as though they represented (as Justinian probably thought they did) a recrudescence of ancient hostility between east and west, between great personified empires. No such backsliding needed to occur.

At the end of the sixth century, the border between Rome and Persia would still be more or less what it had been 200 years earlier. Blood and treasure had accomplished nothing except the exacerbation of hostility and an impediment to mutual understanding. The stage was set for bloody and desperately ill-advised conflict in the seventh century.

SHOCK AND AWE IN AFRICA

The flotilla that Belisarius led to Africa was arguably the largest force of sea power ever assembled to that date, unless we believe that the emperor Leo's ill-fated assault on the Vandals in 468 had numbered the 100,000 troops our sources imagine. Nothing like Belisarius's flotilla would sail in the Mediterranean until the wars of Turks, Venetians, and Spaniards in early modern times. Ten thousand infantry, 5,000 cavalry, and another 1,000 light-armed mercenaries from amid the Huns and Heruls filled 500 carrier ships, accompanied by another 100 or so light warships for defense and maneuvering. Setting out from Constantinople in June 533, with the prayers of the patriarch filling its sails, the flotilla made its leviathan way from Constantinople down through the Aegean with halts and delays, including one for a bout of dysentery among the troops. It passed Crete, then accepted the hospitality of Theoderic's successors, who let its ships port and water in Sicily. From there it struck out bravely at just the right season for the African coast at the shortest crossing, heading for the Tunisian coast south of Carthage.

The flotilla's size was both its strength and its weakness. Laden with soldiers, drawn mainly from Balkan provinces that could ill afford to spare them, it probably carried enough weapons and food to sustain the trip on limited rations, but fresh water was a trickier business, as always with the transport of human beings on a salt sea, whether it was crack Roman legions or African slaves more than a millennium later. If rainwater failed to supply enough, the ships had to land periodically, with consequent devastation to all those on shore wretched enough to come within reach of hungry, thirsty, libidinous soldiers.

The Africa the flotilla approached was far from ready for it and easy to misread. Justinian was sure, Procopius was sure, and therefore every modern reader is sure that his troops were invading the "Vandal kingdom of North Africa," which sounds like a very different thing from the Roman Africa that had gone before. As everywhere and every when in this period, it's important to catch both the continuities and the discontinuities, region by region and place by place, to make sure we don't deceive ourselves.

The war band we call the Vandals had crossed the Rhine in 406, far from Rome, when Honorius's and Stilicho's attention was focused elsewhere. They appeared in Africa more than twenty years later, under disputed circumstances. At a minimum, we must account for the romanization of a generation that elapsed between the crossing of the Rhine and the crossing of the Strait of Gibraltar. The young men who fought in Africa had all been raised to manhood inside Roman boundaries, and however romanized they were as its neighbors, they were assuredly more so now. Their role in Africa, moreover, was not that of men from the moon, but that of participants in local political dramas. It was said, very likely falsely but said nonetheless, that they had been invited into Africa by one of the Roman generals there, seeking allies against rivals. In the course of a decade, they supplanted those generals and constituted the sole military power between Gibraltar and Cyrene. Carthage fell to them, less by main force than as a result of their growing rootedness in Africa itself. The advantage shared by all these rogue war bands—the ones we call barbarian—was their willingness to settle down and make a place their own. Rome had flourished by building professional, rootless armies that could go anywhere. Armies like that make excellent attacking machines, but if the task is defense, troops close to their homes have a great advantage: short supply lines, easy recruitment of replacements, and a passionate commitment to what they fight for. Roman government in Africa in the fifth century was a plant that lost its roots and so consequently lost its branches and flowers.

The new regime in Carthage owed nothing to anyone and saw no reason to regret its independence. From an African point of view, the heavy taxation that had drawn the produce of Africa, and much of its wealth, across the water to Italy could be done without very easily. The harbor of Carthage was renovated in the fifth century and trade clearly continued, though on terms more advantageous to the Africans than in the days of Roman taxes. Scholars continue to explore just how far the economic relations between Africa and the rest of the world were different in the last years of the fifth century from what they had been a century earlier, but the volume certainly subsided.

In Carthage itself, you might not notice the change. The Vandals, if we have to call them that, are famous for the decadent luxury of members of their upper classes, who clearly prospered well in their capital city. If archaeology were freer to pursue its business in Algeria than has been the case since before the war of independence half a century ago, we would know better just how much the decline of involuntary trade was reflected in the fading of prosperity in the Numidian uplands and the valleys where Augustine had grown up and lived. But the Vandals ran their province much as it had been run before. For the rest of the Roman world, the experience was a bit like the "oil shock" of 1973. Prices went up, and the sellers did just fine, while customers learned to make do with less for their money. The real blow of the Vandal conquest, in other words, was felt outside Africa.

Carthage was still Carthage. We have remarkable works of literature written there under Vandal rule, none more remarkable than Martianus Capella's *Wedding of Philology and Mercury*, nine books in which old myth and new erudition dance together in what amounts to a handbook of the liberal arts for the most refined of literary tastes. The collection called *Anthologia Latina*, which we have in an eighth-century manuscript, was put together in Carthage c. 532–534: that is, just on the brink of the moment when Justinian's forces would shatter a very civilized regime. Its riddles, epigrams, and showpiece verses that can be read backward and forward reflect a highly sophisticated audience, and the Vergilian centos they contain—that is, fresh poems made entirely out of lines of Vergil—required a well-educated audience to be appreciated at all. Thrasamund, Theoderic's contemporary on the throne of Carthage, appears as a benevolent monarch building and restoring the glories of his realm, as any Roman might. Latin was the only language in use, and when the Vandals were overthrown and we come to a period where more documentation and narrative survive, the life of a traditional Roman province was so easily resumed that we have to believe it was never really interrupted. Fulgentius, a writer both traditional (in his *Mythologies*) and orthodox (for his books of Christian theology), came from a family that had recovered its ancestral estates, where he spent his early years managing the business. (We met him on a pilgrimage to Rome when Theoderic was there.) If we did not know the story of Africa and its conquests, the archaeological remains we can see would not encourage us to think of great disruptions.

Only in the matter of religion was the regime idiosyncratic. The reputation of Vandal Carthage has been stained by the polemics of the Catholic Victor of Vita, whose account of life in his province under the Vandals is a deliberate attack on the persecution of true religion by the Arian state and its clergy and minions. Even in his account, the passage of time mitigated the hostilities, until Hilderic, ruling in the 520s and bearing in mind that he was descended from Roman emperors as well as from Vandal kings, allowed Catholic bishops to return to their sees and sought to make peace with the empire. A sober reading of Victor of Vita's lurid text, "against the grain," as one recent scholar put it, suggests that Victor overstates his case, not least to dissuade his fellow Catholics from sidling across the street into the churches of the majority and the mainstream. Just as the Donatists of Africa accepted a government-mandated religious change in and after 411, when Augustine and his henchmen succeeded in having their opponents suppressed, it is clear that when the new flavor of religion in power became Arian, most Africans, eager to stay right with their god and unfastidious about doctrinal nuance, found the bigger and more prosperous churches good places to go. When Justinian's troops returned and imposed another regime change, the movement back to official Christianity was easy, natural, and untroubled.

For a generation after they arrived, the new Vandal African leaders retained the military prowess that had brought them to power and that gave them confidence. Self-assertion and a vision of opportunity brought an African fleet against Italy in 455, succeeding where the Carthaginians had failed three times. The symbolic value of an attack on the city of Rome itself by barbarians remained and remains strong, and so this event and Alaric's earlier sack in 410 remain the benchmarks of terror and destruction in the minds of readers of easy history.[1] The events of 410 and 455, however, were nothing compared with what nominally Roman troops would bring about in the sixth century. The emperor Leo's attempt to attack the Vandals in return in 458 ended in ignominious failure—a failure that would have been much on the mind for Justinian and Belisarius most of a century later.

The Africa of the late fifth century, however, settled into a stable and enduring pattern, increasingly at peace with those around it. In particular, under Odoacer and Theoderic, in the age of rational coexistence and stabilization, the Vandal rulers were respected as equals and left to flourish. There are worse fates. When the heroic conqueror Gaiseric died at Carthage in 477 at great age, a sequence of more and more romanized successors managed the realm rationally and strategically. Gaiseric's son Hunneric had been married to Eudocia, the daughter of Valentinian III and granddaughter of Galla Placidia, and so in 523 there came to the African throne Hilderic, grandson of the conqueror—and grandson equally of Valentinian III. He succeeded Thrasamund, who had been married to Theoderic's sister Amalafrida and thus bound to the Italian regime in a network of dynastic politics following African raids on Sicily in 491. Under Hilderic's rule, from 523 to 530, Theoderic's widowed daughter was imprisoned and died, and the regime was nothing but friendly with Constantinople and its powers. At the same period, Justinian, just coming to the throne in his own name, would observe a similarly complaisant and apparently friendly regime in Italy under Amalasuntha during the regency of her son Athalaric. On one reading, Justinian's ambitions at reconquest arose from his sense of both Africa and Italy as now so close to friendly that only token force would be needed to restore regimes which would be loyal to him in every important way.

The overthrow of Hilderic by his cousin Gelimer in 530 gave Justinian his pretext, and the fleet set out on its mission in 533, doomed to succeed. It should have failed, and failure would have been better for all. Instead, victory was facilitated by a catastrophic breakdown of intelligence on the part of the Africans. News of a rebellion against African rule in Sardinia had sent Gelimer's own fleet and forces north on what proved a fool's errand and left the African mainland effectively undefended. Belisarius, meanwhile, knew not his own good luck, and so steered to land far south of Carthage, more than 150 miles from his goal. At best, it would be ten days' cumbersome march, with the fleet following close beside and the army staying in sight of the sea. Good luck along the way, in finding local officials who preferred capitulation to slaughter, eased the journey. A single battle, ten miles from Carthage, in which the defenders' bad luck in some opening skirmishes was followed by Gelimer's timid generalship, won the day for Belisarius's cavalry and his Huns, long enough for the infantry to catch up with them and march triumphantly into Carthage on September 15, 533.

Historians from Herodotus to Procopius recount ancient battles with discouraging sameness over most of 1,000 years, for good reason. Fortified vehicles are the most dramatic weapons any military force can bring onto a battlefield where forces oppose each other face to face, but they are regularly rendered obsolete. The war chariots of the early Iron Age, known in Egypt, in Persia, and at Rome, had proved no match for real cavalry, when the breeding and mastery of horse allowed mobility and agility to triumph over heavy machinery. The ancient world gave the edge to cavalry. Greeks versus Persians in the fifth century BCE and Romans versus "barbarians" in the sixth century CE were battles remarkably similar in appearance. The irreducible minimum of violence lay in brute force and blunt objects, parried by man-made shields and battlefield tactics. Sharpened iron weapons—swords and spears—had much greater power and did much greater damage, but were at risk of loss and destruction. The thrown spear, in particular, could return to its owner and do him damage.

On foot, men of immense strength, stolidity, and bravery—for by such qualities we must characterize the willingness to suffer privation on privation and the very great likelihood of ending by being hacked to death under the open sky or enslaved by more forgiving brutes—these were the cheapest and most reliable of forces. They needed food, weapons, and some faint prospect of retirement to small farms as a gift from their general. The life of the ancient soldiers was grim, and grimmer for the realization that some chose it over far worse.

Cavalry, the embodied power of the bow and arrow on horseback, took advantage of mobility and ingenuity to run rings around foot soldiers. The decisive difference in battle after battle in the ancient world lay in the intelligent deployment of numerically advantaged cavalry. Using the landscape of a well-chosen battlefield to give the cavalry its freedom made the difference between victory and defeat. In Africa in 533, Justinian's wealth, the experience of his troops and officers, some intelligence in tactics, and a great deal of good luck carried the day.

The defeated Gelimer went to ground a few dozen miles west of Carthage and lurked there until Belisarius sent out the cavalry once again to pursue him in December, and a second battle, fought with equal timidity, won the day decisively for Belisarius. Belisarius's forces had known warfare well, but the Vandals had been mainly peaceful for fifty years and more by this time. Such quietude does not produce warriors or generals. Gelimer retreated farther west himself and held out against capture a few months longer, finally surrendering in the spring of 534.

Belisarius returned to Constantinople from what appeared to be his greatest success, bringing along many prisoners. He was accorded the oldest of Roman honors, the triumph—a generous gift from the otherwise usually jealous emperor, Justinian. The site in these times was not the forum but the circus, the center of secular ritual in Constantinople. Gelimer followed Belisarius on foot, chained and to all appearances doomed. The official piety of the historian had Gelimer look about and quote Ecclesiastes ("Vanity of vanities, all is vanity"), but any sobriety of that sort was quickly undermined. Due diplomatic courtesy prevailed, and Belisarius offered the Vandal a fine estate in Galatia in central Asia Minor, there to live out his days as a private citizen. It is even said that Belisarius would have given his prisoner a grand title, but Gelimer refused to convert to Constantinople's anti-Arian creed and so missed a chance at even greater dignity. Some of his troops reappear in the years afterward in one or another Roman battle on the eastern front.

The story told in Constantinople was that the treasures recovered included the golden vessels of Herod's temple, supposedly seized by the emperor Titus at the sack of Jerusalem in 70 CE, then seized again in Rome in 455 by the Vandals. If we did not know that Justinian was well along in rivalry with Solomon on many fronts—in building Hagia Sophia in Constantinople and the great new church in Jerusalem—we might be more inclined to believe this tale.

Procopius confines his story to wars, not peace. As a result, he gives us only the tip of the iceberg for the story that follows Belisarius's conquest of Africa.[2] The long history of Byzantine rule in Africa is familiar to few. For a century after Justinian, however, the province lived through its least prosperous and most challenged age since the destruction of Carthage in 146 BCE. Most writers make much of the fact that Berber raids rendered life miserable for a generation of Roman generals, without pausing to realize that the Berbers' increasing organization, self-awareness, and self-confidence was a sign not of the decline of civilization but of its spread. As early as 508, a man named Masuna was called "king of the Moors and the Romans" (*rex Maurorum et Romanorum*) in an inscription on stone far off in the western part of what is now Algeria, almost at the Moroccan border, and this inscription is one of more than 100 discovered from that period, far beyond the reach of Roman taxation and government.[3] The Berbers, more than halfway to civilization on that evidence alone, became in the sixth century a force to be reckoned with in and beyond the Maghreb, and they remain so today. Without ever holding power in their own name, without ever being objects of more than grudging toleration by their rulers, they have made a name and place for themselves and have kept at least some cultural traits undiminished far more effectively than many other peoples of late antiquity.

Carthage eased back into its old new role of provincial capital for the most part well. It was a fresh idea that the metropolis of state to which it looked should be Constantinople and not Rome, but Rome was now—and for the rest of the middle ages, at least—over and done with as a city to which others would look as a seat of any worldly power. Ideas and people moved back and forth now mainly from southern Italy to Africa to Constantinople, and this new Carthage would touch a significant piece of the history of the Christian churches in the sixth and seventh centuries.

Resolute in their attachment to Chalcedon and to western ideas generally, the Carthaginian Christians at first reinforced Justinian's biases, thus making it less likely still that ecclesiastical peace would come to the eastern realms. When Justinian made his final bid to pacify the east, however, it was precisely through Carthage that some of the most ardent western resistance to compromise came, thus fatally weakening Justinian's efforts at a crucial stage. The most articulate opponents of his edict against Theodoret, Ibas, and Theodore of Mopsuestia were African—Liberatus of Carthage and Facundus of Hermiane. No sooner had Justinian liberated Africa's orthodox Christians than they turned on him. By the end of the sixth century, the inclusion of Carthage in Constantinople's theological world had done much to drive another wedge between Latin west and Greek east. An Arian Carthage would have been to Justinian's advantage in many ways, had he but the vision to see it.

QUAGMIRE IN ITALY

Theodahad, supreme ruler in Italy at the moment of Justinian's invasion, is a character straight out of Evelyn Waugh. If the stakes in Italy from the 530s to the 550s had not been so high, his story would be grimly funny.

Theodahad was the son of Theoderic's sister Amalafrida. She spent more time in Constantinople than Theoderic did, living there as a companion to the empress Ariadne[4] before coming west to Theoderic's realm, and Theodahad was probably born there. (Amalafrida was the one who died in prison when her second husband, the Vandal ruler Thrasamund, left her widowed in Africa in the 520s.) Theodahad appeared by about 510 as a local strongman in Tuscany, using his connection with Theoderic to dominate and domineer the land he lived in. His presence was felt as far south as the northern suburbs of Rome, but there's no sign that he was active in the city itself, which was shrewdly left mainly to the old aristocrats and their families.

Theodahad is known for two things: Platonism and brutality. The Platonism is usually treated by scholars as a mild surprise, but if Theoderic could boast of his attachment to *civilitas* and his long colloquies with his learned ministers, it should not be a surprise that another member of the family would choose ancient philosophy as his claim to dignity and reputation. It's unlikely that Theodahad saw much of Plato in the original Greek, but not impossible that he had a house philosopher to read for him and adorn his dinner parties; that would have been a very Roman thing to do.

Theodahad first shows up in the record in a strongly worded letter to him from Theoderic, who had to remind him that scripture says avarice is the root of all evil, then added that the royal family should be above ordinary cravings. Theodahad's private army of thugs had evicted a junior member of the senatorial class from his own property and seized it for their lord. A few years later, a similar story: this time, higher-ranking dig-

nitaries had been abused, when property given to them by Theoderic himself was seized, once again by Theodahad's men. When Athalaric comes to
the throne and we get a glimpse of Theodahad again, he is now described
as a "man who takes no undue pride in his nobility, modest and prudent, a
man who adds to the glory of anyone"[5] who can call him a relative, including Athalaric.

Athalaric's brief reign was similar to the first years of the young Bashar
al-Assad in Syria today. Appearances continued unbroken from the reign
of the deceased great king, with reasonable prospects of stability and success, but with a glaring and potentially fatal weakness at the very top. But
it was by no means clear that anything was at risk. At Rome we find an
inscription from the year 533, erected by a man whose many names and
ranks make clear his claim to high family: Praetextatus Salventius Vere-
cundus Traianus, *vir clarissimus et spectabilis* (a senator, then; therefore
of good family but not of the highest rank of officeholders), who memorialized a brother also named Traianus, who had served as a provincial
governor, "preserving the empire" (*servans imperium*). There may have
been people in Italy who thought the empire had fallen in 476, but there
were at the same time plenty of voices describing the empire there as very
much alive.

So when Athalaric died and legitimacy and continuity were at risk, the
choice fell on Theodahad, improbable as he might be. Amalasuntha could
not and did not marry Theodahad, who had a wife already, Gudeliva, herself of good Gothic nobility. So in an odd *royaume à trois*, Amalasuntha
became queen (*regina*), Theodahad king (*rex*), and Gudeliva an elegant
spare tire.

It couldn't last, and it didn't. Within a year, Amalasuntha was dead,
spirited off to imprisonment on an island in a lake in Theodahad's part of
Italy and murdered there shortly afterward. Gudeliva now appeared in the
documents as queen. Theodahad, the boy who grew up in Constantinople
with royal lineage, was now the ruler of Rome.

And Italy was at risk. For once in its history, as not again for many
centuries, Italy became a thing, an object, a target. No Italy had existed
until Rome grew up inside the peninsula, linking Latium and Tuscany,
then Campania and the Sabine Mountains behind, then reaching gradually south and again north until the whole peninsula south from the Alps
answered to a single legal jurisdiction and conferred a single legal status

on those who lived there. By the time that happened, at the end of the republic, there was no other point of view—no Carthage, no Athens, no Troy—from which to gaze on the thing created. Vergil's shepherds in the *Eclogues*, complaining about the last expropriations of land that created Rome's realm, are among the first Italians, but they hardly knew it.

Theoderic had re-created Italy, a thing to inspire both envy and avarice. His domain and that of his successors ran beyond the mountains to north, east, and west, but those were only outlying lands. What Justinian and Belisarius saw was Italy proper, and they craved it, though they can have known little of it. They understood it mainly as a long meandering line, from Naples up the coast to Rome, then up the Flaminian Way, which is how they also understood the old Roman highway northeast through the mountains to the Adriatic coast, and from there, across the negligible Rubicon that had once divided Rome from its provinces, to Ravenna. The line might then extend west, to Pavia and Milan, but that was the farthest reach of the imagination Constantinople could manage. Of the irresistible and fertile landscapes of Umbria and Tuscany they may have heard rumors, as also of the fertile plains in the north, from the Piedmont through Lombardy to the Veneto, and of the less opulent but still resilient lands of what are now Calabria and Apulia. But their Italy was a limited thing, and they would ruin it, and thus nearly ruin all the rest of Italy besides.

And so in 535, Amalasuntha's death gave Justinian the pretext he needed—supposed instability and illegitimacy—to set his fleets on the water again, this time with a base of operations in Africa and doubtless still more confidence that he could seize and use Sicilian ports along the way.

Belisarius worked his way up the coast. As he took Naples against almost no opposition, the shudder of his impact cost Theodahad the throne. The last of Theoderic's family to rule, Theodahad was overthrown by one of his own hard-nosed senior officers, Witigis. Then, as he fled from Rome to Ravenna, Theodahad was cut down and killed, probably by people wanting favors from the new king.

The Italians were luckier in choosing Witigis to lead them. After forty years of mainly peaceful tenancy of a fertile, prosperous land, they had found a leader who was a gifted and able general and who would marshal them fiercely and well in combat, but to no avail in the end.

Witigis inherited an unready force facing a serious invasion, and so he yielded Rome by November 536, in the rainy season, but there was strategy in his concession. By January, with Belisarius thinking himself settled comfortably and even a bit triumphantly inside the capital city, the Italian forces reappeared and laid siege to the city, the first in a series of three dismal standoffs, which would batter and batter a city that had not been prepared to withstand ordinary warfare, much less such a wearing, tedious siege. In these desperate moments, the occupiers of the city became themselves enemies of the residents and destroyers of the city's fabric.

A year of sallies, skirmishes, and inertia passed before Belisarius broke out at last. Leaving behind a garrison, he pursued Witigis north for two years, through 538 and 539. He called for and received reinforcements from the east, and eventually his underlings took Rimini and Milan. At length Belisarius succeeded in cornering Witigis in Ravenna and, in 540, gained the capital of the kingdom that Theoderic had refounded and led from there.

No victory in this war would be a true one, and distraction followed distraction. The defeated forces in Ravenna made a quite rational choice, offering the heroic conqueror the throne he had just earned. The irony of Justinian's reign—that he was a military man who sent other soldiers to fight his wars for him—was no business of the Italians, who simply sought to make the best possible deal.

Belisarius rejected the offer, but it compromised him nonetheless. Though he returned in victory to Constantinople with a retinue of dignitaries—captives, hostages, or guests, Goths or Romans, depending on your point of view—he was denied a second triumph and instead sent to fight again the Persians on the eastern front. Every surviving member of Theoderic's Amal family was by now either in Constantinople or pacified and tamed back in an Italy that supported Belisarius's new regime.[6] Witigis himself was scorned and rewarded with a genteel retirement. The war in Italy, after all, was over.

But it wasn't. First, the Franks chose the moment of destabilization to assert their presence, sacking Milan while all the attention was on the other end of the Po valley, not so much to claim land on the peninsula as to ensure their own dominant position in Gaul by projecting their power across the Alps. In the disarray of that moment, a general—briefly king in the eyes of his followers—named Ildibad rallied the native forces of the northern corners of Italy, Liguria and the Veneto. Then a few months later a new leader emerged at the head of the Gothic-led remnants in those parts of northern Italy that Belisarius's forces had not directly subdued: Totila, a general every bit the equal of Belisarius.

Totila led that Gothic resistance for more than a decade. His ability to recruit forces all through the 540s, starting north of the Po, gives the lie to any thought that the regime of Theoderic's successors was inauthentic or poorly rooted. By all rights, an Italy that had been invaded and defeated, and whose capitals and leaders had been captured, should have subsided into surly dependency. But Totila was able to capitalize on the boorishness of Byzantine colonial rule. Very quickly, the alien presence in Italy realized that it would be confined to cities and safe zones, and from there would have to sally out to fight the unrelenting natives.

Totila was smart, strong, and patient, and so his forces began to recruit directly from the other side. There was little difference between the two sides in origins or loyalty, and if anything those who fought for their homeland had the advantage, and could even offer turncoat mercenaries the prospect of a home in the new land. We know, for example, of the general Herodianus, who had commanded a captured Naples for Belisarius, had accompanied Belisarius to Constantinople in the time of false peace, and then in 545 was sent back to command Spoleto, in the mountains between Ravenna and Rome. There he surrendered to an attack from Totila and fought at the side of his vanquisher.

The years of Totila's war were dismal for much of the peninsula, and one gets the sense that Constantinople had trouble keeping its attention and enthusiasm focused on the conflict there. In 545, Totila had made his way south, picking off Naples, and focusing his intended siege once again on Rome. Belisarius, now back in Italy, tried both by land and by sea to force his way into the old capital, but failed. The siege dragged on through 546 and ended with victory for Totila in December. By the time Totila had his way with the city, there were said to be only about 500 civilian citizens left inside; the rest were dead from starvation or (many more) had escaped during the siege to take refuge elsewhere. For Totila, the city was only a token and not a real goal, so far had its lingering symbolic value outstripped its practical importance. He left it behind for Belisarius to reoccupy and attempt to restore. It stood empty for forty days after the departure of the victor who despised it and before the return of the general who felt obliged to maintain it.

Totila's story was not that of a desperate last stand resistance, for he could muster considerable force and considerable ambition. Even late in his war, he took control of Corsica, Sardinia, and Sicily and sent an impressive fleet against the coast of Greece. He is traditionally thought to be the last barbarian freedom fighter, but it is fairer to think of him as the last Roman general defending the ancient order against the blundering hammer blow of Byzantine ignorance.

Stories of gloom and doom are everywhere in the literature, and saints' lives in particular capture fragments of a pervasive atmosphere of misery and fear. Boethius's surviving daughter Rusticiana, one of the last offspring of the old senate to be seen in the city, is said to have been reduced to begging for food by the end of this siege, throwing herself on Totila's mercy when he took the city. She fled then to Constantinople to start a new life, and that is when she made a good marriage for a daughter with a wealthy family from Egypt; the family flourished at the court of Maurice late in the century. (And she still drew revenues from property that others managed for her near Syracuse and near Rome.) We know a few stories in more detail, and they give us a sense of what it was like to endure in these years: how hard it was, but how in the end endurance was possible.

Consider a landowner, Gundila, by name associated with the new order of Theoderic and Gothic Italy, by now a long-established presence.[7] He lived somewhere in Theodahad's country, north of Rome on the edge of Tuscany. In 539, as the tide turned against Witigis, Gundila lost his property to Justinian's armies, but by a timely conversion from Arianism to Catholicism at the hands of Pope Vigilius in 540, he took advantage of the victor's generosity and got his property back. He even had a certificate from the Arian bishop of Rome to confirm that he had apostasized. Grateful, generous, and prudent, Gundila gave some of the land to the Catholic church of Saint Mary in the town of Nepi, north of Rome in territory swept back and forth repeatedly by the conflicting armies.

Wars did not let up. At some time in the early 540s, when Totila brought the native forces south again, he seized Gundila's land a second time and gave it as a reward to one of his own officers, the count Tzalico. In 544–545, Belisarius returned to Nepi and Gundila's hopes rose, but when Tzalico was expelled, Belisarius gave the land to the Catholic monastery of Saint Aelia in Nepi.

Gundila was resourceful, and so he went over Belisarius's head, so to speak, to Pope Vigilius and persuaded the pope to order the monks of Saint Aelia to return the property to him. Still grateful, generous, and prudent, Gundila shared his recovered property by donating some of it back to the monks of Saint Aelia and some more to another community of monks, Saint Stephanus's.

The war dragged on, and at some point Totila returned; we have some indication that Gundila lost land again. After the war was over and a settled regime was in place, Gundila took the case to law before a magistrate at Rome—and this is how we happen to know his story. From that perspective, the case was a mess, with, for example, heirs of Tzalico still able to claim ownership by right of the grant from Totila, and to hope the new regime that owed allegiance to Constantinople would recognize the grant. We don't, alas, know the outcome, but Gundila had made it through the two decades of war in one piece, fighting for his property and status.

In the southern reaches of Italy, in modern Calabria, Tullianus was a landowner whose family came from nowhere, yet who had broad power in his region and good connections beyond it.[8] When the Byzantine general Johannes came south to claim and exercise control over the cities of that region in 545—while Belisarius was making his great effort to regain the control he thought he had won in 540—Tullianus appeared in his presence. He represented the population of this region as independent but prudent. They would go along with whatever regime was in power, out of a desire for self-preservation rather than by conviction or design. The people said they had gone along with Theoderic's regime reluctantly, but then they felt aggrieved when the emperor's men treated them as though they were the barbarian enemy. Johannes won Tullianus's loyalty by pledging generosity. When in the next wave of conflict Totila again sent forces south to this mountainous area, Tullianus was ready to take sides and lead, and so rounded up a militia of peasants from the region. At this point he anticipated medieval feudal lords and their retinues, heroically holding a pass against the enemy. Totila was able to recruit others from the region, however (this must have happened frequently), and won the day.

Tullianus's brother, Deopheron, encountered Totila in those days not far from what is now Crotone in modern Calabria. Another general, Godilas, came with Deopheron. Godilas is identified as a Thracian, with no indication whether he had come through the Balkans on Theoderic's side or had been an officer with the forces sent from Constantinople. Together

Godilas and Deopheron pleaded for the safety of people around Crotone in the face of Totila's arrival. Usually, Totila could afford to be magnanimous, but he made an example of the commander of the fortress there—a man of Massegetic origins, therefore probably a captive or refugee from Persia—for not living up to an earlier truce agreement. He had the man castrated, and cut off his hands besides. The Italians in the citadel with him lost all their property, but the surrounding people were allowed to keep theirs if they joined with Totila. Eighty of them did.

One more glimpse can help us capture something of the mentality of the higher classes. A minor figure in the old and long-powerful senatorial family of the Anicii, Maximus, betrothed to Mathesuentha, sister of the dead king Athalaric, was quickly and probably rightly suspected by Belisarius of supporting Witigis in the 530s. He sought refuge under the protection of Totila, who put him out of the way by sending him to Campania, south of Rome, where he lived as a sort of hostage on property of his own for many years, waiting out the war. In the end, something went wrong and Totila's short-lived successor Teia had Maximus executed in 552—one of the myriad of personal tragedies in the aftermath of that war.

The church of Rome was ever itself. In 537 Belisarius, in command of the city of Rome, forced the election of a pope, the wretched Vigilius, who would comply with Constantinople's wishes in matters of political loyalty and doctrinal agreement. Vigilius was heavyset, and his enemies snorted that he brought down columns the way Samson did, but only by accident. He had been the Roman church's representative in Constantinople and Theodora sent him back precisely to see him installed as a pope likely to comply with Constantinople's wishes. Nothing we know about him suggests that a fragment of talent, principle, or wisdom disturbed him in his assiduous exploration of his anxieties and in his search for new ways of truckling to the powers that controlled him.

In the years between the sieges, Christian culture sprouted some wings. Arator, a sometime lawyer and public servant—and therefore a beneficiary of the old education—took up the churchly life, and Pope Vigilius made him subdeacon in the church of Rome. In 544, with the city under siege, he presented Vigilius with a grand poem, in two books, of the Acts of the Apostles. The pope prevailed on him to offer a reading there and then in Saint Peter's church on the Vatican hill, after which the poem would be deposited in the church's archives. The sample was so effective and so well received that the pope immediately made arrangements for a complete reading in the church of Saint Peter in Chains a few days later. That reading lasted four days (a few hundred lines of Latin a day), proceeding slowly because the audience continually interrupted the poet with requests to reread particularly delightful bits.

Here's how it began:[9]

> When Judea, polluted by the blood of its crime, had dared to perpetrate wickedness, and when the creator of all things had given back, to redeem the human race, the body he had taken in human form without stain of sin, then he deigned to touch the very bottom of hell without leaving the heights of heaven.

From Jesus's crucifixion to Paul's arrival in Rome (a fitting ending for a poem created there), Arator colors and tones the Acts in traditional solemn hexameters, and cuts no slack for Jews in this context. For a tasteful audience accustomed to showing mild learned distaste for the roughness of biblical language, such a version did not erase the authoritative text from their minds, but it produced the equivalent of a modern video dramatization: untrue to the original in any number of ways, but faithful to the audience's tastes and therefore unlikely to draw criticism. No wonder the poem was a success. If we did not know the circumstances, we would read Arator's lines exalting the eternity of the city, the glorious claims of the papacy, and the merits of Vigilius as without a sense of irony or, more to the point, as admiration for the stubbornness with which Christian structures and ideals were now integrated into old Roman ones and able to survive even the city's most lugubrious misfortunes.

In 545, Justinian's doctrinal maneuverings convinced him that he needed the figurehead of the papacy to support him in Constantinople, and so shortly before the second siege of Rome, he had Vigilius shanghaied from the city, abducting him in the very act of presiding at the Eucharist. Intention crossed with ineptitude, and Vigilius was held for a year of humiliation and impotence in Sicily before finally being taken to Constantinople, where he arrived just as news came from Italy that Totila had captured Rome. We will follow his misfortunes in Constantinople on later pages, but we may note now that whatever leadership the church might have offered in the abysmal times of the late 540s was crippled by his absence.

Nevertheless, the church lived on, and more besides. In a footnote to history, in 549, when Totila was again in Rome, the circus races were held for the last time. Through the vicissitudes of these years, the active damage of military attack and capture, the running sores of times of siege, and the inattention and lack of resources at other times conspired to do to Rome (at the hands of both sides of the conflict, both of which could make a persuasive claim to being "Roman") what no one had done in more than 900 years, since the Gauls' seizure and sack of the city in 390 BCE. The Visigoths of 410 and the Vandals of 455 had been short-term visitors, plundering rather than systematically destroying, and were soon gone. Under leaders like Aetius, Odoacer, and Theoderic, the city had survived, endured, and even been restored to some of its former glories, while its aristocratic leadership remained in control. But now the depredations were widespread, continuing, and (as it proved) irreversible. The destruction of the aqueducts left the city, for one thing, without the means to support anything like the population it had held in antiquity. Most of the damage done to the ancient city and its splendors, the damage that left it a malarial wasteland for most of the middle ages and its heart a ruin long after, was done in this war between Romans and Romans seeking the preservation of whatever they thought valuable in Roman civilization.

What must it have been like to be in the Italy that suffered these waves of war back and forth for seventeen years? Many people, away from the beaten path, were spared direct experience of savagery and loss, though even those who saw no battles saw soldiers and worse coming to seize what they needed by the brutal informal taxation of wartime. Famine in Emilia and Etruria in 549, Procopius tells us, left men desperate enough to grind acorns into a kind of wheat and bake bread from them, and there were rumors of cannibalism.[10] A few people, most of them probably among the wealthy elite whom we know, preoccupied by dreams of Romanness and very likely power, may have wished or even schemed for a Justinianic invasion, but none can have taken any satisfaction in the melancholy sequence of events that unfolded or in the devastation of society and landscape that came afterward. No good thing came from this war. Most people simply suffered, dreaded, and hoped for release.

Belisarius was gone by the time it ended, and Totila was dead. Unable to resist the temptation to achieve a lasting victory, Totila risked a pitched battle at Busta Gallorum in 552, and there defeat and death caught up with him. Procopius gives us a rousing picture of the wild war dance the king performed on the threshold of battle, but for a man whose whole experience of war had come fifty years after Theoderic's settlement in Italy, anything that risked attracting such a parody must have been a gesture rather than a living tradition, like a modern army officer carrying a sword with his dress uniform. The Amalization and gothicization of the army and regime in Italy during Theoderic's last years could have encouraged such posturing, but the almost instantaneous evaporation of Gothic culture in Italy when the war was finally over suggests how little could now be credited to barbarian vitality.

The eunuch general Narses had replaced Belisarius a few months before Busta Gallorum, coming from the Balkans, up the coast from Salona, making his way to Ravenna by June 552 with an army of 30,000. Fresh troops, they faced Totila and defeated him. Only a fragment of resistance faded away into the lands north of the Po, there to go to ground and disappear. Procopius says the Goths were expelled, but his successor in the writing of semiofficial history, Agathias, says not. It may have made no difference.

Military occupation was now the formal means of Roman governance in the land that had known the oligarchic liberty of the Roman republic. Narses would remain in Ravenna off and on until 568, and Byzantine rule would continue there until the eighth century, always based in the cowards' capital—marsh-girt for defense—with a port nearby offering the most direct boat route to Constantinople. (Narses's departure coincided with the Lombards' arrival in Italy, leading later generations to tell an improbable story about Italians who were unhappy with his rule complaining to the emperor Justin II, and Narses retiring in a snit to Naples as a result. It is just as likely that Narses thought the Lombards would make useful soldiers and so invited them in, then lost control of them.)

Justinian's response to the victory—after a quarter century on the throne, at the end of a dispiriting decade—was to try, ever the man of legal codification, to define and shape the society he controlled by writing a prescriptive text. In this case, the text was legal, not ecclesiastical: the "Pragmatic Sanction," issued in 554.[11]

The document is not without fantasy. It annuls all of Totila's acts, a dangerously destabilizing decision, tearing open wounds that would otherwise have begun to heal. Those who had sold property under duress in Totila's time could now recover it by refunding the price they had collected for it. It restored exiles, prisoners, slaves, and indentured farmworkers to the status they had enjoyed before Totila, on the assumption that the state of affairs in the early 540s, after Belisarius's first victory, was legal and Roman.

This disposition still favored the rich, such as Gundila—those who had something left—over those who had been forcibly uprooted and fobbed off with a pittance. Someone who could keep a low profile, however, could very often succeed in hanging on to what he had owned, especially if he and his family had remained in a particular place for all the years since Odoacer and Theoderic entered Italy. A man like that who had been calling himself a Goth under Theoderic's successors may just have forgotten to answer to this label any longer.

One windfall came to the church, naturally, when Arian church lands were confiscated and made over to the orthodox church. We know of surprisingly few such Arian churches—especially if one considered Theoderic's Italy an Arian, Gothic kingdom—but they faded away quickly at this moment.

Power began to fragment. Provincial governors—there would be a dozen in Italy at one moment now—could be nominated locally by the traditional local luminaries, but also by bishops. Tax collection, moreover, now devolved away from Ravenna and fell to the hands of the governors. Troops were to be provided for gently, as it were, by purchases of food and goods at market prices, not by tax, confiscation, or forced sale; and it was stipulated that in the toe and heel of Italy's boot, such purchases could be made only at the regular public markets. Civil law was to be restored, but in the absence of a strong central administration, this meant effectively the drumhead justice of local potentates, in some places generous and wise, in others doubtless extortionate and cruel.

The city of Rome was to be brought back to life. On a bridge over the Anio River not far outside the city's walls, an inscription made in 565[12] speaks of "the restoration of the liberty of the city of Rome and the whole of Italy." When Boethius was executed for hoping for "liberty for Rome," he could scarcely have had this in mind. Free grain for the citizenry and subsidies for the fine professors of the liberal arts were ensured at Rome, as well as funds for the repair of public buildings and aqueducts. We know that the old schools in which those professors taught were on their last legs by now. Of other restorations, there is not much evidence.

Ravenna told a different story. There, an infusion of energy and subsidy from the east kept the city's golden age alive a little longer. Theoderic's capital had seen art and architecture of substance and value, but it was now Bishop Maximian, placed in power in the church there under Belisarius in 546 and remaining until 556, who became the senior churchman in Italy in the absence of Vigilius and brought the new capital to architectural glory. Maximian was the first bishop of Ravenna to be called archbishop, and his rise is a sign of Constantinople's willingness to turn away from the city of Rome, which was socially messy, indefensible, and (from Constantinople) hard to reach. Ambitious building had continued past Theoderic's death, and his tomb and the great church of San Apollinare Nuovo reflect the wealth and very Roman taste and style of that generation. We wish Theoderic's palace, an elaboration of what he found on arrival, had survived as more than a faint rumor. A banker, Julian, dedicated a new church to Saint Michael the archangel and finished it before Maximian became bishop.

At the same time, a greater church had been abuilding from 526, dedicated to Saint Vitale, a bogus patron of the local church. Vitale was the father of saints Gervase and Protase, who had been martyred under the last of the bad emperors before Constantine. Their bodies had been conveniently discovered by Saint Ambrose in the 380s and played a dramatic role in solidifying the authority of the Nicene bishop in Milan when Arian forces seemed destined to prevail.[13] According to the legend in Ravenna, all three had been martyred on the site there where the church in honor of the father would be built. The astonishing church, still intact and richly adorned with famous mosaics continuing the tradition that had flourished under Theoderic, was completed and dedicated on May 17, 548, when the empress Theodora lay dying in Constantinople. Anyone who thinks he knows what Theodora and Justinian looked like draws his ideas from the mosaic procession here, which shows them and their retinues at the moment of ritual entrance to a church they never saw. Maximian finished a second new church in Ravenna, San Apollinare in Classe, in 549, after a visit to Constantinople.

Then funding slacked off, and Ravenna settled into its destiny as a provincial capital. No emperor ever set foot there again.

A COUNTRY FOR OLD MEN

Some men survived in ravaged Italy and even came to prosper again. Three of the senate's dignitaries from the days of Theoderic lived past their ninetieth birthday and remained atop the greased pole of public life—or rather, leaped from one greased pole to another, deftly and just in time. Least known to us of the three is Cethegus, sole consul of the year 504, master of the offices not long after, and patrician from 512 until his death almost half a century later in 558. Ennodius praised him in writing as a younger contemporary in his little work on the best way to educate young gentlemen; and Cassiodorus addressed a puzzling document to him consisting partly of family boasting, partly of social climbing, and partly of a biographical index of a few famous contemporaries. Cethegus persisted and persisted in Italy, holding out until 547 or so, after the fall of Rome to Totila in 546. He was by now *caput senatus* ("head of the senate" by dignity and seniority). He fled Rome before it fell because he was suspected of pro-Gothic sympathies, as many of the veterans of Theoderic's time would be suspected. When he came to Constantinople, he was regularly seen around and with Pope Vigilius, supporting doctrinal rapprochement and a more vigorous prosecution of the war at home. He seems to have stayed in Constantinople until the last dog had been hung back in Italy and the war finally ended, but we glimpse him one last time at home, now in Sicily, receiving a letter from Pope Pelagius I in about 558.

Liberius, the patrician who had been praetorian prefect in Italy before Theoderic, then served him and his successors in that role in Gaul for a quarter century, appeared in Italy in 535; there, Theodahad put him in a delegation sent to Constantinople to make peace. The sources we have credit him as the one voice who spoke up in Constantinople to report the murder of Amalasuntha, the deed that more than any other gave a pretext for Justinian's invasion. Liberius was unable, as a result, to return to any Italy not ruled from Constantinople, and so stayed on in the east, where his long experience won him appointment at an advanced age (he must have been well over seventy by then) as Augustal prefect in Alexandria, effectively Justinian's representative to and governor over Egyptian society.

In Egypt, Liberius was the grand avenging inquisitor, sent from Constantinople to bring a restive province to civil and ecclesiastical heel. He did as well as could be expected—which is to say, he left no lasting result. Justinian soon turned on him and sent out a replacement without bothering to recall Liberius. Remarkably, Liberius prevailed in an unfair fight, sending his would-be supplanter home in disgrace. Officially recalled shortly thereafter, Liberius still succeeded in defending himself before a court of inquiry on his return to Constantinople in the early 540s. There we must imagine him as part of the circle of western adventurers that also included Cassiodorus and Cethegus, eyes wide open for the main chance.

Even then, his career was not over. When Justinian prepared to send his nephew Germanus west to complete the war in Italy, Liberius was variously the stand-in and deputy as preparations dragged on, eventually going on in command ahead of Germanus, who then died before he could undertake the campaign. Justinian is said to have had second thoughts about the elderly general, but too late to stop his last success. He arrived at Syracuse to find the city under siege by Totila's forces. Undismayed, he forced his way through the barbarian lines, sailed into the harbor, and got his entire force into the city. While this was going on, Liberius's appointed successor, an erratic Armenian named Artabanes, was trying to catch up with him to relieve him of command. But Artabanes encountered a terrific storm off the coast of Calabria and wound up, temporarily, on Malta. Liberius, meanwhile, was in the beleaguered Syracuse. Procopius reports that he found himself unable to carry out successful military actions while constricted by Totila's siege forces, and that this military impotence made his troops an unwelcome burden on the limited supplies of the besieged city; so he once more embarked his troops and slipped out of Syracuse for a better encampment at Palermo—all this, while Totila was plundering Sicily at will. Artabanes finally caught up with Liberius in Palermo in 551 and relieved him of command. One story has Liberius going on a last mission to command Justinian's forces in Spain, but we find his tombstone in northern Italy, near Rimini, with a fine inscription in eight elegiac couplets, suggesting either that he retired to Italy directly from Sicily or that he made his way back into Italy after the "Pragmatic Sanction" to live in the shadow of the new regime from Constantinople. He was about ninety when he died. There is a hint that a descendant was still wealthy and well connected as late as the 590s.

Cassiodorus's story is longer, and far from over in these days at the end of the war. We saw his father briefly many pages ago, a local potentate from Squillace, in modern Calabria, keeping his feet among the shifting allegiances of the moment when Theoderic grappled with Odoacer for power, but the family story is a snapshot of survival techniques in late antiquity. We know of a single line of four fathers and sons, dying out with the one who witnessed most of the sixth century's adventures.

The family arose in the eastern empire and took its name from the ancient god worshipped on Kassios, a mountain just south of Antioch. They called the god Zeus Kassios in Greek times, claiming that the local god and the Greek lord of gods were really one and the same, though connoisseurs knew better. The family name, meaning "gift of Kassios," recalls that lineage. By the early fifth century, someone from this family was on the make in Constantinople, for it was then that we saw one member turn up in the entourage of the young emperor Valentinian III, sent west to take the throne in Italy after the death of Honorius in 425. The family stayed at court then, and that man's son turns up in an embassy, side by side with the son of the great general Aetius, seeking out Attila's court in mid-century. Between the second and third of the Cassiodori of the west, the family acquired its estate and base of operations at Squillace, on the southernmost coast of Italy, probably as a reward for service to the throne. The place wasn't special, but it was useful for its olive trees and horse pasturage. (George Gissing, an English novelist, traveling there a century ago found Squillace a squalid, muddy village, with a dump of an inn and, quite remarkably, the only undrinkable wine in Italy.) The third Cassiodorus was closely associated with that landscape until the time Theoderic called him to court as praetorian prefect. We have seen that this was an astute choice, bringing to court the wealth and influence of the most remote part of Italy, ensuring loyalty and connection to a region that Theoderic would never himself see.

The last of the Cassiodori made his first appearance in his father's spotlight, then and afterward having a Zhivago-like glow of learning and conscience—or at least conscientiousness—in a setting where rougher virtues often prevailed. But the young man would show himself equal to almost any challenge, just as Zhivago proved heroic enough in combat surgery or in facing down guerrilla chieftains, while always preferring retirement and learning.

Cassiodorus made his debut while still a very young man, as his father's *consigliere*[14] at court in the early 500s. The father retired by 507, and at that point the son became quaestor, sitting at Theoderic's right hand, spinning his words for him, engaged in the policy conversations of the inmost circles of court. Born in the south, Cassiodorus was precociously learned and eloquent: he came to court barely out of his teens, and so must already have followed the family's ambition to study in better places, most likely Rome. He was more a courtier than Boethius ever was; more dependent on, or at least loyal to, Theoderic's regime; but still very nearly Boethius's equal in intellect and education. Unlike Boethius, he was as unfailingly sure as a cat at finding his feet in any upheaval.

Cassiodorus served most of five years as quaestor, drafting laws, but also writing the official correspondence of the monarch. These letters, and others he would write in later years for the kings in Italy—so masterful was he at turning them into Roman rulers of the most impeccable eloquence—are collected in a book called his *Variae* ("Letters on Diverse Subjects"), and are a splendid source for the internal and external affairs of the kingdom for thirty years, from 507 to about 538. What they do best is show how Theoderic and his court sought to normalize his rule as a Roman—literary, dignified, cultivated, and sane.

Out of office for a few years and presumably looking after his estates and interests, Cassiodorus was rewarded with nomination as consul for the year 514, a mark of both the wealth that followed him from home and the favor he had found at court. He did not come from the most Rome-centered aristocracy, though in one fragmentary document he seemed to claim a family acquaintance with Boethius and Symmachus. The consulship gave him a chance to do a little of what we would now call relationship management with the old families there.

Even out of office, Cassiodorus was Theoderic's man. In 519, on the occasion of the great consular celebration of Eutharic's role as heir to the throne, Cassiodorus delivered public addresses in praise of the regime and wrote two important books in courtly, impeccable Latin. His *Chronicle* was a traditional account of kings, consuls, and emperors from darkest antiquity to the present, easily and naturally showing Theoderic's regime as the continuation of all that was Roman and ancient. The *Gothic History*, now lost and a subject of much speculation, was a more ambitious attempt to write of the Goths and Theoderic's Amal family as full participants in the history of the ancient world going back many centuries. They embody the ambivalence of Eutharic's moment in the spotlight, asserting Gothic identity as a way to ensure Roman authority.

Cassiodorus then vanished from the stage for a few years, until he was called back to court to be master of the offices following the downfall of Boethius, his predecessor. If we are supposed to believe that Boethius was a great man and nearly a saint, then Cassiodorus sometimes looks a little shady to his biographers for advancing at the cost of the martyr. If Boethius really had to die, then Cassiodorus was the kind of loyal servant brought back to court in a crisis.

Cassiodorus was still at work as master of the offices when Theoderic died in 526. The air was full of crisis and threat—how real we cannot tell, but Cassiodorus is credited with some bold action of a military nature. Most likely, he looked after the Adriatic fleet based in Ravenna, against the possibility that a direct visitation from Constantinople would attempt to influence, control, or terminate the young Athalaric's succession.

Cassiodorus went out of office again after writing for young Athalaric, then returned in 533, this time to the highest civil office in the land, that of praetorian prefect. He still wrote letters for Amalasuntha, Theodahad, and then Witigis, because he was so good at it, but he had higher responsibilities than wordsmithing—effectively those of prime minister. From this period we have official letters in his own voice. He was in office when the Belisarian invasion began, and he held on for three years, through the coup of Witigis and through the dismal time of the first siege of Rome.

The latest date when we see him in office in Italy is 538. The *Variae* were published about then, a monumental presentation of 440 letters that show the years of Theoderic and his successors in a bright, dignified Roman light—a publication, in other words, of undoubted relevance and even controversy at a moment when Constantinople's forces were fighting to destroy and replace what Cassiodorus had served all his life. By not mentioning the disasters crashing down on his country from all sides, Cassiodorus makes his most eloquent commentary on Justinian's ambitions.

When Ravenna fell in 540, Cassiodorus was one of those taken from there to Constantinople along with the defeated Witigis, but his dignity doubtless spared him having to be paraded as a prisoner in Belisarius's triumphal parade. He became instead one of those émigré Roman dignitaries of learning, leisure, and a keen interest in church and public affairs who by now had no choice but to side with Justinian in seeking the reconstitution of Italy on a Byzantine—that is, no longer a Roman—basis. He devoted himself to theological writing, producing a commentary on the Psalms meant to introduce to a devout audience not only that text but a finer knowledge of language and rhetoric. Learned retirement was a very old, even Ciceronian, model for Roman gentlemen who did not quite let go of their interests in the great world, but churchly pursuits would sometimes make such retirement more serious and permanent. He appears on the periphery (but was perhaps also discreetly active in the back rooms) of ecclesiastical controversy in Constantinople in the years of the wretched Vigilius (whose story we still defer, poor man). With the "Pragmatic Sanction" of 554, he returned to Italy, to Squillace, and to the ruins left by Justinian's awful war.

There, Cassiodorus spent the rest of his life on his family estates, simultaneously a great man in the neighborhood and a monk. Like many other rich Romans, he had artificial ponds carved out on his estate to hold living fish, ready for the catching and cooking. From them he gave his monastery the name *Vivarium*, "fishpond," with a whiff of ancient dignities and at the same time a touching new metaphor. Humankind, in Cassiodorus's version of Augustine's doctrine of free will and predestination, resemble fish in an artificial basin, sensing themselves free, unaware of the larger captivity and control that loom over them.

In this place, far from Rome, Ravenna, and Constantinople, but not so far from the revived Carthage, Cassiodorus had a small corps of translators and copyists working to build up a library of Christian theology. He told the story of how in the 530s, when he was praetorian prefect, he had worked with Pope Agapetus I to establish a school of Christian learning at Rome, on the model of the one that flourished in Nisibis. It came to nothing as war overtook the Italian peninsula, and what Cassiodorus could do in Squillace was of little importance by comparison with what might have been done in a flourishing Rome. The gesture should make us notice most of all that the formal teaching of theology was still essentially unheard of anywhere in Christendom west of Nisibis. Monasteries were places of doctrine and training by default, because there was nowhere else, but it was a very long time before they devoted themselves to the task systematically, and not until the twelfth and thirteenth centuries would a robust, organized theological education begin to appear in the west.

CODICIBVS SACRIS HOSTILI CLADE PERVSTIS
ESDRA DO FERVENS HOC REPARAVIT OPVS

Cassiodorus in his library—as seen in an Anglo-Saxon Bible copied from one that Cassiodorus's monks produced. The image is notionally of the scribe Ezra, but the bookcase anachronistically contains the New Testament as well as the Old, and all the furniture, clothing, and appurtenances are characteristic of Cassiodorus's time.

Cassiodorus had another thirty years of life in front of him, to spend in learned retirement and close correspondence with at least some of the world outside. The audience he had in mind for his commentary on the Psalms was mainly the small group of monks he had around him in Italy—for they may already have been there, ornaments to a secular dignitary's estate, for many years.

Cassiodorus was eccentric enough to believe that the great minds and pens of Greece and Rome had in fact derived, not to say stolen, their wisdom and their eloquence from the ancient Hebrew scriptures. For hundreds of years Christian intellectuals had retold a story many of them knew was untrue, that Plato had studied at the feet of Jeremiah in Egypt and had gotten his best ideas from the prophet. Inspired by that illusion, Cassiodorus thought that now was the time to teach true rhetoric and eloquence to monks, whose classic texts would be those of scripture rather than secular literature. For the moment, let us leave him, Zhivago fleeing Petersburg, Moscow, and the great world for retirement and infatuation (scripture playing the part of Lara here) in a remote province, where the habits and culture of wealth could forestall the worst effects of rustication and isolation.

There can have been few if any other men in Italy in Cassiodorus's time who matched him in more than superficial ways, but the redirection of ambition to property and province must have been typical, at least of those who survived.

Cassiodorus himself lived on there until at least his ninety-third year, still writing and reading. Many like him did not survive nearly so long.

MYOPIA

The glory of the ancient world, we are regularly told, is the emergence of the critical tradition of Greek philosophy. What is fundamentally "western" about us goes back to Athens, as our educational tradition has long assured us and sought to demonstrate.

Justinian, the man who would restore the Roman empire, did not agree. The overpowering force of his Christianity and the thinness of his own educational attainments made him blind to the traditions in his own backyard.

The traditions of classical Athens remained vibrant as late as the reigns of Anastasius and Justin. Plato's Academy, almost 900 years old, was still alive and well, doing business on its original site at the foot of the Acropolis. Where once the neighborhood had echoed with the debates of many philosophical schools—Academics, Peripatetics, Cynics, Stoics, and Epicureans chief among them—the teachings of Plato had won the day.

Why should Justinian know or care about Athens, after all? No city beyond the walls of the only one he ever knew meant anything to him. When Justinian took the throne, the cities of northern Syria were in the midst of their period of greatest prosperity. Farther south, the Ten Cities of northern Palestine, between Jerusalem and the Sea of Galilee, were building and prospering, as was Caesarea on the Mediterranean coast. Did the emperor know? Could he respect such prosperity and think creatively about how to protect and extend it? Harder still, could he see the way such prosperity, near a desert border with another empire, might be a way to reduce tension and build a community of interest across that border? Not likely.

His ignorance of Athens and its glories, however, is inexcusable.

Athens, the ancient capital of Greek culture, had kept its place in Hellenistic and Roman times as a citadel for philosophers. The names and reputations of Socrates, Plato, Aristotle, and their successors and rivals had survived in formal philosophical schools visited over the centuries by Roman senators such as Cicero and future emperors such as Julian. Like any cultural center, it had periods of obscurity, but it never lost its place, and by the fifth century it came back into its own as one of the two centers of philosophical argument and disputation in the Roman world. Athens remained untouched, moreover, by Christianity, at least in its philosophy—in contrast to Alexandria, whose long history of inclusiveness, going back to the days of Philo the Jew and others, made it a place where traditionalist philosophy was still carried on with sometimes disconcerting Christian overtones and even melodies. Cosmas's rival John Philoponus was in the sixth century the most distinguished practitioner of that line of thought.

Even long after the emperors had become churchgoing Christians, listening to monks and building houses of worship, Athens and its school flourished. Students came from all over the Greek world, proudly wearing the distinctively flamboyant student's gown of the city. Early in the fifth century, the leading teacher, Leontius, sent his daughter to Constantinople to be the bride of the young emperor Theodosius II, changing her name from Athenais to a Christianized Eudocia. Proclus, the most profound and prolific leader of the Platonic school that flourished there in the fifth century, wrote inexhaustibly, and his *Elements of Theology* survive as a handbook of the core of philosophic doctrine in his school. His successor wrote Proclus's life story as the tale of a paragon of "pagan" piety. We are told he observed all the holy days of peoples and nations, undergoing purification rites of the Great Mother, of Orphism, and of the Chaldeans. He wrote hymns and worked wonders: he could end a drought or cure a child by praying to Asclepius.

The school was quite sure that it was the authentic and direct descendant of Plato's Academy. Proclus's successors were not up to his standard, but they were professional and passionate. Proclus's immediate successor, Marinus the Samaritan, left behind the stiff-necked monotheism of his origins and wrote commentaries on Plato's *Philebus* and *Parmenides*, but his books were refuted and rejected by his own successors. Hegias, the leader of the school in the years immediately after 500, conducted frankly non-Christian religious rites, but philosophically the school was not at its strongest.

In 515, the school fell under the leadership of a more impressive figure, Damascius ("the Damascan"). He had studied under the great Ammonius at Alexandria, emphasizing astronomy and Platonism, and he taught rhetoric there as well before moving to Athens, where he completed his education in the other disciplines. He wrote commentaries on Plato and also on the mystical Chaldean oracles that formed the link between late antique neo-Platonism and traditional religion. One later writer even attributes to him a collection of 572 "tales of the supernatural," religio-mystical stories implicitly criticizing the prevailing Christian interpretation. This collection must have included the story he told elsewhere of the man who could infallibly tell which statues of the gods were divinely inhabited and which were not, dropping into an ecstatic trance when he encountered the real thing. Two of the students Damascius recruited capture the ambiguities of the moment: Epiphanius and Euprepius were both born in Christian households in Alexandria, but the first had become a priest of Osiris and the second a priest of Mithras, before turning to the work of academic philosophy in this environment suffused with traditional religion.

Left to their own devices, these leaders of the Academy would have been an interesting and important center of speculation and analysis in later ages for Greek and even Latin Christendom to hear and refute or hear and heed. They were not to be left to their own devices. The religion of Justinian not only expected and promoted conformity but demanded it, and set out to uproot all rivals. Justinian's hostility against surviving pockets of what he interpreted as paganism exceeded even the hostility he showed toward Christians whose thought differed from his own. With other Christians he at least attempted diplomacy before preferring suppression. Anti-paganism had reached Athens in the fifth century; the old shrine of Asclepius on the southern slope of the Acropolis was destroyed and replaced by a church by the year 500. The replacement was strategic, for the church was built so as to take over and efface completely the traces not only of the temple itself but of the sacred spring, the porch where the sick had lain to wait for divine healing, and the shelter where visitors stayed. At the same time, the cult statues were removed from the temples of the Acropolis, and we must imagine how that striking outcrop of rock loomed over the city, dramatic then as now because of the astonishing Parthenon—but then with the hilltop dark and silent, vaguely threatening (at least to some) as the ancient home of demons.

Damascius didn't think highly of these officially sanctioned Christian vandals who were cleaning up the town. He described them in his *Life of Isidorus*: "A race dissolved by every passion, destroyed by uncontrolled self-indulgence, cringing and womanish in its thinking, close to cowardice, wallowing in all swinishness, debased, content with servitude in security, such is the life of those who belong to the present generation."[15]

What exactly happened next at Athens is disputed to this day. In the year 529, shortly after taking the throne in his own name, Justinian went on the warpath against paganism. In Constantinople, his purge amounted to what one scholar has called a "reign of terror" against traditionalists in many walks of life:[16] not just professors and sophists, but lawyers, bureaucrats, and noblemen, of whom many were jailed and many others tortured. The same steps taken in the provinces had the effect of forcing the teachers of Athens to abandon their school and their ways. "Closing the university at Athens" is the melodramatic description that moderns use for this event, and it makes a milestone for those plotting the fall of an ancient pre-Christian culture. Nothing quite so simple happened, for Justinian's actions did not directly attack the schools but rather attacked the religious practices of traditionalists who continued the old ways. Here is one version of his decree from a historian of the time:

> During the consulship of Decius, the emperor issued a decree and sent it to Athens ordering that no one should teach philosophy nor interpret astronomy nor in any city should there be lots cast using dice; for some who cast dice had been discovered in Byzantium indulging themselves

in dreadful blasphemies. Their hands were cut off and they were paraded around on camels.[17]

If the schools at Athens were well populated with such people, whose astronomy was astrological and whose dice playing was fortune-telling, then the schools were affected. Archaeologists have excavated the largest house on the Areopagus, between the ancient agora and the towering symbol of the Acropolis. During the 530s, the house underwent renovation with religious overtones. The decoration was Christianized by removing old statues and putting a cross in the handsome mosaic floor. Outside the house, archaeologists discovered a well containing seven unambiguously traditional religious statues, all carefully preserved—and probably hidden in fear of Justinian's enforcers.

Whatever the sequence of events, the teachers of the school, many of them having come from homes in Syria and Palestine, left Athens and moved east. In such a scattering, people landed in many places, but the group whose fate we hear about went all the way to the Persian border, there to seek refuge. The story has it that Khusro at Ctesiphon welcomed them and made them feel at home. The Christian storyteller suggests with amusement that they thought they would find the ideal Platonic state there. Disillusioned or homesick, they retreated soon afterward to more familiar territory, and in particular to the long-resistant religious traditionalism of Carrhae (or Harran), on the Roman side of the border. Damascius, their most sophisticated thinker, was still in his native Syria a few years later, writing poetry.

Not much changed in Harran in spite of Justinian. Later in the sixth century, Maurice ordered bishop Stephanus of Harran to convert his pagans to Christianity, but ordered as well that recalcitrants should be killed, and their bodies mutilated and paraded through the town. The bishop was smart enough to forget to comply. Then or later, someone collected prophecies from pagan sources to persuade the philosophers of Harran to convert to Christianity. Tabit bin Kurra, a court astronomer from Baghdad, wrote the history of late antique religion in Harran in 901 CE, offering a memorial to the city's resistance to the "error of Nazareth."

Even long-pious Edessa had its relapses, as when a wave of persecution of pagans found sacrifices to Zeus there in the 590s. The culprit turned out to be Rufinus, a Christian clergyman of Antioch, who was tracked to a temple in Edessa where he committed suicide by ripping his bowels out with one of the implements with which he had made sacrifices to the king of the sky. The witch hunt culminated with the show trial and condemnation in Constantinople of the praetorian prefect's vicar in Edessa, Anatolius, who confessed to being part of a high-placed ring of heathens, and who told a lurid story of sacrificing a boy on the high altar at Daphne, outside Antioch.

Elsewhere, paganism survived and adapted itself in surprising ways. In southern Asia Minor, a saint's life from the sixth century has the saint himself "sacrifice" seven calves in the chapel of Saint George; crowds of cross-bearing faithful then recline on couches for the banquet of meat and bread and wine that the saint offers. There is nothing in the description that does not exactly match traditional pagan practices.[18] At Aphrodisias, a handsome city in southwestern Asia Minor, we come on the old festival of the Maioumas, once an object of intense Christian hostility. The puritanical Jacob of Serug, connoisseur of village paganisms, railed against it, and the woman-fearing John Chrysostom a century earlier allowed himself to imagine the horror of naked water sprites frolicking in the festival's pool. But at Aphrodisias, we have evidence of the festival under direction of a Christian, and we see the festival surviving—somehow innocuous by now—at Constantinople into the eighth century.

BALKANIZATION BEGINS

Justinian came from the Balkans, from the land now clumsily called the Republic of Macedonia. As he fell in love with the show of empire in Constantinople and sought to transplant it everywhere, his mind went not least back to his hometown, which was now made to labor under the name of Justiniana Prima and was bathed in a flood of money for appropriately pompous public buildings in a tiny city of less than twenty acres and with only seven churches. Archaeologists find no sign there of traditional urban buildings for administration and commerce: in this region, such towns were now only church-centric forts. Where once there had been modest cities (mainly in the east, in what is now Bulgaria) and passably prosperous estates, the fifth century saw less and less prosperity and fewer of both characteristic domiciles of the wealthy. This was soldiers' country now.

Justinian also insisted—and his insistence lasted for a generation or two—that his particular city would now become the capital of its region, in preference to more strategically situated towns.[19] Justiniana Prima (probably modern Caricin Grad) was last reported as occupied in 615 CE and has seen its grandeur shrink to nothing, with barely archaeological sketches to show how it was laid out. Justinian's patriotic generosity was misplaced, and wasted.

While Justinian pursued this show of imperial glory, he neglected his plain duty. The Balkan provinces were now the prime source of manpower for the imperial military, and so Justinian regularly sought to fill his ranks from them. His best source of men lay not within his own domains but across the Danube in modern Romania, among the Venethi, dwelling where once the original Visigoths had lived.

To read the chronicles of Balkan warfare in this period is to wonder what Justinian could have been thinking. Bulgars and Sclavenes—new names on the frontier—raided the area every year from the late 520s to the mid-530s, and Gepids gained control of strategically placed Sirmium in 536. Constantinople's walls themselves saw raiders in 540, and almost every year of the 540s brought news of another war band on the loose somewhere in the Balkans. The 550s were quieter, but a fresh group of Huns crossed the Danube in 558, opening a season of terror all the way to Constantinople and down into the ancient land of Greece. They finally accepted a bribe sent out from Constantinople and went away.

Bit by bit, we hear more often from the sources for Balkan affairs in this period a word that begins to take shape as a name we know: *Slavs*. Old maps and histories show Slavs as invaders, but now we recognize them as a people that emerged and shaped itself by virtue of its proximity to Rome and also by Rome's resistance to its presence. The Slavs' language (the ancestor of the Slavic tongues) was not independent, but a lingua franca, a frontier argot common to a mixture of people who came to live in proximity to one another. We first hear of these people in the year 527, in exactly the area across the Danube that provided the most soldiers for Justinian's armies later going to Italy. Coin hoards found there show that the people were in regular commercial touch with the Roman empire during the reigns of Anastasius and Justin. It was convenient for Roman observers to give them a name and to portray them ill, but they were a very Roman phenomenon.[20]

Time and again, Justinian would go back to this well looking for soldiers, to build forces to march against the Persians, the Africans, the Italians, and the Spaniards. While doing this, he treated the local disturbances of the Balkan region as a matter of little importance, at least at first. He also saw the region as a place where he could manipulate the local peoples to play them off against each other and keep the peace at low cost to himself. So, for example, when he found the Lombards (their name comes through Latin from a Germanic word for "long-beards") pressing on his own forces, he suborned them to move west, up the Danube valley, to take on the Gepids, flourishing then in the vicinity of modern Budapest. The success of those Lombards resembles the success that Ronald Reagan had in supporting the mujahideen of Afghanistan, not foreseeing the role they would play as members of the Taliban years later. So too the Lombards, emboldened, enriched, and entrenched, would produce the invading bands that came to plague post-reconquest Italy for Justinian's successors and victims, making peace and order in that province impossible for many years. (These Lombards were the usual polyethnic mix, including Saxons, Bulgars, Sarmatians, Pannonians, Suebians, Noricans, and others. It is no wonder that they would fail to create a united kingdom when they arrived in Italy.[21])

Worse was to come. Justinian sought soldiers across the Danube, but was unhappy when people there showed signs of organization, ambition, and military prowess—in other words, when they came to resemble Rome itself. Limited in resources, knowing full well that he could not in the midst of his other diversions spare forces to cross the river and pacify territory that had always eluded direct Roman control, he chose a short-term strategy: fortification. He made the Danube what it had never been before, a fortified dividing line between the inside and the outside of empire. He built forts along the lower lengths of the river, where Bulgaria and Romania face each other east of the Iron Gate that separates the central Balkans from the lower Danube valley. Now Roman soldiers treated the river as a boundary they protected but did not cross, and so abandoned the other side to hostile and almost entirely unobserved forces. Periodic breaches of this barrier, for example by the Cotrigur Huns—*not* themselves native to the border region—in 538 and 558, only reassured Justinian that resistance and fortification were the right policy. He never thought that those Huns had been encouraged and aided in making their way against him by the very peoples he despised, excluded, and set against himself: those longer-settled populations genuinely native to the area.

None of his precautions made the difference Justinian hoped for. His string of small forts, with a few hundred soldiers in each, hanging back from the Danube itself on the more easily fortified higher ground of the Stara Planina (the Balkan Mountains), made a fine show of repelling the feared hordes but had little effect. Trade was largely interrupted, but recruits still came south across the river to join Roman forces, and in the meantime communities of the newly isolated and rejected peoples grew in size and self-consciousness.

So Justinian won the day and lost the war. Effectively denying himself the services of those who lived across the river, he at the same time encouraged their organization and their identity. Nothing did more to shape and encourage the growth of the Slavs as an eastern European power opposed to Constantinople and its purposes than Justinian's decision to draw the line against them. In the end, the Slavs *would* invade—when, in the early seventh century, Emperor Heraclius in Constantinople was distracted by Khusro's life-and-death threats on the Persian front.

The long history of Slavic culture from that day to this owes everything to Justinian and has to be thought of as a mirror image and involuntary outpost of Byzantinism. At the outset, this worked to Constantinople's advantage, after the Greek monks Cyril and Methodius ensured the success of Christianity among the leaders of those peoples, and after their expansion to the northeast into modern Ukraine and Russia made them not the first of the barbarians (from a Roman point of view) but the first outpost of western civilizations that the steppe peoples of later centuries would encounter. If today we draw the line arbitrarily between Europe and Asia along the Ural Mountains, it is Justinian's unwilling and self-defeating contribution to the creation of Slavic identity and ambition that we implicitly endorse.[22] When we look at all the opportunities Rome squandered to advance "civilization" beyond its borders, this one deserves our attention. Justinian brought about a good result by ignorance and bad policy, at needless cost.

PLAGUES OF THE FLESH

Humankind does not live by edifices alone. The constant temptation of ancient monarchs was to seize grandeur rather than earn it, by coercing resources from the margins to the center, to invest in ostentation and display. The Justinian who is remembered for what he built is not the Justinian of history—or, rather, is an embodiment of the weakness of that Justinian. To see Hagia Sophia and the great church Justinian built in Jerusalem as testimonies to his weakness and shortsightedness is to see them as they really are. The outsize scale of his buildings shouts aloud the ego and insecurity of their creator. Justinian and his great empire proved vulnerable to the tiniest of enemies, the plague bacillus.

The years in which his military campaigns in the west went bad and he found himself in his Italian quagmire were dismal ones spent close to home. So much Justinian scholarship has concentrated on the self-glorifying legal, military, and architectural self-assertion of the early years that an important recent scholarly work was impishly called *The Other Age of Justinian*[23]—precisely to signal the long years of frustration and decline that formed part of the career of this grandiose monarch.

The outward sign of the unreliability of the flesh appeared in an outbreak of plague on a scale unlike anything the ancient Mediterranean world had seen since the disease Thucydides recorded more than 900 years earlier in his history of the Peloponnesian wars, or would see again until the black death of the fourteenth century.

The facts of this plague and its impact are disputed and easy to exaggerate. Even the medical diagnosis is uncertain. Many think it was clearly an early instance of the later medieval bubonic plague, but matching ancient reports to the undoubted features of the bubonic plague we know is hard. Similarly, we cannot say just what the impact of the disease was. The stories are vivid enough, as in this example from John of Ephesus: "Others who perished fell down in the streets to become a terrible and shocking spectacle for those who saw them, as their bellies were swollen and their mouths were wide open, throwing up pus like torrents, their eyes inflamed and their hands stretched out upward, and the corpses rotting and lying on corners and streets and in the porches of courtyards and in churches and in shrines and everywhere, with nobody to bury them."[24]

We can plot its course easily enough. Evidently it came by ship and cargo from Africa. Word of its arrival spread from Pelusium, at one of the mouths of the Nile east of Alexandria, in July 541. It quickly moved inland through the Nile valley and east to Gaza, leapfrogging to Constantinople in the spring of 542 and plunging inland from Antioch through Syria that summer. By the end of the summer, it spread as far as Azerbaijan, where

the Persian army felt its lash. Sicily as well was touched in 542, north
Africa and Rome by 543. It ran farther afield in the next few years—to
Ireland in 544 and Wales in 547, for example. Other evidence suggests that
it reached Finland and Yemen. (The speed of its spread in the bad year of
542 is evidence of how well the Mediterranean Roman empire was inter-
connected at this period.)

And it came in waves.[25] At least five times before the year 600 it broke
out again around the Mediterranean, and we can trace aftershocks through
western Europe as late as the middle of the eighth century.

Other dramatic reports from witnesses are easy to come by. Procopius,
usually a skeptic, emphasized the impact on the imagination: "Supernatural beings in human guise were seen by many persons, and those who encountered them thought that they were struck by the spirit they had met
in one or another part of the body, as it happened, and immediately upon
seeing the apparition they were seized also by the disease."[26] Similarly,
John of Ephesus said: "When this plague was passing from one land to
another, many people saw shapes of bronze boats and in them the shapes
of people with their heads cut off. The spectres held staffs of bronze and
moved along on the sea. . . . They were seen everywhere, a terror to all,
especially by night."[27]

Many died; some survived. The great might-have-been of history for
this moment is Justinian's own illness—and his recovery, seen as a godsend by many, though better thought of as an ill-starred blessing. Then
and now, it is impossible not to see such events without overinterpreting
them and overattributing importance to them. If we follow anecdotes, the
plague's horrors are unmistakable. If we scrutinize the rest of the historical record, especially the archaeological record, it is hard to find any lasting impact in the physical world.

Plagues of the flesh weigh heavily on the mind. A few years earlier,
in 536 and 537, men across the world spoke of a year without a summer,
twelve to eighteen months of faded sunlight, spreading from Italy to China.
"The sun looked blue, and at mid-day bodies do not cast a shadow and
the heat of the sun has faded—not just for a moment as in an eclipse, but
for a whole year. We had a winter without storms, a spring without fair
weather, and a summer without heat."[28] The evidence of shrunken tree
rings on wood dated to that period (astonishingly thin in the years 536,
539, and 540, even in North America) confirms the story, which appears

as reports of severe winters in the west, drought in Persia, and famine in China. In Scandinavia, the summers were cool. Mesopotamia saw snow. A volcanic eruption in the Far East could explain the data, but there is no corroboration that science has yet been able to detect for such an event. Inevitably, there was a mild agricultural depression; there were localized outbreaks of famine; and there was overinterpretation then, and now as well. Moderns looking for simple, dramatic explanations for complex events can turn the sequence of events into a fatal concatenation and blame it for the ruin of Rome.[29] Better to let it explain a state of mind that went well with the military reverses and other more human catastrophes of the age. Monophysites associated it with the journey of Pope Agapetus from Rome to Constantinople, to plot against them, as they thought. Procopius saw it as an implicit divine judgment on Justinian and the beginning of bad years for him and his realm. A comet in 539 made men nervous again, and the disasters of the 540s (Persian attacks in Syria and Asia Minor, Bulgars in Thrace, and plague by 542 in Constantinople) kept bad omens in memory.

We need to keep the frailty of the flesh in mind at this point in Justinian's and his empire's career—the cancer that took Theodora from his side in 548. Theodora is impossible to see clearly, so effectively has her maligner Procopius made her out to be the wicked witch and harlot of Babylon who explains all of Justinian's malignity, but her loss left Justinian without his only rudder.

We lose the thread of historical narrative not long after Theodora's death, mainly by accident. Procopius ends his history of Justinian's wars with the truly silly attempt to recapture parts of Spain in 550. Procopius is followed by other historians, particularly Agathias, but the grand narrative of Justinian's reign runs out just at this point. It was never a very accurate or comprehensive narrative for Justinian, for Constantinople, or for any of the ordinary business of empire, and that is one reason modern scholars themselves have tended to treat Justinian on terms he would not have minded—as builder and dispatcher of armies—but it is impossible not to feel the lack of a source as circumstantial and apparently helpful as Procopius.

If Justinian were a modern ruler, we would have been able at every step of the way to assess not only the architectural, legal, military, political, and theological dimensions of his affairs, but also the financial aspects. Ancient empires kept abundant financial records, but hardly any of those documents survive. (Palaces and their archives are designed to be plundered, sooner or later.) A recent scholar has made some sober estimates of the profligacy of Justinian's expenditures.[30] A summary of the bad news runs something like this:

✱ Justinian is reported to have begun his reign with 28 million solidi "in the bank," reserves that Anastasius built up and Justin preserved.

✱ Justinian's wars cost him about 36 million solidi, with some interesting proportions:
  • About 5 million on the eastern front
  • About 8 million in Africa, half of it after "victory" was achieved in Belisarius's short campaign
  • About 21.5 million in Italy, fully half of it in the last two ruinous years 552–554
  • Another 2 million on other fronts.

✱ By comparison, his annual revenues for a good year of his reign amounted to about 5 million solidi; when Africa and Italy were added to his domains, they brought about another ten percent each, or 500,000 solidi each. Most of that revenue was expended locally on governing those restive provinces.

When he began to feel the financial pressures of such extravagant wars, Justinian took the natural action of a martial but improvident ruler: he plundered his own subjects and attacked his own currency, progressively thinning out the amount of bronze in the coinage and profiting handsomely at the treasury as a result. The effects of such a devaluation were slow but inevitable.

Justinian's successor inherited (with Italy and Africa) greater responsibilities than Justinian began with, and had far more restricted financial capacity to address them. No emperor at Constantinople after Justinian had the opportunity for both lavish construction and warfare that Justinian had squandered so unwisely.

PLAGUES OF THE SPIRIT

The Christians of Scythopolis in Palestine, Salona on the Adriatic coast of the Balkans, or Braga in what is now Portugal lived directly with their church and their god. They needed no one beyond their immediate acquaintance to guide their beliefs and practices or assuage their fears concering this life and the next. The lived experience of late antique Christianity, in other words, was local, present, and urgent.

I chose those three cities on purpose. In Scythopolis, imperial authority and religious dissent would run crosswise with each other. Churches under construction there changed the landscape of the town, while non-Christians—in this case Samaritans—rivaled the Christian building programs with constructions of their own.

In Salona, church authority would be divided and then reshaped by other church and imperial forces outside; and a well-established, powerful bishop found himself brought up short with accusations of inappropriate self-indulgence from the bishop of Rome. We will meet this bishop of Salona later and see how he escaped rebuke but left his successor to capitulate.

By comparison, Martin of Braga (a few miles from the Atlantic in northern Portugal, where he died in 580) is a more predictable figure, not unlike the Severinus we met in Noricum a century earlier. Martin had come from another end of the empire, in Pannonia (modern Hungary); he then set out on pilgrimage to Palestine. There he met Spanish pilgrims who inspired him to come to Galicia to convert the people from their ways of error—some from heresy, some from paganism. We can observe his interventions in local practice because we have his letters and can watch the flashes of controversy they ignited. He reminds us how often outsiders were elected bishop in this late Roman world—outsiders who brought spiritual charisma undiminished by familiarity. In many towns, the election of strangers was the vehicle by which ideas and practices trickled along the highways and seaways of the empire to propagate themselves and to advance the cause of catholicism—the elusive notion of a single common religious spirit that would animate all men everywhere to think, speak, and act as one under the power of the god that was in Christ.

In thousands of towns on thousands of days during the reign of Justinian, Christianity played a role in such dramas. Justinian's world could have thought itself now long and securely Christian. His reign was separated from the last official pagan religious rites of Rome by a century and a half, and it looked back to the converting emperor Constantine as we look back to the founding fathers of the United States.

Christianity under Justinian in his core provinces in the east now *mattered* in a way that it had not before, and this mattering came from the top down to meet zealotry, fear, and piety in many different ways in many different places. The Justinian who had made himself the scourge of paganism settled with the years into a similar—and arbitrary—extreme against any form of Christianity that he disapproved of. The specific controversies are important enough in themselves, but they represent even more a transformation of the empire into a place where religion was now to be a fundamental fact of who you were, in all your relations with your fellow mortals from the top of the government down to your neighborhood or village.

The western middle ages, by contrast and in spite of their reputation for religiosity, took much longer to settle into any such obsessive concern with religion. For many centuries, the Christianities (quite various in shape and practice) that populated the Latin west were to be a common color on the maps of the continent, but more because there were no alternative interpretations than because of any excessive devotion. The relative absence of heresy hunters and doctrinal sectarianism for centuries in the west (until the Reformation, ten centuries after Justinian) made it a far more civilized and easier place to live in, and nurtured a religious culture that could be obsessive without being immediately divisive. Jews would suffer increased oppression from time to time, and the presence of Islam on the Iberian peninsula created a shadowland of anxiety reaching into southern France that nurtured murderous sentiments against the rise of the Albigensians centuries later. In the long run, however, the west needed the east and its Muslims in order to find a real self-definition; and in the crusades, western Christianity would teach itself how to organize for purposes of fanaticism and cruelty rooted in religion.

The modernity of this invention in those times needs to be reemphasized. Paul had told the Galatians that traditional identities of Jew and Greek, slave and free were obsolete, and his brand of Christianity was open-minded and inclusive—or, a skeptic nowadays would say, totalizing. Christianities that exclude and define have forgotten this part of Paul's doctrine, and it is far from clear which model should be preferred by believers or by outsiders.

Justinian was the great innovator in this kind of oblivion. Watch the sequence. In the beginning, belief—not belief in large abstract principles, but belief in divine power, the power to heal, the power to destroy, in this world and the next.

Our categories get in our way here. When moderns speak of a believer, we unconsciously adopt Christian terms of reference that blur together at least:

1. Habitual assertion of metaphysical propositions (God is all-powerful) or historical propositions (Jesus was born of a virgin) impossible to verify.
2. Ethical principles sometimes lofty (loving thy neighbor), sometimes quite heavily determined (rhythm method as preferable to barrier method), and sometimes violently unethical (burning heretics at the stake or launching crusades against infidels) in form.
3. Confident performance of finely defined cultural practices (churchgoing, sacraments, pilgrimages, rosaries, bingo, incense, Bible study).
4. Expectations of benefits arising out of the foregoing beliefs and practices, ranging from the eternal (salvation) to the worldly (recovery from grave illness, or a better score on school examinations, or a double down the right field line).

No such set of practices can claim to make complete sense *except* as a lived collection of embodiments and demonstrations of commitment and solidarity. If I attend a religious assembly on a given day of the week, I may improve my chances of heaven, but I also certainly reassure others in my community that I am at one with them and that I honor and share their expectations.

So far, so good: in some way all communities evolve like this, with their limitations and their possibilities. When villages turn into cities, moreover, they find within themselves room for diverse smaller communities and demand less conformity of all inhabitants than face-to-face communities can expect.

Where late antique Christianity introduced novelty to the development

of cities and societies was in the step that came after belief led to practice. Practice itself, the place where the real future of the community was
negotiated, led to structures of doctrine and authority that ensured the
perpetuation and propagation of the saving practices. A simple example is
Augustine's move to construct a theology of original sin around the—at
first to him puzzling—practice of infant baptism. The parents who sought
to baptize infants too young to comprehend the faith they were joining
did not have a theologian's grasp of doctrine; they had only a loving fear
for the well-being of their children. The theologian, however, then built
a theory to fit the practice, reassuring the practitioner and baffling those
who did not share the practice. Even among those who venerated Augustine, the fullness of Augustinian doctrine proved impossible to sustain,
and so a diluted doctrine of original sin remained alongside a baptismal
practice that was universally accepted in spite of doctrinal debates and
inadequacies.

Such behavior baffles outsiders and many insiders, and so fragility
surrounds itself with obstinacy. Western Christianities do not know how
to take a step backward from an overstatement. Doctrine evolves from
one new truth to another, without prior examination of the consequences
of each step, of the *next* move that will be made in the theological chess
game. Each doctrinal step generates controversy and a further reach into
the improbable with another new definition.

This inability to climb down and back from branches of the tree and
the limbs they lead to is a defining feature of post-antique western civilizations, emphatically including that most quintessentially western creation,
Islam. The moments at which regression has in fact occurred are painful and disruptive: the Protestant Reformation, most notably. The Roman
church's recent gingerly attempt to abandon its long-taught but never defined doctrine of limbo—as unbiblical a doctrine as can be imagined—
testifies to the difficulty. The Roman church is regularly encouraged to
rescind many other doctrinal and disciplinary assertions, from the definition of life to the gender of clergy. The intransigence with which it resists
such invitations is an ancient inheritance.

The Council of Chalcedon was ancient Christianity's bridge too far.
In its teachings, clearly evolved in order to deal with the impossibilities
of the preceding generation of doctrinal definitions about the person and
nature of Jesus, the official church reached a dead end and declared that

dead end to be a creed of enduring value. No one who met the living Jesus in first-century Palestine could have guessed what Chalcedon would say, or even understand it.

The emperors who reigned in the decades after Chalcedon, as we have seen, sought to evade the burden of obsession by expressing their acceptance of it in limited and restrained ways. They did not quite take the step back of declaring it to be in error (although there were plenty of people who wanted them to do that), but they did some sidling, some edging, some shuffling away from the outright assertion of the most convoluted and improbable parts of the creed. All through the eastern churches, there was unease at the thought that the God in Christ had been divided in two and his power fatally weakened. If unity could not be restored, then it could be asserted.

Justinian may have wavered at the outset. He comes to us in history as a fanatic—not so much a fanatic for Chalcedon (but he never wanted to reject Chalcedon outright) as a fanatic for getting it right, for finding a solution that he could impose successfully on all his subjects. The evidence for his wavering is of two sorts.

First, Theodora was more than passingly interested in the propositions of the unitarians we call monophysites, and ancient literature and modern literature alike are full of discussions of how Justinian's Chalcedonism and Theodora's monophysitism were deployed alongside, and balancing, each other. No one ever manages to imagine what evidence would show us the imperial couple engaged in theological bedtime conversation, amicably agreeing to disagree.

Remember that odd conversation in 532, discreetly hidden away down in the waterside palace of Hormisdas behind the main palace, when Syrians—that is, monophysites by this time—and Chalcedonians met to look for a way out of their theological logjam, with the emperor himself hovering almost in the next room to encourage their progress. It took a lot for Justinian to convince himself that there was no progress in this direction.

In the years after 532, Justinian felt himself caught between two exasperating poles of ecclesiastical recalcitrance. Many eastern churches asserted their independence from Chalcedon's decisions and proclaimed their faith in God's oneness, unity, undividedness, and uniqueness. They were clear, unrelenting, and unmanageable.

As late as 542, however, Justinian had not made the break. In that year, he sent John of Ephesus as a missionary to convert pagans in Asia Minor, in the area around Constantinople and down the western coast. John reclaimed 80,000 souls, we are told, and built ninety-two churches and ten monasteries. (The building was good politics, for the building of churches and the generosity of churchmen would infuse the remote neighborhoods John visited with imperial funding and encourage—it was so awkward to say "buy"—orthodox belief.)

John himself, born around 500 in Mesopotamia, deserves some attention not only as a missionary but also as a writer. He fell in with monophysites when very young and from his teens wandered in the eastern realms from Egypt to Constantinople. He was ordained somewhere on the run in 529, and by 540 made his way to Constantinople, where Justinian—or Theodora?—found him and sent him on his missionary way, accepting his beliefs and hoping for the best.[31] Notionally the rightful bishop of Ephesus, by the 560s, at the time Justinian died, John became the leader of the monophysites in Constantinople, but he was sent into exile not long afterward by Justin II and died in 589 without returning. In those last years he wrote eloquently and accurately the history of his times and the decades before, to justify and explain the emergence of the monophysite community as the voice of true Christianity; and we have his book, the implicit intellectual autobiography of a man who never changed his mind, but went from promising courtier to banished heretic as the views of emperors hardened.

The recalcitrance of the monophysites exasperated Justinian, but he also clearly felt that they could be retrieved, persuaded, and kept in harmony with himself and his vision of Christianity and even its Chalcedonian basis. What was unresolvable was the intransigence of Rome.

Justinian's uncle Justin had begun his reign in 519 by restoring unity between eastern and western churches, unity based in acceptance of Chalcedon. In all the years of his own reign, however, there was never a point at which Justinian was entirely in harmony with the bishops of Rome, and he found that dissonance maddening. Bishops of Rome mattered to him because they mattered ecclesiastically as the see founded by Peter and attended by Paul in his last years, and they mattered as well because of Justinian's expansive view of the imperial reach of Rome. Justinian deserves credit for consistency and ambition, if nothing else—for not simply dismissing the westerners as heretics and worse and building an orthodox empire for himself. Justinian still needed Rome.

The bishops of Rome, meanwhile, made sure they were needed. The long war between Symmachus and Laurentius over the papacy had ended with remarkable unity there. Whatever divided the church of Rome in those years did not arise again as a divisive issue to divide, and instead the city and its clergy stood fast and together. The end of the Acacian schism on Justin's rise in 519 was easily and naturally taken as a sign that Rome and its intransigence had been right all along, that the daughter city had capitulated to the mother. Something of this must be credited to the skill and intelligence of Pope Hormisdas, who succeeded Symmachus in 514 and still presided when Justin made peace in 519. In the years that followed, Constantinople often tested the Roman church. Pope John I was summoned to Constantinople in 525, abused, and sent home to die, and then a series of other short-term popes in the 530s sent embassies and showed their support for the regime of Theoderic's successors and their resistance to Constantinople's new demands. Throughout the long war of the 530s and 540s, the church of Rome and the kingdom of Theodahad and Witigis were remarkably aligned with one another, although the kings were notionally Arian and thus heretical.

The defeat of Witigis in 540 and the supremacy of Constantinople's forces in Italy encouraged Justinian. That is how Pope Silverius was deposed and the puppet Vigilius put in his place. But even when he was arrested in Rome and dragged to Constantinople, Vigilius was not always entirely spineless. Justinian at that moment was preparing to impose the kind of compromise he had always intended. Chalcedon would be preserved and venerated, but as much of its baggage as possible would be thrown to the wolves to placate them. That might work.

A shimmering vision of truth led him on. Truth was timeless, he and his church could believe, and could be separated from men and controversy. A successfully worded creed could live and guide teachings forever, without requiring that the process by which it was written be remembered in any accurate detail. None of the global councils of the early church deserves much respect as a process when viewed either as an operation of the holy spirit or as an operation of deliberative democracy among episcopal equals.[32] Justinian's own historian had only disdain for the process when he wrote of clergy traveling to Rome "on account of an article of faith that the Christians dispute among themselves, holding different opinions. I will by no means mention the points of contention, though I know them well. For I think it is insanely stupid to investigate the nature of God, and ask what sort it is. For I do not believe that human beings have a sufficiently exact understanding of human things, far less of anything that bears on the nature of God. . . . I would say nothing else about God than that he is entirely good and holds everything within his power. But let each say about these things whatever he thinks he knows, both priest and layman."[33]

Of all the councils and confabulations that took place from the reign of Constantine to the reign of Justinian, the few that emerged as authoritative were understood—or at least argued—to have had a privileged access to the truth and to have left behind concise formulas that could stand beyond controversy and time and guide right belief. Reciting a proper creed with heartfelt assent was the Christian shibboleth, the phrase whose utterance revealed and ensured identity and loyalty. God's power frowned so heavily on insincere assertion that no one would utter a creed he disbelieved—or so men thought. Why did God require the assertions of his creatures to capture so accurately and precisely his own nature and report it back to him? No one asked that question loudly enough to unsettle the obsession with definition.

Public compromise and private coercion both played a part in Justinian's strategy. One way to go forward was to rewrite history, and so in the 540s, Justinian began to throw historical baggage over the side.

The first victim was an astonishing one: Origen, the greatest scriptural interpreter in the history of early, and arguably of all, Christianity, had always been slightly suspect. His name was a code word for a style of intellectual Christianity that had partisans but was also easily sacrificed to make a political point. Barsanuphius of Gaza, for example, had no time for these elite intellectuals: "These are the speculations of the Greeks; these are the dreams of people who fancy themselves to be something. . . . But these doctrines do not lead those who believe them to the light, but rather to the darkness." The teachings of the monastic innovator Evagrius Ponticus (d. 399) had shaped the way Origen's ideas integrated with monastic pride. But Origen had written things that could embarrass even his followers, such as his defense of "apocatastasis," the doctrine that at the end of all things even hell would pass away and the damned would be rejoined to their benevolent creator. What Origenists had in common by the sixth century was resistance to the emperors, attachment to freedom of thought, a mystical impulse, and Platonic intellectualism. They were too smart, too well read, too independent, too little attached to party politics for their own good.[34]

There were monks around Jerusalem who invoked Origen's name in support of positions too far outside Justinian's comfort zone to be tolerated, and so in 543, Justinian himself condemned Origen and his works. This condemnation went far afield in several ways. For one, it led loyal believers to destroy most of the surviving works of Origen himself in Greek. (We depend for our knowledge of his contributions on surviving fragments and on works translated into Latin by 400 or so.) For another, it let the emperor be seen and known as the arbiter of theology in his own voice and his own name.

This imperial ukase ran afoul of deep conservative traditions. Living theologians could find their work and doctrine disputed, controverted, and praised, but once they had died, their fate and the approval or disapproval of their teaching was traditionally to be left in the hands of God. To condemn the dead because of their teaching seemed dangerously arrogant. But Justinian knew what others had not fully internalized, that books were now forces in their own right, and there was no necessary difference in authority between the books of the dead and the books of the living.

A deeper strategy animated Justinian. By attacking the dead, he could implicitly attack the living at little cost. Firing over the heads of the monophysites to attack Origen was one thing, and turning then to attack Theodoret, Theodore of Mopsuestia, and Ibas of Edessa—the authors condemned in what came to be called the "Three Chapters" of an edict—brought the extreme Chalcedonians within firing range. Attacking the three extreme "dyophysite" ("twoish") authors would frighten any contemporary sympathizers, who may have been few enough in number, except for those who rightly venerated the contributions of Theodore of Mopsuestia, but it would also reassure the monophysite ("oneish") faction that attention was being paid to their concerns.

All this almost made sense. Once Vigilius was in Constantinople under virtual house arrest, Justinian went to work on him. In his first years in Constantinople, Vigilius toed the party line, condemning those who would not condemn the "Three Chapters," issuing an official *Judg-*

ment (*Iudicatum*) in 548, then retracting it under extreme pressure from his own retinue and from Latin writers in contact with the recently revitalized orthodox church in Africa. Justinian returned to the offensive in 551 and insisted on having Vigilius's support, but the pope showed a trace of backbone in taking refuge in the church of Saint Peter (the first pope, after all) at Constantinople and excommunicating those who accepted the new imperial edict. Not long after, Vigilius fled across the water to Chalcedon to the church of Saint Euphemia, symbolic home of orthodoxy since the council there a century earlier.

Then came the point, just as the war in Italy was finally winding down in 553, when Justinian had the confidence to do what no emperor had done in a century: call a council. Meeting in Constantinople under the emperor's eye in May and June 553, just over a century after Chalcedon, the Second Council of Constantinople did the emperor's exact bidding. It made no new contribution to theology; it clarified nothing; but it also ceded nothing. In formal words, Chalcedon was reaffirmed, but the "Three Chapters" authors were condemned, and with them the still resistant Vigilius.

After the council, pressure was again applied to Vigilius, and in 554 he finally issued another *Judgment* that did his master's bidding, condemning the "Three Chapters" and supporting the council. Vigilius was now superfluous and of no interest except as a symbol of the unity of realms. (The acts of the council were even doctored after the fact to make it seem that Vigilius had supported Justinian all along.) Dispatched back to Italy in 555, he died at Syracuse in Sicily en route, the most convincingly humiliated bishop of Rome ever seen. When his successor, Pelagius I, was finally elected in 556, there were too few bishops in the neighboring region to be found to conduct his consecration, and an embarrassing delay ensued.

Vigilius was lucky that he didn't make it to Rome, for he would have found that, whatever effect the "Three Chapters" condemnation had on the monophysite opposition, it shocked many westerners. If Justinian was having enough trouble ensuring the stability of his rule in Italy on military terms, the "Three Chapters" edict was decisive in weakening the *idea* of ecclesiastical authority exercised from Constantinople. No pope after Vigilius ever truckled as he had truckled, and for many decades afterward whole segments of the western church remained in continuous rebellion against the idea of condemning the dead and condemning *those* dead.

Justinian never relented, and in his last years he devised a new variant on theological subtlety, "aphthartodocetism," which tried to preserve the serene divinity of Christ by making his sufferings entirely voluntary and even his physical body incorruptible in its godhood. This Jesus only *appeared* to suffer and die on a cross. Few disciples followed this flag willingly.

No emperor after Justinian would attempt the kind of theological authoritarianism that he practiced, and for good reason. It had failed. No figure of late antiquity believed in the universal unity and consistency of Christianity more than Justinian did, but no figure did more to ensure that it would never be achieved. The monophysite rebellion in the east proved enduring and subsists today in the Jacobite churches. The Nestorians' withdrawal to the Persian empire proved permanent as well. The disaffection with and suspicion of the western church endured. Vigilius was the weakest of popes, but his failure made all the popes after him stronger. As late as the fifth century, it might have been imagined that Christianity would be genuinely catholic, that is to say, universal. At no point since Justinian has it been possible to imagine such a thing.

PART III

GREGORY'S WORLD

Rome's Remains
(565–604)

The final scenes of our drama: in which it has begun to seem normal that the city of Rome is a pale shadow of its old self and that the older order of life in much of the Roman world has given way to new routines and new figures of authority. During these scenes, "noises off" will remind us of what is to come, while memories of a more robust imperial past will remind us that the medieval future was made possible—or necessary?—by the hubris of an empire that did not know what was in its own best interest.

6

Learning to Live Again

USTINIAN DIED ON November 14, 565. We will visit his airless palace and witness his botched succession in a few pages, but we will see best what he left behind if we look first to the four corners of his earth. The affairs of the court at Constantinople were now, almost suddenly with Justinian's passing, diminished in scale and importance. One can almost look around the world of 565, take a deep breath, and say, *Well, that's over*. Justinian had worn out his mandate and his throne, and even the Ottomans would never match what Constantinople had known in antiquity. We are suddenly in a different world, where people were learning to live again, with very different expectations.

NORTHERN EXPOSURES

Julius Caesar conquered Gaul, but left the job unfinished. What he left undone made the European middle ages possible. Nowhere in the Roman world is the question of "decline and fall" more irrelevant, for northern Gaul was the part of the Roman empire that rose under Rome's rule, rose again as that rule faded, and continued to rise almost without interruption for hundreds of years.[1]

Consider again Theoderic's fortunes in Gaul. He succeeded in staking a claim for himself across the Alps—a remarkable achievement for a king based in Italy and rivaling the success of the Roman republic in expanding into this territory after the Punic Wars. But Provence and the Rhône valley up to about Lyon were all he could manage. Aquitaine—that is, southwestern Gaul from the Mediterranean coast to the Atlantic and up to Bordeaux on the Garonne—was always beyond his reach. Farther north, another world.

Formally, of course, Roman rule of law had extended throughout the land. Gifts of land to colonists created nuclei of romanization, and more prominent figures came to possess extensive estates over which they presided from dignified country villas. But at no point did the landscape of northern Gaul—a landscape we now associate with the heart of what is French, from Normandy to the Île de France to Champagne and Burgundy—ever become the home of the kind of aristocracy, first arriviste and then eventually quite settled and self-satisfied, that marked the lands of the south. More than that, northern Gaul, like the other western provinces, lacked the healthiest form of premodern culture, the village of peasant farmers. The villa and its plantation dominated in Africa, Italy, Spain, and Provence; they never had the kind of well-rooted local communities of people who farm the land because they care about it. That absence is what made these provinces most unlike the eastern realms of Syria and Egypt. It doesn't matter so much whether peasants owned the land or rented it, as long as they had control over their lives and produce and had opportunities to benefit from what they did. The great Roman estates in southern Gaul offered few such opportunities, and created a population dependent on its "betters" for social leadership and economic development. Farther north, until you came to the Rhine valley and Rome's military presence, there was even less structure.

When Theodoric crossed the Alps into Gaul, therefore, the advantage he had over Julius Caesar's armies almost 600 years earlier was that there was already a natural community of interest and even family relationship between southern Gaul and northern Italy, and a long history of collegial association. By contrast, northern Gaul was terra incognita—dark much of the year on winter days shorter than the Mediterranean ever knew, dank, and too close to the military frontier for many travelers to venture that way. Militarily, the Roman momentum ran out at the Rhine, true enough, but the force of Roman civilization had truly dissipated hundreds of miles before reaching it. If Rome had really been ready to preserve and even extend its northern frontiers, it would have built cities in places like Trier and Strasbourg that were not merely camps and markets but centers of influence and radiation well beyond, supporting the growth and enrichment of people inside and outside the boundaries of the empire.

We mustn't imagine a stable and unchanging world in northern Gaul. The fourth century saw a real infusion of money and attention from Rome to that territory, but little of it involved aristocrats, villas, or economic development. Instead, the empire's increasing militarization made northern Gaul the headquarters and base for connecting the Mediterranean world to the British outposts of Rome and the Rhine frontier. Emperors began to spend more and more time in Gaul, tending to their borders, and candidates for empire arose more and more often in Gaul or Britain. The city of Trier underwent the kind of revolution that occurs when a provincial town becomes a de facto capital of empire without having become a real city in the process. The stories we know from Trier are all those of visitors—Augustine tells one in his *Confessions*, and figures like Jerome, Symmachus, and Ausonius, the most well-connected and literary men of the late fourth century, all made their way to Trier, not for the cuisine, the culture, or the business opportunities, but to pay court to the emperor in residence at the time.

This looks like a great leap forward for romanization, and the student of history who knows that intruders made their way across the Rhine and pervaded Roman Gaul in the early 400s can look upon those visitors and that prosperity with a sense of opportunity lost. But archaeology politely yet firmly disrupts our easy assumptions. Of all the provinces of the Roman empire, northern Gaul is the one where the old ways faded earliest and fastest. The scattered villas that signaled the presence of Rome and gave a few wealthy Romans opportunities for exploitation and self-glorification began to be abandoned by 350, just when emperors began to be a real presence and half a century before historians can possibly try to blame any barbarian invasion. By 450, northern Gaul still had its veneer of Romanness, but the substance was not there and it needed to chart a new future. How to explain this?

First, bear in mind that the Roman presence in this part of the empire was thin and insubstantial, compared with the strong, deep roots elsewhere. The landscape itself was very different from what is there today, for the agricultural revolution of the moldboard plow did not come to the Rhine and Moselle valleys and the land east to the Elbe until only 500–1000 CE. What would become a network of well-tilled, productive farms was in 450 a cold, wet forest frontier. But beyond the frontier and even well beyond the Elbe, as early as the first centuries of the empire, traffic in the precious commodity called amber linked what is now the Baltic to the Mediterranean, and there is evidence of cultivation of cereal grains reaching almost that far, almost that early. The natural community of northern Europe was romanizing cheerfully without regard to Roman policy, borders, or intent: Roman civilization without Romans.

Take as well the telltale question of languages. Jerome, the translator of the Latin Bible, had a worldly career as a minor bureaucrat before devoting himself to religion. Between his secular and his religious careers, he traveled widely in Roman domains west and east. Himself a native of the northern Balkans, educated for success at the city of Rome, he came to Trier as a young man in the 370s, but later spent long periods in Syria and finally in Palestine, doing much of his scholarly and literary work in a monastery at Bethlehem. He tells us that when he passed through the province of Galatia in the interior of Asia Minor, he discovered there natives who spoke a language very like the one he had heard from natives in northern Gaul. This makes sense in a long view of Roman history, for in the 300s BCE, Gaulish warbands had ranged widely through the Balkans and into Asia Minor. The province of Galatia itself took its name from their settlement there. This story can tell us something about the provincialism of Galatia, but we must also see the same trait manifested in Gaul. Latin was the imperial language of the Romans and made its way permanently throughout ancient Gaul. Nowhere in the western provinces did any Germanic language dislodge Latin when Roman rule went away, except in Britain. (Latin is still spoken today in most of what was Roman Gaul, though in a debased, corrupted form of which its native speakers, who made it their own imperial language long after the Romans left, are inordinately proud.) But up north, away from the Mediterranean and away from the villas and military towns, out in the country, the old languages could live on, separate from the Roman camps and cities. The eventual linguistic boundary between French and German falls not far west of the Rhine in old Roman domains.

Second, the imperial presence in Gaul in the fourth century marked the beginning of a new militarization of the province that represented a change in the model of what it meant to be Roman. When the future emperor Julian was first put in charge of troops under his cousin Constantius in the 350s, he came to Gaul and tightened up both borders—and also, remarkably, tax collection. In so doing, he subtly asserted imperial and military authority over a matter left elsewhere to civilian and local control. As the power and the organization became increasingly military rather than civilian, camps, fortified cities, and finally a wealthy officer class replaced dignified civilians. In this part of the Roman world, where such dignified civilians had never really taken root, the rise of the military was easy.

The people who embodied this culture and did not much care what its links to the city of Rome might be are the ones we call Franks—the way we call another community of border folk Tex-Mex. And now their time had come to flourish.

Their flourishing is strangely irrelevant to the other military upheavals of this age. The bands of Vandals and others who passed the Rhine in 406 and scooted through the northern countryside, down to Spain, and on to Africa left no mark here. The wars of the fifth century came and went as well, with a decided breakdown in the authority exercised from Rome and the Mediterranean. As with Britain, part of the problem started here, when Roman generals, seeking advancement, revolted and headed south to make their claim to imperial titles and glory. The vacuum they left behind was not always filled by the victors in those contests. Thus some areas simply lost their relationship to the rest of the world, and so we have challenging evidence to decipher, identifying pockets of what sometimes seems like rebellion but sometimes appears equally strongly as an attempt by local leaders to establish and maintain order in a world no one else would settle for them. Historians often identify the Bagaudae we have heard of as robber bands and worse, but a modern journalist might choose to call them local militias, as we see the term used today in societies where a breakdown in central authority has left communities thinking they have few other options for self-defense. In their embodiment of local autonomy, they are not necessarily alien forces—often, quite the contrary.

In that environment, the Franks along the border made out just fine. Their survival, prosperity, and rise to eventual ascendancy in all of Gaul—and eventually under the Carolingians well beyond Gaul—is a sign of the success, survival, and resilience of what was most precisely

Roman about the Roman world. The Frankish leaders were military men, as made sense in the circumstances, but the extension of their authority through Gaul was remarkably rapid, consistent, and effective, a sign of how naturally Roman they were. The decisive date is 451, when the battle of the Catalaunian Plains did away once for all with real threats posed by external invasion to the Roman lands west of the Rhine. The retreat of Roman-led forces after that battle left a vacuum that the Franks moved efficiently to fill. Their great king Clovis (r. 481–511) deserves as much praise as Theoderic for effective leadership and visionary ambition, but he had the good fortune to live farther from Constantinople and so never came under Justinian's hungry, Sauron-like eye. In some alternative universe, the Italy of Theoderic and the Gaul of Clovis probably became the core of a surviving, thriving western Mediterranean polity that finally achieved Julius Caesar's ambitious goal to extend itself firmly and successfully to the Rhine and beyond. Without Theoderic's Italy, the Franks were on their own, and they deserve much credit for making the most of their opportunity.

When Justinian began his war of Italian reconquest, the Franks saw an opportunity and seized it to make essentially all of Roman Gaul their own. On occasion, especially when encouraged from the east, they made forays into northern Italy, but they had the sense not to overcommit themselves. Eventually the Frankish king Theudebert I wrote to Justinian boasting of a realm that stretched from Pannonia (that is, modern Hungary) to the Atlantic, comprising the upper Danube, the Rhine, and all of Gaul and the Low Countries. He had reason to be proud.

The Gaul that the Franks created, called Merovingian after Clovis's grandfather Merovech, had its own landscape and economy. It was a country of small fortified cities and—the secret of its success—an increasing number of small communities of landholders: villages, at long last. The cities were the places of the kings, their military lieutenants, and the bishops of the Christian church. We know a lot, for example, about sixth-century Tours because of the abundant writings of Bishop Gregory there. He was famous for his history of the Franks and other books about churchmen, but his city's walls enclosed only about twenty-five acres of land, an area about one fortieth the size of New York's Central Park. There would be no great or ambitious cities in Frankish realms for a very long time, but there was increasingly order, stability, a monarchy, and a lordly class made wealthy beyond its dreams by a level of taxation low enough to allow many others to feel prosperous as well. From the late fourth century to the late sixth century, military talent and good fortune had largely replaced noble birth as the basis for success and prosperity. Now birth began to matter again, as it would matter there until our own time.

The Merovingian kings particularly favored and fostered the growth of monasticism in their domains, first invoking the heavenly patronage of Saint Martin of Tours and then in later centuries (from Charlemagne's time around 800) under that of Saint Benedict. Monasticism on this western model combined two contradictory impulses. First, an ideology of austerity and self-sacrifice gave structure to the days and the lives of those members of the community. Second, they were places of wealth and conspicuous consumption. All that land and all those hands were removed from the normal economy, providing an assurance of comfort and care for all those who lived on it, an assurance that no secular landlord or sharecropper could know. Land that fell into monastic hands was like an old master's painting that comes today into the hands of a public museum: it would never be sold again, and the monastery would grow richer with time. The architecture of the monastery soon grew more and more impressive, as gift followed gift and the small community of privileged ascetics would live on the produce of rafts of farmers, be they freemen or serfs.

The right way to think about the Franks, in other words, is to imagine them as a fragment of the Roman empire, cut off and abandoned by the Mediterranean-centered government. This fragment grew, flourished, and prospered, precisely in realization of its Roman cultural DNA. (The Franks' native way of putting it was to claim descent from the ancient Trojans, the ancestors of the Romans themselves.) When Frankishness encountered other fragments of the Roman world—for example, the Burgundian kings who flourished for a time between the Franks and the Mediterranean province but were then vanquished—different expressions of what the Romans had planted competed with one another. The Franks prevailed.

In their prevalence, something fundamental to the geopolitics of the whole Eurasian landmass was finally accomplished. The outpost of civilization that had crept around the shores of the Mediterranean in the Hellenistic age was able now, decisively, to plant a replica of itself on the northern shores of the European mainland. From the middle ages onward, it has been fashionable to speak of a "transfer of empire" and a "transfer of culture" from the Mediterranean northward. The history of the period 500–2000 CE has been profoundly influenced by this coherence of culture on the northwestern fringe of Eurasia's westernmost peninsula. Until very recently, those who grew up in that part of the world and its colonial dependencies found that introduction to the history of the world, or of western civilization, or of Europe, effectively meant indoctrination into the history of England and France, with attention to Germany during wars or reformations and to Italy during renaissances, but little more. In the twenty-first century, such a picture of the past already seems provincial, threatened, and precious all at once. The Franks, that is to say the Romans of the Rhine, made it possible, and their success should be taken as the last western *triumph* of the Roman order. If we hear that Bertram of Le Mans died in 516 and from his will we learn that he left behind property of about 740,000 acres in fourteen communities, separated into more than 100 individual properties he had accumulated, we should realize that to some people any talk of decline and fall was just sour grapes on the part of the unambitious or unsuccessful.

To take the story only a little farther forward, the next steps in the advance of that northern world were commercial rather than imperial, and the commercial stamp on that particular form of "western civilization" remains to this day. If Tours was a traditional Roman city shrunk in on itself as a military encampment, take by contrast Dorestad, on one of the streams by which the Rhine enters the North Sea. An old Roman fortress, it became a trading city, one the economic historians call an emporium, with no aristocracy, no military, and no royal presence: just a community that existed to welcome the ships of the North Sea and the boats of the Rhine and to build a market for their exchange of produce and products. Think of it as a Frankish Hong Kong. By modern standards still small, it nevertheless enclosed within its city walls 105 acres, four times the area of Tours; was successful enough to be taken over as a personal possession by Charlemagne and raided repeatedly by Vikings; and did not fade until flood control over the lower Rhine put it out of business in the ninth century. In its moment, it embodied a future that could almost imagine naval powers on the Atlantic, powers that could descend from the Vikings of Scandinavia and their seafaring innovation and daring. Dorestad was rich in its time, and its riches foreshadowed the immense wealth the western naval powers would draw into their heartlands from all over the globe. That too, I must insist, has to be taken as a sign of the success and growth of the Roman empire—or at least its most successful fragment.

A BARBARIAN CODA

The story of the fall of the Burgundians is alive today in the headset of the passenger next to you on an airplane listening to Wagner's *Götter-dämmerung* on an iPod, and it is a story that captures all of our narrative from a distinctive angle. We mustn't think it true, but we must recognize how it could have taken root. The vehicle by which the story makes its way through the middle ages and into Wagner's atelier is the German saga called the *Nibelungenlied*. It is as important and true as the tales of Romulus and Remus or David and Solomon.

As early as the fifth and sixth centuries, fragments of stories began to circulate, blurring together pieces of the history we have explored and rewriting them for effect and added glory. These were not the latest descendants of an ancient German saga, but the first creations of a new tradition. One of the oldest clearly and explicitly goes back to the days when Theoderic (called Dietrich of Bern in the saga) and Odoacer were at war, but it rapidly became entangled with memories and tales of the days when Attila (Etzel in the saga) roamed the Danube valley almost at will. The importance of the *Nibelungenlied* is its perspective: it captures the point of view, with many variations, of the people who lived north of the Danube in modern Bavaria and Austria.

We met these people, and saw a piece of this story from still another point of view, in the life of Severinus of Noricum many pages ago. While that story was told from a Roman perspective and treated barbarians with hostility and skepticism, the saga version preserves the ethos and angle of those for whom the Danube was home, Rome was far away, and heroism and villainy were distributed in the ordinary way, not arbitrarily assigned to ethnicities. A medieval reader who knew the *Nibelungenlied* and came on a manuscript of the life of Severinus would have felt as habitués of the Royal Shakespeare Company do on first watching *Rosencrantz and Guildenstern Are Dead*.

The saga as we have it offers an alternative ending for Theoderic, who appears as an exile from Verona now living in the Balkans, where he allies himself with Attila (Etzel), and where the Burgundians—with whom the saga's narration sides—are his enemies. The exile probably reflects the experience of a few Italian refugees heading north around 600, then entering trading relations—the archaeologists tell us—with the new powers they found. But this Attila is far from being the scourge of God that Roman propaganda would make of him, and it is quite historical that he and Theoderic's forebears had been allied, as late as the great battle of the Catalaunian Plains of 451. Here is how one modern critic thinks the story went in its earliest form:

> Attila, wedded to a Burgundian princess, lusts for her brothers' treasure, succeeds in luring them to Hunland despite the warnings which she sends them and other warnings given in "Burgundy," fails to extort an answer from them as to where they have hidden their hoard, has them killed, and, together with his sons by this wife, is in turn killed by her and burned in his own hall.[2]

This story combines the fall of the Burgundians with the wooing of Brünnehilde and the death of Siegfried. Connecting Siegfried to the Burgundian royal family makes the two stories intertwine and gives epic scope to the family tragedy. The real Burgundians were battered by the Huns in 437, but then yielded the Rhine and settled westward after Attila passed west from Passau to Worms to Metz on his way to the Catalaunian Plains. The Franks in the 520s and 530s brought Burgundian independence to an end. By the standards of epic, the *Nibelungenlied* comes surprisingly close to historic truth.

The politics and drama of the Danube, however, meant less to the saga maker than the personalities within the Burgundian royal house, and it is here that Wagner found the domestic drama he then projected on a grander stage—in more ways than one—in his *Ring* cycle. But catch the spirit of Brünnehilde as the *Nibelungenlied* has her and you can begin to smell the smoke wafting from Wagner's stages: "Over the sea there dwelt a queen whose like was never known, for she was of vast strength and surpassing beauty. With her love as the prize, she vied with brave warriors at throwing the javelin, and the noble lady also hurled the weight to a great distance and followed with a long leap; and whoever aspired to her love had, without fail, to win these three tests against her, or else, if he lost but one, he forfeited his head."[3] The doom of Siegfried is already palpable in those lines, and he appears thus in the *Nibelungenlied*, ever obedient to his fate, ever the legend from a past that never was.

CELTIC FRINGES

Gaul and the Franks made one future out of the Roman heritage. When the plug was pulled on Roman power in the northwest, Rome's nearly sudden abandonment of Britain left behind the most mysterious landscape of late antiquity. Britain (mainly what is now England) had been Roman and Latin, but in the last years of the fourth century it suddenly vanished from the consciousness of historians, lawgivers, and generals, and in very short order it was almost completely de-latinized—with no invading barbarians to blame.

The vanishing of Rome was a self-inflicted wound. When local Roman generals took their troops with them to the continent to seize the imperial throne for themselves, they assumed that they could leave the island province stripped of forces. But when Theodosius defeated the usurper Magnus Maximus in 388, he had other challenges in front of him and so could be understood as acting very reasonably in not sending troops he did not have back to an island that would (in his eyes) only nurture other competitors for his own throne. For Britain needed Rome and its tax-supported soldiers more than Rome needed Britain.

This point must be emphasized: the part of the Roman empire that lost its Romanness the most completely did so most voluntarily. Arabic replaced Latin in North Africa as the result of systematic invasion and cultural transformation, but the Angles and Saxons who arrived well after the province had given up on Rome and who gave England its tongue were more like the Franks than like anyone else. Their groups of fighters and followers found their way to the British mainland by a variety of paths, with the larger forces that we see eventually emerging over time out of a long series of opportunistic local conflicts. They filled a vacuum. The farther north one reached to find Caesar's conquests, the thinner the romanization had been, and the more artificial the Roman presence. In Britain, there were no people like the Franks at hand, and so the successors of Rome needed to be imported. Perhaps.

A curious shadow of Rome falls over this Britain and stretches into our own time: the shadow of Arthur. If the name represents a real person, then our imagery of Camelot must be discarded and a late Roman general must be seen in its place. This Arthur would be the British equivalent of Clovis, but bereft of supporters, land, and luck and so doomed to failure. The moralizing historian Gildas from sixth-century Britain tells the story of one doomed general, Ambrosius Aurelianus, whose ancestors had worn the imperial purple, and who may be a piece of the history that was later rewritten as part of Arthur's story. (The name Arthur begins to be mentioned briefly in early medieval Welsh poetry and in scattered historic references, but the full Arthurian yarn does not get told until the twelfth century.)

People like Ambrosius Aurelianus were as often usurpers of authority as they were loyalist generals, and the barbarians they fought were as often the official federate troops of the emperor as they were irresponsible invaders. If we knew all the circumstances behind the battle of Badon Mount that Gildas tells us about, we might once again have great difficulty deciding just who was fighting for and who was fighting against the traditions and legitimacy of the Roman world.

The revival of Britain after the departure of Rome was long in coming, and had to do with the growth and flourishing of the border peoples, including the Angles, Saxons, and others who came in dribs and drabs to Britain across the North Sea. Christianity had found various homes in Britain in the centuries before Roman power dissolved, and it hung on for dear life.[4] In the eighth century the Venerable Bede from his monastery in northern England tells a stirring story of lapse in the face of barbarian hostility and then dramatic reconversion by Augustine of Canterbury, sent out by Pope Gregory the Great. Bede minimizes the presence, persistence, and diversity of the Christian communities Augustine found surviving there, but his story is so good that it dominated medieval and modern awareness. A more complicated, less barbarian story is closer to the truth.

So consider a young man from a Christian family in western Britain in the years just after the Romans abandoned the island. His father and grandfather were clergy in this age before lifelong clerical celibacy, and life went on with or without a Roman empire to think of. The young man was kidnapped by pirates and sent into slavery in Ireland, where he tells how he found true religion while herding pigs. In due time he ran away to sea and made his way, through various adventures, across Gaul, which he makes sound like a far more desolate wasteland than it ever could have been.

> And after a few years I was again in Britain with my kinfolk, and they welcomed me as a son, and asked me, in faith, that after the great tribulations I had endured I should not go away from them. But in a vision in the night, I saw a man whose name was Victoricus, and it seemed he was coming from Ireland with countless letters. He gave me one of them, and I read the beginning: "The Voice of the Irish," it said, and as I was reading it, I seemed to hear the voices of the people near the wood of Focluth, which is close to the western sea there, and they were crying out in one voice: "We beg you, holy young man, to come and walk among us again." And my heart was so moved with compunction that I could not read any further, and so I awakened. I give God my thanks, because after many years, He sent me to them, as they had cried out for.[5]

This man was Patrick, that is, *Patricius,* "patrician," a name left behind by the Romans. He undoubtedly traveled afoot through Ireland, mainly in the north, preaching, converting, and dealing with the local potentates. Did he really convert Conall Gulbain, a son of the nearly legendary Niall of the Nine Hostages and founder of the O'Donnell clan? The story that he did so was, for many centuries, important quite without regard to whether the event really happened or not. Just in the last decade, research has brought legend perilously back to life with the suggestion that a high proportion of Irish people can trace their genetic descent back to a single male figure of the mid-fifth century, a point of origin that coincides neatly with the legends of Niall, Conall, and their like.

If Patrick did not convert all of Ireland to Christianity, he nevertheless came at a moment when the Christian wave was breaking across the island, planting monasteries formed in the Gaulish tradition, monasteries that dominated the landscape, which would have no cities or real villages for centuries to come. The Ireland that claimed him was otherwise little touched by the tendrils of Mediterranean civilization and remained economically backward until the 1990s, but it already had a complex social structure, a distinctive culture, and an impressive learned class—the more impressive for flourishing in a society entirely without cities.

By 600, Ireland was able to export its version of Christianity, which had become slightly eccentric by now, from time spent growing in a hothouse far from its original home and without regular contact with the continent. A religious-minded prince from the family that came to call itself O'Donnell fled local quarrels for the Hebrides and settled on Iona. His name was Columba, Latin for "dove." Later stories would have it that he was sent away in penance for his part in a war, to a place he could never set eyes on Ireland again, and Iona was closest. The contemporary accounts of Saint Brigid make most sense if we keep in mind that her home, Kildare, had been the center of worship of the ancient goddess Brigit long before anyone heard of Christianity. The "voyage of Saint Brendan" with his followers in a tiny boat into the north Atlantic need not have happened in just the way the medieval legend tells it, but it captures the omnidirectional zeal of an island society gone mad for monkery.

That Irish church would flourish in its often daffy way until the twentieth century, though now it is in retreat. The Irish stressed some aspects of continental Christianity—particularly a long tradition of intense, learned biblical exegesis. But the conversion of ancient Ireland's druidic class happened too quickly and easily to be entirely transformative. Ireland remained a center of missionary activity, monastic zeal, and frequently idiosyncratic practice, intermittently subject to military invasion from the east (Britain) or northeast (Scandinavia), rarely exporting anything. On a later page we will meet a few more Irishmen wrestling with angels in the middle of the sea.

The Irish share with the citizens of Iberia, southern Gaul, and Italy—the last of these all ruled by distant offshoots of Theoderic's family and relations—the pleasure of being the last Christianities to thrive in the west before the rise of imperial Christianity radiating from the Frankish and Byzantine courts.[6] The rulers of these ancient Christian societies generally cared about Christianity enough to practice it in some form, to support it, and even to discourage its enemies, but they had no vision of a society wholly Christian that they could insistently impose on their followers. Augustine of Hippo himself, writing *The City of God* in Africa in the early fifth century, provided the makings of such a vision, without being able to imagine a world in which Christianity was unopposed and sovereign, unpersecuted and persecuting. The reality was emerging before his very eyes, but it had not yet established itself. Much of the most intolerant Christian language and practice arose among people who assumed that intolerance was necessary for a battle always fought but never won.

Patrick's story is of the mid-fifth century. The story of Augustine of Canterbury, whom we mentioned above, is of the late sixth century, when Pope Gregory in Rome sent out a mission to convert the heathen Angles to Christianity. A small band of monks made their way from Rome north, crossing Gaul and making visits to the chief churchmen along their route. They found it easy enough to cross to Britain and had the serene confidence to introduce their faith to the people they found there as though they had come from another world with a great gift. In fact, they had little sense of what they would encounter when they arrived. In a society already sprinkled with pockets of Christianity, they quickly found themselves involved in local politics, winning kinglets here and there for their cause, only to find that other kings and other peoples were already affiliated with their creed through their other dissonant parts.

The various communities of British Christians argued not about doctrine but about practice. In one year the royal household of King Oswin, or Oswy, of Northumbria found itself divided at Eastertime by a disagreement over the calendar. Finding the date of Easter is not a straightforward calculation, inasmuch as the four gospel texts in the canonical scriptures differ among themselves about the precise timing of the crucifixion and resurrection, and so it took a very long time for all communities to approach agreement on this matter. In this case, Queen Eanfleda, daughter of King Edwin of Kent in the south, had brought her own chaplain, a priest named Romanus, and he insisted that she follow the Roman calendar. It scheduled Easter a week later than the clerics of the king's end of the palace, who observed the date calculated by the Irish tradition of the time.[7] The pre-Easter period was a time of austerity and self-control, especially the last week, and so there was some tension, not least sexual, in the household when the menfolk in the king's retinue came to the end of their austerity and were prepared to celebrate in many ways, but the womenfolk around Eanfleda were just entering the week of their greatest renunciation. Differences of practice were visible every day, as when the island's monks observed the ritual haircut—the tonsure—in a different style from the continent.

The drive toward unity and authority in Christianity finally brought together representatives of churches up and down Britain in 664 CE to meet at Whitby, on the northern English coast, where they made peace and the Roman interpretation prevailed. Soon one standard monkish haircut was seen everywhere. The version of Christianity that had arrived from Rome long before thus yielded to the combined forces of the more recently arrived churchmen and the official form of Christianity sent out from Rome itself. Roman soldiers and governors were long gone from Britain by now, but Rome remained a powerful presence.

There is more paradox here, for as early as the sixth century it was the Irish Christians (call them traditional) who had begun to trickle back onto the mainland of Europe, and one of them, Columban (or Columbanus, no relation to the Columba of Iona we met a few pages ago), founded monasteries, met secular rulers, and lectured Pope Gregory by writing him letters on correct doctrine. Columban's Latin poetry—by a man born where Latin was a late arrival and no tradition of Latin writing existed until Christianity brought its texts—is quite the best of his age. His monasteries (particularly at Luxeuil in Switzerland and Bobbio in northern Italy) flourished long afterward as centers of learning and culture. Such movements have led some moderns to think, with the hearty agreement of Irish exiles everywhere, that they could speak of the Irish as the saviors of civilization.[8] With all respect to my ancestors, the Irish were no such thing.

It is truer to say that in the centuries after Patrick, the Irish worked and won their way into the framework of the world Rome left behind. Their religion may have been a kind of cargo cult: a mixture of ancient Irish practices and Christian importation, and they were economically and socially backward, inward-looking in the extreme. The great Irish seaports of Belfast, Dublin, Waterford, and Cork were not to be settled and exploited until centuries later by the Vikings, and the native societies remained landlocked and poor. The renegades who left Ireland found a role for themselves in other European societies that were still very much the heirs of Rome and that hardly recognized themselves as the beneficiaries of any Irish gift. The inclusion of Ireland in Roman Europe progressed slowly, not reaching stability and success until the prime ministership of Garret FitzGerald in the 1980s, following the deposition of the last of the ancient sacred high kings, Eamon de Valera.[9]

THE END OF THE EPIC OF CHRISTIANITY

Augustine had welcomed the relics of Saint Stephen, the first martyr, to his church in Hippo in the 420s, and Stephen's march across the Mediterranean was an influential example for later generations and other places.[10] A high-minded writer could explain the mystery of relics with great elegance:

> The noble souls of the victorious traverse the heavens and join in the dance of the immaterial beings. Their bodies are not hidden away each in its single grave, but the cities and villages that have divided them among themselves call them saviors of souls and bodies and doctors and honor them as protectors of cities and guardians and treat them as ambassadors before the master of the universe and through them receive divine gifts. And even though the body has been divided, the grace has remained undivided, and that minute relic possesses the same power as the martyr, just as if he had never in any way been divided.[11]

By 600, Pope Gregory was steward of the shrine of Peter that lay beneath the basilica Constantine had built in his honor just outside the traditional walls of Rome. When people wrote to Gregory asking if they couldn't have just a small piece of the saint for their very own, or perhaps something that had touched his body, he answered that it was impossible, for a very devout reason: there was so much power in that tomb, and in his relics, that anyone who was imprudent enough merely to touch them could easily lose his life. Something resembling an electric charge was striking down those who came into contact, as when workmen repairing the shrine inadvertently brushed the saint. This kind of living power would spawn later practices that at this distance seem preposterous, such as the obsession with stolen relics in later centuries.[12]

The original great relic was the "true cross" that the bishop Macarius discovered in Jerusalem in the fourth century, excavating it at the behest of the emperor Constantine. It proved a friable discovery, for the first sighting of a relic from the cross in another land dates from as early as 359, in the north African city of Sitifis (now Sétif). In 540, another piece of the

cross protected the city of Apamea against a Persian invader, so successfully that the story was told far and wide and soon Justin II had the relic
transferred to Constantinople. The emperor Maurice used a golden lance
containing a fragment of the cross when he went campaigning in the Balkans in the 590s, and Heraclius did likewise when he went out to fight the
Persians in 622, as part of a campaign to recapture the remains found in
Jerusalem of the one and only true cross. Down to the present day in the
Roman church, the consecrated altar of any church is required to have a
saint's relic embedded in it.

The buildings and rites of Christianity were traditionally Roman
as well. Earliest Christianity is reported to us as a thing of people and
common meals, with leaders but not clergy and homes but not architecture. Rituals and the priests to manage them emerged early enough for
Tertullian (c. 200) to have to defend Christianity against salacious rumors
of cannibalism and sexual orgies carried on behind closed doors. (One
story had it that the Christians tied dogs to the candlesticks, then startled
them into knocking over the candlesticks, thus dousing the lights and providing a cover of darkness in which brother was expected to fornicate with
sister.[13]) Architecture emerged later, with respectability, and the buildings
of Christianity departed from their models, the ancient temples, in several
ways. But a religion of priests, rites, and looming handsome buildings is
something that Jesus practiced in moderation and criticized firmly, occasionally without moderation. He would have recognized the Christianities
of 500 and 600 for what they were, and perhaps not disowned them.

Those puritanical bishops who emerged in the fifth and sixth centuries, men like Martin of Braga, who kept trying to water down or eradicate
customs they knew were marked by the old religious ways, represented
something genuinely new, a wave of the future that could still, with some
difficulty, connect itself to the message of Jesus and the distinctly Christian
past. They were the true men of the book, joined in their textual obses-
sions by the men of monasteries, whose numbers now began to explode.

As late as 400, most bishops and churchmen were of modest social
and educational background, from the periphery of imperial culture. At
that time, figures such as Ambrose and Augustine already foretold the
future, in which the textual practices of the imperial bureaucracy became
the order of the day within established Christianity. There would be more
copies of scripture and more readers, but that meant there were also more

books written about scripture, and the library of the writings of the venerated "fathers of the church" began to hedge the Christian past with contemporary authoritative interpretation. Knowing scripture alone was no
longer enough.

The Christian library of theology would be accompanied by the Christian bureaucracy of ecclesiastical administration, and never more so than
in the oldest home of bureaucracy, Rome itself. By the time of Pope Gregory I, the administration of the papal household and office had aligned
itself almost perfectly to the hierarchical structure of Roman imperial
government. A complete bureaucratic structure of offices and documents
grew up and flourished. The simple Christian bishop had once spoken
to an audience within the sound of his own voice, but now the powerful Christian patriarch in Rome, Constantinople, Antioch, or Alexandria
wrote to an audience far beyond his ken, and expected his words to be
taken seriously.

We can even see the textualization of charisma in the church building
itself, when someone like Augustine would have stenographers trained as
the Roman government had trained them sitting by his side to take down
every word of his sermons, and would send authorized copies to selected
friends. In the fifth century we have the story of Sidonius as bishop in Cler-
mont going into church one day only to have the *libellus* (a small folded
piece of writing) on which he had written the prayers for the day snatched
from his hand by a prankster.[14] The account praises the bishop for carrying off the ceremonies as if nothing had happened, thereby indirectly confirming that premeditation and a prepared text were by now the expected
supplements for divine inspiration. A century later, great bishops celebrat-
ing the Mass were surrounded by books, probably four in all, handled by
different minor clergy: one for scriptural readings, one for prayers, one for
songs, and one for stage directions for managing the comings and goings
around the altar.

The sixth century saw an explosion of Christian books and books
about books. The *Pseudo-Gelasian Decretal* is a guide to books you
should read and books you should not, and assumes that there is an audience that has access to books and expects to find its Christian experience
supported there. (Pope Gelasius had nothing to do with it, but it was taken
as the archetype of the much later papal *Index of Forbidden Books*.) At
the boundary of empires in Nisibis, a flourishing school of exegetes of-

fered their example to others. In Constantinople, one imperial quaestor, Junillus, wrote a book to report the wisdom of the Nisibis school (probably to misrepresent it in support of Justinian's views). Even farther west, in remote Squillace, the former quaestor Cassiodorus had Junillus copied as part of his ambitious program to bring together all the important books of Christianity.

To moderns accustomed to a textual culture, such actions have a reassuringly familiar appearance, and speak to us of a Christianity that was normalizing itself. In fact, guidance of everyday experience by a *written* text was a very new idea. The codes of Roman law can be said to anticipate or parallel its Christian development. In very similar kinds of texts, Christian writers sought to regulate the cares of the heart and to extend the even longer arm and farther-seeing eye of a heavenly father who cared about every act and every person.

Christianity everywhere claimed to be universal and everywhere became parochial. The challenge of languages was overcome by the implicit acceptance that Christianity could exist in any language in which its books could be read. Translation for Christianity began early, and by the fifth and sixth centuries it became the rule of the day. Earlier churchmen's limited efforts to cling to original languages and close study of original texts faded away. Very few Christians by 600 knew any Hebrew at all, few knew or spoke Aramaic (though at least one village in Syria speaks it still), and even those who spoke Syriac, the language closest to Hebrew, were unable to approach scriptural texts in the original. Greek churchmen and Latin churchmen settled into the comfortable cultivation of religion in their own language and made effectively no attempt to go behind the translations they received.

This meant that the Greeks had the advantage of seeing at least the New Testament in the original, but the Syriac and Latin churches, and after them the Slavonic churches as well, were entirely cut off from original sources. The finest points of theology were regularly debated and then taught on the basis of translations that were—even when they were as good as Jerome's versions of the Bible—hugely imperfect. Even more than scripture, this parochialism meant that the theology of the Greeks, and in particular the language in which powerful figures like Origen and Cyril had written, would be a nearly closed book to churches in the rest of the world until modern times.

And almost everywhere, official, urban, bureaucratic Christianities were matched, especially during the fifth and sixth centuries, by the rise of monasteries as alternative centers of power and homes for Christian observance and identity. The word "monasticism" hides a multitude of stories and things. Starting in the fourth century, in parts of the Roman world where barren deserts came close to urban centers—in Egypt, Palestine, and Syria—holy men fled "the world" to leave temptation and sin behind. Of course, even when they went out into the wasteland to wrestle with the devil, they were not so far from civilization as to keep at least somewhat less austere people from following along and writing down their stories. The popularity of tales of the desert grew from the fourth century onward, when the life of Anthony, in particular, was a best seller in many countries, and when rumors of the wonders to be found in the desert drew tourists and dilettantes. Egeria, a gentlewoman of the church from Spain or, more likely, Gaul, made the grand tour of the Holy Land in the late fourth century and wrote an account of her journey for the benefit of her sisters back home. She was thrilled to write about the tourist trap that had sprung up at Mount Sinai, where you could see, all on the same day, the burning bush and the rock where Moses received the Ten Commandments. She wrote in equally loving detail about the grand liturgies of Jerusalem. Jerome, as a young man ambitious and well connected in a traditional way, went to try out the ascetic life in the monastic communities of Syria. He came scurrying home quickly enough, but he boasted of his heroic austerities all his life. Years later he found a better way to combine influence and austerity, taking a wealthy patroness along to set him up in a monastery in Bethlehem, convenient to the prosperity and power of the church in Jerusalem, but suburbanized in a town whose name was recognized all over the world.

Such stories about monks depend on two stereotypes. There's the authentic monk, the loner, the purist, the man who turns his back on society and flees to the desert; and then there's the riffraff of monkdom, including the half-disciplined communities of followers of fashion, ill-disciplined, too attentive by half to the ways of the wicked world. The two groups overlap.

So what were monks?

Traditional societies offer few roles for the socially mobile or the ambitious—mainly, these societies offer the army or government. Mediterranean society told you who you were by where you were born, where you lived, and who your family was. Movement beyond the confines of that identity was relatively difficult and relatively infrequent. Merchants probably succeeded best, yet they have mainly stayed off the radar of historians and moderns who know the past best from the surviving written record. Soldiers could move around, and many found the military life liberating, but it still was confining even at the best of times and often enough led to an early grave. "Barbarians" in that light are people whose mobility has not yet been anchored and tamed in Roman reality.

Christianity offered fresh chances for such mobility. Often, ordinary Christian clerics were ordained after marrying and having children, though lifelong celibacy became more fashionable from the fourth century onward. The celibate cleric gave up family to achieve his status, but gained as well, in independence and ambiguity of social position.

But the institutional church, if it allowed you to reposition yourself, tended to freeze you where you were. A bishop of a church might have come from anywhere, but once he landed in his position of leadership, he was ordinarily bound to remain there for life. Houses of clergy were filled with people who had detached themselves from the expectations of their communities only to find new and permanent homes. (We have seen how, in the fourth century, attempts by government to keep rich taxpayers right where they were failed repeatedly.)

Monks, on the other hand, were out of all bounds. They had an ideological reason for departing from the midst of civil society, but the effect was to create individuals who were not connected to the societies through which they passed and had no obligations to these societies—but who could demand financial and moral support as their due. Spectators are meant to see the sacrifices of asceticism, without noticing the power it could bring.

Monks, to be sure, found themselves in communities more often than not, and a social expectation developed that only the holiest could be allowed to live on their own, entirely detached. They were the ones most willing to expose themselves to public view by enacting a visible role, or the ones most willing to retreat entirely and genuinely from human contact. Others were expected to remain in houses with fellow monks and place themselves under some supervision. One sixth-century monk whose views would have long influence, an Italian from the hill country southeast of Rome, began his set of rules for monastic life by sternly insisting on stability—that is, on regular residence in one place under a particular authority. He had stinging rebuke for the monks he called "sarabaites" and "gyrovagues"—the kind who went about on their own, begging for sustenance, and offering contact with their presumed holiness promiscuously to one and all. Such a vigorous rebuke must mean that the practice was common, and one man's fraud is another man's saint. To see those figures as atypical and necessarily either virtuous or vicious is a mistake. We should instead see and admire their instability and their ability to elude the nets their society would set out to control them, even when monasteries themselves began to wield such nets.

In different parts of the Christian worlds, monks took on different appearances and had different fates. In Egypt, they were by now long settled in desert fastnesses not far from the cities of the Nile, and they also thronged the cities, particularly Alexandria. The financial resources that went into the churches, and that grew as churches acquired property, were the underpinnings of the communities, the implicit tax that sustained unproductive hands. The urban oppressed poor of classical antiquity were now joined by the urban privileged poor, these monks. A monk might be poor by choice, but he had little risk of starving to death. The monasteries in town and outside it were hotbeds of spiritual authority, which some would call charlatanism. Wanderers and the renegades might be reined in not by sage teaching but by their own desire to settle down and share the power of great monks and great houses.

The first monks and in many ways the real monks were eastern, whether they spoke Greek, Syriac, Coptic, or, eventually, Slavic. That eastern monasticism is what we find east of the Adriatic to this day, most notably in the ancient communities of Mount Athos in Greece, a whole landscape of celibate communities. Western monasticism was different.

Westerners heard about the monastic founders of the desert before they met any of them or their followers. Here and there imitation broke out, but it was not until long after our period that there were any appreciable numbers of western monks. "Desert" in the west didn't mean a barren landscape so much as it meant a remote wasteland, and the earliest houses were forest hermitages and huts, well away from towns and cities. The most austere landscapes of the eastern monastic desert were often (as in Egypt and around Jerusalem) only a few miles from bright lights and

326 of THE RUIN OF THE ROMAN EMPIRE

big cities. In the west, monks were more likely to be in genuinely remote locations.

Until the turn of the fifth century, there were few communities, and there was not much excitement outside their walls. Augustine called the household he led at Hippo a monastery, and his sister led a house of religious women there, though they didn't always get along well. The reputation of the eastern desert came west, inspiring deeds and words. The former soldier Martin drew a small community around him in the last years of the fourth century near Tours in central Gaul. When he was gone, Sulpicius Severus, a writer who had never met him, told his story of piety and power in a book that made him out as a western rival and worthy competitor of the legends of the east. If you think, Sulpicius's argument ran, that there are holy men in the east, well, we have our own, and here are astonishing stories to prove it. Those stories never really found a readership or a reputation until more than a century later, when the Frankish kings began to present Martin, for their own political reasons, as a locally grown saint and sage.

The monastic ethos finally broke into the western provinces with full strength when one man, John Cassian, arrived from the east in the early fifth century. Cassian was something between a monk and a tourist of monkery in his early days, traveling through the eastern deserts and cities, and sitting at the feet of the revered fathers he found there. Bethlehem, Egypt, and Constantinople saw Cassian come and go, increasingly entangled in the religious controversies of the time. The seasons changed and he found himself in the west, settled at Marseille, where his role became that of sage and guru; in a series of writings over the last decades of his life (he died in 433) he embodied the ethos and offered the anecdotes that would become archetypal in western monasticism. In *Institutes* and *Lectures*, he told of life in the eastern deserts and reported the words of the fathers he met there. Invariably, the result takes on a cast of its own that makes us unsure where the received tradition leaves off and Cassian's interpretive genius takes over.

His example and books inspired a remarkable place and its people, the island monastery of Lérins in the harbor of what is today Cannes in the south of France. For a long generation in the early fifth century, Lérins was the thrilling center of monastic inspiration, sending its monks as bishops and missionaries throughout Gaul and into the British Isles. Even Patrick of Ireland may have spent time there, for he shows traces of the spirit of Lérins, and he permanently shaped Irish monasticism. In the other direction, Cassian's influence stood behind the three next most influential western authorities on the monastic life: the *Rule of the Master*, which comes from an anonymous teacher in northern Italy around 500; the too famous *Rule of Benedict*, from the mid-sixth century; and then the multiple writings of Pope Gregory I in the late sixth century. For austerity and guidance, Cassian's texts and his imitators' rules were authoritative. On many days, in his sermons on Job, Ezekiel, and the gospels, Gregory could keep pace with Cassian's most demanding biblical meditations; and Gregory's *Dialogues*, four books of tales of ascetic heroes we will hear of again, created a powerful textual image of self-denial in obedience, austerity, and a life's devotion. Benedict's short, practical *Rule* did not come to the fore until the ninth century, when Charlemagne's administration actively promoted it as a standard, at a time when many monasteries were founded.

Eastern monasticism grew and flourished, and its ascetics probably numbered in the tens of thousands, some even in double monasteries, communities with men and women living separately in the same house. In the west, even with such intellectually powerful figures as Cassian and eventually Gregory, monasticism long remained in small houses, scattered and finding their respective authority in different ways. In Ireland, abbots were bishops and monks ruled the church, but elsewhere, some houses stood alone and rose and fell in a generation or two, while wealth and patronage began to build more powerful houses near royal courts and cathedrals.

Despite all the quarreling of monks, in the generations after Justinian, particularly, but not only, in the western provinces, something important faded from view: heresy. For Justinian's great effort to bring the whole world into doctrinal alignment with himself not only failed; it failed catastrophically and permanently. Egypt and Syria settled into their versions of monophysitism; Constantinople clung to its increasingly nuanced and impenetrable version of Chalcedonian orthodoxy; the western churches gradually tumbled together under something like the authority of the bishop of Rome—an authority that would sometimes be contested, but rarely on doctrinal grounds. The history of the development of the core doctrines of Christianity henceforth comes to an end, and what will occur in the future are occasional revivals and repetitions of old arguments. Christians in the west during the ninth, sixteenth, and seventeenth centuries fought over free will and predestination. Westerners could never agree on these questions, though they held little interest at any period for the eastern churches. Now and again, communities would need to act out their hostilities, as when the Greek and Latin churches, long adrift and estranged, found it necessary in the eleventh century—just when harmony would have begun to be valuable—to declare their enmity with mutual excommunications not lifted for 900 years.

The drift to relative harmony brought all the Latin provinces quietly into the ark of orthodoxy. The last to hold out for the old religion of the frontier was the regime in Spain that remembered a Visigothic past. By the late sixth century, of course, anything one might call barbarism there had been part of the Roman empire for 200 years, since the day when Fritigern and Alavivus brought their small refugee band across the Danube. The gradual retreat from Gaul into Spain in the late fifth century and early sixth century, as the Franks made themselves masters of Gaul and in 507 finally drove the Visigoths into Spain, had accidentally put the losing side in a position to build a lasting regime. The gradual establishment of the kingdom that would form the heart of Andalusia produced governance that was Roman, military, and at least modestly prosperous. By the late sixth century, the moment of Justinianic invasion had faded and a few pockets of imperial presence remained on the southeastern coast of the peninsula, but King Leovigild (r. 569–586) succeeded his brother Athanagild and married Athanagild's widow to solidify his reign. In short order, he seized Córdoba back from the Byzantine garrison that had lingered there.

Leovigild's administration was marked by expansion of control and authority, entirely in the Roman and Byzantine traditions. In the way of such kingdoms, he brought his sons Hermenegild and Reccared to the throne with him, and married the former to a Frankish princess, to ensure peaceful relations northward. Catholic historians of later generations want to make it out that for a year or so in 584, Leovigild dug in his heels and insisted on appointing Arian bishops and opposing the spread of Catholicism. Something snapped then in the royal household, and Hermenegild revolted, ostensibly in the name of authentic religion, and was jailed and then killed. Leovigild prevailed for another five years, extending his control over the whole peninsula. As soon as he was gone, Reccared took the throne in 589 and declared himself for Catholicism—and suddenly the struggle was over. The Catholic bishops who had been in resistance emerged immediately as dominant figures in the realm, especially Leander of Seville, a friend and correspondent of Pope Gregory, who was in the process of taking the Roman see in 590. Whatever the true story, the divisions in the kingdom had been just that, divisions, not controversies in any way rooted in distinctive beliefs and practices of different religious communities.

And so by 600 Christianity became, in most of the world that knew it, something entirely normal, a part of the background, a part of the everyday, an object of practice and occasional obsession, but not a focus of much thought or any controversy. The epic of the rise of Christianity was at an end.

CHILDREN OF ABRAHAM

Abraham has a lot to answer for. Half the people on earth know his name and revere him as an ancestor for their religious traditions: 2 billion Christians, 1 billion and more Muslims, and about 15 million Jews. We take it for granted that these three families eye one another warily, occasionally falling into fraternal warfare. So it is easy to forget that, at least to the man in the moon, together they probably resemble a single exuberant growth, swallowing half the globe. Each has so decisively excommunicated the others that observers and participants alike accept them as three different beasts.

What do they have in common? They have a set of books originally written in Hebrew that tell a more or less connected story of the chosen people in Palestine, followers of a god who set himself up, quite bravely for such a provincial deity, against all the other gods of the world. The books are full of all the famous names: Adam, Eve, Cain, Abel, Methusaleh, Noah, Abraham, Isaac, Jacob, Moses, Joshua, David, Solomon—those are the great worthies of the old scrolls. They and their leaders were, in the accounts by later generations, swept away, their Jerusalem and their texts all but destroyed and the heart of the movement gutted in the time of the Babylonian captivity. The people of Judaea became decisively entangled then with the great nations of the world and fell under the sway of the Persian monarchs ruling in Mesopotamia. That captivity dates to the sixth century BCE, to the 100 years of Persian ascendancy that ended with the great wars the Persians fought to try to make the Greek-speaking western shores of the Aegean part of their empire. All later Judaism, all later Abrahamic faith, depends on the stories of ancient days, when the Israelites lived alone and isolated, outside history.

The story of the Babylonian captivity cannot be trusted. It was written by Jerusalem's leaders long afterward to explain how they came to hold power and to justify their claim that they were descendants of the ancient worthies. The ostensible story is one of sweeping exile, then sweeping return, accompanied by a nearly magical restoration of authority. The exact text of destroyed scriptures was magically recovered after decades of oblivion. Just how much destruction accompanied Assyrian suppression of the revolts in the lands where Yahweh was worshipped we cannot yet be sure. Who left to go into exile in Babylon is far from clear.

The restoration after the captivity, under Cyrus in 537, was not a victory for the Judaeans, but rather a new, insidious domination. The Persians preferred not outright subjugation and oppression, which the Assyrians had occasionally practiced, but domination in place, and so they allowed people who had been living in Babylon for fifty years (therefore adults, the grandchildren of the original captives, therefore people who had been acclimated to their new society) to go to Judaea to seize control and rule at the expense of the people they found there. The support of Persian soldiers and the determination of Persian authority to make its own settlers—dare one say pawns?—dominant are unmistakable.

But the settlers sent from Persia were not the only children of Abraham in those lands. In the long history that follows, the Jews who didn't go away became known as the Samaritans, from the zone north of Jerusalem where they lived (and where a few remain to this day). Needless to say, they do not accept the story of the Persian-supported returnees or the legitimacy of the rule they imposed.

The real history of Jewry begins from that moment in 537 when Cyrus sent his own selection of the chosen people back to Jerusalem—or, perhaps better, from the moment twenty years later when the temple that had been razed in 587 was restored. These subjects first of Persia, then of the successors of Alexander, and eventually of Rome loved to tell stories about themselves as an autonomous, proud nation, descending from the doughty past when they were a chosen people living by themselves in their own special land. But those stories were being told by people increasingly cosmopolitan, international, civilized, prosperous, and, frankly, happy with their lot as subjects of great kings elsewhere.

The scriptures that tell their ancestor stories claim to have come into being before the captivity and were all but destroyed during the captivity. But even when the temple was restored, the scriptures were, somehow, left in neglect. Just what the Judaism of that period, from the 510s to the 450s BCE, was like is a hard subject, made harder by the confidence we see displayed when Ezra proclaimed the restored Torah in the 440s, a century after the return from Babylon and almost a century and a half after the captivity began. He and his immediate circle had not been part of Jerusalem Judaism until they were sent back themselves from Persia—more Jews from exile—in 459. But yet it was Ezra who was able to make the holy book new again. Again? Perhaps it was even newer than he made it out to be.

The Judaism that Persia created lived and flourished in the niches of the world of Persia's greatest son, Alexander the Great. Alexander's lasting achievement was to extend empire and the pomp of great citites from Mesopotamia to the shores of the Mediterranean. The Alexandria he founded and the Antioch he came on, seaports for the worlds of the Seleucids in Mesopotamia and the Ptolemies in Egypt who succeeded him in rule, were the places where Judaism enjoyed its greatest prosperity, always staying just a little outside the mainstream, harking back to its often angry god in his remote mountaintop city.

The coming of Rome to the eastern Mediterranean and the borderlands of the east changed remarkably little at first. Taxes went to different overlords and the soldiers spoke a new language. Over time the hand of distant authority began to weigh more heavily. In the age of Rome's own revolution, Judaea was on the rise again, to a new position of advantage as a client kingdom under Rome. The local princeling, Herod, was a man of good family, but because he was Idumean, from south of traditional Judaea, he was never Judaean enough for everyone in Jerusalem. His connections to Rome—the new Persia—were excellent. His father had been the Roman governor (procurator), and he himself ruled Galilee for Rome as a very young man. When Rome's rule was imperiled by a Persian invasion in the 30s BCE, Mark Antony welcomed Herod, declared his support for him as "king of the Jews," and sponsored his return. Herod was more successful than his patron, but when Antony was gone it would be a long time before any Roman ruler had as coherent an eastern policy in mind.

Though suspect because of his family, his religion, and his Roman sponsorship, Herod was the most successful ruler who ever sat in Jerusalem. He ruled for more than thirty years and oversaw economic success unexampled in local history. His Judaea was a country of cities, palaces, and—for its time—industrial wealth. His support for the port city of Caesarea was decisive in shaping the economy and culture of the coast. Most spectacularly, he rebuilt the temple at Jerusalem on a scale that still flabbergasts. The temple he inherited had been built after the Babylonian captivity and attracted visitors for centuries on what must have seemed a paltry scale by the time of Herod. In 19 BCE he began a reconstruction that entailed erecting the vast platform we now call Temple Mount, home of the Dome of the Rock and al-Aqsa Mosque. (The "Wailing Wall" or Western Wall dear to Jewish worshippers is a fragment of the footings of Herod's complex.) When Herod's work was completed, it was the largest and grandest temple in the Mediterranean world. When we read in the gospels of Jesus expressing disdain for the commercialization of the temple and its precincts, we must force our imagination to a scale large enough to envision the huge spaces involved, something resembling the grandest of modern shopping malls. Then we can understand what magnetism would bring droves of people there daily. We should also read with caution the story of Jesus "cleansing the temple" and not imagine that one man could drive out all the merchants and moneychangers from this vast space.

Take a broad view of the fate of Jewry in the reign of Augustus or Tiberius and you will see a prosperous province settling in to anchor the Roman empire in the east and Judaism at a peak of wealth and prosperity. Jesus spoke as a prophet not to a declining culture but to one at its absolute zenith. But the Romans' high-handedness toward the Judean religion evoked a response that proved suicidal. Tension rose, from the time in 6 CE when Rome insisted on appointing the high priest to the moment in 66 when rebellion broke out. We depend not only on Christian New Testament texts for our view of that time, but chiefly on Josephus's account in *The Jewish War*, which captures a privileged local perspective. From those accounts, the Romans seem overbearing and obtuse to local religious sympathies— but those texts would obviously make exactly that point. When serious insurrection broke out, the emperor Nero sent his general Vespasian to suffocate it. Vespasian landed at Caesarea, taking control of the coast and the north, leaving Jerusalem to itself to fester. He eventually succeeded Nero in 69, and it was Vespasian's son (and the future emperor) Titus who carried out the final devastating siege and destruction of Jerusalem in 70. The temple itself was destroyed in a hideous fire that consumed the marble of the vast edifice. Its treasures were carried off to Rome, where the arch of Titus still memorializes the event. Those treasures, you may recall, were said to have been captured again and carried off from Rome by the Vandals in 455. In Judaea, the last stronghold, the hilltop fort of Masada, fell in 72; Rome had mastered the landscape. New Israeli soldiers today are taken to Masada to swear their oaths of allegiance.

Jerusalem was sacked, but the religion survived. Deprived of its Temple and its sacrifices, forever (as it seemed) deprived of its political identity and influence, this people that should have been relegated to marginal prosperity at the fringe of empire turned out to have become something quite unexpected and quite modern. The god the people knew in Judea turned out to be portable, and the religious identity they had shaped was able to move with them.

And some part of Judaism's survival is owed to Christianity. It's a subtle question just when in history it begins to make sense to speak of the followers of Jesus as practitioners of a religion separate from Judaism.[15] Talk about Jesus flourished among practicing Jews, and on at least one occasion those who revered Jesus came nearly to blows in discussing whether non-Jews should be allowed to share in the new movement. The New Testament collection of texts represents a retrospective choice, not confirmed until the fourth century, to tell the story of Christianity in terms of Pauline inclusiveness, but among the many kinds of Christian community that flourished until Constantine's conversion forced them into the open, these groups were Jewish in every way that mattered.

The eventual compromise of orthodox Christianity validated the Jewish past and rejected the Jewish present. When official Christianity ended by defining itself as rigorously new and different, it was a divorce without complete disengagement, and Christianity and Judaism still define themselves in terms of each other to this day.

Judaism itself had to be reinvented repeatedly in late antiquity and the middle ages, reinvented with a new kind of clergy in the rabbinical class, reinvented with synagogues that imagined only a future or past temple as their point of departure, and reinvented with a Bible in the canonized Masoretic text of scriptures. Judaism settled for being identified with religion rather than nation or place, before eventually descending to being identified as well with ethnicity. In Judea and Syria, the fifth and sixth centuries CE were the greatest age of construction of synagogues, buildings decorated with elaborate mosaics, dazzling with sometimes gaudy imagery (of the temple and the Torah, and also of biblical scenes, animals, and the signs of the zodiac), places where prayer had replaced the defunct and obsolete business of sacrifice. (Judaism had no rituals to surrender when Theodosius banned pagan sacrifice and had the advantage of having already reinvented itself to live in a Christian world. If Titus had left the temple standing, we have to wonder what the fourth-century emperors would have made of it.)

From the fourth century onward, villages in the east began to be more and more religiously homogeneous, developing an apartheid that remains in deadly force in many places today. Until then, religion had not been a criterion for selecting your residence, but by about 500 it was clear when you came to a place whether the inhabitants were Christians, Jews, Samaritans, pagans, or whatever. Persecution of various kinds was now easier than ever.

Most striking of all, the late sixth century is the heart of the period when the Jews of Babylon developed the elaborate exploration of religious law called the Babylonian Talmud. Christians seem to have been entirely oblivious of this scholarly, subtle activity, even centuries later when the precious copies of the Talmud were the focus of religious intellectual activity. This religious invasion from what was strictly the domain of the Persian emperors gradually spread through the domains of the caliphs who succeeded them, from Persia to North Africa, long after working its way north into Christian Europe. (Never mind the irony that the Jewish scriptures originally came from people who had been sent from Babylon to Jerusalem, and now the Talmud itself took decisive form in the city symbolic of all that was worldly and unclean.)

Meanwhile, the Samaritans went on their way, quite convinced of their ancient seniority to the Jews. What Judaism suffered in 70 CE, with the sack of Jerusalem, the Samaritans had experienced and survived in 107 BCE with the destruction of Shechem by the Hasmoneans. (Shechem was, credibly enough, said to be the place where Jacob dreamed of the angels' ladder to heaven, where Joseph's bones found rest, and where Abraham was tempted to sacrifice Isaac. Official Jewish tradition argued with some of that history, but could not uproot it.) The Samaritans regrouped and made nearby Flavia Neapolis ("Flavian Newtown") their chief city; it was founded just after the destruction of Jerusalem and today is known as Nablus, on the west bank of the river Jordan. There they lived and made their way, on the wedge of land between Judaea and Galilee that still bears their name, and down along the coast in the cities, reaching a height of prosperity in the fourth century. They spread around the Mediterranean well enough that in the late sixth century Pope Gregory had to deal with their issues: Samaritans bought pagan slaves and circumcised them (Gregory insisted that they be set free); or a Christian was enslaved by a Samaritan, then set free, then reclaimed by his former master's son, who had in the meantime converted to Christianity (Gregory was outraged and freed the man again).[16] At Khirbet Samara, on the road from Nablus to Tulkarm, a Samaritan synagogue about ten by fifteen yards in area was built over an older Roman building in the fourth century and then restored much later, in Arab times. Other synagogues were destroyed or turned into churches; at least one was turned back again to Samaritan use under the Arabs.

Christians knew what Jews were, but Samaritans were a puzzle, and often a source of friction. Pressed hard enough, they rioted in 484 in Nablus, and full-scale revolt broke out in 529. The historian John Malalas told the story this way later in the sixth century:

> In the month of June of the seventh indiction [529] a riot broke out among the local people when the Samaritans fought with the Christians and Jews, and many parts of Scythopolis were set on fire by the Samaritans. On hearing of this the emperor was angry with the governor Bassus, and so he relieved him of his office and had him beheaded. When the Samaritans learnt of the emperor's anger against them, they rebelled and crowned a bandit chief, a Samaritan named Julian, and they burnt estates and churches and killed many Christians. On entering Neapolis Julian watched chariot races [like an emperor] with a large number of Samaritans, and the first event was won by a certain Nikeas, a Christian charioteer. There were other charioteers at Neapolis, both Samaritans and Jews, whom the charioteer Nikeas defeated.

When he approached the rebel to be honored as was his due, he was asked what his religion was. When Julian learned that he was a Christian, he took the fact that the very first victory had gone to the Christians as an ill omen against himself, which in fact it proved to be, and so he immediately sent for the charioteer and had him beheaded in the circus. He also abused the bishop of the city. When the governors of Palestine and the general Theodoros the Snub-Nosed learned of this, they immediately reported the daring rebel to the emperor Justinian. The general set out against Julian with a large force, taking with him the phylarch of Palestine. On learning of this, Julian, the Samaritan rebel, fled from Neapolis. The general pursued him with his army, and they joined battle. The general cut down a large number of the Samaritans and captured Julian, whom God delivered into his hands. He beheaded Julian and sent his head with the diadem to the emperor Justinian. The news of the rebellion of the Samaritans and the ill-fated Julian arrived at Constantinople at the same time as the rebel leader's head. 20,000 fell in the battle. Some of them fled to the mountain known as Gerizim, and others to Trachon, to what is known as the Iron Mountain. The Saracen phylarch of the Romans took 20,000 boys and girls as plunder from the Samaritans. He took these as prisoners and sold them in Persian and Indian territory.[17]

To say 20,000 in both cases is doubtless an exaggeration, but the defeat was decisive. Bad as that was, worse lay ahead in 566, when one last revolt led to a decisively crushing response from Justin II. Though the Samaritans survived and found tolerance again from the Muslim Arabs, their days as more than an insignificant minority were over.

THE THIRD SIBLING

Everything I have said to this point imagines Christianity and Judaism in the traditional dyad of a European encounter, in which Christianity congratulates itself on its refreshing advance over the relatively primitive religiosity of its elder sibling in the tribe of Abraham. It has taken the shock of the twenty-first century's opening confrontations to remind western Christians that they are not the last-born of their family, but rather the middle child, in a household joined by Islam about as long after the rise of Christianity as the time that stretched from the Babylonian captivity to the life of Jesus.

The story of Islam is easy to tell, hard to understand. In the 630s, on the death of Muhammad, Arab armies seemed to arise magically from the desert sand, driven by a new force and an ambition that were hard *not* to attribute to divine blessing. By 641 Egypt and Syria had fallen to them. From then into the 660s their forces went deep into Asia Minor, eventually besieging Constantinople in 673. Carthage fell to them in 689, and by the early eighth century they had made the crossing to Spain and pressed north into Gaul. Modern readers have wondered if they might have gone farther:

> A victorious line of march had been prolonged above a thousand miles from the rock of Gibraltar to the banks of the Loire; the repetition of an equal space would have carried the Saracens to the confines of Poland and the Highlands of Scotland; the Rhine is not more impassable than the Nile or Euphrates, and the Arabian fleet might have sailed without a naval combat into the mouth of the Thames. Perhaps the interpretation of the Koran would now be taught in the schools of Oxford, and her pulpits might demonstrate to a circumcised people the sanctity and truth of the revelation of Mahomet.[18]

Patient investigation has made the story less astounding, to be sure. We now understand the growth of a prosperous and self-aware Arab community along the frontiers of Rome and Persia in the Arabian peninsula, just at the fissure separating the empires. The swift spread of Arab rule did not mean an instantaneous and total conversion of all the conquered peoples to Islam, for Christianity and Judaism survived quite well for a long time. The spirit of Theoderic was in the air when the Caliph Umar ordered that a mosque in Damascus was to be destroyed because it had been built on the site of a house wrongly taken from a Jew. The Umayyad caliphate of Damascus, the first pan-Arab polity, sitting in the oldest continuously inhabited city in the world (unless Aleppo can claim that title), reigning from 661 until its overthrow in 750, was a typical ancient empire in its diversity, inclusiveness, and rapacious ambition. (The Egyptian city of Aphrodito, where we met the poetic aristocrat Dioscoros many pages ago, supplies us with another trove of documents from around the year 710, letters of a local official to the Umayyad governor of Egypt at Fustat—near what is now Cairo—letters in which little has changed since the days when Aphrodito gave its loyalty to Constantinople.)

Only gradually did the domains of Islamic conquest become assimilated to the demands of Islamic religiosity, as the baleful spirit of Justinian made itself felt in this branch of the household of Abraham.

What remains to be explored, and may not be properly explored for a great many years to come, given sensitivities and caution on all sides, is the connection between Muhammad's religious movement and the Christian, Jewish, and Roman past that had permeated the world of the Arabian deserts as firmly as it had the northern lands across the Rhine and Danube. Just how quickly Muhammad's teaching took the shape of Islamic religion as medieval and modern peoples would receive it is a subject that has so far successfully deterred investigation.[19] One way to read Islam is to make it the Wesleyanism or Mormonism of late antiquity, an offshoot of the existing religions of Abraham and, unimpressed by the complexity of its ancestors, seeking clarity, simplicity, and extreme portability. The Christianities of late antiquity had grown to bloated proportions in wealth, power, and doctrinal complexity during the 300 years after Constantine. Against that baffling facade of lavish piety, the simplicity and power of the Muslim message were an alluring new song. If you were a monophysite Christian, aggrieved at being an object of condemnation by Christians you thought had lapsed into virtual polytheism with their two Christs and three persons in God, then Muhammad's "There is one god!" could be a refreshing return to what you considered authentic religion.

No matter how Islamic we may conclude the earliest followers of Muhammad were, they were read by contemporaries in more conventional and predictable ways. The seventh-century Armenian historian Sebeos sees only the refreshed claim to descent from Abraham, treating the new movement with guarded respect. About the same time, the earliest testimony from outside is a Christian treatise, *Teaching of the Newly Baptized Jacob*, written in the 630s, ostensibly in Carthage, recording a conversation between Jacob, who had recently been forced to accept Christian baptism, and other Jews, in which they discuss among other things the terrifying appearance of a false prophet in Arabia. Palestine is being overrun by this false prophet (for this report seems to treat Muhammad as still alive and in command), and a traveler named Abraham lands at Sycaminum (modern Haifa), there meeting an old man and asking him about this prophet. "He is a false prophet, for the prophets do not come armed with a sword." The old man speaks of the new prophet as the Antichrist. "So I, Abraham, inquired and heard from those who had met him that there was no truth to be found in the so-called prophet, only the shedding of men's blood. He says also that he has the keys of paradise, which is incredible."[20]

The monotheisms of Palestine manifested themselves in different ways through the fifth and sixth centuries. Absent the authoritarian style of Christianity, many forms of worship of a single god would have doubtless continued and differentiated themselves. We will soon meet the un-Jewish Jews of Medina, but of even greater importance are the people called *hanifiya*,[21] claiming Abraham as their father in religion, denying all false gods and star worship. A time traveler dropped down unexpectedly in their midst could not easily tell whether he had found a rogue form of Judaism, or of Islam, or of neither. Similarly, the fifth-century Greek Christian historian Sozomen makes up stories about Saracens, claiming that they were the descendants of Hagar but *pretending* to be descended from Sarah, and so using her name. They are somehow Jewish, abstaining from pork, practicing circumcision, and in other ways following recognizable ritual and tradition.

In this zone of ambiguity, can we hear the voice that became Muhammad's before the prophet appears on the scene? Can we hear the voice of the future before the future arrived?

The Kaaba in Mecca had been, after all, a religious center long before Muhammad. Protected by the Quraysh clan, the looming black-box shrine stood in a city which considered itself a center of commerce and trade, but whose real appeal was as a religious site on the caravan routes north from Yemen. The Kaaba was filled in Muhammad's youth with images and artifacts of hundreds of gods, the accumulation of generations of passing fancy and fervor. Muhammad himself, the story goes, cleansed the Kaaba of its paganism far more effectively than Jesus cleared the Jewish temple of its merchants. We can credit the story of idols and icons hacked with a sword and humiliated, though we might linger thoughtfully over the report that he left one image, of Jesus and his mother Mary, reverently untouched. Though Muhammad and his followers originally turned to Jerusalem to pray (as did many Christians), eventually Mecca and the

Kaaba would become the remarkably purified chief focus of Islamic piety and pilgrimage.[22]

Were there really days when the Arabs before Muhammad cheered at the contests of poets in their festival, then hung the texts of the winners on the Kaaba in letters of gold? We have some texts of these.[23] Tarafah's ode is virtually a love song addressed to his camel:

> Her long neck is very erect when she lifts it up
> calling to mind the rudder of a Tigris-bound vessel.
> Her skull is most like an anvil, the junction of its two halves
> meeting together as it might be on the edge of a file.
> Her cheek is smooth as Syrian parchment, her split lip
> a tanned hide of Yemen, its slit not bent crooked;
> her eyes are a pair of mirrors, sheltering
> in the caves of her brow-bones, the rock of a pool's hollow,
> ever expelling the white pus provoked by motes, so they seem
> like the dark-rimmed eyes of a scared wild-cow with calf.

Labid loves a camel less favored in appearance:

> . . . with a lean camel to ride on, that many journeyings
> have refined to a bare thinness of spine and shrunken hump,
> one that, when her flesh is fallen away and her strength is spent
> and her ankle-thongs are worn to ribbons of long fatigue,
> yet rejoices in her bridle, and runs still as if she were
> a roseate cloud, rain-emptied, that flies with the south wind,
> or a great-uddered she-ass, pregnant of a white-bellied sire worn lean
> by the stampeding and kicking and biting of fellow-stallions.

The poet Tarafah was himself ambitious but realistic:

> Had my Lord willed, I'd have been another Kais bin Khálid,
> and had my Lord willed, I'd have been another Amr bin Marthad;
> then I'd have been a man of much substance, visited
> by all the sprigs of the nobility, chiefs and sons of chiefs.
> I'm the lean, hard-bitten warrior you know of old,
> intrepid, lively as the darting head of a serpent;

I have vowed my loins cease not to furnish a lining
for an Indian scimitar sharp as to both its edges,
trenchant—when I stand forth to take my revenge with it
its first blow suffices; I need no repeat stroke; it's no pruning-hook—
a trusty blade, recoiling not from its target.

In another ode, ascribed to Zuhayr, we see lovely ladies borne along in litters on their journey:

their howdahs hung with costly cloths, and fine-spun veils
whose fringes are rose-red, the very hue of dragon's blood;
issuing from Es-Soobán, they have threaded its twisting course
mounted on Kainite camels sleek and excellently nourished,
swerved through hollow Es-Soobán, ascended its rugged ridge
wearing the sweet coyness of the luxuriously nurtured.
It is as though the thrums of dyed wool littering every spot
where they alighted were uncrushed berries of the red faná.
With the dawn they arose, and sunrise saw them stirring,
then into Wadi Er-Rass they plunged like hand into mouth,
and when they came to the waters blue in the brimming well
they cast down their sticks, as one who pitches his tent to stay;
a sweet diversion are they to the gentle, a pretty sight
well worth the scrutiny of those who like looking at beauty.

Islam is, among other things, what Abraham made of that magnificent world when Muhammad gave him the chance. In Arabia as in Judaea and all up and along the eastern frontiers, life could take its own course in these communities, barely touched by the twitches on the strings of authority that ran back to Constantinople.

7

Constantinople Deflated:
The Debris of Empire

HE STORY OF Justinian's empire after his death is an embarrassment to all who try, still, to praise him. Count no man happy, the old Greeks had said, until he has died; and one should count no emperor a success until one knows what becomes of his creations after he is gone. Justinian falls rapidly from his pedestal when we look at what he left behind.

THE POET CORIPPUS gives an account of the night Justinian died, which reads like a fragment of Soviet Kremlinology in the latter days, when Brezhnev gave way to Andropov, who yielded to Chernenko, each a more preposterous parody of Bolshevik loyalty than the one before. You can almost hear in Corippus's lines the purring engines of big black limousines sliding through the streets around the palace as the word got out among the leading courtiers that the time had finally come. There were many choices, at that point, for emperor; but the deal was clearly done and the fix was in: Justin—Justin II in the history books—was the man.

Justin was in his mid-forties, a nephew of the emperor, married to a niece of Theodora's: his relationships gave him a claim to power. He had a cousin, also named Justin, the son of a cousin of Justinian's: Germanus, who had been moving into leading military commands in the late 540s until premature death removed him from the scene. This other Justin showed promise, often a strong disqualifier in imperial politics. Worse, he was away from court doing useful military service in the Balkans when Justinian's end came, and thus was at a disadvantage in any competition requiring stealth and intrigue at court. The successful Justin had waited there in a discreet administrative role since 552 and had won the support of the church in the person of the patriarch, John Scholasticus—and of the military in the person of the count of the excubitors, Tiberius, a Balkan officer of real talent, as we shall see.

Justinian died in the palace he had scarcely left for years. Callinicus, the majordomo of the imperial residence (we might render his official title "provost of the sacred bedchamber"), claimed obligingly that Justinian had named his nephew to succeed him. The machinery of court spun into action. The excubitors blockaded the palace, the patriarch raised the crown on Justin's head, and before anyone was the wiser, the new emperor was installed.

Corippus wrote ceremonial verse that makes it all sound charming.[1] The senators rushed to the palace through the silence of the night, balancing grief and optimism ("rejoicing but you could scarcely say their faces were happy" was Corippus's delicate method of letting them have it both ways). Answering the summons, the senators reached the palace just as the cocks crowed and the first birds sang their dawn melodies to a day new in more ways than one. Justinian's body lay on a bier covered with a pall depicting him trampling the defeated Vandal king Gelimer thirty years earlier. Rows and rows of kings and others he had conquered flanked him in those images, under the benign gaze of female figures representing Africa and Rome in the ancient way. Corippus's awkward metaphor made Justinian out to be an ancient tree that had fallen, leaving courtiers to flutter about looking for new perches (the poet mercifully refrained from extending the metaphor to bird droppings), but the octogenarian body itself was unchanged in color, "shining with its customary glow." By the time the poet finished, the corpse itself rejoiced at the new day, turning (in some people's eyes) into the shape of an angel. (The corpse continued rejoicing in the Church of the Holy Apostles until western crusaders sacked Constantinople in 1204.)

The humbug of empire covers weakness in glory. Justin, doomed to an inglorious reign, appears now in Corippus in a garment not unlike the corpse's pall, but woven with purple, on which the whole series of Justinian's achievements (that is to say, the factitious, ruinous military victories that others won for him) were picked out in gold and gems. We are told to envision again the scene at court when Emperor Justinian stood resplendent in his great hall with his foot on the Vandal tyrant's neck while happy, liberated Libyans brought tribute and applauded. So too the figure of Rome herself, invoked in particularly desperate rhetorical moments of every century of the ancient era, appeared on the garment, extending her arms, breast bared, the nursing mother of empire and liberty, both of them dead or doomed.

Later the same day, with creaking insincerity, the old Roman ritual of imperial selection was reenacted. This was a rite not of the senate, but of the army, whence since the first century had come the most effective choices. Four sturdy young men were chosen to lift up a huge ceremonial shield, and then the emperor was lifted up—delicately, delicately!—to stand on it. There he remained for whatever moment, "as brave as they come, bright shining as the sun."

Some were impressed, some were pleased; all understood that the realities of power were unchanged.

Justin did well enough at the outset, as younger replacements of superannuated leaders often do, complaining about and then paying off debts that Justinian had incurred to ensure peace abroad and to keep up appearances at home while forgiving tax arrears into the bargain. Never mind that rumor ran wild after the other Justin passed through Constantinople for an amicable visit, went on to Alexandria, and there was found murdered in his bed. The empress was said to have ordered his head brought back to Constantinople, to be kicked about like a football. Even her supporters would have known that story, and the guilt or innocence of the imperial couple was irrelevant: the court was, as courts will be, a world of spin. When two senators, Aetherios and Addaios, were executed for conspiracy to poison Justin, one of them confessing, few cared for the truth, for all recognized a regime in thrall to its insecurity.

Abroad, Justin played the diplomatic game too nonchalantly, and disaster ensued. The Balkans had clearly slipped beyond imperial control, so he was content to send support or just empty promises of support to the players there. Such machinations always run the risk of replaying the last war, and since Justin knew that the Gepids were a threat of old, he both offered them support and then withheld it, leading to the triumph of the relatively obscure Lombards. The empire came out of the Lombard-Gepid war with its own position momentarily protected, but two strong powers now divided the Balkans between them, the Lombards to the west and the newly materializing Avars to the now neglected east, where they had made their way through and around Justinian's failed line of forts on the Danube, acquiring an identity and support as they prospered. The Avars would remain there to plague Constantinople until the emergence of the "Slavs"; the Lombards, shortly afterward, in 568, moved west to take a place in Italy.[2]

The final dismemberment of Italy is the most lasting accomplishment of Justin's reign. In the new balance of power, there were centers and hinterlands, but no Italy. Constantinople remained in firm control of Ravenna and in notional control of Rome, though control of Rome deteriorated over the decades that followed. Narses, who had succeeded in stabilizing the Constantinopolitan presence, died at Rome in 574, and no figure of substance ever succeeded him. Between them, a string of Lombard enclaves we call duchies straggled down the spine of Italy, headquartered at Spoleto to the north (in the mountains behind Tuscany) and Benevento in the south. They maintained at Genoa and Naples other outposts loyal to Constantinople. The ports, in other words, maintained contact across the water with the capital city, while the rest of the country became irrelevant.

Old histories see the Lombards as the last great wave of barbarian hordes swooping down into Italy, but they were far more normal in Roman terms. Relocated in Italy, seizing the high ground, cowing their neighbors into grudging submission (for there was no one from whom to expect rescue), they promptly subsided. Their great leader Alboin, who had won the war against the Gepids and then led his forces into Italy, was overthrown and murdered in 572 at the hand of his wife Rosamund and a henchman, and his successor Clef lasted barely a year. For another ten years, the Lombards in Italy made do without a single leader. You could draw a map to show for every square foot of Italy at that time whether Lombards or Romans claimed suzerainty there, but over considerable stretches of country local lords held sway and the patterns we saw already under the rule of Theoderic's successors grew stronger. A few landlords and a few soldiers could give a valley a semblance of government, whatever its notional relationship to some ruler elsewhere might be. Many of those landlords, moreover, were newcomers, military figures of sometimes ambiguous provenance, who had settled in Italy on vacant lands—sometimes forcibly vacated, of course—after Justinian's great debilitating wars. If no one thought of them either as warlords or as barbarians, they were still men to be reckoned with in their petty domains, and were for the most part left undisturbed by more ambitious rulers elsewhere, who had enough to do just to maintain their own pretense of power.

The best—not truest—yarns about them come from a writer more than a century later: Paul the Deacon. Admiring frescoes in the church at Monza, just north of Milan, commissioned by a very philo-Roman and Catholic queen of the Lombards, Theodelinda, Paul created what was for a long time the standard picture of the Lombards: "They exposed their forehead and shaved all the way round to the neck, while their hair, combed down on either side of the head to the level of the mouth, was parted at the centre. Their clothing was roomy, mainly made of linen, like the Anglo-Saxons wear, decorated with broad bands woven in various colours. Their boots were open at the big toe, held in place by interwoven leather thongs. Later on they began to use thigh boots, over which they put woollen greaves when out riding, in Roman fashion."[3] Theodelinda had been the queen of Authari; when he died in 590, she chose to call Agilulf to the throne as her spouse. While he reigned she undertook to advance the cause of Nicene Christianity, winning Pope Gregory's friendship and flattery. In the treasure house of the cathedral at Monza there survives today a splendidly detailed small-scale gilded silver sculpture of a mother hen and its chicks, probably a gift from Gregory to her.

At the time Theodelinda married Authari and then Agilulf, the duke of Spoleto was named Ariulf, who first appears in our records commanding the left wing of Byzantine forces against the Persians at the battle of Nymphaeum on the Tigris in 582. Constantinople had reason to dislike and distrust the Lombards, but it was hard to see them as anything other than leaders of an insurrectionary province, scarcely as invaders.[4]

Elsewhere there was not much better news. Revolts in Africa killed a senior general and two praetorian prefects between 569 and 571, and the Visigoths were just then pushing the last Byzantine forces back closer to

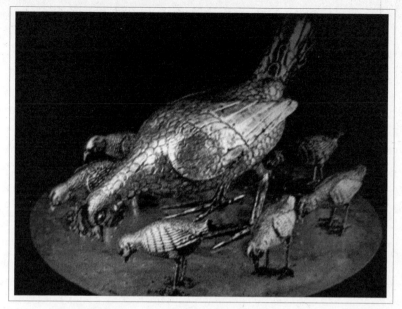

Mother hen and chicks: a papal gift for a queen.

the sea. So naturally the emperor Justin—dumber than his predecessor, if
this can be believed—chose to provoke Persia. Having to his name only
about a quarter of the forces that some of his imperial predecessors could
muster (one contemporary numbers his army at 150,000 empire-wide), he
could ill afford this imprudence.

Justin took the lofty view that Rome did not pay for peace. Unfortu-
nately, the only peace Justinian had been able to achieve was one he had to
pay for and could barely afford. On pretext of protecting Armenian Christians against the Persians' imposition of Zoroastrianism, Justin rattled his
saber, only to see Apamea leveled and Nisibis and Daraa taken and held
by Persia.

Justin may have been encouraged in his folly by dreams of a grander
alliance. In 568, an embassy arrived at Constantinople from far-off Sogdiana in central Asia, offering a long-term contract for the silk trade to
Rome's advantage, one that would cut out the Persian middlemen. In
August 568, Justin sent a general, Zemarchus, to the Turks of Sogdiana to
seal the arrangement. The delegates came and went by a northerly route
along the shores of the Black and Aral seas. When they arrived in Sogdiana,[5] they and their baggage were ritually purified—with drums, bells,

incense, and chants—and then they were led to meet the khan. By the time they got back to Constantinople, they were ready to tell of unimaginable luxuries—thrones of gold surrounded by vessels of gold and silver, and furnishings and clothing of silk. The alliance lasted a decade or two, but it was hard to maintain contact at such a distance, and the Persians had every incentive to prevent their enemies to the west and north from staying in communication. Rome seems to have gained no real benefit from the contacts.

While the traditional northern and eastern frontiers absorbed attention, there is no sense that Constantinople was aware of what was happening to its south. Having outsourced its southeastern frontier to the management of the Ghassanid Arabs, the empire was in no position to appreciate developments there. By now, the frontier belonged to the Arabs, whom no one took seriously. Rome's Ghassanids and Persia's Lakhmids skirmished occasionally—but only occasionally. History repeated itself in this growth of a power both romanized and un-Roman sitting on the frontier and waiting for its opportunity.

Constantinople was blind to all this. So when, in the 570s, the Persian king sent a force south to Yemen to support the local Himyarite rulers in shaking off Ethiopian control, a domino at the farthest frontier fell silently into Persian hands. The future did not lie with the forces from remote northern Constantinople.

Justin, meanwhile, ordered the end of the "fifty-year peace" that Justinian had struck with Persia. By 573, the Mesopotamian frontier was in tatters, with the bulwark city of Daraa seized, and Khusro conducting raids at will far behind it into northern Syria and Asia Minor.

This was the time Justin picked to go mad, perhaps his most astute strategic decision. We needn't linger over his precise medical diagnosis, for the outlines of a palace coup are clear. The empress Sophia, with a bit of her aunt Theodora's backbone, gained control. She did this in alliance with Tiberius, the promising count of the excubitors who had smoothed the imperial transition in 565. In 574, Justin named him (was prevailed on to name him, the story went) to the rank of Caesar, second only in imperial title to Augustus, and heir presumptive to the throne. Khusro accepted an offer to buy a few years' peace, and Constantinople subsided into self-absorption.

Sophia and Tiberius sparred with each other, but it was Tiberius who knew he had the upper hand. By the time Justin died in 578, Sophia's efforts to cling to power were obvious enough to raise stories of an attempted coup against Tiberius, but there must not have been much to the story, for once he had installed his own wife as his empress, Tiberius allowed Sophia to remove herself to a palace across the Bosporus.

Tiberius II brought back to the throne the name last borne by the successor of Augustus almost 600 years earlier. Whereas Justin had been parsimonious, Tiberius was a spendthrift, and such lavishness is always a popular quality in a ruler. While Justin was still alive, he sent a general to try to help his Italian outposts against the Lombards, but to no avail; and when in 578 the senate of Rome (making its last formal appearance in history) sent him money to try to purchase protection, he told the senators they would be better off taking it to the Lombards or the Franks instead, to see what deal they could make for themselves. He expanded the palace and bought peace in the Balkans from the Avars—who promptly reneged on the deal. His one lasting blunder was to yield to his impatience with the Ghassanid leadership, arresting their leader al-Mundhir in 581 on grounds of his religious (monophysite) sympathies and exiling him to Sicily.[6] With that gesture, Tiberius lost the support and reliability of the Ghassanids, and he unwittingly smoothed the path to Syria and Asia Minor for any forces that would arise in Arabia. Tiberius cultivated a reputation for generosity: tax cuts marked his accession as sole emperor.

In a subtle way, Tiberius also marks the end of imperial religion's ancient obsessiveness. Emperors before Justinian had supervised doctrinal strife without caring about it; Justinian had cared deeply about it and thus created a new intimacy of union between state and church. Tiberius inherited an empire in which state and church were now so identical that an emperor could cease to care about theology himself.

Justin II had inherited his predecessor's talent for dithering, trying to conciliate the monophysites and at one point in 571 issuing what was spoken of as a "second *Henotikon*," in memory of Zeno's attempt of 100 years earlier to find a formula of words that would bring unity. Nothing worked. Tiberius, on the other hand, enforced orthodoxy without a moment's care for what it meant. The emperors after him who did care about theology knew in their hearts that they were playacting and that nothing they did would change the religious landscape. Tiberius was not unwise to let things be. Emperor Heraclius would stir the hornet's nest again briefly, giving his enthusiasm to a factitious doctrine called monotheletism.⁷ His enthusiasm faded into irrelevance when the Arabs took Syria and Egypt away from the empire. Chalcedon prevailed by disaster and default as the religion of the Byzantine empire.

In four years Tiberius was dead, and a younger, better general, Maurice, replaced him. In this Maurice and his two successors, Phocas and Heraclius, you saw the Byzantine empire at its best. These men were good officers, knew the difference between victory and defeat, and knew how to avoid disaster. Maurice and Heraclius (both, as it happens, Armenians by origin) have good reputations with moderns, whereas Phocas is reviled as a butcher. For he was leading troops in the Balkans when Maurice overplayed his hand and ordered them to remain on frontier post through the cold winter. The troops revolted and Phocas seized the throne and murdered Maurice. If we put aside our fastidiousness and affection for Maurice, the three men were of a piece. Maurice came from Cappadocia, deep in Asia Minor, and reigned for twenty years, from 582 to 602; Phocas lasted eight years; and Heraclius, the improbable Armenian from Carthage, survived for thirty-one years on the throne.

Historians like and approve of Maurice: "He is described as intelligent and self-possessed, reserved in manner, and living a life of moderation and restraint; he maintained his dignity but displayed kindness to others and was free from pride and arrogance. . . . He enjoyed poetry and history. . . . Described as rich, kindly and charitable. . . . Said to have summoned his family to Constantinople and enriched them."⁸ If he was a typical Roman of his age, no less typical was Comentiolus, an officer from Thrace who first appears in 583 on an embassy to the khan of the Avars. In the next year we see him as the commander of forces attempting to drive the Slavs from Thrace, and for the following five years he is active in the Balkans. He then turns up in 589 in the Byzantine outpost in Spain, where a Latin inscription records his work strengthening the fortifications at Carthago Nova. He next appears fighting on the Persian front, supporting Khusro II's claim to regain the Persian throne as a shah friendly to Byzantium. Another four years pass and we see him fighting the Avars again in Thrace. Loyal to his emperor, Maurice, he fought in defense of Constantinople against Phocas's coup, and was executed when the coup succeeded.

These emperors took turns seizing a tired throne. Justinian's long neglect of the Balkans, his uncomprehending disdain for the realities of power on the Persian frontier, and his failure to secure the loyalty of ecclesiastically unreliable provinces from Syria to Egypt severed the empire completely from any population that connected its own salvation to the empire's success. Empire was now merely a bargain, a transaction, an opportunity. If we want to understand what happened when Muhammad's forces loomed up half a century later, we must understand the tottering emptiness of the late sixth century.

Maurice understood the Balkans, pressed hard, and failed catastrophically. The Avars made inroads, with their *chagan* in a church at one point donning imperial robes taken from people he had captured and setting himself up to mock Maurice. They were bought off for a time by outright bribes, but they may also have regrouped in view of a perceived threat from the Turks in the direction of Scythia-Ukraine; during this period, we begin to hear more and more of these Turks. Phocas forswore conquest in the Balkans, maintained the status quo in Persia, and knew that he could not succeed.

Phocas ascended by the sword and descended by it, quite literally. In 608, the elder Heraclius, governor, or exarch, at Carthage and Maurice's colleague, friend, and appointee, revolted. He had a nephew and a son to deploy, so he sent the nephew, Niketas, to secure Egypt in 609; then he sent the son, Heraclius, to Constantinople in 610. There, the younger Heraclius allied himself with Priscus, the count of the excubitors (the platform Justin and Tiberius had used to ascend to the throne themselves). Consequently, Phocas was overthrown and the younger Heraclius installed as emperor on October 5, 610. Heraclius beheaded Phocas with his own sword, just as Theoderic had murdered Odoacer more than a century earlier.

Heraclius at this time was in his thirties; he had been born either in Armenia (his father's native land) or in Africa. He imitated Maurice and was only the second emperor at Constantinople to take the field and exercise the original role of commanding general since Theodosius more than 200 years before. Heraclius lived the role unrelentingly for the thiry-one years of his reign, also finding time to marry two wives who bore him at least eleven children. Many of those children were disabled in various ways, leading to whispered stories of divine vengeance for—incest? or worse? His thirty-one years on the throne should—if the gods were kind—have established him as one of the greatest of emperors. But the gods were not kind.

The apparent triumph and real tragedy of Heraclius's reign lay on the Persian frontier. Phocas bought peace there for cash, while letting his grasp on the Balkans slip as well. The disruption of Roman attention that came from Heraclius's revolt made things easier still for Khusro II, the worthy successor of his grandfather, who now ruled Persia. In short order, Persian forces led by Khusro swept into Roman domains. Damascus was lost in 613; Jerusalem, and with it the true cross, in 614; and Egypt in 619. Raids in Asia Minor reached as far as Chalcedon across the Bosporus from Constantinople, and persuasive rumors flew that Persia was in touch with the Avars for what could have been a fatal pincer maneuver. Persian forces seem at the end, however, to have backed off an attempt to establish themselves permanently to the north and west of Antioch. Some of what Asia Minor lost at this moment came from warfare and its destruction, and some from consequences as populations declined and economic vitality sank. Things were never the same.

A monk, Antiochos Strategos, recounted the desperate struggle in Jerusalem, as an eyewitness to it all. The Persians besieged the city for twenty days, from April into May. Eventually their siege engines succeeded in breaking through the city wall. Cisterns offered useful hiding places for a few, but many who took refuge in churches were discovered and hacked to death. Hundreds died in Justinian's vast new church alone, just one part of a gruesome body count Antiochos provides, totalling 66,000 who lost their lives in the siege. This total is high but not impossible, and the sheer awfulness of the event is certain.

For his first decade, Heraclius stayed mainly at home, apart from one failed campaign in 613, and let his empire take its punishment. Desperation reached such a point that people said the emperor was thinking of moving his own headquarters, the capital of the remnants of empire, from Constantinople to Carthage. The thought that the Roman empire would find itself led now from the city of its ancient enemy, the city it had razed to the ground 750 years earlier, was too delicious for words. But it is reasonable to believe that Heraclius, raised in Carthage, would have been aware of the tactical possibilities of recruiting his forces from the west. He might have been smart to do so. To regain the advantage in the east, he bought his own peace in the Balkans, buying off the Avars for a time in 619. That was in the long run the real defeat, but these emperors in Constantinople were never able to discover that their long-term interests lay in the Balkans.

Heraclius was wiser than most of his predecessors and concentrated his efforts in the 610s on rebuilding his army. Tradition ascribed to him the reorganization of civil government into "themes"—roughly, military recruiting districts—that after centuries would be made standard. The Byzantine empire was a stranger to irony, and none would sense it when the realm was organized into units whose functional purpose was to provide soldiers in order to preserve the existing entity.

Despaired of, pressed hard, and finally becoming venturesome, Heraclius took the field in 621. For the first years of his wars, the issue remained in doubt. In the summer of 626 the Avars were at the gates of Constantinople in what could have been its last gasp, trapping the city while Heraclius and the main forces were away on the northern part of the Persian frontier, in Lazica, but the Persians' attempts to cross the Bosporus and aid the Avars were repulsed by the Byzantine navy on August 10, and the Avars withdrew. There have been more famous battles in history, but few with greater lasting effect.

Gradually, Heraclius built his alliances. Instead of marching east through Mesopotamia, as Romans so often had, he went north and then east from Constantinople along the Bosporus and Black Sea, approaching the Persian frontier from the north through Armenia. Embassies to the Khazars and other Turkic forces on the northern steppes found a good reception, and even inside the Persian forces there were opportunities to discover turncoats. In December 627 at the battle of Nineveh, Heraclius prevailed against Persian forces led by Rhazates—even though the Khazars failed him in the crisis. Holding the front, Heraclius looked south. Alliance with the Axumite Ethiopians—his fellow Christians—brought him support in winning back Yemen and the Red Sea provinces in 629 and afterward. Shaken on the south and now overextended—as would inevitably be revealed when any leader succeeded in opposing them—the Persians tottered. Heraclius finally moved on Ctesiphon, the Persian capital on the Tigris; and Khusro's court revolted, deposing him, effectively surrendering the war. Heraclius claimed back as his terms for peace all that Khusro had taken from Rome, and the Persian government sank into anarchy and a series of short-lived rulers of no distinction.

Every sign pointed to a lasting victory for Rome over Persia. Heraclius took for himself the ancient Persian title "king of kings," dropping the traditional Roman imperial title Augustus, just as Alexander had Persianized himself more than 900 years earlier. Back in Constantinople, Heraclius now styled himself *basileus*, the Greek word for king, and that title would be part of Byzantine pomp for the next 800 years. His reign also marked the effective end of Latin as the official language of empire and the permanent triumph of Greek. To this day, "Rum" is still an eastern name for the empire founded by the descendants of Romulus, but all the *romanitas* had gone out of it by now.

Heraclius's ostentation of empire culminated in 630, when he traveled to Jerusalem, there to return the true cross of Christ to its rightful home. He marched into the city barefoot, as befitted a pious Christian pilgrim, carrying the cross himself, and brought it to the Church of the Holy Sepulcher. The church stood on the site now occupied by an elaborate, labyrinthine basilica shared among various Christian denominations, the spot identified 300 years earlier when the true cross was discovered in Constantine's reign.

The trip to Jerusalem was Heraclius's last moment of glory. He fell ill soon afterward; and in the field in the 630s he was represented by other generals, who saw his most important frontiers collapse.

The future lay to the south. Muhammad died in 632, leaving behind a whirlwind prepared to move north, east, and west. The pummeling that Byzantine and Persian forces gave each other and the relative detachment of Syria, Palestine, and Egypt from Byzantine control gave the men of the desert their chance. Just as the northern barbarians had found their strength shadowing the empire they admired, so the Arabs of the desert marches had grown in strength and confidence and were prepared to seize an opportunity. If it was not divine providence that brought them to this moment, they seized it as though it were.

In 634 the Arab armies invaded Syria and defeated Theodore, the emperor's brother, in a string of battles. Heraclius raised a large army that attacked the Arabs near the Yarmuk River, a tributary of the Jordan, in the fall of 636. After a successful beginning, the larger Byzantine army was defeated and put to flight. Roman Syria was easily taken at that point. The Arabs capitalized on Persia's disarray by quickly taking the whole of the frontier lands (including Mesopotamia and Armenia) and then Egypt not long afterward. Alexandria fell in 640 after a siege that lasted more than a year. At that time, Muhammad had been dead less than a decade.

What was left for ancient empire? The Balkans, the suburbs of Constantinople, most of Asia Minor, and the African outpost around Carthage that Justinian had seized at such cost. Italy remained, with as much cost as benefit, but the African base would support Constantinople for the sixty years remaining before the Arabs seized it at the turn of the eighth century. (Sicily remained Byzantine much longer: without it, the whole of Byzantine pretension might have fallen.) By the end of the seventh century, the economics of empire had caught up with Constantinople and the city population collapsed.

Heraclius died on February 11, 641, his empire fully and finally in tatters. His two sons failed to establish themselves, and it was his grandson Constans II who became emperor later that year at age eleven, at the onset of what would be a long and pointless reign. Irony alone would accompany him as he visited Rome in 663, the first emperor seen there in two centuries. He was assassinated in his bath in 668, and his successors forgot the west.

ALEXANDER'S DREAM REBORN

The only truly sane monarch in antiquity was Alexander, the wild child, who came to within an inch of creating a world in which we now most wish we could live, one marked by community and not by conflict of cultures. His only really rational successors were Mehmet the Conqueror and Genghis Khan. All were unquestionably destroyers, and all wrought terrible suffering in the world, but all three knew in their bones something that few others have seen or said and no others have been able to bring to reality. Can we dream their dream a bit?

We should be able to see their truth more clearly, with the hindsight of many centuries of recorded history and the accurate topography of modern cartography, and indeed, their truth is a simple one. The great fault line that runs across the landmass of the Old World, separating north and west from south and east, and occurring again in the geography of empires and wars of every generation since the rise of the Persian empire, has the ability to bring humankind to its ruin. In our own time, it has the potential to set loose unspeakable terrors.

The fault line of geography has remained a fault line of peoples. Four human agglomerations divide the Eurasian landmass among them, while sub-Saharan Africa and the Americas stand dangerously outside the stories of those families. Americans—thought dangerous by many because of our self-satisfied exceptionalism—speak to the Europeans as to siblings or cousins, and Africans of the Sahara and the south are marginalized by all, their skin color a frivolous pretext for exclusion. Europeans, west Asians, south Asians, and east Asians compete over the right to define the main story of our species.[9]

The separate world of east Asia has mainly stood outside the Eurasian psychodrama and may well yet prevail over all its rivals. The two other boundaries of peoples, defining the two directions in which west Asians must look, have been killing fields and chasms of misunderstanding. The United States chose to go to war in 2001–2003 in both those regions.

Alexander had his chance.[10] He was too young, too provincial (Macedonian, not Athenian or Corinthian), too libidinous, too fond of drink, too daring—too extreme in every way. Or at least that's how we explain his ambition and his failure. And he conquered the Persian empire, only to die, deep inside Persian lands, too suddenly and too soon. His generals succeeded beyond what should have been their own wildest dreams in consolidating a remarkable amount of his power, and the Ptolemies of Egypt and the Seleucids of Asia succeeded in establishing Alexandrian kingdoms in lands that had never before thought of owing homage to the Greeks.

Another young man once created and faced similar uncertainties, uncertainties he succeeded in putting to rest by living to a ripe old age. I am thinking of Augustus, who had the world at his feet by the time he was thirty-one, after the battle of Actium, and whose wisest next choice was to live another forty-five years. By the time Augustus was gone, his Roman empire was as assured of success as any such thing can be.

Persia slipped away. What would Persia have become had Alexander lived longer? It would have become—it would have remained—Persia.

What would have existed then was a greater Persia that linked the highlands of Iran with the Fertile Crescent from Baghdad to Gaza (and thus with Egypt) and with Asia Minor and the Aegean as well. The counterhistory of the world that might have been if Alexander had sustained his achievement is impossible to trace with anything more than a fantasist's confidence, and it is certainly an open question whether even Alexander could have stitched together and united that disparate empire.

In the limited accomplishments of those who came after Alexander lay the roots of unceasing future conflict. When Alexander was gone, the

Persians stayed home for a good long time and the Hellenistic world that linked the Aegean to the Levant to Egypt was created—a splendid world in many respects, but dangerously out of touch with the world to its east and heedless of the possibilities to its west. The creation of Judaism as the religion of those who found themselves self-consciously between empires put the seal on the world making of the generations before and after Alexander. (Where would Alexander's capital have been? Mesopotamia would have had a strong claim as his permanent residence, but if he kept palaces in the traditional heartland of Persian monarchy, then surely he would have had others in Damascus and Jerusalem.)

What even Alexander could not have foreseen was the rise of western Mediterranean sea power under the Carthaginians and land power under the Romans. The long struggle for mastery between the two had the effect of forging a bizarre new threat, a military state capable of basing itself on tax revenues and compulsory military service drawn from the lands of the west. For the first time, it became possible to imagine a community of peoples bound together by water among the many small seas that make up the Mediterranean. When Roman ambition met Hellenistic civilization, the Mediterranean as we know it was invented. So successful were the Romans that we moderns tend to take such a community for granted, as somehow natural, forgetting that it is in many ways an artifact of militarism and military technologies.

The Mediterranean as the heart of a civilization was possible under the following conditions:

1. Seafaring had to advance to the point where ships could carry appreciable cargoes, including when necessary human cargoes, and overcome the currents and winds of the several Mediterranean seas to move at will from place to place. The Romans prevailed when that kind of seafaring (powered by slave labor, a form of human power that assorts well with ambitious empires) was possible.

2. Seafaring had to fall short of mastery, and so leave seamen imprisoned inside the Pillars of Hercules (that is, Gibraltar) and marooned ashore for several months every winter, while the rains and winds owned the seas. The Portuguese of the generations before Columbus made the seafaring Mediterranean obsolete, by opening up all the seas of the world to European traffic.

3. Land transport, on the other hand, had to be expensive and of limited usefulness. As long as land transport around the Mediterranean was limited to human and animal power, the sea would be the highway of choice. The Romans imported their grain from Africa, not from the Po valley, both because bulk shipping needed to go by water and because Africa is far closer to Rome than any place on the Adriatic coast of its own peninsula. Much of the coastal land of the Mediterranean basin is cut off by mountainous hinterlands from easy land communication with even close neighbors. Those mountain lands are what drive men out onto the water and assure the Mediterranean of its power. The railroad and especially the internal combustion engine would finish off the seaways and drive apart the northern and southern shores in consequence.

4. Northerners and easterners and southerners had to leave the Mediterranean alone. Africa and Mesopotamia and the western shores of the northern steppes had to be inhabited by people with limited ability to force Mediterranean attention to themselves. Whenever barbarians, Berbers, Arabs, or Persians came knocking at the door of the Mediterranean world, the enclosed prosperity of that fragile community was much at risk. The Romans had a constant, unforgiving need for a lot of luck and a lot of military organization to preserve the conditions under which they could flourish.

That last point is the most important for understanding both the Romans' success and the long abeyance into which Alexander's dream subsided. In particular, Alexander's success (and that of his successors) at cowing the Persian monarchy into retreating to Iran left Rome with more than 400 years of comparative "privacy," so to speak, and the Romans took full advantage of that respite in every way but one.

But that one was critical. Though they knew the story of Alexander, the Romans never really learned his lesson. The fatal flaw of the Roman empire—if we must think empire is a good thing—was that it had forgotten how to be imperialist. It had no strategy for north, south, or east, and when from any of those directions enemies arose who understood the Romans and their achievement full well and better than the Romans understood their rivals, then the Roman venture faltered.

The prosperity and peace of the Roman empire were unmistakably good things, however one assesses the price that was paid to achieve them. It is reasonable to lament their passing, or at least to wish that more could have been preserved. In the absence of strategy or vision, though, Rome had few unexploited advantages left.

The city of Rome, once Justinian's wars did their worst, never rebounded to more than a shadow of itself, rising in the time of the Renaissance from long misery as a malarial swamp, then settling from the Renaissance until the present for being a showplace—that is, a tourist trap. To be sure, in the irony of history, the final lesson that societies learned from Rome was a variant on Tacitus's quip about making its emperors somewhere else. The long-term lesson now was that "Romes"—new Romes—could themselves be made someplace else, no longer just on the Tiber. Nowhere west of Tibet have we seen, since late antiquity, the emergence of great powers with wide territorial ambitions that weren't imitating Rome in one way or another. Constantine was the first to imitate it, with his parody of the seven hills plunked down on the Bosporus, and the Arabs would make Damascus and Baghdad Romes in their own time. To the northeast, Kiev would become the third Rome and Moscow its rival, the latter clinging to the word *czar* (which is merely Caesar heard at a distance) to the end of its ambitions. The Frankish king Charles, whose spin doctors persuaded us to call him Charles the Great (Charlemagne), and the later Frankish monarch Napoléon, sought restoration of empire on various pretexts. Charlemagne thought empire was his for the taking because the throne in Constantinople was inappropriately held by an impossible pretender; Napoléon, observing the panoply and political disunity of the last days of the Holy Roman Empire, compelled it to dissolve in 1806 to make way for his own imperial pretensions. Each of these rulers of the Franks made sure that Rome's religious power—in the person of the reigning pope, who crowned him—would underscore the legitimacy of his role.

New continents could play with old images as well. A few years ago, while walking through the construction sites of the post-Soviet Unter den Linden in Berlin (another place of post-Roman imperial pretensions, at least twice), I found myself grumpily commenting that the city was home to a lot of pompous imperial architecture. Then a companion reminded me that I reside in Washington, D.C. Americans take their capital city for granted, without thinking how preposterous it must appear to many without their heritage. To place a massive white pile of building on a modest outcropping of land in Potomac bottomland and call it a Capitol building on Capitol Hill is to invoke the Roman past and Roman pretension in a way that should have alerted the earliest observers of the American republic that it too would aspire to wide-reaching empire.

The end of Justinian's pretensions gave birth to an age in which Alexander's dream could have been restored. The caliphates of medieval Islam contented themselves, however, with advancing Asia's claims while leaving Europe in the main to itself. It took the Turks, and eventually then Mehmed II the Conqueror, to bring the Islamic vision to fruition, and even they bypassed Constantinople for a very long time, making a de facto Asian-European empire in Asia Minor and the Balkans, leaving only the shrunken island of Byzantine—that is, Roman—pretension in place. The sack of Constantinople in 1453 was of little military value and had little effect in the centuries that followed on the evolution of the polyglot, poly-theological capital of what became the Ottoman empire; but the symbolic value of placing himself on the throne of Rum was evident to Mehmed and to all his contemporaries. The Turkish empire, indeed, is the only one since Alexander ever to link Europe and the Fertile Crescent,[11] surviving even the conquests of the Mongols in the thirteenth century.

In the same centuries as those when the Turks raised themselves to status as an imperial power, the only credible alternative rendition of Alexander's vision yet to emerge swept out of eastern Asia and for a brief time sought to impose itself. Genghis Khan understood his world more deeply than any of his contemporaries did, and he had the brilliant idea that the north could finally exercise dominion over the south, that the hitherto marginal steppes of Asia could become the superhighway for an equine empire that would stretch from western Europe to the Gobi Desert and Mongolia. He too was technologically challenged, yet he accomplished far more than could reasonably have been expected by those who look to the rich and the cultured to beget empires. That real empire across the Eurasian landmass has come so often from improbable peoples—from Romans, Turks, Arabs, Persians, and Mongols—should teach us to be realistic about the wellsprings of power.

Technology in the end temporarily trumped geography in the competition for shaping the human community. Just when Mehmed's success established him as worthy rival to the western monarchies of his time—paltry though most of them were—the chance and coincidence of the development of oceangoing navigation tipped the balance decisively in the direction of the Europeans. Opinions can reasonably vary, but the most likely subsequent outcome of the rise of a Constantinopolitan Turkish empire seems to me either that the Turks would have continued to extend their dominion westward (as they certainly sought to do) or that a counterbalancing European response would have brought the two competing powers together in a way destined to be marked by war in the short run and by the emergence of a common culture in the long run.

Vast wealth flowed into western Europe as a result of its global seaborne adventures, easily trumping earlier Chinese and Muslim successes.[12] Consequently, just when benign obsolescence might have set in for European—that is, Roman—exceptionalism, and when a community of nations from the Atlantic to Tibet might have been possible, Europe was suddenly reinvigorated. It now had ample reason to devote itself to devastating internal wars from the sixteenth to the twentieth centuries, and its vast wealth enabled it to treat all the other peoples of the earth with a mixture of rapacity and disdain, leavened with the expression of the west's best quality, its fair-minded curiosity and quest to know and understand.

I have not spoken much in these pages of east Asia, for good but perilous reason. The long history of the emergence of China—as much the fruit of geographic and technological forces as was Rome—should not be separated from the history of the rest of the world. The isolation of the Middle Kingdom in practical terms, however, has made for separations of narrative and separations of peoples to a remarkable degree for a small planet. Without the Huns, the Turks, and the Mongols to terrorize both western and eastern powers, their histories could easily have been left separate and alone.

I mention China now to raise the question whether history might yet repeat itself. At this moment of human progress (the year 2008), the old fault line between northwest and southeast has become an aggravated, suppurating wound. A historian can only shake his head at the spectacle of the European Community debating with anguish whether to allow the citizens of Istanbul to join their tribe, when the word "Europe" itself was born to describe the ground on which that city stands. Intelligent but ill-educated people the world over have discovered that the Shiite community of Islam, which we had learned with difficulty a generation ago to associate with the peoples today occupying the Persian highlands, not only pervades but even nourishes its roots in sacred shrines and cities of southern Mesopotamia, and politicians struggle to make sense of the way borders carved on the map at Versailles have blinded Europeans and their cousins to the true ethnic and religious geography of western Asia. Just at the moment, it is fashionable to express deep anxiety at two complementary phenomena: the globalization of western capitalist culture and the Islamization of western Europe. Some lament the former's invasion of traditional societies, including those of the east; many bemoan the growing demographic presence in the northwest of peoples owing their origins and much of their religion and culture to the southeast. Readers of this volume should recognize many of the rhetorical blunders of antiquity—mistaking Rome for civilization and the opponents of Rome for opponents of civilization, for example—still living and flourishing in our midst.

The opportunity that slipped away in the aftermath of Mehmed's conquest, driven off when European seaborne activity expanded, has returned. Humankind might yet be able to find a way to build commonality of culture and purpose to link the peoples of Europe, western Asia, and south Asia—to achieve, in other words, Alexander's dream. Such a confrontation and eventual coming together would be painful and difficult to imagine, and neither devout Muslims nor devout Europeans at this moment will accept any future we could now envision—but the importance of finding one is undeniable.

Two risks present themselves. The peoples whose stories are not part of the Eurasian narrative—those of Africa and of east Asia—can distract us once again. Africa offers the lesser risk, but a real one; poverty and disease will find for themselves literal and figurative weapons with which to claim the attention of the world's wealthy and healthy, and to exact redress of grievances. Nothing says that the rich nations yet have it in themselves to respond to such a challenge.

More than that, China imposes itself on the world's attention. This is not a place where I would need to repeat the exaggerations, the euphoria, and the sheer numerical inevitability that accompany the rise of China at this moment to a place of global authority. Technology has now trumped isolation, as Beanie Babies designed in Illinois, manufactured in China, and sold over the Internet calmly supervise me from the desk where I write. There is every reason to think that China will continue as it has begun, at least in the long run; if it fails in the short run, the costs for many will be immense.

8

The Last Consul

HE FIRST CONSULS of Rome took office in 509 BCE, when the kings were expelled and the republic was established. From the time of Augustus, the consulship ceased to be the effective chief magistracy of the empire, but the office continued to be filled, year in and year out, and continued to attract the aspirations of the wealthy and well connected. After the founding of Constantinople, one consul normally came from the western empire and one from the eastern—though there were exceptions—and if anything pride in the office intensified. In earlier chapters, we have seen a parade of such proud families.

All this ended in the sixth century.[1] The last consul, Basilius, gave his name to the year 541, 1,050 years after the first consuls of 509 BCE. He had ancient and recent lineage, his father having fallen afoul of Theoderic along with Boethius. To choose him as consul in Constantinople the year after the surrender of Witigis at Ravenna was to declare the success, such as it was, of the Justinianic notion of a restoration of empire over the western provinces to be led from Constantinople.

Henceforth, however, the dignity of consul was reserved for emperors alone, and they tended to take up the title as an appurtenance of office on accepting the throne, but the old annual rituals came to an end. With the end of the consulship, we have to expect the end of the senate of Rome, for without a pinnacle, the community that supplied the senate's ranks lost a chief method of replenishing itself.

There is one more "last consul" to be found, in the crypt of Saint Peter's basilica on the Vatican hill. He lived in a bleak Italian world. The waves of warfare killed off most of the old aristocracy and impoverished almost all that was left. The old separation between civilian and military leadership in Roman society vanished, and the landlords of the new Italy of the late sixth century were army officers; their retainers looked like the *condottieri* of a much later Italy.[2] "Recession" is a polite name for the economic disarray into which the country fell, while economic and social institutions disintegrated. The senate of Rome is last seen in action in 578, sending an embassy to Constantinople. What few senators we see in this period were south of Rome—twenty-seven in Campania, Sicily, and the south; only four in Rome; and another three or four in Ravenna. If the appearance of ancient Roman Italy survived anywhere for a time, it was in water-bound Sicily, but much of the land had fallen into the church's hands by this time.

A preacher quoted Luke's gospel on the coming end of the world and said that all he could read there had come to pass or was coming to pass in his own times. "We see nation rise up against nation and press upon the lands more in our times than we read in the scriptures. You know how often we have heard of cities overthrown by earthquakes. We endure plagues without ceasing. We do not yet see signs openly in the sun, the moon, and the stars, but the air is full of their coming." On another page of his works he describes his world as one of "cities emptied of their peoples, fortresses overthrown, churches burned, monasteries of men and women destroyed, farms abandoned by their owners and devoid of farmhands. The land is a desert and the wild beasts now roam where once a throng of humankind lived. I do not know what is happening elsewhere in the world, but here, where we live, the world is not predicting but displaying its end."[3]

The last consul? He wrote those words of desolation I have just quoted. Gregorius was his name, a name Greek in origin and meaning effectively the same as the Latin name Vigilius—"wakeful," "watchful." We see his family in the fifth century advancing to office and we can trace ancestors through several generations. His great-great-grandfather was Pope Felix III (r. 483–492).

Gregorius's father, Gordianus, was a mid-level functionary for the church, probably not himself an ordained cleric, but we know that he was wealthy enough to have estates in Sicily and a mansion on the Caelian hill in Rome a few hundred yards from the ancient forum. His three sisters—Gordiana, Tarsilla, and Aemiliana—were amateurs of the religious life and set up housekeeping as a kind of convent, but when two of them died, the third sister, Gordiana, whom Gregorius makes out to have been frivolous and irresponsible, went so far as to marry the steward of her estates, and it is not clear whether Gregorius was more indignant at her broken religious vows or the low social standing of the object of her affections. (Aunts can be very disappointing.)

Gregorius was born in the 540s, the worst years Rome has ever known. He grew up in the midst of his family's wealth, but saw ruin on all sides. Gregorius is famous for anticipating the end of the world, a thought that must have come easily to a young man reading the scriptures while surrounded by ancient, war-pounded glories now left to decay. The baths of Caracalla, for example, lay a few minutes' walk from his family's home, but we think they saw their last visitors in 537. Over Gregorius's lifetime they began their descent into ruination before his eyes.

The evidence of his writings tells us that Gregorius was the last polished product of the ancient schools of Rome. He shows all the signs of a traditional education that was rapidly becoming impossible for young men in his city, and he is the last signal figure of ancient latinity that the city produced. He could have written something like Arator's poem about the apostles, but by the time he held high office, there were no young men left around him who could accomplish anything similar.

We now know that Rome was fading irreversibly, but Gregorius and his contemporaries only suspected it. As for an old family of Beijing in the first years of communist rule,[4] it was possible to imagine that all would blow over and ancient prerogatives would be restored. Gregorius had the kind of career his ancestors dreamed of, for he ascended to the office of prefect of the city at a young age and was called to serve at the imperial court not long after. He eventually returned to Rome, where he reached the highest civil office in the western empire, serving fourteen difficult years.

Gregorius was endlessly busy and distracted by the demands of his office, and we can track his concerns through the happy chance of the survival of his official register of letters. More than 900 such missives show him as an attentive and mainly effective administrator. He controlled official estates at a distance through stewards and managers, he conducted diplomacy with the leaders of neighboring provinces, and he paid particular attention to ensuring the continuity of local governance in Italy and beyond. He assembled a leadership team, as we would say nowadays, following the model of Roman bureaucracy of the last three centuries, and we can see some of those leaders themselves advancing to higher responsibility over the years. He was not directly accountable for military affairs, but he was in constant communication with generals and he advocated strenuously for a vigorous, vigilant defense.

Personally, he was an austere and challenging leader, attacking corruption and demanding the highest and most self-denying personal integrity. In practice, his patronage fell on those who, like him, had come through a difficult training to reach a high ethical standard. When he died, his epitaph called him a consul,⁵ but his successors, restive with regard to his personal style, execrated his name and sought to forget all he had struggled to teach. His successors of the seventh century were, in the aggregate, far less effective as rulers and far less well known to posterity than he, and they did not prevail in their effort to make us forget his name.

That personal style was the most remarkable thing about him. If Theoderic looked forward pragmatically to a continuing and more or less well-led Roman empire, and if Justinian looked forward delusionally to a restored grandeur that was never in the cards, Gregorius anticipated doom. The apocalyptic last things of the Christian religion preoccupied him, and he regarded the civil and military setbacks that the western provinces underwent in the late sixth century as signs of the impending end. Though he struggled hard to advance the physical and material well-being of the population entrusted to his care, his frank expectation was that the struggle was of little use. The horrific disaster and judgment that Christianity promised as waiting for humankind in the vestibule to an eternity of happiness was the best that Roman society could look forward to. Gregorius was the most effective and best-documented orator among Roman rulers since the age of Cicero, but his surviving speeches counsel not civic responsibility or imperial ambition, but resignation and moral preparation for disaster.

When I describe Gregorius in this way, those who recognize his name and already know his story will feel somewhat disoriented and perhaps unhappy. I hope at least they would agree that everything I have said here is true. For when you find Gregorius in the reference books or the Wikipedias of our time, you discover that the title under which he exercised authority as ruler of the Latin west (or of the fragments of it that acknowledged his power) was not consul or emperor but *papa*, and his formal office was not consul, prefect, or emperor but bishop of Rome. I speak of the man commonly known as Gregory the Great, Pope Gregory I, who sat in the see of Peter from 590 to 604.[6] What I have said is all true, even if I have played fast and loose with the reader's expectations, the better to make a point.

A system of government centered on the city of Rome was the result of the work of many generations and stood at this historical moment as humankind's most venerable living achievement. The British monarchy in our own time can stretch itself to imagine a similar pedigree and a slightly longer past, but little else in history save the dynasties of ancient and modern China and those of ancient Egypt can rival Rome. To be sure, the Roman idea had already begun replicating itself elsewhere, but if we allow the papacy its claim to have perpetuated the Roman idea, then that idea now stands at 2,500 years of continuity. We would be reduced to quibbling with the rulers of China over the criteria by which to judge which is older.

By 590, that Roman system of government had been repeatedly eviscerated and stripped of authority over a period beyond the scope of a man's years. From the mid-third century at least, the city had seen less and less of emperors, and from the time of Diocletian (r. 284–305), the rule of the vast Roman empire had been increasingly decentralized, then recentralized in ways that made the city of Rome a backwater. Whatever dignity had been restored to the city in the age of Theoderic had been firmly and finally stripped away, not to say savagely destroyed, in the ostensibly benevolent wars that Justinian visited on the Italian peninsula.

Rome held on, Justinianic ruins and all. Within the traditional city walls, the population shrank dramatically, no longer divided between mansions on the hilltops and hovels in the valleys, but mainly crowded together in the old Campus Martius, the flat land between the capitol and the Tiber, or around the edges. The church that Gregory led made itself at home in the basilica of Saint John Lateran and in other buildings around it on the east side of the old city. North and south, what the Italian middle ages came to speak of as the *disabitato*, the uninhabited space, was already returning to nature. We do not see proof that malaria had made its way into the city at that date; and at least some remnants of the ancient aqueduct system may have brought water to the diminished population. When cows first grazed in the forum is not recorded, but they made it their own soon enough.

We mustn't imagine a pleasant place. Strip away, in imagination, all the modern construction (and by modern I mean post-1400), leaving only the hulks of antiquity, battered by Justinian's wars. Recall that the city's economic livelihood had always been dangerously focused on a single main source of revenue that was now gone: taxes no longer flowed to the seven hills, nor did the food supplies sent in lieu of taxes at the order of a distant government. The secondary source of economic power in the past had been the wealth of the large landowners who crowded to the city to make up its senate. They too were gone. Absent a bishop of Rome and absent pleasing stories about the activities in Rome of the apostles Peter and Paul, there would have been no reason for Rome to survive as more than a derelict.

The pious tenacity of place that kept the church present and let a resourceful leader extort prestige and submission from Christians elsewhere represents ancient survival of a religious tradition that long antedates Christianity. At some date, Roman bishops began to claim a supreme religious title that was appropriate for a river town: *pontifex maximus* ("bridgebuilder in chief"), which had been suborned into the service of political power by Julius Caesar's exercise of the office and had long attached itself to the emperors themselves. The emperor Gratian abandoned the title in the 380s, when he was persuaded by bishop Ambrose and others to de-paganize his regime. Centuries later we see popes using the title, but they may have adopted it in the fifth century, as part of the church's attempt to persuade the Roman aristocracy to look to the pope as the supreme religious authority. To this day, the oldest religious title in the western world belongs to the pope, inherited or borrowed from the native religious tradition of the city of Rome.

When wasteland invaded and made the city its own, one reasonable reaction was to choose to live in the desert—that is, the monastic desert. Gregory tells us himself of his disillusion with the world and then of his conscious choice to sell his property for God's benefit. His estate was extensive enough to establish seven monasteries in the neighborhood of Rome and in Sicily. He became a monk in the family mansion, there devoting himself to the contemplation of divine things and the study of scripture.

It wouldn't last. Gregory was too prominent, too well connected, too promising. The reigning pope, Pelagius II, dragooned him into papal service and sent him to Constantinople, there to serve for six years as *apocrisiarius*—roughly, ambassador to the imperial court. For a man who wanted nothing to do with the wicked world, Gregory found himself at the center of all the power, wickedness, and hope there was.

POPE ON A DUNG HEAP

So he started thinking about the book of Job. He lived with a few monks in Constantinople and for them he began a series of meticulously detailed homilies on the Latin translation of Job's story. This is one of the great unknown works of all western literature, great in its ambition, great in its execution, and great in its readership for centuries afterward, but it started as sermons. Eventually revised and completed in a comprehensive exegesis running to thirty-five books—about 500,000 words—*Moralia, or Moral Teachings in the Book of Job*, became a standard of medieval monastic spirituality, sometimes read in full, sometimes read in part, and known also through abridgments. A book like this defeats every form of literary criticism and so escapes attention far too easily for a work so influential in method, tone, and doctrine. It is known today only to specialists.

Formally, the *Moralia* set out to provide a fourfold allegorical interpretation of Job's story in the ancient Alexandrian tradition. The theoreticians of interpretation believed that there were four main ways to render a biblical text credibly intelligible to its audience. Everything in scripture points to one end and thus speaks allegorically—that is, it says something beyond itself underlining the core Christian message. Much of the New Testament achieved this in cold prose, telling the story of Jesus or preaching the Christian faith, and thus required no rewriting. On the other hand, much of the Old Testament outwardly seemed to tell the story of Judaean antiquity and thus needed revision to be made Christian. If David was a forerunner of Christ, for example, then everything Davidic could be declared ipso facto Christic—and the Psalms of David became Christian prayer par excellence. The believer who said that the Lord was his shepherd could mean Jesus in good conscience, even though the Psalmist had spoken of Yahweh.

The stories of the Old Testament were true, Gregory thought, and in that truth lay what allegorists suddenly realized they must take as the literal sense of the text, a most artificial and arbitrary concept. Until exegetes tried to distinguish the two, it was easy to read in multiple registers unconsciously, and the seven days of Genesis did not trouble either the credulous or the skeptical. Once it was decided that a literal sense had to exist in the first place, so that the allegorical sense could improve on it, then all sorts of artificially naive and frankly silly things had to be imputed to that literal sense (and to the Jews who were supposedly its slaves). Modern Christian literalism needed the allegorical exegetes to build a rest stop on the way to the fundamentalist misprision of scripture.

Between literal and allegorical poles, the Christian sophisticates of late antiquity would argue, the whole of scriptural interpretation plays out. Whatever does not tell the Christian story with its literal sense must, a priori, have a deeper sense, accessible to the interpreter inspired by the church and the church's god, and inaccessible to the benighted Jewish author.

The most subtle schemata of interpretation saw as well that the allegorical message of scripture (the basic truths about Christianity) had two further subsets: the moral (what is true for the individual reader) and the mystical, prophetic, or anagogical (what tells of things to come). In principle any and all of these senses of scripture could be present anywhere, leaving the believer or the interpreter the pleasant task of exhuming them from beneath the letter of the text. If Jerusalem is a name for a city in Judaea in literal truth, it is also a sign for the church (allegorical sense), for the redeemed human soul (moral sense), and for the heavenly kingdom (mystical sense—much reinforced by the heavenly Jerusalem of the book of Revelation, of course).[7]

So Job is a natural. The original scriptural book is scarcely likely to be anything except exemplary fiction, and remarkable for its prestige in the Jewish tradition in that it tells the story of an errant gentile. Put against the schema, Job seemed simple: he was the gentile he was, literally, but he represented Christ allegorically (his trials anticipating the passion and crucifixion), while he was a model for ordinary believers morally, and in his ultimate redemption he stood for the redeemed and perfected believer of the afterlife mystically.

Does saying this in a few words truly give away the plot of a book that had no surprises of plot? Hardly, but the magic of the book—and I must admit that it has magic—is in the patient, elaborate, luxuriant practice of meditative reflection on the difficult and holy words, rarely more than a few at a time. The work may strike some readers as bizarre, but it is serious and even artful, and it has the power to move many. Job on his dung heap is Christ accepting incarnate life and its ills; Job's four sons represent the classical cardinal virtues of justice, wisdom, fortitude, and temperance; and his three daughters stand for the theological virtues of faith, hope, and charity. The book can be read as a mechanical parlor game, but its function is to give rise to a loosely connected series of meditations on the Christian life. The wide readership and influence of the *Moralia* indicate that it evidently did what it needed to for its church.

We cannot follow Gregory this way without remembering that the book of Job is a book that appeals especially to self-absorption and self-pity. Back in Rome, we saw Gregory regularly lamenting the fall of Rome around him, and though he never quite made himself out to be Job in so many words, the link is unmistakable. On the last pages of the *Moralia*, he comes as close as he ever does to telling us a version of his own story—what we might call his confessions. There we capture behind the rhetoric some flavor of what it felt like to be wise, holy, and saved; to be unsure and anxious at the same time; and still to be Roman as well.

Now that I have finished this work, I see that I must return to myself. For our mind is much fragmented and scattered beyond itself, even when it tries to speak rightly. While we think of words and how to bring them out, those very words diminish the soul's integrity by plundering it from inside. So I must return from the forum of speech to the senate house of the heart, to call together the thoughts of the mind for a kind of council to deliberate how best I may watch over myself, to see to it that in my heart I speak no heedless evil nor speak poorly any good. . . . For when I turn inward to myself, pushing aside the leafy verbiage, pushing aside the branching arguments, and examine my intentions down at the very root, I know it really was my intention to please God, but some little appetite for the praise of men crept in, I know not how, and intruded on my simple desire to please God. And when later, too much later, I recognize this, I find that I have in fact done something different from what I know I set out to do.

It is often thus, that when we begin with good intentions in the eyes of God, a secret tagalong yen for the praise of our fellow men comes along, waylaying our intentions from the side of the road. We take food, for example, out of necessity, but while we are eating, a gluttonous spirit creeps in and we begin to take delight in the eating for its own sake. So often it happens that what began as nourishment to protect our health ends by becoming a pretext for our pleasures.

. . . But I think it's worthwhile for me to reveal unhesitatingly here to the ears of my brothers everything I secretly revile in myself. As commentator, I have not hidden what I felt, and as confessor, I have not hidden what I suffer. In my commentary I reveal the gifts of God, and in my confession I uncover my wounds. In this vast human race there are always little ones who need to be instructed by my words, and there are always great ones who can take pity on my weakness once they know of it. Thus with commentary and confession I offer my help to some of my brethren (as much as I can), and I seek the help of others. . . . I have not withheld medicine from the ones I can help, but I have not hidden my wounds and lacerations from the others. So I ask that whoever reads this should pour out the consolation of prayer before the strict judge above for me, so that he may wash away with tears every sordid thing he finds in me. When I balance the power of my commentary and the power of prayer, I see that my reader will have more than paid me back if for what he hears from me, he offers his tears for me.[8]

That extraordinary self-mistrust epitomizes his description of the ideal life of the Christian in the world. "Our life is all a temptation" (Job 7.1). Trial, temptation, travail: that is human life in this world for Gregory. Job's story is not merely a story, not merely a case study, but an archetype. The world is not evil, but the world is a testing ground, shaped by man's sin into a place imperfect in many ways, where death and suffering have power over human life and human hope. Augustine never took his innovative theory of original sin this distressingly far.

This reading of Job proposes a further allegory about the world in which a person lives. The good things that happen and the bad things that happen no longer represent mere chance and blind causation, but neither must they be taken as rewards or punishments in themselves. *Why do bad things happen to good people?* Gregory implicitly asks. *To test and try them and make them ready for eternal life.* To the classic question of theodicy, this has the form of a plausible answer. The wealth and luxury of the blasphemer and the travails of the pious need not scandalize, for a greater game is afoot. What matters is not what happens to the believer, but what the believer does in response to the experiences that come along.

The life of a man buffeted by temptation is no pleasant thing. It is incongruous and baffling, and painful besides. The alternative life offered to the Christian believer is one of contemplation.

At this point, we must suspend our attention to Gregory's argument, look around, and see where we have come. The Christianity of which he speaks has escaped from the upper room, and escaped again from the churches and basilicas of late Roman cities. It now offers different practices for different people, and we meet various experiences of Christianity in various places in the same community. Resisting the forces of temptation by means of contemplative meditation on scripture is arguably beautiful and Christian, but few individuals in his Rome or Gregory's Europe would be able to devote themselves wholeheartedly to that strategy. It is tempting but premature to speak of a spiritual elite here, though inevitably a social distinction emerged. The baseline religion of a broad Mediterranean community was now differentiated not only by physical location and tradition but by choice and social location as well.

Gregory's contemplative approach is firmly in the western monastic tradition. John Cassian's *Institutes* and *Lectures* were the raw material from which westerners built their version of the eastern spirit. Gregory had read the scriptures mainly in Jerome's versions, and had read Augustine as well. His merit, reflected in his reputation in later ages, was his integration of scriptural tradition, monastic ideology, and Latin theology.

Gregory gives us little *physical* sense of his notion of contemplation, no manual of meditative techniques. He left in his *Dialogues* and sermons many pen portraits of contemporary religious figures in Italy, in which we are rarely admitted to the primal scene of mysticism: the tranquillity of the adept who reads his sacred texts. More often we see the monk or bishop at prayer—the second stage of contemplative activity, marking the movement from textual intake to internalization; and more often still we see him engaged with those around him, embodying the contemplative life without letting us see how he acquired it. It's not clear how far Gregorian practice approached what later generations of medieval and modern readers would turn into a regular practice of textual absorption. He surely knew and practiced the hours of prayer that were common in late antique monasticism and that would become more fully canonized in Benedictine ritual centuries later, but he covers those moments with a veil of privacy.

As a result, his writings have an abstract quality that lends them to use as mediated tools of instruction under a monastic superior—and he may well have meant them to serve this purpose—rather than to functioning as self-help manuals. "Contemplation" alone is a hollow prescription. Gregory's texts assume a specific direction of thought: recognizing the temptations of the world, falling back on scriptural authority as a contemplative guide, and engaging the believer through what Gregory calls *discretio,* usually translated in western religious traditions as "discernment." Gregory's believer retreats to an inner space where a mental act, the correct interpretation of experience informed by biblical contemplation, is the critical step from darkness to light, from sin to redemption. He may live in a community, but he faces his god alone.

Beleaguering, relentless temptation offers no opportunity for taking one critical step; rather, the step must be taken over and over again. Temptation recurs, contemplation enlightens, and discernment chooses yet again, and the path leads forward. In a similar representation of the workings of the self, Augustine equated the moment of relief with delight, the spontaneous upwelling of authentic love for goodness, the love that when set free would lead irresistibly to right action—*dilige et quodvis fac,* he said, "love and do whatever you like"—for righteous love would assuredly mean that "whatever you like" would work out for the best.[9] The danger was that false delights would lead to false loves, and thus to perdition.

Augustine thus left the experience, and the technology, of the moment of true delight mysterious, wrapped in the difficult doctrines of predestination and free will that puzzled and outraged his readers in his lifetime and after. Gregory belongs to the Latin church that had decided, by the time of the Council of Orange in 529, to let its Augustine be an optimist and at least a bit of a Pelagian. There isn't much optimism in Gregory's depiction of a falling, temptation-fraught world, the place where he implicitly identifies himself with Job on his dung heap. But his gloom masks a belief that, whatever the explanation in deep divine terms, salvation is in the hands of the believer, who will watch, pray, read, and find within himself the God-given spontaneous act of discernment and thus the ability to choose the right over the wrong. "Discern, and do as you will" is Gregory's message, one in which a little of the vitality of Augustinian religion has ebbed away.

Gregory's book on Job was with him in Constantinople and accompanied him back to Rome. Modern scholars detect in the surviving text the remnants of oral sermons to a monkish audience revised into textual dignity, probably originally in a master copy sent along to bishop Leander of Seville, an old acquaintance from Constantinople and one of the triumphant generation of Catholic Christians of post-Arian Spain. (Leander's brother, Isidore, was the most abundantly learned man of his generation and of his century, and his books would be textbooks for centuries. To modern eyes, he is medieval, not classical; to his own contemporaries, however, he represented the inherited tradition of Latin learning. The twenty-first-century Roman church has declared him the patron saint of the Internet.)

BURDENS OF OFFICE

Relieved from his mission and called back to Rome, Gregory was a senior cleric in 590 when another wave of the plague that had seeped through the Mediterranean for the last half century carried away Pope Pelagius II. The election quickly and obviously fell on Gregory, and he was heartbroken. To hear him tell it, anticipation of the burdens of office was more than he could face and he tried every possible way to escape what was being laid on him. It would have been surprising if he had succeeded in escaping, though later legend had him halfway down the road to missionary work in England (work he would later send others to perform) when he heard—a poetic moment here—the chirp of a locust. He thought of the Latin name *locusta* as though it told him to stay where he was (*loco sta*—"stay in place"), and he returned to Rome and to duty.

He did insist on waiting for formal confirmation of his election from the emperor Maurice, and seems to have hoped it would not be forthcoming. He stands near the head of a long line of Christian rulers and leaders who take up responsibility while harboring grave doubts about the value of what they do, about their own ability to fulfill their responsibilities, and about the ultimate moral damage they might inflict on themselves. No one, Gregory thought, should become a bishop unless he doesn't want to.

The office he took up was now more papal than it had ever been, partly by design and partly by default. His letters show us a city without food, without defense, and racked by disease. His first public appearance outside churches found him organizing a mass procession, starting from every city neighborhood with people in streams coming together at one church to pray. This gloomy search for relief set the theme for his fourteen years in office, years increasingly miserable for him as his health deteriorated. (His stomach difficulties probably had something to do with his ascetic practices of self-denial and a ritually abusive diet.)

Part of what he inherited was the consulship that I suggested at the beginning of this chapter. Among his first surviving letters are the instructions he sent to the deacon who represented him in Sicily, where two centuries of inheritances had made the bishop of Rome a landowner on a vast scale hitherto seen only among the most elevated and imperious aristocrats. Gregory, before he abandoned his wealth and property, was without question the richest and most powerful man in Italy, probably in all of what had been the Roman empire west of Constantinople and Alexandria.

And so his performance in the papacy was also an enactment of the responsibilities of a wealthy Roman. Though the city of Rome itself was an emaciated relic, the people needed to be fed, and it fell to the church—that is, the pope—to ensure nutrition. When the Lombards in the mountain duchies of Spoleto to the north and Benevento to the south threatened the city with raids and more, it was the responsibility of the church—that is, the pope—to negotiate with the Byzantine generals and the exarch at Ravenna for support, and then, when the support failed, to negotiate with the Lombards themselves for truce and mercy. From Ravenna, Gregory was considered too prone to appease the Lombards, and it is a hard question what the best strategy in that moment would have been.

In addition, Gregory saw smaller cities within the sphere of Rome's most ancient influence, down into Campania and up into Tuscany, at risk of falling apart when they lost their bishops, so he sent clerical delegates to oversee elections and sometimes to merge bishoprics. The urge behind his actions had a spiritual origin, but at the same time it made him more and more the de facto ruler of central Italy. What looks now like nascent, grandiose papal ambition was in him a combination of ecclesiastical ideology and traditional noblesse oblige.

And the pope had his *secretarium*—the staff of writers, clerks, and messengers who could express his will in words and make the dignified pages reach the courts and churches of the whole Mediterranean. Bishops of Rome had written like this for most of 200 years, but in Gregory's time, the sheer quantity of the correspondence, as well as its attention to detail and the urgency with which the pope claimed attention and authority, gave it for the first time a genuinely imperial quality.

Monarchs were the most dignified of his correspondents. At Constantinople, Gregory had met and been received amiably by the emperor Maurice and the empress Constantina, and he seized the cleric's privilege of continuing to write to them, as he delighted in their responses. His letters to them are a mix of pastoral advice—especially to the empress—and political exhortation. The emperor's formal support for his own office and for the imperial forces deployed in Italy, as feckless and ineffective as they mainly were, had to be maintained at all costs. When Phocas overthrew and murdered Maurice, Gregory switched his allegiance instantly and has distressed many generations of well-wishers by the transparent sincerity with which he gives his new overlord the same loyalty that he gave his friends. His fickleness disappoints, but a high moralistic line would have done no one any good.

There were other monarchs to write to, chief among them the Lombards in Italy, whom Gregory flattered and cajoled as best he could. Gregory's hand reached even to Gaul, where Queen Brünnehilde, though she may have resisted his larger claims to papal authority, was happy to assist the party of monks assembled under Augustine on their way to Britain. (Gregory had seen slaves for sale in Rome and, when he asked what kind they were, he was told they were *Angli*, Angles; he said their name and beauty reminded him of *angeli*, angels, and so they deserved salvation.)

Gregory's eye also reached the Balkans, where the question was churchly authority. The birthplace of Justinian, Justiniana Prima, had been declared the church metropolis of an ill-defined region, and the shifting military and political fortunes of those lands made the definition even more obscure. Gregory asserted that Salona, the principal city of the Adriatic coast, should pay heed to the bishop of Rome, who reasonably imagined both sides of the Adriatic shore as his.

Natalis, the bishop of Salona at the time of Gregory's accession, was a hard case.[10] He was clearly accustomed to being lord of his own domain, and as Gregory's church had become essentially autonomous of civil authority in its sphere, so too many other Christian leaders far from the capital went their way unconcerned about what any authority might say. Gregory, on the other hand, was by nature a meddler, and he spent his first years seeking, by the medium of dignified correspondence, to get Natalis to change his ways. Called to account for his high living and dinner parties, Natalis parried reproach by reminding Gregory that Abraham had been said in the Bible to offer lavish feasts to visitors, meaning the three mysterious strangers in the eighteenth chapter of Genesis. "Ah," Gregory replied, "dinner parties like that are all well and good, as long as your guests, like Abraham's, are angels."[11]

Such sparring leads to nothing. Soon enough, age and excess took their toll and Natalis died. Gregory had his candidate for succession in the person of Natalis's senior clergyman, the archdeacon Honoratus. But Natalis's allies had their own candidate, Maximus, and to advance him they had two strategies. First they got Honoratus approved as bishop of a smaller neighboring city in Dalmatia. Since episcopal election was permanent and a bishop once enthroned could not move to another city, the elevation of Honoratus effectively disqualified him from the see of Salona. When Gregory challenged the legitimacy of this hasty rustication and election, Maximus appealed to the bishop at Justiniana Prima and beyond to Constantinople, on the grounds that they were his real superiors.

Gregory worked and worked through a long chain of years and letters to wear down his opponent. What we cannot intuit well in such a case is the frisson of spiritual fear and the authority that could come with the commands of a figure like Gregory. What if, the rebuked miscreant had to wonder sometimes in the small hours, that really is the voice of the shepherd that God has put over me? In the end, Maximus consented to come to Ravenna—closer to Salona than to Rome—for trial of his various offenses before bishop Marinianus. He chose to confess to a lesser charge of having performed church rites while under sentence of excommunication, and the last we see of him is the day he performed his penance, lying facedown in a public street in Ravenna for three hours, crying out at the top of his voice, "I have sinned before God and most blessed pope Gregory!"[12]

Gregory did not stint at defending his own ecclesiastical turf in such material terms, but he was also vigilant for his authority in other ways. The bishops of Constantinople had no ancient standing in the church, for their town was a backwater until Constantine. The incomparable advantage of imperial presence, on the other hand, gave them doctrinal authority and patronage second to none. Gregory had seen the patriarchate there at first hand, and as pope he watched with evident unhappiness when the patriarch, to describe his own authority, used the title "ecumenical patriarch"—spiritual father over the whole inhabited world. Gregory's campaign of remonstrance had no effect on his rival (whose predecessors had used the title as long ago as the reign of the emperor Anastasius), but in a world where none of his western readers knew any Greek or saw any eastern texts, Gregory's polemic at least defined papal supremacy to the satisfaction of many and thus laid the groundwork of a long future for the western papacy. Gregory has been a sympathetic model for many progressives in recent generations, including Pope John XXIII and Hans Küng, but in his own time his every gesture had the effect of establishing, or at least establishing the foundations for, later papal pretensions that went well beyond what he himself undertook. The historian Hugh Trevor-Roper gave vent to a familiar anticlericalism in calling Gregory "the Stalin of the early church." He was mostly wrong but a little right: wrong in that Gregory's ambitions, intentions, and effects were entirely different, but right in that the connection between power and ideology that Gregory piloted in the Latin west would return in many baleful forms in modern times.

Administrator and exegete, Gregory also shows himself to us taking a private refuge, not in the act of contemplation, but in telling stories. His *Dialogues* begin with him sitting in a quiet place suitable for sadness and melancholy and finding solace in telling the deacon Peter stories of the holy worthies of Italy in his time and in the preceding decades. Some are as simple as this:

There was a monk living in the same abbey, who was the gardener. A thief used to climb over the hedge to steal the vegetables. The holy man, seeing that some went missing and others were trampled down, went out to see where the thief came in. On his way, he found a snake, which he commanded to follow him over to where the thief had found entry. He commanded the snake this way: "In the name of Jesus, I command you to watch this passage, and not allow any thief to come in." So the snake immediately obeyed and laid itself across the path and the monk returned to his cell. Later, when the monks were at rest, the thief came and was climbing over the hedge. Just as he put a leg over, he saw the snake and froze, dangling downwards head first with his shoe caught in the hedge. When the gardener came and saw him, he spoke to the snake: "Thank God, you have done what I commanded: go now on your way." And so the snake went away. The monk spoke to the thief: "What does this mean, brother? God has delivered you into my hands, as you see. Why have you been brazen enough to steal the labor of monks?" And so he untangled the shoe and let the man down, bringing him to the garden gate, where he gave him the vegetables he had come to steal and said to him sweetly, "Go on your way and steal no more. But when you need food, come here and I will give you willingly, for God's sake, what you would otherwise sinfully steal from us."[13]

Paganism in its old dress had continued to fade in the sixth century along with the aristocratic traditions that sustained it, and here we can taste a distinctively Christian superstition. Dragons were always spoken of in ancient legend, but direct assertions that real dragons had been seen and dealt with begin to mark Christian texts from about the fifth century, when a pope was shown destroying a man-eating dragon that lived somewhere near the temple of Vesta in the heart of Rome.[14] This useful snake is his relative.

Gregory's *Dialogues* are so famously full of stories that leave the world of bureaucracy and predictability behind for the realm of charming or terrifying fancy that one recent scholar has mounted a vehement attack on their authenticity.[15] The wise and spiritual Gregory could not, he argues, have written these fairy tales. This is not the place for that argument, which has not proved widely persuasive, but suffice it to say that the stories contain a language operating by its own laws, and they offer a persuasive portrait of a world that runs beyond the documentary and the sane.

The world of Gregory's *Dialogues* is one in which holy monks and bishops offer the interpretive key to understanding and surmounting a chaotic landscape and society. In the Greek church, contemporaries were writing "lives of the fathers" in a similar spirit during the same decades, and the combined impact is to make us realize that these books marked the end of an age of famous and influential monastic leaders. Henceforth, stories about these men would dominate the conversation surrounding monastic holiness, and real monks would take second place in a world of routinized charisma.

The second of the four books into which the *Dialogues* are divided had its own special impact, for it tells the story of Benedict of Nursia, a monk and abbot who had died fifty years earlier at his community's house at Monte Cassino, south of Rome. Gregory could never have met or seen the man, and by his day the community had been sacked and destroyed by Lombards of the Benevento duchy, no great thing considering how small and poorly housed monastic communities then were. Monte Cassino was restored, if that is the right word, early in the eighth century by a refounder who knew of the place and its fame from reading Gregory. (It was sacked and rebuilt again in the ninth and twentieth centuries.)

The structured series of stories that Gregory tells of Benedict and his equally pious and monastic sister Scholastica had the effect of providing the backstory that would accompany the monastic rule attributed to Benedict through the middle ages, after the *Rule* became a standard in Charlemagne's realms. Pope Leo III crowned Charlemagne emperor in 800, and Charlemagne was generous in his support of popes and papal ideas thereafter. So when his bureaucrats of God selected Benedict's rule as the best and began to promote it throughout western Europe, the availability of a suitably edifying biography from the pen of the best and most spiritual of popes had the effect of cementing his authority. (Britain lay outside Charlemagne's power, but Gregory's prestige there had another source: his influence in sending out Augustine of Canterbury to organize the churches in Britain, leading to wide acceptance of the Benedictine model there as well.)

The obvious and distracting effect of the *Dialogues* is to fill the mind with stories of magical divine power that are in every way ancient and predictable, despite their Christian flavor. Christianity supplies authoritative figures, now usually bishops and monks, who prevail in a landscape thick with demons and angels, but the believer and unbeliever are still ancient peasants or patricians, baffled by the unintelligibility of good and bad fortune and seeking interpretation, consolation, and power. Gregory's stories offer what was needed, not to the people who lived the stories, but to an admiring wider audience.

The book is usually taken as the charter document of medieval superstitious Catholicism, as though there were something new in the world about credulity and divine powers bending to the will of those who knew how to use them, or perhaps something so distinctively lofty about Christianity that it would not be associated with such vulgar religion. But look again, and you will see that Gregory's intellectual seriousness is what was important and what carried the day. To be sure, people in those days told each other stories every bit as wacky as those of UFO sightings in the 1950s, but it is far more important that a serious intellectual, literary, and cultural leader wrote down the stories for his peers and readers. The peasants are characters in stories, but the literati, the people who had been given a new way of understanding their world, are the ones who are now different. Miraculousness existed for them—as it always had—but now it had a theoretical and textual warrant and control in Christianity.

Gregory was able to persuade his readers to think of themselves as living in the world Jesus lived in. His stories of power, mystery, and miracle are shaped and formed by biblical antecedents, as a way of asserting that the improbable was now intelligible, in "modern" religious and textual terms.[16]

Domesticating the implausible makes credulity respectable, as we see in our own time with the canonizations of Padre Pio and Juan Diego of Guadalupe. But connecting the imagination of the credulous with the authoritative texts of a society means that credulity is now at least a bit under the control of educated people. It would take a long time for modern skepticism to manifest itself and it still has had little effect, to be sure, but the long and slow struggle to assert the reasonability of the world against the ignorance of the credulous got a critical assist even from Gregory.

Thirteen centuries after Gregory, a Sicilian aristocrat who might well be a character out of Gregory's letters told a not very miraculous story of his own great-grandfather. Giuseppe Tomasi di Lampedusa's *The Leopard* (*Il Gattopardo*) was written in the ruins of a great ancient family, in a time just after World War II when Sicily had seen all the depredations and few of the benefits of modernity. Lampedusa tells the story of the arrival of

384 ✦ THE RUIN OF THE ROMAN EMPIRE

modernity, seen through the grim lucidity of the last dynastic prince of an old family, who greets the coming of Garibaldi and Garibaldi's men with rueful intelligence. He knows that his nephew and heir is a wastrel and consigns him in marriage to the arms of a domineering upstart woman of transient beauty, recognizing what he cannot accept or change. Lampedusa's prince harbors in his character the last of the polymathic *sprezzatura* of the Renaissance man, combining learning, libido, and a keen sense of the working of worldly power.

Gregory was like and unlike the prince, as fully sensible to the disasters that had visited his world, but with a lugubrious optimism that gave rise both to his grim determination to act and to his glad embrace of the miraculous and the untrue. The disarray and political disunity into which Italy had fallen in Gregory's century would not begin to be healed until the revolutions of the nineteenth century, and it may reasonably be argued that the *unification* of Italy was not finally manifested until the power blackout of 2003—taken as the first genuinely national common experience shared by all of Italy and Sicily since the wars of Justinian.

Long after being recognized as a great administrator, spiritual leader, and writer, Gregory at his death was not universally mourned. He had imposed a monk's spiritual discipline on the clergy and administration of the wealthy Roman church that many found unsettling. His immediate successors were at pains to forget him and his ascetic zeal, in favor of a more comfortable stewardship of church affairs. The influence of his writings tipped the balance in favor of Gregory's memory, with the help of his mission to England. His reputation was always high among the heirs of his converting monks, and British and Irish readers ensured the preservation and dissemination of his works and his early biographies. All life is a temptation, as he kept quoting Job, and Gregory surmounted that temptation only in leaving this life.

In the end, Gregory the Great was wrong to anticipate the end of the world. It had already arrived.

Epilogue

"Every angel is terrifying."
(RILKE)

"The archangel loved heights."
(HENRY ADAMS)

REGORY'S ELECTION HAD come at a grim moment. In September 590, a great flood overran the banks of the Tiber and spread across much of the city. It destroyed buildings and ruined storehouses in which the church kept grain to feed its members. The plague followed in November, carrying off Pope Pelagius and leaving the deacon Gregory to protest in vain that he had no appetite for the church's supreme office. Gregory of Tours, the contemporary Frankish historian, records a sermon that the other Gregory delivered in this moment to the people of Rome.[1]

> For behold, the whole people is stricken with the sword of heavenly wrath, and individuals are smitten down with sudden death. . . . Each one who is struck is taken away without even a chance for repenting his sins. Think what it would be like to appear in the sight of the strict judge above with no time to weep for what you have done.

Gregory ordered a grand procession of prayer and repentance. A hundred years earlier, his predecessor Gelasius could still rant (probably to no effect) against the survival of the old festival of the Lupercal, originally a fertility ritual but by then claimed to prevent epidemics. The Lupercal rites began in ancient times by sacrificing a goat in the cave where the wolf had suckled Romulus and Remus, but that had been put aside under the empire. It was no longer the aristocrats who ran in the streets brushing women with branches to communicate fertility, but paid hands from the lower classes.

Now, a century after Gelasius, the bishop was firmly in charge and the Lupercal was gone. What Gregory ordered was the "sevenfold litany," dividing the population in seven parts, each assigned to one of the city's churches, from which they would come together in prayer and procession. The clergy were to gather at the church of Cosmas and Damian (on the Via Sacra, close to the heart of the ancient city, in a building that had been the ceremonial hall of the city prefect), while abbots and monks would gather at the shrine of the martyrs Gervase and Protase. Religious women and their leaders were assigned the church of Marcellinus and Peter; children the church of John and Paul; widows the church of Saint Euphemia; married women the church of Saint Clement. The men of the city—laymen— would gather at Saint Stephen's. From those dispersed points they would come together at the basilica of Saint Mary, which is now called Santa Maria Maggiore. Many of them gathered in the valley between the Caelian and Esquiline hills not far from the papal Lateran church of Saint John, while others huddled in shrines a few yards from Santa Maria Maggiore itself on the Esquiline.

But first, for three days, the groups stayed at their assigned churches, singing Psalms with prayer and weeping. On the climactic day, at about nine in the morning, they came out in procession, chanting the Greek prayer for mercy, *Kyrie eleison*, "Lord, have mercy." A deacon who was there reported that no fewer than eighty of the faithful fell down dead within one hour, no doubt exhausted by the fasting and prayer and affected by the crowding of the populace.

In later times, the story of this dramatic opening of Gregory's papacy was improved with the report that as the procession passed Hadrian's tomb, the archangel Michael appeared, sword flashing in hand, atop the great hulk—never mind that for such a spectacle the goal surely must have been Saint Peter's church across the Tiber and that does not match what we know of the actual procession. A few years after Gregory's papacy, a chapel in honor of Michael was established high up in the tomb, so the story must be very early. Today the angel, cast in bronze in more modern times, brandishes his sword atop the tower once again.

Let's let them have their story. What happened when the lamenting procession looked up to see the angel there, dazzling, brilliant, beggaring description, standing at the pinnacle of a glowering stone tomb? What did people think? In his right hand, a fiery sword slashed the air. So Apollo had brought plague to the Greeks at Troy on the first page of the *Iliad*:

> [Apollo] came down furious from the summits of Olympus, with his bow and his quiver upon his shoulder, and the arrows rattled on his back with the rage that trembled within him. He sat himself down away from the ships with a face as dark as night, and his silver bow rang death as he shot his arrow in the midst of them . . . and all day long the pyres of the dead were burning.

In Michael's moment, before gaping onlookers, the dealer of death paused, then plunged his sword deep in a bright scabbard that hung at his belt. A gasp, then exhalation ran through the crowd as the people realized that the warrior from the court of heaven was showing them that mercy had been decreed and the plague would come to an end.

That story was enough for the tomb to be called to this day the Holy Angel's Castle (Castel Sant'Angelo). The rooftop would be fortified to defend the medieval city, a tunnel would run from there to the Vatican, and Giuseppe Verdi in the nineteenth century would make it the setting for the climax of *Tosca*.

The "coming out" of the archangel is a sign of the times—hard to miss, easy to overstate. To understand the archangel and read this sign aright, it is best to see where he came from and where he was going.

The Michael of that moment in Rome might resemble the Apollo of Greek myth, but angels are Hebrew in origin, Greek in name. *Angelos* was a word any Greek-speaker would easily hear as "messenger, herald," a courtier from the halls of a great king. Ancients who had seen nothing of kings and courts still knew how to imagine them, and many had seen at least some modest visitation from a royal or imperial world beyond their

The angel on Hadrian's tomb sheathes his sword.

ken. Courtiers of every rank dressed lavishly for their station, were terrifyingly calm and poised in demeanor, and were arbitrary in the use of the
power their master secured to them: they were the kind of men children
would have nightmares about and grown men would view with caution if
not alarm.

The courtiers of this great king of heaven were more powerful still.
They appeared suddenly, they outran other mortals in all the ways and
shows of power, and they were immortal. The sixth-century writer we call
Pseudo-Dionysius the Areopagite, whom many thought to be the friend of
the apostle Paul who had heard directly from Paul what he had seen in his
vision of heaven, described the court of angels in his *Celestial Hierarchies,*
a book quietly influential in both Greek and Latin churches for many centuries. (He is the one who sorted out the angelic orders: seraphim, cheru-

bim, and thrones on high; virtues, dominations, and powers between; and principalities, archangels, and angels in the lower ranks. Pope Gregory and the seventh-century Greek theologian Maximus the Confessor, who spent time at Rome, took up this ranking and made it the standard treatment.) In a rigidly monotheistic world, to speak of angels was to speak of beings who had once been undoubtedly divine but who now offered no threat to the one supreme god. They incorporated the powers of Apollo and Hermes and more besides.

One of Hermes's roles, for example, was psychopomp—attendant of souls on their way to the next life. In ancient myth, the underworld was far off and the road dangerous—hence the need for a safe guide. For Christianity the risks were different: devils lay in wait on all sides, in this life and in death, to seize the dead and carry them off to hell. A conventional story of saints' lives concerned a monk who died alone, when all his brothers were away. The saint was granted a vision of the newly deceased and the devils that assailed him, and led all the absent brothers in prayer, which kept the devils at bay until good angels could rush to the rescue and guide the blessed one to a heavenly reward.

All this still made sense in ways barely past those of ancient traditional religion, for it was generally agreed that the ancient gods were not a figment of the imagination, but only the fallen angels roaming through the world in pursuit of the ruin of souls, passing themselves off as beneficent divinities, just long enough to seduce and destroy the gullible. (The idea that devils could snatch souls made an absolute mockery of everything Augustine, for example, had taught, to say nothing of Jesus, but made absolute sense at the same time.)

The messengers of the Lord had taken on names now familiar to us—Raphael, Ithuriel, Gabriel, and especially Michael—in the Hebrew scriptures. Listen to the prophet Daniel introducing Gabriel:

> And I lifted up my eyes, and looked: and behold, there was a man dressed in linen and his loins were girded with worked gold; and his body was like topaz, and his face like the appearance of lightning, and his eyes like a burning lamp; and his arms, and from there to his feet, like shining bronze; and the voice of his words was like the voice of a multitude. . . . And I heard the voice of his words; and when I heard, I threw myself on my face in confusion, and my face I pressed to the earth.[2]

Michael is Gabriel's colleague there but came into his own in the biblical book of Revelation:

> And there was a great battle in heaven: Michael and his angels fought the dragon, and the dragon fought, and his angels; and they did not prevail, and there was no space for them further in heaven. And the great dragon was cast down, the ancient serpent, who is called the devil, and Satan, who seduces the whole world.[3]

In the guise of Michael, Christianity found its warrior god, protector, and avenger, threatening but—to the faithful—benign. He had churches all over Asia Minor and would survive by name into the Koran. The earliest visible wings are pinned on his shoulders on a sarcophagus from around the year 400, but Isaiah had already given six wings to the seraphim, followed by Tertullian around the year 200.[4] One of Justinian's few trips outside Constantinople took him to a church dedicated to Michael at Germia, in Galatia, where there were also to be found relics of Saint George the dragon slayer.

And Michael loved the high ground. It is hard not to give him a personality as he makes his appearances in western Europe, a visitor from the east, gradually spreading his cult and name throughout western lands far from his native Israel, far from the Greek lands where he had been naturalized into the religious consciousness of the Mediterranean.

Gargano Promontory on the Adriatic coast of Italy captured him first. On a volcanic headland projecting into the sea, in caves high on the hillside, he first appeared in the days of Theoderic. Stories are told from the years 490, 492, and 493, when the local bishop was reputed to be a relative of the emperor Anastasius (who hailed, we recall, from just across the Adriatic). If we do not quite trust the later text that recounts this origin, we might note that there are churches at Larino and Potenza, not far from Gargano, dedicated to Michael in 494 and 496 and known from sober and reliable letters of Pope Gelasius.

There was in that place—so the medieval tale goes—a wealthy man named Garganus, who would give his name to the mountain. His vast herd of cattle grazed everywhere on its sides. One of the bulls wandered off by himself and did not return home with the rest of the herd that evening. The master took a group of his slaves, went out through all the rough country looking for him, and found him at last on the top of the mountain in front of the entrance to a cave. Furious that the bull would go off alone like this, he snatched up a bow and a poisoned arrow to shoot him. But it was as if a gust of wind caught the arrow when he shot it and it blew back and struck the bowman instead, killing him. The people watching were thrown into an uproar and confused at how this had all happened—but they didn't dare go close to the body to see. They asked the bishop what they should do. He told them to fast for three days and pray to God for guidance.

When they did that, the holy archangel of the Lord appeared and spoke to the bishop in a vision, saying, "You have done well to say that men should seek explanation of God for what baffles them. That this man was struck with his own arrow—that was done by my will. For I am the archangel Michael, and I am always in the presence of the Lord. I set out to protect this place and its people and so I wanted to prove by all the things that happened there that I am the watcher and guardian of this place."

Who could resist? The cave was excavated further and arranged as a church, Michael's church, and so it remains to this day. The Lombard rulers of the seventh century ensured its fame and position. You can still see inscriptions there in the old runic alphabet in honor of Michael, by Lombard visitors, pilgrims with names like Hereberecht, Wigfus, and Herraed. Grimoald I, the duke of Benevento, defended the sanctuary against Byzantine raiders from the sea in 650 and made much of Michael's protection that he had enjoyed. When Grimoald ascended a greater Lombard throne at Pavia in 662, he took with him his devotion, building a church to Michael in his palace there.[5]

By such means and by other bearers, Michael found his way west and north. To appear in Rome in 590 was no difficult thing for him, for his fame had run ahead of him, and Gregory's faithful would know him well enough to recognize him. His footfall on the top of Hadrian's tomb reflected his predilection for heights, which his votaries recognized by building his chapels on high ground and even in the towers of great churches. It became conventional in later centuries for a magnificent cathedral to have a chapel to Michael in one of the towers at the western entrance, or to build one over the entryway, guarding the approaches.

The most famous shrines of Michael take us farther north and west, and we can hopscotch from high ground to high ground to find him.

Mont-Saint-Michel, on the coast of Normandy, won his favor early and grew eventually to the Romanesque church and monastery on the hill-top that ultimately won the veneration of even Henry Adams. Facing the famous Mont-Saint-Michel, on the coast of Cornwall about 200 hundred miles across the water, Saint Michael's Mount, with a story of the angel appearing to fishermen there in 495 CE, looks like a scale model of the more famous shrine, as though the angel had leaped across the water just there, and pilgrims were shown his footprint preserved on stone where he stepped.

We must go farther, across Britain where Celtic and Roman Christianities found each other, across the Irish sea, and across Ireland itself. We must go not to the northeast of the country, where Patrick had preached, but now to the southwest, to the ring of Kerry and beyond into the waters of the north Atlantic, waters into which a few fisherman and a few saints would venture.[6] Some of the hardy, or foolhardy, men who set out in those boats did not go far to find land. Eight miles off the coast of Kerry, there are two prominent rocky outcroppings called the Great Skellig and Little

Skellig Michael.

Skellig, and the larger of them is Skellig Michael. High up on the rock survive, astonishingly well preserved, the buildings of a tiny monastery that clung to this spot. Almost 500 feet above water level on a rock rising still 200 feet higher, six stone conical huts and two small oratories made of stones without masonry have weathered more than 1,000 years—weathered because to survive at all they had to be fiercely built.

No old book tells us a story to go with this astonishing site. Visible from the shore, these rocks are virtually the first landfall that storms coming north and east off the ocean find, making the southwest of Ireland the rainiest place in all Europe. All the water that is scooped up in the atmosphere, when prevailing southwesterlies that follow the gulf stream north and east, reach first land here and pour down rain. When storms catch up in those clouds, the prominent Skelligs pull the lightning from the clouds as well, and so it has always been. In those days, the faithful ashore, in whatever lee of the wind they could find, gazed out on the rocks to see the flashes of lightning strike and wonder at the angelic and demonic powers at war there.

The size of the community on Skellig Michael could never have been more than a dozen or two, even if there were more buildings than survive today. Its monks fed themselves with fish and with what they could grow in tiny gardens of soil they found on ledges among the rocks. It was an arduous life beyond our imagining, and dangerous as well. To live on that rock, even with the protection of the stone huts, a monk had to assume and accept that he would be cold, wet, and hungry almost every day of his life. We do not know how long men would stay out on the rock—for a season or for a lifetime, though in those conditions a few seasons could feel much like a lifetime.

A few years ago, archaeologists found traces, even on that rock, of a monastic practice familiar everywhere else in the world—a lust for hermitage. On a piece of the rock higher still, an arduous ascent from the small cluster of huts and tiny chapels, stood another minute dwelling—one for the monk so holy, so enraptured with God's power, that he would have to flee the noise and conviviality of the community of rock clingers for this piece of solitude and, if such can be imagined, still greater misery, along with the proximity of the angel.

Michael made it that far. His disciples were all but entirely ignorant of the story we have followed in this book, ignorant of the failure of humankind to build a society that could bring together Europe, Africa, and the reaches of Asia in neighborly respect, ignorant of the task that lay ahead for the generations of the remote future, our generations. They had excuses for their ignorance that we do not.

Old errors are easy to reenact—as fading empires, bereft of self-awareness, struggle again to use their old power to preserve themselves, and in so doing risk weakening beyond repair; as religious communities mistake their faith for destiny and find pretexts for behavior that goes beyond even the unconscionable and the imaginable. Today, as in the sixth century, a calm sense for the long view, the broad view, and a pragmatic preference for the better rather than the best can have a hard time overcoming the noisy anxiety of those who would transform—that is, ruin—what they do not understand.

Civilization is a thing of the calm, the patient, the pragmatic, and the wise. We are not assured that it will triumph.

LIST OF ROMAN EMPERORS

A simplified table. For fuller information, see the website "De imperatoribus Romanis" (http://www.roman-emperors.org), in which this is based.

31 BCE–14 CE	Augustus
14–37	Tiberius
37–41	Caligula
41–54	Claudius
54–68	Nero
68–69	Galba
69	Otho
69	Vitellius
69–79	Vespasian
79–81	Titus
81–96	Domitian
96–98	Nerva
98–117	Trajan
117–138	Hadrian
138–161	Antoninus Pius
161–180	Marcus Aurelius
180–192	Commodus
192–193	Pertinax
193	Didius Julianus
193–211	Septimius Severus
211–217	Caracalla
218–222	Elagabalus
222–235	Severus Alexander
235–284	Approx. 64 emperors, claimants, rivals, none too successful

284–305	Diocletian
285–ca.310	Maximianus Herculius
293–306	Constantius I Chlorus
293–311	Galerius
305–313	Maximinus Daia
305–307	Severus II
306–312	Maxentius
308–324	Licinius
306–337	Constantine I
337–340	Constantine II
337–350	Constans I
337–361	Constantius II
361–363	Julian
363–364	Jovian
364–375	Valentinian I
364–378	Valens
367–383	Gratian
375–392	Valentinian II
378–395	Theodosius I the Great

REIGNING IN THE WEST

393–423	Honorius
425–455	Valentinian III
455	Petronius Maximus
455–456	Avitus

457–461	Majorian
461–465	Libius Severus
467–472	Anthemius
472	Olybrius
473–474	Glycerius
474–475	Julius Nepos
475–476	Romulus Augustulus
c. 476–493	Odoacer
493–526	Theoderic
526–534	Athalaric
535–536	Theodahad
536–540	Witigis
540–541	Ildibad
541	Eraric
541–552	Totila
552–553	Teias

REIGNING IN THE EAST

395–408	Arcadius
408–450	Theodosius II
450–457	Marcian
457–474	Leo I
474	Leo II
474–491	Zeno
491–518	Anastasius
518–527	Justin
527–565	Justinian I
565–578	Justin II
578–582	Tiberius II
582–602	Maurice
602–610	Phocas
610–641	Heraclius

NOTES

I have referred where possible to English versions, especially those of the Loeb Classical Library, but there are many sources of this period not available in translation and there I have given reference to standard editions of the original text in the ancient language.

OVERTURE

1. Standard edition with French translation by W. Wolska-Conus (Paris, 1968–1973). The only English translation is quite old and available in only a few research libraries in book form, but currently available online at http://www.tertullian.org/fathers/#Cosmas_Indicopleustes.
2. W. H. C. Frend, *The Rise of the Monophysite Movement* (Cambridge, 1972), 204.
3. See R. Sorabji, ed., *Philoponus and the Rejection of Greek Science* (London, 1987), and the long series of English translations of Philoponos's work published by Cornell University Press in recent years.
4. *Barlaam and Ioasaph* (London and New York, 1914), trans. G. R. Woodward and H. Mattingly, in the Loeb Classical Library.
5. C. Wickham, *Framing the Early Middle Ages* (Oxford, 2005), 615.
6. For Nisibis and its school, see A. Becker, *Fear of God and the Beginning of Wisdom* (Philadelphia, 2006).
7. G. W. Bowersock, *Hellenism in Late Antiquity* (Ann Arbor, 1990), 60–67, for Horapollo and for Dioscoros in juxtaposition.
8. Wickham, 245ff.
9. I take this theme from W. Treadgold, *Concise History of Byzantium* (New York, 2001), but take his idea farther than he might do.
10. A. Dalby, *Flavours of Byzantium* (Totnes, 2003).
11. Cassiodorus, *Variae* 12.4; hereafter abbreviated Cass. *Var.* (Turnhout, 1973). (The *Variae* published by Cassiodorus in his own name comprises the official letters written in the name of the monarchs he served, so texts quoted from it usually speak in the voice of rulers.)
12. A. Dalby, *Empire of Pleasures: Luxury and Indulgence in the Roman World* (London, 2000).

13. Averil Cameron et al., *Cambridge Ancient History*, Vol. 14 (Cambridge, 2000), 368. See also P. Garnsey, *Famine and Food Supply in the Graeco-Roman World* (Cambridge, 1988), 20–37.

14. Sidonius Apollinaris, *Epistulae* 9.13.5 (Cambridge, Mass., 1936–65 [Loeb: *Letters and Poems*]), quoted in H. Maguire, "The Good Life," in G. Bowersock et al., *Late Antiquity* (Cambridge Mass., 1999), 238–257. Hereafter abbreviated Sid. Ep.

15. The treasure is rarely seen and is kept mainly in a bank vault, while arguments rage over its rightful ownership and even provenance: Lebanon, Croatia, and Hungary all claim that it was found on their soil.

16. K. Randsborg, *First Millennium AD in Europe and the Mediterranean* (Cambridge, 1991), 158–160.

17. O. R. Constable, *Housing the Stranger in the Mediterranean World* (Cambridge, 2003).

18. Theodoret reported in P. Brown, "The Rise and Function of the Holy Man," *Journal of Roman Studies* 61 (1971), 86–88.

19. Cass. *Var.* 10.30.

20. N. Purcell, "Literate Games: Roman Urban Society and the Game of Alea," *Past and Present* 147 (1995), 3–37.

21. R. West, *Black Lamb and Grey Falcon* (New York, 1941), 274–275.

22. On Gibbon, J. G. A. Pocock, *Barbarism and Religion* (Cambridge, 1999–2005).

23. *Memoirs of the Life and Writings of Edward Gibbon* (London and Boston, 1898), 144.

1. ROME IN 500: LOOKING BACKWARD

1. As argued by L. Cracco Ruggini, drawing on A. Chastagnol, *Le sénat romain sous la règne d'Odoacre* (Bonn, 1966).

2. We call it the Colosseum or, less correctly, the "Coliseum," because it stood in the vicinity of a giant statue of Nero; but the word was not applied until centuries after the time of which we speak here. M. Beard and K. Hopkins, *The Colosseum* (Cambridge, Mass., 2005), captures the whole history of the building vividly and concisely.

3. Anonymus Valesianus 2.12 (Cambridge, Mass., 1939 [Loeb]). "Catholic" is a contested word in this period, usually applied by moderns to the ancestors of later Latin orthodox creeds and churches, especially the modern Roman Catholic Church. But almost no people in the period of which I write would have admitted that *they* were not Catholic, and so I try to avoid the word. "Orthodox" can mean less controversially the prevalent body of beliefs in the Roman world under imperial domination and approval, at a time when Greek and Latin churches had not drawn apart. Later pages of our story will show how the later separation of creeds begins to manifest itself.

4. M. Hendy, *Studies in the Byzantine Monetary Economy* (Cambridge, 1985).

5. Ennodius, *Panegyricus* (Berlin, 1885: *Panegyric Spoken before Theoderic the King*).

6. Agnellus of Ravenna, *Book of Pontiffs of the Church of Ravenna*, trans. D. Deliyannis (Washington, 2004), 146.

7. W. Goffart, *Barbarians and Romans, A.D. 418–584* (Princeton, 1980). Goffart, followed by others, controverted by some, and most recently expanding his arguments in *Barbarian Tides* (Philadelphia, 2006), is the leading scholar of this difficult subject.

8. Cass. *Var.* 1.1.

9. Ennodius, *Epistulae* 3.10.

10. We have to be careful not to overgeneralize about the languages of these northern peoples. The way Ulfilas wrote down his gospel would have its own effect in propagating a standard written form of language among people who might not have known their kinship with each other. P. J. Geary, *Myth of Nations* (Princeton, 2002), 75, points out that not until the ninth century did a general sense of the kinship of "Germanic languages" develop.

11. Standard church histories sometimes make it hard to see just how far Christianity moved away from the beliefs of Constantine and his court bishops when the Nicene orthodoxy prevailed in the late fourth century. R. P. C. Hanson, *The Search for the Christian Doctrine of God* (Edinburgh, 1988), may be the fairest survey in English, but it should be read along with a more traditional presentation, e.g., J. Pelikan, *The Emergence of the Catholic Tradition* (Chicago, 1971), in order to grasp what is at stake in the modern debates.

12. I owe the development in this paragraph and similar observations below to Anthony Appiah, "What's Special about Religious Disputes?" paper read at Georgetown University September 12, 2006.

13. P. J. Geary, *Before France and Germany* (Oxford, 1988), 1.

14. Cassius Dio (Cambridge, Mass., 1914–1927 [Loeb]), 56.18.2.

15. The logic of that line underlies two beautiful books (and perhaps someday will underlie a third), Patrick Leigh Fermor's account of his walk in 1933 from the Hook of Holland to Istanbul: *A Time of Gifts* (London, 1977) and *Between the Woods and the Water* (London, 1986).

16. C. Whittaker, *Frontiers of the Roman Empire* (Baltimore, 1994), is brilliant on the culture of those borderlands.

17. Who were Rome's best emperors? The list is terrifyingly short. Augustus, cold-eyed brute that he was, reduced the power struggles of the late republic to exhausted order and established mechanisms for ruling the wide empire from a small center; Trajan and Hadrian understood empire and its demands and solidified and professionalized an army and a government after a century of Augustus's successors had done no more than terrorize; Diocletian rescued and restored empire, by force of a vast expansion of government; and Constantine made permanent what Diocletian had initiated (and what might very well have collapsed entirely). There is also Anastasius, whom we will meet again. Just a few.

18. Modern Edirne, today the first city of Turkey as you approach from Bulgaria or Greece; in the fifteenth century, it would be headquarters and capital for the Ottoman Turks before they captured Constantinople itself in 1453.

19. Orosius, *Seven Books of History against the Pagans*, 7.43 (Washington, D.C., 1964).

20. Peter Heather's *The Fall of the Roman Empire* (Oxford, 2005), drawing on his earlier work, offers a very traditional and, to my mind, flawed narrative of the barbarian overthrow, but I owe a great deal to his interpretation of Aetius and the Huns in these years, even where I disagree with him.

21. I have told this story briefly in my *Augustine* (New York and London, 2005), especially 209–244; a fuller but more partisan traditional view is that of W. H. C. Frend, *The Donatist Church* (Oxford, 1951).

22. This "fiscal collapse" is one theme of many interwoven in Wickham's *Framing the Early Middle Ages*.

23. This paragraph and the next are based on the translation of Priscus in J. B. Bury, *The Later Roman Empire*, Vol. 1 (London, 1923), 279–288, revised for readability.

24. Jordanes, *Getica* 39 (*Gothic History of Jordanes in English Version,* trans. C. C. Mierow, Princeton, 1915).

25. Geary, *Myth of Nations*, 98.

26. Procopius, *Wars* (Cambridge, Mass., 1914–1940 [Loeb]), 3.7.16–17.

27. Sid. *Ep.* 1.2. On another page (*Ep.* 1.7.5) Sidonius admits that he prefers Goths to Greeks, and on another (*Ep.* 5.6.7) that he prefers the Burgundians to the government of the official emperor, Julius Nepos. But he professes himself surprised (*Ep.* 5.5) by a friend who has "gone over" to the Burgundians and learned their language in an astonishingly short time—which is evidence both for Sidonius's reservations and for his friend's no less interesting enthusiasm.

28. Ibid., 5.17.

29. Sidonius, *Poem* 5.

30. Eugippius, *The Life of Saint Severin*, trans. L. Bieler and L. Krestan (Washington, D.C., 1965).

31. Augustine, *Confessions* 9.7.16, trans. M. Boulding (New York, 1998).

2. THE WORLD THAT MIGHT HAVE BEEN

1. Marcellinus, *Chronicle* under the year 508 (in *Monumenta Germaniae Historica,* "Auctores Antiquissimi," vol. 11 [Berlin, 1894]).

2. By the seventeenth century, the anti-Pelagian doctrines for which Augustine had fought intently for the last two decades of his life had been effectively disowned by the Roman church. See L. Kolakowski, *God Owes Us Nothing* (Chicago, 1995).

3. Cass. *Var.* 1.45.

4. It resembles in many ways another book of the same period, the Rossano Gospels, a Greek gospel book in Italy, written on purple parchment with letters in silver and first lines of important sections in gold.

5. No German reader would miss the quotation in this last line of the other great hero ancestor of German independence, Martin Luther at the Diet of Worms— "Here I stand: I cannot do otherwise, God help me."

6. Not much mention had been made of the Amals during Theoderic's first thirty years in Italy.

7. Cass. *Var.* 3.52.

8. Ibid., 2.27.

9. Ibid., 4.43.

10. *Edict of Theoderic* 111 (*Edictum Theoderici* in *Monumenta Germaniae Historica,* "Leges in folio," vol. 5 [Berlin, 1889]).

11. Cass. *Var.* 7.10.

12. Ibid., 4.22.

13. Greg. *Dial.* 1.4. (*Dialogues* [Washington, D.C., 1959]).

14. Cass. *Var.* 2.3.

15. Ibid., 4.51.

16. Ibid., 1.27.

17. Ibid., 3.51.

18. Ibid., 3.39.

19. Gregory the Great, *Homilies on Ezechiel* 2.6.23 (no English translation; see *Homélies sur Ezechiel* [Paris, 1986–1990]).

20. Cass. *Var.* 3.48.

21. *Corpus Inscriptionum Latinarum* 10.6850–2 (Berlin, 1876–). Another inscription (*Inscriptiones Latinae Selectae* 825 [Berlin, 1892–1916]) of the time stops just short of this one: *salvis dominis nostris Anastasio perpetuo Augusto et gloriosissimo ac triumfali viro Theoderico*—"in the age of our lords Anastasius forever Augustus and the most glorious and triumphant Theoderic." The most skeptical modern scholar attributes these expressions to the optimism of the senatorial class—which is to say, the people who were trying to come as close as they could to understanding Theoderic's rule as a legitimate imperial continuation, in the face of others who were reluctant to do so.

22. Cass. *Var.* 2.32–33 records the order Theoderic gave to have this project carried out.

23. Psalm 14.1.

24. Matthew 28.19.

25. R. MacMullen, *Christianizing the Roman Empire* (New Haven, 1984); and K. Harl, "Sacrifice and Pagan Belief in Fifth- and Sixth-Century Byzantium," *Past and Present* 128 (1990), 7–27.

26. R. MacMullen, *Christianity and Paganism in the Fourth to Eighth Centuries* (New Haven, 1997), 33.

27. Sozomen, *Eclesiastical History* 7.22 (London, 1855).

28. Those scriptures had not yet been commonly gathered into a single book or called a "Bible." For one thing, they were too bulky for late antique bookmaking technologies to manage in one lump; for another, there was a long tradition of treating a loose collection of texts as scriptural—a book of Psalms here, a Pentateuch there, gospels over here, epistles in another manuscript, etc. The sharp definition of the official list of "canonical" books was only settling into place in the fourth century; and even so, one-volume Bibles were slow to come into use and were rare as long as manuscript technology remained dominant.

29. A straightforward discussion of the history and doctrines can be found in J. Pelikan, *The Emergence of the Catholic Tradition* (Chicago, 1971); for much greater detail, see A. Grillmeier, *Christ in the Christian Tradition* (Atlanta 1975–1987), vol. 2 (in 2 parts).

30. John Malalas, *Chronicle* 16.16 (Melbourne, 1986); two other early sources, Evagrius and John of Antioch, tell the story of the battle without this weapon of mass destruction. A more elaborate such compound in liquid form, known as "Greek fire," is attested to first in 670 CE and was a standard and powerful weapon in Byzantine arsenals for centuries.

31. Boethius, *The Consolation of Philosophy*, book 1, prosa 4 (Cambridge, Mass., 1973 [Loeb]).

32. Cf. Plato, *Republic* 5.473D.

33. The cord around the head and the bulging eyes are reported as torture inflicted at Theodora's orders on a suspected homosexual at Constantinople a few years later (Procopius, *Secret History* 16.23 [Cambridge, Mass., 1940 (Loeb)]).

34. Procopius, *Wars* 5.2.

35. S. J. B. Barnish, "*Religio in stagno*: Nature, Divinity, and the Christianization of the Countryside in Late Antique Italy," *Journal of Early Christian Studies* 9.3 (2001), drawing on Cass. *Var.* 8.33.

3. BEING JUSTINIAN

1. I owe this observation to Professor J. F. Matthews.

2. J. Freely and A. Çakmak, *Byzantine Monuments of Istanbul* (Cambridge, 2004).

3. Rome's *original* success came exactly for economic reasons, for it sat at a crucial ford in the Tiber controlling passage and commerce north and south between the prosperous regions of Tuscany and Campania, and had salt to sell besides. These advantages had long become irrelevant by the time of Cicero and Caesar.

4. G. Downey, "Earthquakes at Constantinople and Vicinity," *Speculum* 30 (1955), 596–600, lists from surviving sources significant earthquakes at Constantinople in 477, 525, 526, 532, 542, 546, 548, 554, 557 (that one took down the dome of Hagia Sophia), 583, and 611.

5. 1 Kings 6–7, 2 Chronicles 3–4, and Ezekiel 40–43.

6. By 626, when Heraclius fought the Avars at the city's gates, the Virgin was seen to appear in front of her church—even the *khagan* of the Avars acknowledged that he could not fight her. Averil Cameron, "Images of Authority," *Past and Present* 84 (1979), 21.

7. Translation by Alan Cameron in his *Circus Factions* (Oxford, 1976), 318ff.

8. The silentiaries were originally the ushers, that is, the higher manservants, who governed life inside the palace. As the palace became the focus of all power, their influence grew. The emperor Anastasius had risen from their ranks.

9. Translated by Archimandrite Ephrem Lash.

10. Freely and Çakmak, *Byzantine Monuments*.

11. Their history has now been splendidly told by K. M. Ringrose, *The Perfect Servant: Eunuchs and the Social Construction of Gender in Byzantium* (Chicago, 2003).

12. "Porphyrogenitus": literally "born to the purple," that is, born in the purple chamber of the palace that was set aside for childbirth when an heir to the throne was prayerfully expected.

13. Constantine Porphyrogenitus, *De caeremoniis* 1.93 (Bonn, 1829–1840).

14. Even in the Greek account of this event 500 years later, this stereotyped phrase, *Justine Auguste, tu vincas*, appears in Latin.

15. The whole code was translated into English in one large volume by Clyde Pharr (Princeton, 1952); long out of print, it is worth finding in a large library if the

reader would like to get a sense of the everyday concerns and controls of the late Roman world. On its making and meaning, see J. Matthews, *Laying Down the Law* (New Haven, 2000).

16. Agathias, *Histories* 2.15, 1–4 (Berlin, 1975).

17. Malalas, 18.168; see Justinian, *Institutes* 4.18.4 (Oxford, 1913), punishing both homosexuality and adultery with death; later ordinances repeat the condemnation; see also Procopius, *Secret History* 16.23.

18. B. Croke, *Count Marcellinus and His Chronicle* (Oxford, 2001).

19. Michael the Syrian, *Chronicle* 8.2 (Paris, 1899–1924).

20. Luis Buñuel's film *Simon of the Desert* reimagines his power; the ruins of the great church may still be seen at Qalat Seman in Syria.

21. Pillar sitting had been a way to speak with the gods in this region long before Christianity predominated: Lucian's second-century *De dea Syria* 28–29 (now edited with translation and commentary by J. B. Lightfoot, *Lucian: On the Syrian Goddess* [Oxford, 2003]) tells of one temple where twice a year a man would go up a pillar and remain, never sleeping, for a week of prayer. (In the absence of a suitable pillar, a tree would sometimes offer sufficient elevation and discomfort.)

22. My translation; original quoted in Alan Cameron, "Wandering Poets: A Literary Movement in Byzantine Egypt," *Historia* 14 (1965), 470–509.

23. Quotation from Frend, *The Rise of the Monophysite Movement*, 214.

24. Sebastian Brock, "The Conversations with the Syrian Orthodox under Justinian [532]," *Orientalia Christiana Periodica* 47 [1981], 87–121. (Whoever translated the manuscript into Syriac was either trying very soon thereafter to advance Justinian's peacemaking or trying at a later date to embarrass him and his successors by showing how amenable he had once been.)

25. The comparison with Stalin was already made by T. Honoré, *Tribonian* (London, 1979), 28ff. Honoré knows Justinian as well as any scholar at any time and sees in him an intellectual snob but not a liar, pretentious and vulgar, narrowly educated and resentful of those who outshone him intellectually while eager to make himself out as a great intellectual and a colleague of intellectuals.

26. A. Grafton and M. Williams, *Christianity and the Transformation of the Book* (Cambridge, Mass., 2006), tell the story of Caesarea's libraries; while excavations continue, K. Holum, ed., *King Herod's Dream: Caesarea on the Sea* (New York, 1988), gives a hint of what was there.

27. Procopius, *Secret History* 14.2.

4. OPPORTUNITIES LOST

1. Paul J. Alexander, *The Oracle of Baalbek* (Washington, D.C., 1967).

2. I know of no one good book on the lost future of the ancient world, but Mark Munn, *The Mother of the Gods* (Berkeley, 2006), and A. Momigliano, *Alien Wisdom* (Cambridge, 1975), capture important elements of it.

3. The great French historian Fernand Braudel, in *The Mediterranean in the Ancient World* (London, 2001), thought Alexander's mistake lay precisely in choosing to look to the east and not realizing that the real future lay to the west. Braudel reminds us that Rome was just expanding out of the Tiber valley into Campania and Latium in the years when Alexander was heading east. The view merits con-

siderstion, but Alexander could scarcely have gone west without fearing attack from the rear, that is to say from the east; it is hard to know how seriously to take the ancient reports that he himself thought he still might try the west, after Arabia.

4. R. N. Frye, *History of Ancient Iran* (Munich, 1984), is standard. Note that I use "Persian" geographically and not ethnically, making no judgment regarding quarrels among modern scholars over whether, for example, the Parthians were really Persians.

5. G. Fowden, *Empire to Commonwealth* (Princeton, 1993), 13.

5. WARS WORSE THAN CIVIL

1. My first professor of late antique history quoted an old wheeze at this point: "When in Rome, do as the Vandals did." The joke and the byword made of their name betray the underlying lazy thought. The colloquial usage seems to have won currency in English by its application to the excesses of the French Revolution.

2. To call this victory a "reconquest," as many moderns do, is to accept Justinian's tendentious interpretation of the event.

3. Wickham, 375; and G. Camps, "Rex gentium Maurorum et Romanorum," *Antiquités africaines* 20 (1984), 183–218, quoting *Les inscriptions d'Altava*, ed. J. Marcillet-Jaubert (Aix, 1968): item 194, but see the whole sequence of texts from 111 to 224.

4. Ariadne deserves her own note: daughter of the emperor Leo I, mother of Leo II, she was wife and empress to both Zeno and Anastasius and spent most of half a century in the heart of the palace at Constantinople.

5. Cass. *Var.* 8.23.1.

6. P. Amory, *People and Identity in Ostrogothic Italy* (Cambridge, 1997).

7. Gundila: ibid., 149–150, 321–325.

8. Ibid., 181–182.

9. Arator, *On the Acts of the Apostles* 1.1ff (Atlanta, 1987).

10. Procopius, *Wars* 6.20.18–33.

11. Justinian Novellae, *Appendix* (in *Corpus Iuris Civilis* [Berlin, 1954]), vii (554).

12. *Corpus Inscriptionum Latinarum* 6.1199.

13. Augustine was in Milan when their bodies were "discovered" and recounts the excitement that greeted them (*Confessions* 9.7.16).

14. The exact Latin word is *consiliarius*, and the role is not very different from that of Robert Duvall's character in the Mafia fairy tales of Francis Ford Coppola.

15. Translated in MacMullen, *Christianity and Paganism in the Fourth to Eighth Centuries*, 60.

16. Ibid., 58.

17. Malalas, quoted in E. Watts, "Justinian, Malalas, and the End of Athenian Philosophical Teaching in AD 529," *Journal of Roman Studies* 94 (2004), 168–183.

18. *Life of Nicholas of Syon*, quoted in MacMullen, 135.

19. F. Curta, *Southeastern Europe in the Middle Ages* (Cambridge, 2006). "Balkans" is a modern word, from the Turkish word for mountains, and it is increasingly common to hear of southeastern Europe, meaning mainly the lands south of the

roughly east-west line carved by the Save and Danube rivers, sometimes extended to include Wallachia (southern Romania) and even Transylvania (northern Romania). What is now independent Greece fits the definition but is usually exempted from inclusion, wrongly. Not only are there disputes with the Republic of Macedonia over the proper understanding of "Macedonia," but in northwestern Greece we find the Greek, Albanian, and Macedonian languages, from three different branches of the Indo-European language tree, swapping vocabulary and even developing common syntactical features where they make similar departures together from their several language families.

20. F. Curta, *The Making of the Slavs* (Cambridge, 2001). No later subaggregation of Slavic peoples in history is without controversies, as each group tries to prove, unsuccessfully, that it is really an independent ethnic entity with ancient lineage.

21. B. Shaw, "War and Violence," in *Late Antiquity: A Guide to the Postclassical World*, ed. G. Bowersock, P. Brown, and O. Grabar (Cambridge, Mass., 1999), 130–169.

22. D. Obolensky, *The Byzantine Commonwealth* (London, 1971), treats this Slavic history with an unusually full account of its dependency on the region's Byzantine connections.

23. M. Meier, *Das andere Zeitalter Justinians* (Göttingen, 2003).

24. Quoted ibid., 334.

25. See P. Horden, "Mediterranean Plague in the Age of Justinian," in M. Maas, ed., *The Cambridge Companion to the Age of Justinian* (Cambridge, 2005), 134–160, for details. See also L. Little, *Plague and the End of Antiquity* (Cambridge, 2006).

26. Procopius, *Wars* 2.22.10.

27. John of Ephesus, quoted in translation by Horden, "Mediterranean Plague in the Age of Justinian."

28. Cass. *Var.* 12.25.2–3.

29. D. Keyes, *Catastrophe* (New York, 2000); Meier, *Andere Zeitalter*, 359ff, is better.

30. Professor Kenneth Harl of Tulane University; details at http://www.tulane.edu/~august/H303/handouts/Finances.htm.

31. S. Harvey, *Asceticism and Society in Crisis: John of Ephesus and the Lives of the Eastern Saints* (Berkeley, 1990).

32. R. MacMullen, *Voting about God* (New Haven, 2006).

33. Procopius, *Wars* 5.3.5–9.

34. B. Daley, in *Origeniana Sexta* (Leuven, 1995), 627ff.

6. LEARNING TO LIVE AGAIN

1. Wickham, *Framing the Early Middle Ages*, is decisive in shaping our current understanding of Frankish history, and in this chapter I follow and explore his interpretation.

2. *Nibelungenlied*, trans. A. Hatto (London, 1962), 385.

3. Ibid., 53.

4. C. Thomas, *Christianity in Roman Britain, AD 100–500* (Berkeley, 1981).

5. Patrick, *Confession* 23 (New York, 1998).

6. R. Markus, *The End of Ancient Christianity* (Cambridge, 1990).

7. Bede, *Ecclesiastical History* 3.25 (Harmondsworth, 1955).

8. T. Cahill, *How the Irish Saved Civilization* (New York, 1995)—and not just "western" civilization but civilization as a whole!

9. I owe this point to the late Professor Proinsias Mac Cana, in a lecture in Dublin in 1973. Like many propositions about Ireland, it was uttered tongue-in-cheek, but was nonetheless absolutely true.

10. For Stephen, see my *Augustine: A New Biography* (New York, 2005), 174–179.

11. Theodoret, quoted in E. K. Fowden, *The Barbarian Plain* (Berkeley, 1999), 46.

12. P. Geary, *Furta Sacra* (Princeton, 1978).

13. Tertullian, *Apologeticum* 8.

14. Gregory of Tours, *History of the Franks* 2.22.

15. See, for example, A. Becker and Y. Reed, *The Ways That Never Parted* (Tübingen, 2003); and S. Schwartz, *Imperialism and Jewish Society 200 BCE to 640 CE* (Princeton, 2001). The differentiation of Judaism from any of its competitors and neighbors was hardly as clear-cut then as it would be later: S. Cohen, *Beginnings of Jewishness* (Berkeley, 1999).

16. Gregory the Great, *Letters* 8.21(Toronto, 2004).

17. Malalas, *Chronicle* 18.45. The "Saracen phylarch" was in fact the leader of the Ghassanid Arab people, to whom Rome had entrusted much responsibility for security in Palestine and Arabia.

18. E. Gibbon, *Decline and Fall of the Roman Empire* (best edition by D. Womersley [London, 1994]), chap. 52. The prophecy of the last sentence has of course now come true in the mosques of contemporary Oxford.

19. Peter Brown's review of P. Crone and M. Cook's hotly controversial *Hagarism* (Cambridge, 1977) in "Understanding Islam," *New York Review of Books* (February 22, 1979), is a splendidly cautious introduction to the issues and possibilities.

20. R. Hoyland, *Seeing Islam as Others Saw It* (Princeton, 1997), 57.

21. *Cambridge Ancient History* 14.685.

22. Muhammad's preference for circumcision and kosher food rules, his reverence for Abraham, and his month of fasting in the same season in which Yom Kippur fell were all signs of common ancestry and mutual respect among traditions.

23. A. J. Arberry, *The Seven Odes* (New York, 1957).

7. CONSTANTINOPLE DEFLATED: THE DEBRIS OF EMPIRE

1. Upcountry in Egypt, Dioscoros of Aphrodito did likewise: "Justin is come to us, the life-giver, bringer of good, Justin is come to us. . . . It is a fine thing . . . to sing the young son of the many-sceptred palace, the much-praised emperor who loves Christ."

2. Archaeological evidence does not reduce itself easily to storytelling, so we don't know what to make of the discovery in 2004 of a cave near Andritsa in the Peloponnese—that is, the southernmost part of the Greek mainland—where a few dozen people took refuge with supplies and utensils that could have lasted for a

sustained period of hiding, but they all died there, without sign of violence. We cannot do justice to the sixth century without finding places in our imagination not only for Cosmas, Theoderic, Justinian, and Liberius, but also for this small group of frightened people, dying in a cave fearing threats that we cannot identify.

3. Paul the Deacon, *History of the Lombards* 4.22, quoted in N. Christie, *The Lombards* (Oxford, 1995), 42ff.

4. G. P. Bognetti, "Tradizione langobarda e politica bizantina," *Rivista di Studi del Diritto Italiano* 26 (1953–1954), 269–305, thinks the Lombard "duchies" were Roman offices.

5. Their destination was somewhere in what is now Kazakhstan, past Tashkent, perhaps nearing Almaty.

6. Frend, *The Rise of the Monophysite Movement*, 330, shows how hard it is for us to decide what to make of a figure like al-Mundhir by cataloging the *contemporary* opinions of him: Evagrius the Syrian thinks him a rogue and traitor; Theophylact the court historian thinks him simply a traitor; John of Ephesus defends him stoutly; Michael the Syrian has no judgment to pass on al-Mundhir but criticizes the Roman officers who arrested him.

7. "One-will-ism": If people could not agree that Christ had a single nature, perhaps they might agree to a single "will." No one was impressed with this hairsplitting.

8. *The Prosopography of the Later Roman Empire*, ed. J. Morris (Cambridge, 1971–1992), Vol. 3, see "Maurice."

9. Each of those four zones of the Eurasian landmass is inhabited by a diverse mix of peoples, religions, and cultures. No racialist theory can make any sense of these issues. The fashionable phrase "clash of civilizations" is no more helpful.

10. There is apparently no limit to the number of books or movies that Alexander can inspire. Peter Green and Robin Lane Fox are the authors I know who have best combined scholarship with interpretative and literary ability.

11. Leaving aside the brief and quickly surrendered venture of the Roman emperor Hadrian.

12. Two recent books help us imagine alternatives: J. Hobson, *The Eastern Origins of Western Civilization* (Cambridge, 2004); and G. Menzies, *1421: The Year China Discovered the World* (London, 2002).

8. THE LAST CONSUL

1. Alan Cameron and Diane Schauer, "The Last Consul: Basilius and His Diptych," *Journal of Roman Studies* 72 (1982), 126–145.

2. Thomas S. Brown, *Gentlemen and Officers* (London 1984); P. Brown, "The Servant of God at the End of Time," *University Publishing* 9 (Summer 1980), 3–4.

3. Gregory, *Homilies on the Gospels* 1.1 (Kalamazoo, Mich., 1990), and then *Dialogues* 3.38.

4. I think of David Kidd, *Peking Story* (New York, 2003), for such a history.

5. The text of the poem placed over his grave was copied down and transmitted in medieval manuscripts. Two small fragments of it were found in modern times and are now on display, with a reconstruction of the complete text to supplement them, in the crypt of Saint Peter's basilica in Rome.

6. See R. A. Markus, *Gregory the Great and His World* (Cambridge, 1997).

7. H. de Lubac, *Exégèse Médiévale* (Paris, 1959–1964; trans. Grand Rapids, Mich., 1998–2000), is the standard sympathetic study, best corrected by comparison with D. Dawson, *Allegorical Readers and Cultural Revision in Ancient Alexandria* (Berkeley, 1992).

8. Gregory, *Moralia* 35.20.49 (Oxford, 1844–1850).

9. Augustine, *Tractates on the Epistle of John* 7.8 (Washington, D.C., 1988–1995).

10. His predecessor Januarius, in the time of Theoderic, had been no paradigm of virtue; the king had to write commanding him to pay his debt for a purchase of sixty barrels of oil, which he had welshed on (Cass. *Var.* 3.7).

11. Gregory, *Ep.* 2.44.

12. Gregory, *Ep.* 8.36.

13. Gregory, *Dial.* 1.3.

14. R. MacMullen, "Cultural and Political Changes in the 4th and 5th Centuries," *Historia* 52 (2003), 465–495.

15. F. Clark, *The Pseudo-Gregorian Dialogues* (Leiden, 1987).

16. The category of the "modern" first appears under the Latin word *modernus* in sixth-century usage, revealing a culture now looking back and defining itself *against* a rival model and not simply seeking to imitate the past.

EPILOGUE

1. Gregory of Tours, *History of the Franks* 10.1 (Harmondsworth, 1974).

2. Daniel 10.5–9.

3. Revelation 12.7.

4. Isaiah 6.2: "Above it stood the seraphims: each one had six wings; with twain he covered his face, and with twain he covered his feet, and with twain he did fly." Tertullian, *Apologeticum* 22: "Every spirit, angel, and demon, upon the account of its swiftness, may be said to be winged, for they can be here and there and everywhere in a moment."

5. On Michael at Gargano, see G. Otranto, *Italia meridionale e Puglia paleochristiane: saggi storici* (Bari, 1991).

6. One medieval legend claimed Pope Gregory himself for this region, telling of his upbringing in Corcaguiney, on the Dingle peninsula just north of Skellig Michael.

FURTHER READING

The student of this period has many choices. Of course, one should read Gibbon, but only with appropriate inoculation—to keep from believing that either his narrative or his facts are complete and accurate. He was a marvel of learning, but he had real limits, and he lived before the great age of modern scholarly investigation. For a short fat man, he was a giant, but many dwarfs in our age know more than he ever could.

Among those who bring erudition and analysis to this field, there is a small war going on, between those who think the empire fell and those who think the story of empire too small to be intelligible and who need the larger canvas of "late antiquity" in order to explain these transitions. For two recent accounts of "decline and fall," see Peter Heather, *The Fall of the Roman Empire* (2005), and Bryan Ward-Perkins, *The Fall of Rome* (2005). The dean of late antique studies, by contrast, is Peter Brown, whose *The World of Late Antiquity* (1971) and *The Rise of Western Christendom* (rev. ed. 2002) tell the story in briefer and longer form. P. Brown, G. Bowersock, and O. Grabar's, *Late Antiquity: A Guide to the Postclassical World* (1999) has the form of an encyclopedia but more resembles a box of very fine dark chocolates of every description and may be sampled to taste.

The reader with more patience for detail and less need for narrative should read Chris Wickham, *Framing the Early Middle Ages* (2005), a masterpiece of learning and judgment. A provost sometimes meets well-wishers who venture to doubt that humanists are engaged on what can truly be called research. I hand them Wickham's book. For learning, erudition, and a conventional comprehensive approach embodying the anglophone scholarly consensus—thus a view much more conservative than my own—the *Cambridge Ancient History* (Vol. 14, covering the period 425–609, published 2000) is a treasure trove.

The Notes beginning on page 397 contain many more titles, almost all of them well worth browsing for the reader willing to take the next step into a fascinating era, whose contours continue to emerge into the scholarly light of day.

CREDITS AND PERMISSIONS

MAPS

Maps designed and produced by Andrew Rolfson, Department of History, Georgetown University.

IMAGES

Barberini: The Barberini Ivory (sixth century), Louvre, Paris, France/
Giraudon/The Bridgeman Art Library.   225

Cassiodorus at Vivarium: Codex Amiatinus Ms 1 f.vr, seventh century,
Biblioteca Medicea-Laurenziana, Florence, Italy/The Bridgeman Art
Library.   276

Chicken and Chicks: "Hen With Her Seven Chicks," Filippo Serpero
Museum of the Treasure of the Duomo, Monza, Italy.   347

Sant'Angelo: istockphoto.com   388

Skellig Michael: Image provided by and used with permission of Fáilte
Ireland.   392

Dr. Carole Sargent, director of Scholarly and Literary Publications at
Georgetown, has supported this work in many ways. My gratitude to
Artemis Kirk, Georgetown University librarian, and to her splendid staff
is equally immense. The wisdom and example of my great friends Casey,
Jerome, and, especially, Horatio have been indispensable.

INDEX